Dedication

Co-Captain Jim Wood was a linebacker and guard on Corsicana's State Championship football team in 1963. His dream was to have a book written about the Acree championship years in Corsicana. This book is dedicated to him.

D1496841

Table of Contents

Run to the Green House

Foreword

If he were writing here, Coach Jim Acree would "Do it right." He'd make sure you found a reason to read the stories in this book. Historically and biographically, the tales show how boys transformed into Acree's men while learning to become winners in football and life. To experience Acree, read the stories, and read some of them more than once. He was a winner. His head coaching record speaks for itself: 130-52-4 with nine playoff appearances (*) and one AAA State Championship.

Bonham High School AA
     1958 10-1-0*
     1959 10-2-0*
Corsicana High School AAA and AAAA
     1960 7-3-1*
     1961 9-2-1*
     1962 8-3-0*
     1963 14-0-0*
     1964 8-2-0
     1965 12-1-0*
     1966 5-4-0
Midland Lee High School AAAA
     1970 2-8-0
     1971 5-5-0
     1972 8-2-0
     1973 3-7-0
     1974 8-2-1*
     1975 6-3-1
     1976 10-2-0*
     1977 5-5-0

INTRODUCTION

Jim Acree was a man who lived to win. He was an exceptional athlete whose expectation of winning carried over into his coaching. As head coach, Acree's authoritarian style pushed players to want to win as much as he did. He cut, hammered and shaped Corsicana boys into men. These men would deliver five football championships in seven seasons, and win the AAA State Championship in 1963.

Acree was zealous about preparing boys to play—and not just play, but play to win. He used the same methods that had formed him—hard work and dogged perseverance. To please him, players had to spend themselves physically and develop a level of mental toughness they didn't know existed.

Growing up on an Oklahoma farm under an abusive father, Acree longed for a place to call home. He traveled the world in the military and found acclaim as a boxer in college. In Corsicana, he found both professional success and a place to belong. He and his wife, Rosemary, with three daughters and a son, planned to settle there. The family constructed a new home. His winning endeared him to many Corsicanans but a few hated him. His opponents feared him.

After ending a disappointing season in 1966, Acree received a surprise phone call. On the other end of the line was a school board official. He reported the results of a University Interscholastic League hearing on the evidence that Corsicana coaches provided medical services to players.

Listening to the report, Acree twiddled the phone cord, pulling, twisting and stretching it, challenging its ability to even function. He did the same

1

with the boys who played for him. He tested their desire and determination. Which ones would stay and pay the price to win?

When Acree hung up the phone, he stood silent, staring at the state championship ring on his huge right hand. He moved across the room and slumped on the couch next to Rosemary. His big, dimpled chin fell. The former boxing champion told her, "The UIL put Corsicana on probation."

Life delivered an uppercut he did not see coming. Dazed, he spoke again, "I don't understand how doing what's right can be so wrong."

With the stiff backbone of a coach's wife, Rosemary replied, "Jim, we need to move on."

CHAPTER 1   HARD ROAD TO A HALL OF FAME

"Good is this Strife for men. So potter with potter contendeth; the hewer of wood with the hewer of wood; the beggar is jealous of the beggar, the minstrel jealous of the minstrel." Hesiod

God gave James Dewitt Acree a double portion of competitiveness. He also gave him an abusive drunk for a father.

On May 3, 1970, hard-nosed Jim Acree attended his father Loy's funeral at the First Methodist Church in Maud, Oklahoma. He sat in a pew, surrounded by his wife, Rosemary and their children.

Rosemary asked, "Jimmy, why are you crying about that awful old man?"

Acree put his feelings into words, "Such a wasted life."

Precisely what wasted life meant was unclear because Jim Acree was a man who talked very little about anything other than football. He didn't speak about having a father who often came home drunk—a brutal man Jim hid from outside the farmhouse in the surrounding trees until Loy fell asleep. Loy was a carpenter who also hit his wife, Veral, as if she were a nail. He forced Jim to plow eighty acres using two mules. If he didn't get his work done, Loy beat him while yelling, "I said, do it right!"

Acree didn't tell stories about having a high school coach who was a native Osage Indian—a coach with disdain for "squaw men," boys who gave up and quit. He also didn't share his experience of eloping to marry his wife, Rosemary, when she was just sixteen years old and he was eighteen.

Coach Acree was silent about all these things, but this rough history speaks volumes about the man he became.

Jim's father, Loy, was the oldest son of James Blanchard Acree who moved by wagon to Oklahoma in 1883. "J. B." was a schoolteacher, a home-building contractor and Chief of Police of Maud.   J.B. had concerns about the title security of 140 acres of unoccupied land that the family owned. Indians kept coming back trying to claim it. But worries over his family's safety prevented J.B. from moving onto the land.

Loy picked up J.B.'s carpenter skills to earn a living, but his body's chemistry turned alcohol into "firewater." He became the black sheep of the family. Drinking often, he had a penchant for poor decision-making, such as the time he hopped a train north to join a circus. He returned to Maud after finding it hard work which only earned a dollar a day. As a carpenter, he drank on paydays and sometimes gambled away his earnings. At twenty-five, he married Veral Raper in October 1927, who was sixteen and expecting a child. Perhaps ill-advised, Loy decided to make a home on J.B.'s land, which became the family farm. Jim Acree, his first son, was born on it in April 1928.

As a young man, Acree was always on the go. With Loy as a father, his home was just a place to eat and sleep. Being stuck behind two mules doing farm work kept him from satisfying his competitive urge. Walking rows of corn wasted chances to organize and play sports with other kids. His hyper-competitiveness resembled a flaw in a design that always pushed him to look for a new angle on how to win. Once, when playing Red Rover, he showed his brother Stan how to lock arms so tight that a girl knocked herself out trying to break through their outstretched arms. He played to win, but life on the farm meant losing...and losing to Loy, a man who Jim thought, "wasted his life." Farming was a life mistake Jim wanted to avoid. Sports competition brought out the best in him—focused effort, innovation and preparation.

"Big Jimmy Acree" developed into a young, athletic man. He was tall with long, muscular arms and had a strong, stout body. In Maud High School, he had a champion's build and a powerful look, like a model in a sports magazine. Other Maud Tigers had strength like him, but Acree's arms were noticeably longer and ended in more prominent than average hands. This enabled his extended reach, which he used to knock out boxing opponents. Later as a coach, he would use

Jim Acree, Maud High School, 1946

those hands to grab a player's facemask, pull their face close to his and in the heat of a moment shout instructions, "Dammit. I said, hit him. Run it again!" As an adult, those unusual hands were also seen at times as a smothering handshake with a dad, accompanied by a smile and a quiet voice whispering a compliment about a son, "You can believe he knows his blocking techniques."

Up close, Acree's eyes carried the force of his thoughts—a glare at a player receiving instruction or a sparkle if greeting a parent, a co-worker, a friend or celebrating a win. But no matter the situation, they beamed an intensity of focus such that a recipient could not hold a gaze into his eyes for long without looking away. His eyes sat deep below his broad forehead, above a Roman nose, inside his prominent cheekbones and angular jaw, which ended in a jutting, dimpled chin. He had a wide mouth with thin lips that exposed perfect incisors. This gave him a fierce look if he was angry or a happy appearance when he relaxed into a smile. His ears were not square but complimented his face, always pinned back in attention when listening to someone speak. His stride was long, especially when irritated; he seemed to be able to cover the width of a football field in three steps.

Acree started competitive running in high school under Coach George Tallchief, a full-blood Osage Indian. The Osage were a tribe of "super warriors" who played any game to win. Acree was just as competitive. He fit in because he played to win like them.

Running was the trait of a warrior, so Acree ran to please Tallchief. He ran from home to school because he didn't have a car. He ran hard during workouts to develop superior conditioning. He ran to neighboring St. Louis, Oklahoma to see Rosemary, an extra payoff being a kiss from the attractive brunette.

He saw running as an antidote to any ailment, not just escaping Loy. For instance, if he was sick, he dressed in a heavy plastic pull-over rain top and ran two miles saying, "The way to get rid of a cold is to sweat it out."

As if he were running away from Loy into the hands of a loving father, Rudyard Kipling's poem "If" inspired Jim. He loved the lines,

> *If you can fill the unforgiving minute*
> *With sixty seconds' worth of distance run,*
> *Yours is the Earth and everything that's in it,*
> *And—which is more—you'll be a Man, my son!*

* * *

Jim took the punishment when jobs around the house were not to Loy's liking. One particular beating left abrasions on Jim's body that his coaches noticed. As a group, several men visited Loy to "discuss" his treatment of Jim. No one living remembers what happened, but after that meeting, the beatings stopped—perhaps because Jim's physical capabilities at age fifteen allowed him to restrain Loy.

Standing up to Loy set a new course for Acree's life. Perhaps he saw coaches come to his aid and decided he wanted to be that kind of man. Regardless, competitive sports were a way off the farm—a chance to become a man and not waste his life like Loy.

Raised in Great-Depression-poor Oklahoma, Acree was industrious about earning an extra nickel. He hunted, trapped and skinned game and sold hides for a few cents. He farmed corn and cotton to add to the house money his mother Veral made by selling eggs. If a job required hard work, dedication and persistence, Jim Acree was first in line to take it. He was not arrogant or egotistical. He equated hard work with success. In this way he avoided a beating from Loy.

As Acree grew into a man, life taught him to respond to triumph and disaster in the same way: "What do we do to improve?"

While Loy wasted his potential, Jim developed himself as an athlete. But where should he focus his efforts? Because of his physical talents, Coach Tallchief recruited him to play multiple sports—his height gave him benefits in basketball. His speed advantaged him in football. His strength aided his track performance. His long reach enabled his boxing. But his toughness made him a multisport letterman—football, basketball, track and boxing.

On the basketball team in the 9th grade, Acree and the Maud Tigers won the 1944 Oklahoma State basketball title. Although he lettered in basketball throughout high school, it was not his second favorite sport. That belonged to boxing, which he began in 1946 as a junior. As a "no-contact" sport, basketball didn't offer the joy of hitting, which Acree relished. He knew firsthand from Loy what a blow could do to a man's will.

Boxing was not a high school sport, but he was likely a founding member of the Maud Boxing Club, which allowed him to participate in state tournaments sanctioned by the AAU (Amateur Athletic Union).

Acree liked seeing his name in the Maud newspaper with headlines like, "Big Jimmy Acree Contributes to Another Win." As a linebacker, he expected to win every play by making the tackle, or as an offensive end, to outrun every defender after he caught a pass. For the Osage, size and speed mattered; but for Acree, the heart mattered most. Play the game to win it or don't play at all. The Osage were enemies of other tribes in the territories surrounding Oklahoma. Likewise, Acree competed with those around him. To best them, he never gave up. Regardless of size, speed or strength, he obtained exceptionalism with a heart that out-hustled any opponent. Work harder. Run faster when your opponent is tired. Run after practice when your opponent is at home lounging. Run while your competitor is riding in a car.

Acree appeared to adopt Tallchief's perspective on quitters, tribally called "squaw men." They were displeasing, not allowed to marry and could never redeem themselves. It was traitorous to accept defeat, making a man untrustworthy. Perhaps Acree saw Loy in this light, a squaw man. Acree pleased Coach Tallchief by boxing, playing basketball and football and running track in the same way an Osage boy performed tribal rituals in a rite of passage.

Jim Acree was charismatic and intelligent. Having benefitted from the help of others, he always offered help to other boys—primarily in helping them reach their potential athletically. Reading sports magazines, he adopted a Charles Atlas philosophy of weight training and dietary habits that would "make you into a man." He utilized store-bought and homemade exercise equipment, including a speedbag for boxing or the use of empty cans filled with dried mud for weight training. He taught boys how to improve themselves.

Watching Indian players aggressively hitting in football attracted Acree, too. It led to winning. He developed a love for hitting and taught hitting techniques to other players. He learned football, not just for his position, but he studied every position on the field.

By 1946, Acree also excelled as a football player, lettering all four years in high school. As an end, he had a record-setting sixteen catches in one game. His senior year, an article headline appeared in the Maud Enterprise, "Acree Stars as Maud Wins Over Bowlegs."

After a win over Tecumseh, a game writeup mentioned, "Acree with his pass-catching would be a credit to any high school football club."

Another article describing a win against Wetumka said, "Big Jim Acree ran up the score sufficiently to win the game."

That year, 494 Maud citizens (almost the whole town), signed a scroll and mailed 1,915 postcards supporting the handsome and popular Acree as an All-State player. Out of 1,000 nominations across the state, coaches voted Acree to the 1946 All-State high school football team. He had been a second-string vote on the 1945 All-State team. With a reputation for being one of the most feared tacklers in the game, opponent school administrators and coaches from surrounding towns extolled his play. For example, a Tecumseh official said, "Acree is the best defensive player I have seen this year in the state."

A coach from Shawnee said, "Good end. Best player I've seen in the state. Swell boy. I just couldn't forget that #66 in action."

And there was an accolade from Bowlegs, "Best offensive and defensive and most outstanding player I have seen play."

With only thirty-seven students in his class when he graduated from high school in May 1947, Acree might have wondered if he could make it in the world. But his way off the farm would be as a football player.

Loy wanted Jim to stay in Maud, but the new head coach at Oklahoma University, Bud Wilkinson, had other ideas. In 1947, Wilkinson shifted the school's player-recruiting strategy from paying former military veterans to offering scholarships to promising high school players. He offered a "full ride" to Jim Acree. Baylor University also recruited him.

Jim didn't tell anyone of his plan to elope with Rosemary Morphew to nearby Coalgate, Oklahoma. They married on April 5, 1947. She was expecting a child and he needed to support a family. Veral didn't want her boy to move away, so Loy argued, "Do it right, stay here and work the farm for a living."

Jim & Rosemary Wedding

Colgate, Oklahoma, 1947

Rosemary's parents in nearby St. Louis, Oklahoma offered the newlyweds better counsel. "Rosemary, you stay home and finish high school. Jim, you accept the scholarship in Norman. It's only forty miles west and you can still see each other."

Baylor was too far away. Acree liked the Morphew plan and accepted Wilkinson's scholarship. Their first daughter, Susan, was born in November 1947. Rosemary became valedictorian of her class in 1949. Aside from being smart, she was attractive with a ready smile and quick wit. Once wearing a fake "fur," a thoughtless person asked her if it was "real." She smiled and replied, "I'll have you know that millions of little polyesters gave their lives for this coat."

She sacrificed an academic scholarship to OU to care for her young family. Perfect for Acree, she decided "to make things as easy for Jim as possible."

Freshman at Oklahoma
University, 1947

Later, when complimented on his mastery of the game, Acree said, "Everything I know about football, I learned from Bud Wilkinson."

Known as the "Great White Father," Oklahoma Coach Bud Wilkinson was a champion Acree wanted to emulate. Before coaching at OU, Wilkinson was a three-time National Champion as a starting player at the University of Minnesota. He became the OU head coach in 1947 and won thirteen consecutive conference championships.

Jim Acree was a Sooner on four of those titles. He suited out when Wilkinson won two Sugar Bowl Championships in 1948 and 1949 and a National Championship in 1949. Acree also traveled to Miami and dressed out with the team when Wilkinson became an Orange Bowl Champion in January 1954. But suit out is all Jim did.

Because of injury, Acree was not a star football player in college, but he was a champion many times over on Wilkinson's coattail. He adopted Wilkinson's clockwork philosophy for practice sessions. Don't be late or "You'll pay the price." With a precise start time, the routine was eight minutes of calisthenics, a two-minute practice overview with the coach, thirty minutes of reaction drills with boys grouped by position, thirty minutes of half-line scrimmage, thirty minutes of dummy drills, fifteen minutes of blocking drills and fifteen minutes of scrimmage.

In the fall of 1947, Acree was one of thirteen All-State freshmen to play against the varsity reserves. Weighing 195, he started at the left end in the Red/White freshman game. In 1948, he competed as a tight end in a Red-White team scrimmage. Bud Wilkinson "platooned" first and second teams each quarter. Acree was second team, right end against Iowa State in October and likely saw some playing time. The competition was tough on Wilkinson's star-studded, 10-1 team that season. Acree was not a member of the varsity squad for the January 1949 Sugar Bowl. He accompanied the team as a reserve to the game but did not ride the train and participate in four days of pregame workouts with the forty-four-member squad. Acree did not letter in 1948. Perhaps this was when he turned his attention to boxing at OU.

* * *

Acree never mentioned his boxing coach, Dewey "Snorter" Luster. In Luster's days as a student at OU, he lettered four years as a football player. The 5'7", 140-pound end was a member of the 1920 undefeated team at OU. That same year he set up the intramural boxing club. Later, during the war, he coached Oklahoma football to Big Six Conference titles in 1943 and 1944. His success continued later in his career, too. In 1956, Luster's boxing team placed sixth in the NCAA Championships. He earned his nickname because he snorted in the ring so much as an amateur boxer.

The usual fear of receiving a blow to the head had no hold on Acree. Instead, he relished hitting opponents. He sought to beat an opponent into submission. Although there are few records, we know Acree was boxing at OU by 1948, and we can see from his results that Luster must have been an excellent coach.

In early 1949, less than two years out of high school, Acree excelled in the novice class as a heavyweight. In January, he won the Golden Gloves title in the Oklahoma City tournament. The Maud Enterprise described this division title fight. "Acree put Gail McGhee of the Elks Southsiders to sleep in the first round of their heavyweight clash."

The newspaper described Acree as "a rugged and willing fighter who took one minute to defeat McGhee, first sending him into the ropes with a successful left hook. When McGhee rebounded, Acree met him with another looping hook to finish him."

As an amateur, Acree didn't earn prize money for fighting. However, with his competitive spirit riding high, he must have had a spark of achievement in his eyes as the referee held up his arm. Winning the division title advanced him to fight Ted Reynolds of the Cameron Aggies in the state-wide Golden Gloves tournament. The referee decisioned their bout in the second round. Again, the referee raised Acree's arm in victory. He advanced to the state finals, but Bob Collins of Northwestern A&M knocked Acree to the floor in the third round and won the match by referee's decision. Jim finished as a runner-up in the state Golden Gloves meet.

Acree was successful as a boxer, but he was on a scholarship to play football. Strangely though, he was not listed as a letterman in 1949. Why?

In March that year, he was one of ninety students to come out for spring practice. Wilkinson selected him as an end on a practice squad run by famous OU quarterback Darrell Royal. None of the players selected were lettermen, except for Royal. That spring, Acree also scrimmaged in the Red/White game as an end. That fall, the Sooners were undefeated, having an 11-0 finish. There is no evidence that Acree even played.

Before the 1949 football season ended, Acree returned to boxing.

Exactly when he injured a knee is unclear; likely, it was in 1949. That year, OU coaches moved him to an interior line position. The injury was bad enough to qualify him for surgery, but he drew a short-straw and received an experimental treatment with horse liniment. The injury limited him as a football player, making it painful to run at full speed.

However, he was still able to jog and box. Acree had surgery for meniscus repair in 1967, but the operation was insufficient. The knee bothered him the rest of his life.

Acree also had his jaw broken in a match that spring. With his mouth wired shut for six months, he could not eat normally, and his weight dropped. The injury would have kept him out of football that August, suggesting another reason he didn't letter in 1949.

As a Sooner pugilist, he fought against North Texas State on December 9, 1949. Two weeks later, weighing 175, he won a light-heavyweight bout on the WKY-Radio boxing show. He earned the nickname "fancy Dan" boxer because of his technique and style.

Acree's name appeared in columns for boxing stories of the Daily Oklahoman, juxtaposed with columns about the Sooner football team sans Acree. His football career wasn't over, but he never suited up again as an end for the Sooners. However, he proudly wore red boxing shorts as an OU Mittman.

After a knockout win over Jack King of Oklahoma A&M in January 1950, his third of the year, Coach Luster selected Acree as the lead fighter for the OU intramural team in the state-wide Golden Gloves tournament. He fought in the open class. Soon after, in February 1950, Acree suffered a severely pinched nerve. But possibly seeing visions of a "squaw man," he wouldn't quit. A tournament doctor intervened and forced Acree out of the competition.

But Acree didn't quit mentally. He decided to fight later in the AAU tournament, losing in a semifinal bout.

These losses were just the start of bad news in 1950.

Acree reported for off-season football duties, but his career as an OU Sooner quickly deteriorated. Following Wilkinson's advice to join the

National Guard for extra money backfired. Unexpectedly, politics and the atom bomb impacted Acree's life at age twenty-two.

* * *

The Army activated his National Guard unit into the 45th Infantry Division, destined for Japan and

Seeks Heavyweight Title

Acree Boxing, 1950

Korea. Interviewed in September 1950, Wilkinson mentioned three other activated players and referred to "freshman" Acree. Calling the other three by name saying, "They will be missed," his lament didn't include Acree. Along with other evidence, this indicates that Acree did not letter at OU before entering the Army. On September 27, 1950, Luster also announced Acree as one of four boxers that would be lost due to activation to serve in Japan and Korea.

Acree reported to Ft. Polk, Louisiana. The Morphews had moved to Kermit, Texas by then and Rosemary moved in with them. A second daughter, Debby, was born in November 1950. After leave to visit his family in March 1951, the Army shipped Acree to Japan, then Korea. Bored on the voyage over the Pacific, he volunteered as a cook. Acree also played center on an Army football squad.

Legendary football coach Vince Lombardi was at the U.S. Military Academy, and the Army asked him to coach an overseas clinic, which Acree attended. Lombardi's piece, "What it Takes to Be No.1," put Acree's core beliefs into words:

Winning is not a sometimes thing; it's an all-the-time thing. You don't win once in a while; you don't do things right once in a while; you do them right all the time. Winning is a habit. Unfortunately, so is losing.

I've never known a man worth his salt who in the long run, deep down in his heart, didn't appreciate the grind, the discipline. There is something in good men that really yearns for discipline and the harsh reality of head-to-head combat.

You've got to play with your heart, with every fiber of your body. If you're lucky enough to find a guy with a lot of head and a lot of heart, he's never going to come off the field second.

I firmly believe that any man's finest hour—his greatest fulfillment to all he holds dear—is the moment when he has worked his heart out in a good cause and lies exhausted on the field of battle—victorious.

Lombardi opened Acree's eyes to what to teach boys about success in life, particularly football. (An autographed photo of Coach Lombardi was one of Acree's prized treasures). In the Army, he served soup, played football and boxed through the summer of 1952.

That September, the Maud Enterprise proclaimed Acree's return to the Big Red Machine, but he was not a returning letterman nor was he a star end, making touchdown catches and running to win games. He returned as a tackle, an unheralded lineman, wearing #58 in a team photo. Acree returned to OU football for the fall of 1952 season; but by

Korea, 1952

then, his dream of becoming a star football player at OU must have ended.

At age twenty-four, he was five years out of high school, married with two children and had a bum knee. No longer a standout player, he thought he had to find another way to stay off the farm.

That month, in an article about OU boxing, Snorter mentioned Acree's return to the boxing team. Luster described other returning fighters as champions, but not Acree—implying he hadn't won a championship at that point. Luster again listed him as a heavyweight fighter because his weight returned to 195.

A motivated, physical Acree finally had success as a boxer. In March of 1953, one month shy of being twenty-five, Acree earned the AAU State Boxing championship. Officials named him the tournament's outstanding boxer. The Daily Oklahoman described the fight. "Acree traded punches with Enid's hard-hitting Everett Wilson through three furious rounds that kept the crowd in an uproar as first one and then the other forged into the lead. The first round went to Wilson by a narrow margin. Acree took charge in the second stanza with a body attack that had Wilson hurt before the bell."

Seeing his opponent's weakness, "Continuing the body assault in the third round, Acree piled up enough points for a well-earned victory and the championship."

Big Jim Acree was the last man standing. With his arm held high by a referee, Acree took pride in a competitive win over a foe. When asked later how he won so many fights, he answered, "I hit 'em in the gut until they couldn't breathe anymore."

Other heavyweights had 6'3" height and weighed as much as or more than 195. Many boxers had equal or greater reach; some were lefties like Acree. But something about Acree made the difference. Undoubtedly his rough home life contributed to his toughness. No son endures beatings from a drunken father without developing a fighter's determination to survive. But in the ring, in the heat of the moment, Acree's level of desire came into play. He simply "wanted it" more than his opponent. No one could prepare more than Jim. His training and willingness to condition himself honed the endurance he needed to fight multiple rounds in a ring. Acree's prior success in football developed his self-image as a winner. But Lombardi-like desire drove him to succeed in the ring.

Acree fought as an amateur and never made a nickel boxing. It was not part of his scholarship requirements. He did it out of his competitive lust.

Oklahoma officials canceled the Golden Gloves competition after the 1958 season. Illegal gambling was a persistent problem. Various states legalized prize-fighting but regulated it. In general, Americans lost interest in boxing as a sport. To many people, the idea of boxing was repugnant. The goal in the ring was to win by injuring an opponent, to destroy their will to fight, to render them senseless, unable to answer the bell.

On August 12, 1953, Rosemary gave birth to their third daughter, Nancy, in Norman. OU celebrated Dad's Day in October 1953 in the football game against Kansas. The program listed Acree as an unlettered senior, wearing #53, a third-string center. Appearing in a team photo was only a showpiece. Present or not, that Dad's Day, Loy's desires must have tugged at Acree. There was no money in boxing, and with a growing family, how would he stay off the farm?

After the 1953 football season ended, Acree, the reigning AAU Champion, surprisingly rejoined the OU boxing team and scheduled an open bout in December 1953 with the reigning Golden Gloves champion, Carl McClure of Cameron College. Acree was not in the boxing shape needed for three-minute rounds. Demonstrating his willpower, however, he thrilled the crowd with a "free-swinging brawl." McClure won by decision with a score of 60-59.

It was Acree's last significant fight.

* * *

Acree rejoined the football Sooners in their January 1954 win over the Maryland Terrapins in the Orange Bowl. He was a third-string center. Later, "Big Jim Acree" fought in his final boxing tournament in Tulsa. He completed his scholarship by serving as a coaching aide in March when 100 men came out for football. He was set to graduate from OU in June at twenty-six with a degree in Education.

Rosemary and Jim in Miami for the Orange Bowl, 1954

As did his time as a star footballer, his days as a boxer ended without fanfare.

With their family of three young girls, he and Rosemary had to decide what they would do next. Loy's advice to move back to Maud and work on the farm was not an option. Coaches Tallchief, Wilkinson and Luster were positive role models for Acree. Coaching became his choice of profession.

Coach Luster had previously taught at Norman High School. Perhaps wanting to keep Acree in Norman, he introduced Acree to the new head coach, Boyd "Bronco" McGugan at NHS. In May, he and superintendent J. Don Garrison interviewed Acree for an assistant coaching job. As a backup plan, Garrison also interviewed Acree for the head football coach at the Norman Junior High School.

After discussing the possibilities with Rosemary, Acree told the Daily Oklahoman, "I'm definitely interested in the junior high position. The program is well developed here."

Living in Kermit, Texas, Rosemary's parents again had different advice for the young couple; "Leave Oklahoma, or you'll starve to death."

Acree applied for an assistant coaching position in Bonham, Texas, and he received an offer of $1,000 per year more than the Norman Junior High position. As if the difference in money were not the deciding factor, Acree told the Daily Oklahoman, "I don't wish to become categorized as a junior high coach."

Like a seasoned professional, he added, "When you're coaching junior high boys, you have to think like one of them, and it's difficult to be then thought of as anything but a junior high coach."

Indeed, that wisdom regarding junior high coaches came from an experienced member of the fraternity, maybe even M. B. Nelson, the new head football coach in Bonham, Texas. Having played professionally two years for the Los Angeles Rams, M. B. was a storehouse of football ideas new to Acree. He learned a great deal about the coaching profession from Nelson, too. M.B. began coaching in Cisco and arrived in Bonham after coaching for four years in Aransas Pass. The soft-spoken coach took control of the 0-10 Bonham Warriors in 1954 and hired assistants Jim Acree and Raymond Anderson. Together, they won three AA district championships in 1955-1957. The last two years were eleven-win seasons.

Speaking about Acree's influence on the confidence of their 1956 Bi-District Championship team, Jerry Moore said, "We were just a bunch of high school boys, but he made us feel like we could gain a yard on the New York Giants!"

In 1957, aided by Acree's hard work, Nelson simultaneously held the job of High School Principal. To Acree's surprise, after the '57 season ended, Nelson retired from coaching to focus on his job as Principal. With Nelson's recommendation, Acree's performance impressed Bonham and they elevated him to Head Football Coach in 1958. No doubt, Nelson was one of several great men to influence Acree's life.

Jim had built strong offensive and defensive lines on the football team, which were key to three district titles in a row, but now he had to step up his game to coach the entire squad. Bonham named Raymond Anderson as Acree's number one assistant. Heavy losses in the line and backfield, due to graduation, concerned Acree, but he noted a critical attribute in the remaining squad members—a desire to play. "The kids are in excellent spirits, which is a good sign."

Acree led the 1958 Bonham Warriors to a 10-1-0 season and a district win. Under his leadership, in 1959, Bonham had a 10-2-0 season and again won their District Championship outright.

James Acree Moved Up To Head Coach; Anderson Top Aide

Head Coach, Bonham, 1958

His physical stamina led him to think he could outwork any opponent. When he did lose, he imagined that he would have won had he prepared better. To him, mistakes were the result of a lack of preparation. If he became known for anything, it was game preparation.

Acree was a popular coach, frequently speaking to boosters at the Quarterback Club and local civic organizations. Rosemary was a member of the Bonham Story League and often shared humorous stories as a guest speaker at organizations such as PTA meetings. They made a home in Bonham, where their only son, James Felix Acree, was born in 1957.

The lure of a competitive opportunity to move up to Class AAA football was too great, and Acree resigned on January 3, 1960 to take a head coaching job in Corsicana, Texas. Full of confidence, he told Rosemary, "Grab hold of my coattails. We're going places!"

He had been instrumental in building the Bonham teams that won five straight district titles, two bi-district titles and one regional title. In 2007, the Fannin County Sports Hall of Fame honored his impact by inducting him and M. B. Nelson as members. Rosemary, Susan and James Felix sat in the audience and listened as Acree received accolades from various speakers. Their eyes were wet with tears. Unlike his father Loy, Jim Acree made his family proud.

In 1960, the boys in Corsicana had not seen a championship-minded coach come to town since the invention of the television. They would soon fall under the powerful spell of Acree's competitiveness.

Jim Acree, Fannin County Sports Hall of Fame

CHAPTER 2 BREAKING THE DROUGHT

"If you are going to be a champion, you must be willing to pay a greater price." Bud Wilkinson

In 1960, Tiger fans in Corsicana, Texas believed big and quick Gary Whistler would be an All-District tackle, but new Head Coach Jim Acree had team rules—no smoking, no drinking and keeping a curfew.

In the first week of August's two-a-day practices, Whistler walked away from the team and kept quiet, not even telling friends what happened. Moreover, Acree gave no explanation why a returning letterman would quit.

Whistler might have thought, "Nobody tells me what to do off the field! I don't have to eat Acree's shit. He can kiss my ass."

Acree tried to get him back. He stood silent in the home of Whistler's good friend and teammate, W. R. "Dub" Garlington, and listened as Dub phoned Whistler at Acree's urging. Dub attempted to persuade Whistler to return to the team, but Gary refused, again without saying exactly why he'd quit.

That was it—the Gary Whistler way. Acree asked him for his uniform, and he was gone.

Like a boxer who refuses to answer a bell, Whistler's desire to play football under Acree dissolved. That was his senior year. He might have had second thoughts but declined to explain his actions to others. He quit high school, as well. Whistler did what was necessary to be his own man. Soon, the Army, a wife and a job declared him to be their man. It's thought that he went to his grave never having forgiven Acree.

* * *

Coaches tell players that football is like the game of life—you win some and lose some. But to Coach Jim Acree, winning was the substance of life, like air, food and water. He focused on winning football games. Seeing a team of boys execute sharply on a green football field was like breathing air with the smell of freshly mowed grass. He would say, "If we don't improve, we are dead."

He likened preparing for a game to taking nourishment saying, "eat too little and we will lose."

And irrespective of talent, he always believed a player's desire could beat back an opponent. "You must have something inside you that causes you to rise above the rest."

Like rising water, the desire to win sought its own level in each boy, regardless of their size or speed. Acree searched for players who wanted to win football games. His problem was finding boys who were willing to work as hard and relished winning as much as he did.

Like his high school Coach George Tallchief in Maud, Oklahoma, Acree disliked quitters. His competitive nature rejected those who lacked perseverance. Boys who refused to sacrifice personally for the team eliminated themselves. Players who wanted to treat talent as the only requirement for winning had no place in Acree's scheme. Football is a team sport, he thought; and the collective desire of the boys determines a team's winning attitude.

Each boy reacted to Acree. Some admired him. Many feared him. A few thought he was cruel. Those who bucked up against him had no choice but to quit. It was his way or turn in your uniform. That year, Gary Whistler wasn't the only boy to walk away from the Tigers.

* * *

Corsicana is a smallish town in Central Texas, south of Dallas. In 1960, cotton fields surrounded it, north to Rice, south to Angus, west to Barry and east to Powell. Row after row of black soil separated tall, green stalks of leafy plants salted with white bolls, the rounded, fibrous fruit of cotton. "King Cotton" was an economic essential. Another essential was high school football, which was racially segregated then. However, the town's interest in the game had waned as team after team disheartened Corsicanans—just as poor cotton crops disappointed farmers in a decade-long drought.

A farmer watches the elements of sunshine, soil and rain turn a seed into a vigorous cotton plant. Likewise, a coach foresees determination, diligence and preparation as ingredients needed to convert boys and a town into winners.

Or viewed the other way around, a city and its boys develop into champions by reaching for and attaining the mindset of a winning-oriented coach—a coach such as Jim Acree. Coaches like him come to town only ever so often.

Corsicanans spoke of Coach Johnnie Pierce when he roused them to a series of football titles long ago. Tiger football hero, Maco Stewart, remembered Coach Pierce leading the Tigers to two successive semifinal appearances in 1930 and 1931. Then in 1932, adopting his ways, the Corsicana Tigers became State Champions, defeating the Mighty Mites from the Masonic Home in Fort Worth. The Texas Interscholastic League (TIL) had only one eleven-man football bracket. Corsicana defeated powerhouse teams from Highland Park, Tyler's John Tyler, Houston Reagan, Waco, Marshall, Temple, Cleburne, San Antonio Brackenridge, Greenville and Masonic Home.

In 1933, Coach Pierce cemented an expectation of winning in the town by capturing the District 11-A title, a bi-district title in 1934 and another

25

district title in 1935. He became a founding father of the Texas High School Coaches Association.

And as if it were the secret to winning Tiger football games, Coach Pierce wore a blue, short-sleeved shirt on the Tiger sideline.

Like a drought strikes farmers, Corsicana failed to achieve football celebrity through the remainder of the 30's and during the war years. But after that long absence and two coaching changes, the town and players again won titles by watching and adopting the fervor of Coach Boyd Payne.

Corsicana's District changed as post-war Texas towns grew. The TIL increased the number of classifications and realigned schools into districts biennially based on student enrollment. The Tigers transformed from "also-rans" (losing) in 1947 to title winners in District 10-AA. They also repeated the win in 1949 in District 13-AA. Corsicanans believed that a coach's leadership held the secret to a team becoming champions.

Despite four coaching changes after 1949, Corsicana experienced another decade of football losses. Corsicanans settled in as "also-rans" and watched their rivals succeed. Nearby towns such as Athens, a District 5-AAA winner, defeated the Tigers, 22-6 in 1958. Another traditional competitor, Cleburne, became the Class AAA state title holder in 1959. When the Yellow Jackets played Corsicana that year, the Tigers walked onto Yellow Jacket field to the sound of a buzzing hometown crowd. They faced big and quick linemen, who stifled the Tiger run game. The match ended in a Tiger loss, 13-14.

The school bus that brought the Tigers to the game sat in the parking lot of the limestone stadium, housing a stone-cold visitor's dressing room. As if stuffed full of losing, the players had lumps in their throats on the bus ride home. That year they came up one game short, losing to the Athens Hornets, 7-12. The thrill of being a champion never materialized under Coach Mark Culwell, known around town as a "good man."

By the summer of 1960, sales of reserved seats at Corsicana's Tiger Field on 4th Avenue dropped from over 400/year to just 62—a decline of about three dozen per year since their last football playoff team. Projected sales for the start of the fall season were just 12 reserved seats. Some folks blamed sagging football revenues on television and the attraction to newer forms of entertainment. But a 32-43-5 record over the previous eight seasons had eroded interest in local football.

Corsicana's overall win percentage dropped below 60%, a first since 1925. Tiger fans had supported multiple head coaches and endured boasts from district rivals—Mesquite, Ennis, Waxahachie and Athens. Football success by neighboring rivals Cleburne, Palestine and Waco became intolerable. Competitors considered Corsicana to be a "good opponent," that is, one they could beat.

All this would change in 1960 under the new Head Coach, Jim Acree.

Acree arrived in Corsicana with a winner's reputation—a champion from Oklahoma University under Coach Bud Wilkinson. Acree was born with a desire to win. He expected to win. And he would do it with players who improved their gameplay through diligence and sacrifice. He'd rather start a tenacious 5'-3", 135-pound defensive noseguard before a larger, more talented man who loafed or didn't like to hit. Left up to Acree, every player would hustle and hit somebody on every play. The more powerful the hit, the greater the player's desire in Acree's mind.

Working as an assistant coach under M.B. Nelson in Bonham, Texas, he learned how to turn a ten-loss team into District Champions. In 1958, Nelson retired from coaching and Acree became Bonham's head coach. He was off the farm home in Oklahoma, but he had learned how to cultivate a crop of boys and townspeople into champions like himself. Under his leadership, the Bonham Warriors won two more district titles in 1958 and 1959.

To lure Acree, Corsicana superintendent Dana Williams offered him an opportunity at the AAA level with a student body nearly double the size of Bonham. That meant the number of tryouts could potentially double in number. Acree's goal was to improve the town's weak football reputation and sagging spirits. Polyester was replacing cotton, and Williams expressed a possible remedy. "Only a state championship in football would put Corsicana back on the map."

After Acree accepted the offer, two coaching resignations immediately challenged him. First Assistant Coach Dave Smith at Corsicana High left to coach in San Antonio. He competed for the head coaching job and didn't get it. Eddie Cook, head coach at Drane Junior High in Corsicana, also resigned. So Acree recruited assistant coach Raymond Anderson from Bonham to follow him to Corsicana and become his first assistant coach.

After moving day, his wife Rosemary stayed at home from church to care for two of their four children who had contracted the measles. She had high expectations, too. "We're happy to be here and all moved in. Maybe somebody will come to see us."

* * *

Acree conceded charge of the home to "Slim," as he called his wife, while he searched for "alert, scrappy, confident players" he could mold into a winning team. It was imperative to do it without breaking any University Interscholastic League (UIL) rules.

Acree's competitiveness created a natural conflict with the UIL, an organization that developed football rules in Texas. Although he admired the UIL and even praised it in public, he perhaps saw its growing control of local coaches as competition, especially if he perceived its rules as coming from uninformed, less football-minded representatives.

Originally known as the Texas Interscholastic League, the UIL began in 1910 with a belief in the need to regulate the natural rivalry between schools in various "extracurricular activities," especially in the growing sport of football. Membership in the League numbered hundreds of schools that selected or appointed representatives to form committees and devise rules to organize, manage and regulate competition between member schools within some educational standard. With UIL oversight, members voluntarily adhered to these rules, disciplining themselves.

When Acree arrived in Corsicana, the UIL had recently banned spring practice for senior high students in Class AAA districts. How could he become familiar with his players if the UIL barred workouts with them? He wanted to work with the players, but the UIL rule book was an inhibitor. He saw parts of it as contrary to his winning philosophy. For example, disallowing spring and summer workouts forced him to find creative ways to engage with the boys that would not break UIL rules. He intended to help them prepare for competition, keep football on their minds and maintain conditioning for the action coming in August. The high school boys may have been aware of UIL rules regarding off-season practice, but they willingly attended player-led workouts where Acree "gave hints" of what to do. Acree became known for stressing the importance of "off-season" programs long before the UIL legitimized them.

In March, Acree responded by coaching the Corsicana track team in the annual Dogwood Relays held in Palestine, Texas. By doing so, he could see the speed of running back W.R. Garlington, the endurance of end Billy Nelson and the strength of tackle Gary Whistler—all footballers in senior high. Interviewed after the meet, Acree revealed what was important to him, "Several boys lowered their own times, but we didn't manage to win anything."

The relays included entrants from the current football opponents, Ennis, Cleburne, Jacksonville, Waxahachie and Athens. Purportedly, Acree watched athletes from the other schools as much as he did his own. To him, the track meet was a scouting adventure.

The UIL had not banned spring football drills for Corsicana's two junior high schools, Collins and Drane, which Acree supervised, including seventh, eighth and ninth graders. Consequently, the ninth graders in 1960 who became high school students in the fall, had a better understanding of Acree football than previous sophomores and juniors, who may have only experienced Acree via informal workout sessions behind closed doors in the high school gym.

In Maud, Acree enjoyed seeing his name, "Big Jimmie Acree," in the Maud Enterprise and understood its effect on player commitment, so he released a list of players participating in the spring workouts. Among the eighth graders attending were boys who later became notable high school seniors: Jim Hagle, Gary Roman, Donnie Denbow, Sam Cooper and Jim Wood.

To allow junior high players to show off their football skills, Acree scheduled two spring games between the schools—seventh and eighth graders mixed against each other and ninth graders against other ninth graders. The town turned out for the scrimmages to see their boys play on Tiger Field, but the city and the boys came to watch Acree, too. Players and fans studied him intently as he roamed the sideline with authority. He only had to call out a player's last name to have him instantly appear at his side, waiting eagerly for instructions. From the start, players wanted to please him. Fans admired his focus and intensity.

* * *

Tiger Field on 4th Avenue was the site of about twenty-five games a year, which wore down the crown turf on the field. Acree acquired two truckloads of barnyard manure and worked beside the players to spread it. He told Coach Anderson, "If the players see me working beside them to help build a better field, perhaps they will put out more energy and pay closer attention to the fundamentals of the game."

Anderson agreed, "If all the players see us working hard with them, we'll have better teams and go further in conference competition."

1960 senior ball carrier W.R. Garlington said, "Acree was an outstanding leader and coach. He led by example and worked harder than anyone I've known to win."

That included Coach Anderson who nicknamed Garlington "Dub."

Dub said, "Coach Acree brought commitment and hard work to an all-new level. He spent untold personal time working physically and mentally, preparing for a championship, not just preparing a football team to play, but preparing the team to win a championship. He set an example for his players on 'commitment to winning' that none of us had ever witnessed. It caused the team to play beyond our physical ability because he expected it and we respected what he was trying to achieve."

Acree believed and practiced an adage attributed much later to Steven R. Covey, "Treat a man as he can and should be, and he will become as he can and should be."

One Corsicana boy, Steve Baggs, shared how a previous coach had driven him out of football by saying, "You're no good."

Baggs had quit football, but as a senior, he approached Acree and asked, "Give me a chance, Coach."

Acree saw his longing and Baggs became a star placekicker and eventually received a Most Outstanding Lineman award. Coach called him a "man." He wanted boys to demonstrate courage, intelligence and a desire to excel. Besides his actions, he never defined what he considered to be a man. Extrapolating from his behavior, 'a man' doggedly worked to complete a task, focused on the job at hand, led others by working harder than anyone else, helped others to improve, prepared for every situation and played the game to win—and win championships. It was as if Acree were saying, "Do as I do and you will win in football and in life."

31

To illustrate the work example set by Acree, former assistant Coach Jerry Moore told the story of how for extra pay, Acree mowed the baseball outfield with a powered-push mower. One day, Acree had the boys working on grooming the infield while he cut the outfield. Moore said, "Acree pushed the mower forward in the tall grass and then pulled it back. He did this over and over, methodically covering the outfield. Suddenly, Acree stood beside us with the top of one of his shoes mangled and bloody."

The boys were shocked; Acree had dragged the mower back over the top of his foot. Calmly, Acree said, "Y'all keep working. I'm going down the road to have Coach Anderson patch up my foot. I'll be back."

Moore reported that after a while, Acree returned with his foot bandaged and proceeded to finish the mowing job.

As if he were preparing eighty acres for farming back in Maud, Acree also tended the grass on the old Tiger field that spring. He seeded, fertilized and watered it, treating each sprig as if it were a player. Through care and mowing, he trained and groomed the grass like it was part of the team. He believed that playing under the lights on a lush, green field, freshly striped, energized the players to do their best. It worked for him. It should work for them.

· * * *

That spring, at his first appearance before the Dads Club, an organization of townspeople that promoted Tiger sports, members queried Acree about the number of boys coming out for football. He reported, "Sadly, not enough."

Acree explained that Corsicana lost many boys between junior high and high school because some parents considered football "too rough."

Rumors of "roughness" limited the number of tryouts. He told the Dads, "If football was a bloody game, I never knew it."

Speaking indirectly to the mothers, "We're going to put bars (facemasks) on helmets and save everybody's teeth."

He assured the Dads, "Size and speed are not everything. We look for an ability to move, courage and agility."

He stated one of his core values, "We believe you must make sacrifices to obtain anything worthwhile. Your boys will learn this lesson and develop into men you can be proud of."

To promote a team mindset in the town, Acree stated, "If you have some advice for the program, please bring it to me, not the boys."

Acree wasn't looking for guidance from the parents through the boys.

Corsicana voted to construct a new football complex on West Highway 31 for use in the 1961 season. The old Tiger Field location lacked parking, and rival stadium improvements embarrassed the locals.

District opponent Waxahachie also had a new coach, creating an unknown. Competition in District 8-AAA changed when the UIL replaced traditional enemy Palestine with unknown Mesquite. Acree and his assistants met their coaching competition at the Texas High School Coaches Association (THSCA) meeting. As if it were a jinx on the Tigers, coaches from Athens, Waxahachie, Ennis and Mesquite picked Corsicana to win District 8-AAA. With a 4-5-1 record in 1959, choosing the 1960 Tigers to be district champs was absurd. Unknown to them, Coach Acree intended to make good on their pick.

* * *

That summer, to stay fit, Acree encouraged the boys to get jobs working outside in the hot sun. He kept in shape himself, distributing fertilizer in the Corsicana area for a company with whom he worked while living in Bonham. To make sure football was on the mind of the boys, he acquired 52 free tickets to an intra-squad scrimmage of the Dallas Texans, who would become the Kansas City Chiefs. Corsicana coaches accompanied multiple car-loads of boys to Cobb Stadium to watch the action. They were amazed at how Acree clued them position-by-position on what to watch in the scrimmage. They started to appreciate his eye for mistakes, too.

Acree brought an Oklahoma-style, Split-T offense to Corsicana. To him, the "most beautiful play in football" was the run-or-pass option to the corner. He searched for a quarterback that could carry it out effectively. His innovative nature expressed itself. He improvised offensive plays, defensive stunts and trick plays for special teams. But UIL notwithstanding, he considered it his purview to specify all aspects of football practice: who, what, when and where. For example, he devised a metal-pipe contraption on the practice field at Tiger Field, designed to keep linemen low as they "fired off" to execute their blocking assignments. If technology could help him win, Acree adopted it.

He relished fan support and often gave them insight into his strategy. He spoke weekly to civic clubs, such as the Lions Club, the Rotarians and the Kiwanians. He described the conditioning requirement for players to go both ways: offense and defense. He told his strategy for controlling the ball, emphasizing the running game. Given four tries to make ten yards, Acree declared, "Gaining 3 or 4 years per carry is good."

He stated, "We'll pass only when there is a better than 50% chance of success."

"We'll also pass if we can exploit an opponent's weakness."

As if he were coaching the fans, he added, "We'll use a 'quick kick' to get out of field-position trouble."

Acree started two-a-day workouts in August with sixty-three tryouts. Returning assistant coach Jim Miller handled the linemen, and Raymond Anderson coached the backfield. The boys dressed out at the high school, and the coaches used an old truck with slatted sideboards to carry them across town to the practice field, located on the north end of Tiger Field.

Using a variety of organized, timed workouts, Acree drilled the boys on football fundamentals—blocking, tackling and ball handling. He emphasized physical conditioning, regardless of size and speed and pushed players to exhaustion only to surprise them with even more challenging work, such as bleacher running or wind sprints. Repetition was Acree's primary teaching tool. After completing a practice play, players expected to hear the words, "Run it again, men."

"One more time."

"Same song, different verse."

To test perseverance, he practiced players using fast-paced, repeated drills until they could "do it right." His goal was to help boys improve, but only if they made up their minds to succeed. He had little patience for anyone who lacked hustle. His harsh methods quickly ended fanciful dreams of football glory for "soft" boys, as he might have called them. He prepared his "men" to play hard for the duration of a game when boys commonly played both ways.

He toughened players for football just as he had learned it. His teams were "well-coached" and possessed all the marks of a good opponent, one where the other team, according to Acree, "would have to try their best if they want to win."

Reminiscing on the difficult practices, former player Don Fuller said, "Near the end of each practice, it was dark. We longed to see that old truck with slatted sides roll up and take us back to the high school."

Boys such as Dub Garlington and Steve Baggs accepted Acree's plan that year, but star baseball player, James Basham, quit Tiger football during the first week of two-a-day practices. He walked off one morning and never returned even though he played as a quarterback, a key man in Acree's offense. As a pitcher, Basham was a two-time District 8-AAA baseball champion. He was also a track speedster on the Tiger mile relay team. Acree needed experienced boys like him to become leaders on the football team. But each boy had to want to become a football player in the Acree way.

When Acree occasionally "eased off" full-speed contact with pads in practice, he allowed the boys to wear just helmets, t-shirts and shorts. However, he made sure they understood they were not ready to play, "I didn't want them to go 'stale.'"

He didn't want the players to quit like a soft drink "fizzes out."

* * *

Probably no district competitor watched Tiger workouts from the fence lining the practice field. Still, in Acree's competitive mind, he might have considered what he would do if he faced an unknown opponent. To finish off summer drills before the start of school, Acree bused the boys on a Saturday to a three-way scrimmage with Henderson and Mt. Pleasant; it was a three-hour bus ride, each way, into deep East Texas. He hoped to learn about the Tiger offense and defense and avoid the prying eyes of any central-Texas competitors.

At the annual BBQ Dinner sponsored by the Dads Club, Acree staged a short scrimmage and introduced a smaller (weight-wise) Tiger squad than the previous year. The team makeup was primarily juniors. Thirty boys were on the A-team and thirty-one on the B-team.

During practice, Acree focused on the A-team and prepared the boys to play every down as though it would determine the game's outcome. He described the ideal player's attitude, "Never do we go onto the field that winning is not foremost on our minds."

But did the team want to win more than their opponents?

Waco High

For their first game of the 1960 season, the Tigers worked hard to prepare for the 43rd meeting against Waco High, billed as a "Battle of the Bengals." Waco was a larger AAAA school with a town population five times that of Corsicana. Corsicana had not defeated them in their previous eight matches. Choosing from a smaller talent pool, the Corsicana players were on average twenty-three pounds smaller than their corresponding Waco players. Preseason coaches' polls picked Waco to win its district. Moreover, it would be Acree's first outing as Corsicana's head coach. Acree told the press, "Things look bad for us."

No fan asked Acree, "Does Corsicana think they can win the Waco game?"

Nevertheless, Acree prepared his Tigers to play hard-nosed football and courageously face a team of larger boys. In the third quarter, a Tiger became frustrated and played irresponsibly, drawing a 15-yard personal foul. With the score 8-13, the penalty gave Waco momentum to score from the Tiger 11-yard line, making it 8-20.

Showing a will to fight, however, the Tiger eleven didn't give up. On the ensuing possession, the offense scored in three plays. They didn't quit when they were behind. Corsicana made a game of it, but the clock ran out. Waco escaped with a win. Corsicana lost 14-20 due to a costly mistake. Acree assured the Dads Club in a game review that Sunday afternoon that the team would make fewer mistakes the following week against Palestine.

Acree was a living library of everything significant to defining a champion. In one visit to his reading room, the players discovered that winners don't beat themselves. He encouraged them to play aggressive football, but they had to avoid crucial penalties, especially personal fouls. Fans were pleased with how the team ran the Oklahoma Split-T offense, the team's enthusiasm on defense and "shooting the gaps," but winning also includes avoiding mistakes. And not just penalties, but missed tackles, too.

Waco won its 13-AAAA District in 1960, and the Corsicana Tigers learned to take advantage of their opponent's mistakes. Waco did not relax when they had a lead. Their desire to win flowed like sweet crude oil from a West Texas gusher.

By not quitting, the Corsicana Tigers demonstrated a fighting spirit and won the town's support. Waco may have defeated Corsicana, but the city and the cheerleaders sensed a new attitude, a will to win. They cheered, "Tigers Fight. Tigers Fight. Tigers Fight, Fight, Fight!"

Acree never said, "just go out there and have fun."

Palestine

His comments to the Dads Club regarding their next opponent, Palestine, give insight into his thoughts about competition. Corsicana had defeated Palestine the previous year, and Acree said, "The Wildcats will come to town with an incentive to even the count."

In other words, if an opponent beat Acree in a match, Acree would come after them the next time they played. Jacksonville, for example, would soon learn that.

Preparing for Palestine, Acree directed Anderson and Miller. "Let's work the second-string players into more practice rotations this week," adding, "with some starters out this week, we need to develop depth in the squad."

Greater squad depth is a characteristic of a "good opponent."

Despite losing to Waco, the town sensed a more spirited Tiger team and came out to support them in their first home game. Rumors reported that Palestine improved over the previous year and that fans would get their money's worth.

The evenly matched teams treated the fans to a "leather-popping" affair. As a player, Acree was known for hard-hitting—a characteristic he passed on to the Tigers. "Move fast and hit somebody."

Mimicking Bud Wilkinson, Acree inserted the second-string team in the second half to see how they performed under game pressure. This included future star quarterback Tom Wilson. The Tigers edged out Palestine, 13-6, and savored a win "on the green grass of home."

Demonstrating their hustle and hitting, the energetic Tigers had to come from behind to win. They made mistakes, but not costly ones as in the previous week.

Cleburne

For the season's third game, Acree shifted the team's focus to defeating State Co-Champion Cleburne. The Tiger B-team coach, Bill Hay, scouted the Yellow Jackets in their losing effort against Irving. He told Acree, "Cleburne is a big, strong ball club. It lost to Irving, but it had some key injuries."

With the Tiger game in mind, Acree expressed his competitive expectation, "But they'll be healed by game time."

The press favored Cleburne over the Tigers. Corsicana's District 8-AAA had a reputation of being composed of weak teams. The powerful Jackets were known for making notable hits. In their previous six games against Cleburne, the Tigers had lost four and tied two. The tie games were moral victories for fans but unacceptable to Acree. Left up to him, tie games would have ended in sudden-death overtime.

Acree drilled the players that week on blocking assignments, defensive stunts and special teams' play. He pushed their conditioning to a new level. For him, repetition in practice translated to repetition in winning. After practicing, he set expectations at the Dads Club. "If our boys are sharp, they can win."

Playing on home turf, the Tigers had an advantage in the number of fans. They defeated the Yellow Jackets 14-6 and ended a six-year jinx. Wind from a northerner affected passing and punting, but Acree's focus on player conditioning produced a win. With more first downs, rushing yards and completed passes, Cleburne dominated the game statistically. But Acree informed the Dads Club, "Hustle won the game."

Corsicanans watched Acree from the bleachers as he worked with the players on the field and the sidelines. The town bonded with him as if they were two cotton plants grafted into one. Like magic, hard work, preparation and conditioning restored their lost confidence. Winning drew the team, the town and Acree into a single knot, securing by a common goal—winning a District Championship.

The Tigers were victorious over a Cleburne team that went on that year to appear in the state AAA Semifinal game. And two Tiger wins in a row stirred excitement like a good, soaking rain enlivens the spirits of Corsicana farmers. After the win, at Coach Miller's suggestion, Coach Acree led the team in singing a victory song in the middle of the field, "When the Roll is Called up Yonder, When the Roll is Called up Yonder, When the Roll is Called up Yonder, We'll Be There."

The other coaches lumped into a group, but Acree stood apart. After the win, the town and the players studied Acree's words and actions. At the close of practices the next week, the red-faced boys gathered near Acree, perhaps on one knee and did not miss a word he spoke. The chain-link fence between the stands and the field no longer marked a separation of the fans from the Coach.

Acree spoke in a direct, informative style—some say he was blunt. Through film review with the Dads and the players, Acree highlighted the Tiger's defensive weaknesses, demonstrated why they yielded sizeable running yardage to Cleburne's backs and pointed out how they succumbed to good blocking.

Acree didn't credit the weather for the Tigers' fortune. The rain had soaked the players and the ball and having a 7-6 lead, the Tigers pounced on a turnover and then scored again. Acree complimented the team for their burst of third-quarter effort.

He acknowledged their weaknesses but noted they played well under adverse conditions. Both the victory and Acree delighted the town. The Cleburne win raised Corsicana's "football fever." Other 8-AAA District foes, Ennis, Waxahachie and Athens, lost that week. Expectations for a championship surged in the town.

Jacksonville

Acree was not one to bask long in a victory. Undefeated Jacksonville was up next, and the Tigers looked terrible in practice. He told the Dads, "They are not ready to play."

Continuing an intimidating sequence of non-district games for the Tigers, Jacksonville hosted Corsicana in the confines of their Tomato Bowl stadium. Five of the Tiger non-district opponents in 1960 became title-holders in their districts.

The visitor locker room in Jacksonville was a humid, uninviting box with bench-lined, cinder-block walls and a damp, concrete floor. Just the kind of place to take a nasty fall.

Acree's pregame talk to the players who gathered before him on a knee or a bench, consisted of last-minute reminders. Having a plan to control the ball on offense, he only stated that Don Fuller would return to start at fullback and Jim Barnabee at a guard slot.

The team pushed out onto the field business-like, wearing serious faces like their coach, ready to hit, sweat and fight to win. To the thrill of the homecoming crowd, the Indians scored two touchdowns, while the Tigers fumbled the ball away three times.

Watchful of down and distance situations, Acree called timely quick-kicks, which kept the Indians from scoring more often. If a starting man's technique weakened from the struggle, Acree replaced him. He inserted second-string quarterback Tom Wilson to try his hand at advancing the scoreless Tigers.

Fans hoped for a score, a long run or a pass completion. The boys knew from the film review to watch their position and not just to follow the football with their eyes. They stood ready for Acree's call to substitute at any moment. His eyes never left the field. He summoned players from the sideline and pushed them into the game to make a specific call, make an adjustment to override how he had prepared the quarterback based on the situation or perhaps call for a defensive stunt.

Acree actively managed the game from the sideline, his actions expressing his intent to win, substituting to force the Indians to fight through stubborn Tigers, responding as he had rehearsed them so many times in practice. Occasionally, he excitedly jumped into action in response to an unexpected event, a fumble, a penalty, a blocked punt and received a warning from a referee to stay off the field.

Just as he focused countless hours preparing for the game, Acree immersed himself during the game as it unfolded, analyzing how the Indians consistently advanced via short gains between the tackles. Hard like the red stone in the stadium, his mind was impervious to distractions. His eyes searched the field for any weakness to exploit, the need to pull a player out for coaching or shift to a throwing strategy instead of running. Acree engaged with action and looked for any opportunity for advantage.

The players saw how a competitive attitude fights even when the opponent is winning. Acree learned from each situation as if he knew he would match up against the Indians again. Jacksonville defeated the Tigers, 0-14.

Gloom overtook the Tigers on the bus ride home. The players mentally replayed their mistakes, which hurt more than their knocks and bruises. The loss hurt, but it did not dissolve Acree's desire. His back-and-forth reviewing of the game film before the Dads Club spoke of the mistakes and how a properly executed block would have freed a runner and led to a score against a formidable Indian defense. The heads of the players and members of the Dad's Club spun dizzy-like hearing and seeing Acree's insights. They started to believe they should have won the game.

That weekend, after the curfew passed, Acree patrolled the downtown streets in his jeep. He found team member Freddy Allison out having fun and kicked him off the team. Freddy was a third-string player, but his father was a key supporter. Acree was willing to sacrifice boys to uphold team rules. The news worsened. Starter Jim Barnabee was out due to injury, and an illness had sidelined key lineman, Joe Allen.

Dallas Samuel

For the fifth week in a row, the press picked Corsicana as the "underdog" against upcoming opponent Dallas Samuel, a AAAA powerhouse. Acree analyzed the Spartans for the Dads Club. "They have a big ball club and probably are one of the better Class AAAA teams in the State. So far, they have not shown much speed, but they relied on power in beating South Park of Beaumont and South Oak Cliff."

What some would describe as a dream, Acree spoke about the matchup, "If the Tigers hit hard and hustle, they have a good chance."

His competitive attitude dominated his thinking, "They don't look invincible."

About practicing to prepare for that week, Acree also told the Dads, "We have had to go back to the fundamentals of our basic offense."

From the Jacksonville experience, he added, "There are some basic things the boys have not yet mastered, and until we do, we have to work on them. For one thing, we need to learn to block."

With a 2-2 record, the Tigers, not ranked in any AAA poll, faced the defending champion, Spartans, ranked sixth in the state in Class AAAA. That Friday night, adrenaline filled the boys when they saw the profound difference in the size of the two teams. Thrown into a fight they could not win before a home crowd that overflowed the stadium, the Tigers surprised the press at the half, trailing only 7-13.

Acree knew the teams were not so far apart in wanting to win. He had seen the determination in the Tigers since they started two-a-days. He noted how they learned the split-T offense, the linemen setting large gaps, with a quarterback running, pitching or throwing the ball. They endured his repetitive practicing of every part of the game and learned how to respond in game situations—open field, short yardage, goal line. He saw their confidence develop into sharp execution no matter what their circumstance.

In Acree's mind, the Tigers were capable of winning. The boys only needed to decide for themselves if they wanted it bad enough. If a determined player chose to execute his blocking assignments better, under Acree's coaching, his blocking improved. The Tigers scored two touchdowns on a AAAA team that had only allowed one score in their previous four games. Although outmatched, Acree relished seeing the Tigers' grit.

A champion's mindset and that of also-rans have little similarity. Player comparisons such as size and power didn't fool Acree. The eleven boys on the field for the Tigers were not there by chance. Acree sifted through boys on the team to find those who craved winning. The size of their desire mattered most to him.

Corsicana was hungry for a championship. Acree recognized in the 1960 crop of smaller Tigers the courage to go full-speed against larger boys. Speaking to Dads and boys at a church function, the audience raised the question of the importance of size. Acree responded, "Size is the most overrated thing in football."

"Most important is determination and heart in wanting to play the game."

Intelligence was also a factor in winning. "If you think hard enough about the game, you can play it."

The pain of losing to Samuel was visible in the tears of the boys. But Acree's endless effort to improve them testified to his belief that they could be champions. Like seedlings ready to sprout, the Tigers were set to transform.

Lufkin Panthers

With a 2-3 record and a 13-41 thrashing from Samuel, the 1960 Tigers had had their fill of losing. Next up, the AAA Tigers beat a ranked AAAA team by surprising the Lufkin Panthers, 17-0.

Playing as if they had something to prove, the AAA Tigers shocked the AAAA Panther's hometown crowd. The Tigers demonstrated precision blocking, shrewd football and a fondness for personal contact. One game writeup reported, "Echoes of the tackles could be heard in the stands."

Hard-hitting doesn't show on the scoreboard, but Lufkin lost forty-seven yards rushing and three fumbles against the Tigers who lost nothing. The Corsicana Daily Sun reported, "Seldom have Corsicana followers seen the Bengals block and tackle as they did against the larger Lufkinites."

The Tiger defense smothered opponent runners, threw passers for a loss and held the Panthers on downs at the Tiger 5-yard line. W.R. Garlington's punting kept the Panthers in a hole. A double reverse by the Tigers in the second quarter brought the crowd to its feet, cheering a 22-yard gain.

On the margin of a Steve Baggs field goal, Corsicana led 3-0 at the half. This stunned the home team and their fans. The Tigers continued to roar in the third quarter. Sending Corsicana fans to their feet, W.R. Garlington returned a punt 73-yards for a touchdown. Later, Billy Nelson caught a 27-yard pass for a touchdown, making the score 17-0.

Steve Baggs kicked two extra points, garnering more ovations from Tiger fans.

Acree-conditioning paid off. The Tigers played tough throughout the game, while the Panther's effort dwindled toward the end. Acree's investment in practice repetitions paid dividends. Corsicana executed well on offense, defense and special teams. Acree liberally substituted second and third-string players throughout the game.

He praised the team's spirited play, but their 65 yards in penalties didn't go unnoticed.

The following week District play began and he drilled them one-on-one between two blocking dummies ad nauseum. He aimed to teach them the difference between not holding while blocking and holding on while tackling.

* * *

Ennis

The team peaked just in time for district play. But their first District 8-AAA opponent was an unexpectedly improved Ennis team. Acree wanted a championship. He spent so much time in preparation that week that the players thought he never slept. Studying his reactions in the film room, they saw his primary concern—what scout, Bill Hay, had reported—the Ennis Lions outweighed the Tigers across the board.

Furthermore, the Lions had speed in their backfield. Scoring on a seventy-yard run against Tyler Lee, they had a big quarterback, who could also pass well and proved it by throwing a forty-three-yard touchdown toss against Tyler Lee. While Corsicana pummeled Lufkin, Ennis surprised Tyler Lee, a AAAA team, outscoring them 12-6. With back-to-back wins, Acree believed Ennis was improving and hence, more formidable than their 2-4 record suggested. What the film didn't show was the size of the fight in the Lions.

Acree affected winning expectations in the town's barbershops, workplaces and grocery stores. Even though the Lions had destroyed Corsicana the previous two years, Acree helped Corsicanans and players believe the Tigers could prevail. He called for "more townspeople to make the 20-mile trip north up to Ennis to cheer for the Tigers."

That week, Ennis occupied the player's thoughts whether they were talking with their families at home, in a classroom discussion at school or reviewing plays in the film room with their Coach, who ran the projector back and forth. Acree could see victory ahead. He believed, "The Tigers can win if they chose to."

Compared to the season opener against Waco, Acree changed the team's lineup against Ennis, starting Steve Baggs at center, Doug Sorenson at guard, George Boyd at halfback and Tom Wilson, an up-and-coming quarterback, played most of the game.

Playing on their home field, the Lions surprised the Tigers and opened with an onside kick. They recovered it and quickly scored. The touchdown fired up the Ennis fans to expect a blowout. They must have imagined the Tigers wrapped up in burlap bales like cotton and made ready for market.

But Corsicana was Acree trained not to give up. The Tigers fought back to win, 16-6. The Corsicana Daily Sun channeled Acree in describing the success, "This is the kind of football that shows desire and sacrifice. That's what it takes to make a winner."

The Lions contested furiously, and the Tigers had to come from a deficit to win the game. Acree praised the improving Lions afterward, knowing his team had escaped a den of passionate players. The Tigers were victorious only through persistent, gritty play. He commended his players but pointed out their need for offensive improvement. Acree could always see room for improvement. For example, a blocker who didn't keep driving his feet but dropped to his knees after first contact, taking himself out of the play.

Waxahachie

Waxahachie had a scheduled off-week before opening their district play against Corsicana in the Tigers' eighth game of the season. The Indians were healthy and rested. The defensive-minded Braves outweighed the Tiger linemen by seventeen pounds on average and outweighed the backfield by eleven pounds. Nevertheless, the press picked the Tigers as a favorite. Acree warned, however, "They are dangerous and we cannot afford to take this game lightly."

Acree repeatedly practiced the Tigers that week on game fundamentals. As always, he included a fumble recovery drill. He taught boys to yell, "Ball! Ball!" if they spotted a football on the ground.

Waxahachie surprised the Tigers on a slippery, muddy Tiger field that Friday night. Six fumble exchanges occurred, four recovered by the Tigers. After one Indian bobble in the third quarter, the Tigers' Steve Baggs booted a field goal from the 17-yard line for the only score in the game.

The Tigers fumbled four other times but expertly recovered them. Acree emphasized reaction to the ball. In total, they snagged eight of ten fumbles on a muddy night. Corsicana squeaked by 8-AAA District foe Waxahachie, 3-0.

The Tigers dreaded Acree's obsession with repetition in practice, his intolerance for mistakes and his "do it again until we get it right" perfectionism. His work ethic appeared to have no limit. Everyone around him fell into an expectation that to win, the Tigers had to outwork their opponent. Thankfully, a day had only 24 hours. He would have lengthened it if it were within his control. Schoolwork demanded attention; otherwise, he would have required players to work around the clock that week after narrowly avoiding defeat by the Indians.

The Tigers went into an open week, but instead of resting, Acree put them through a routine of intensive workouts focused on the fundamentals of football. He drilled the team on blocking and tackling, keeping the boys late each evening. With no game scheduled, he didn't see a need to rest.

Athens

Corsicana was a district leader over Athens by two games. However, a loss to the Hornets would mean a tie with Mesquite and a battle for who would represent the district in the playoffs. Four years had passed since the Tigers defeated the Hornets. In the ninth week of the season, fans repeatedly asked Acree, "Can the Tigers beat Athens?"

His response didn't vary. "If they want to and if they are willing to pay the price."

Acree believed the Proverb, "All hard work yields a profit," but it doesn't take much to suppose he read it as "*painfully* hard work." The boys didn't just imagine they could win; they had confidence they would do their best to win. They had given their best in practice. They would do the same in the game.

Acree saw teamwork in their unified huddle break, their simultaneous attack off the line of scrimmage and the coordinated backfield movement to conceal the ball carrier. Their transformation on defense was apparent in how a linebacker shed a blocker, a tackler hit a ball carrier or a cornerback attacked an oncoming sweep. Seeing a reflection of himself in the determination expressed on players' game faces delighted him. The locker room had no mirrors. Otherwise, the Tigers might double-take their image if they understood that Acree saw his face in theirs.

The change in the boys was not unexpected. They listened to Acree each day, absorbed his play descriptions, visualized the outcome of their blocks and saw a ball carrier racing through an opening and the crowd jumping up to signal a touchdown.

49

Carefully watching Acree's powerful demonstrations, reactions and moves, the Tigers acted out his example on the field. His motions became their automatic reactions. Through repetition, they improved as a team together. And the profits of their labor came.

In game nine of 1960, Corsicana destroyed district rival Athens, 28-0.

Mesquite

In game ten, Mesquite fell, 20-6.

W.R. Garlington recalled the fierce contact, "I remember our guard Jon Ed Ingham on a 4th down punt I made that was perfect as it sailed over the Mesquite receiver's head. He scrambled back to recover it, arriving at the same time as Jon Ed jumped on him, causing the ball, receiver and Jon Ed to bounce completely off the ground and high enough that I could see daylight underneath them as I rushed down the field."

A near-capacity crowd saw the match against Mesquite on Tiger Field. The game was a weird experience for the Tiger players. They peered into their opponents' faces across the line and perceived their thoughts of defeat. Their opponent had given up. They had searched in vain for a play that would work against the Tigers but found nothing. The Corsicana players recognized the anguish they once knew. The darting eyes that gave away the direction of play, a stance that betrayed a pass versus a run, the bickering over who caused a miscue and the frustration and desperation of losing after so much work.

The Tiger teammates understood each other's intent and actions with minimal communication. The opponent players watched as they executed, machine-like, to create a victory. Admiring the Tigers, they wondered at the mystery of being a champion.

In defeating Mesquite, the 1960 Tigers completed their transition to undisputed District 8-AAA champions. They experienced the change through Acree's strategy to couple painful work in practice to winning on Friday nights.

They had broken the drought.

For the first time in a decade, car horns honked up and down the main drag in Corsicana.

Don Fuller said, "The Town went crazy after winning the championship. The Palace theater gave each team member two tickets to see 'Jail House Rock,' starring Elvis."

Corsicana enthusiastically committed to Acree football. A record number of fans—over four hundred attended the annual Tiger Loyalty Banquet sponsored by the Lions Club. Unrelated to Corsicana ISD, the Dads Club collected $900 from members and in a public Club meeting gave it as a show of appreciation to the seven football coaches in the high school and two junior highs. The practice established a tradition associated with winning in Corsicana.

The Tigers were still boys in appearance, but they had become men under Acree. They now had a "can do" mindset. They triumphed because of teamwork. Individually, they would never be the same. The players bonded together and produced a championship.

* * *

After the Mesquite game, Raymond Anderson won the coin toss with the District 7-AAA representative, Jacksonville who defeated the Tigers in game four. A week later, the Indians came to Corsicana for the bi-district title game.

An estimated 5,000 fans overflowed the stadium to fill 250 temporary bleachers and another 1,000 fans lined the fence surrounding the field. The Tigers played the undefeated Indians to a 7-7 tie. Jacksonville advanced on penetrations, 2-1, their last one coming with 28 seconds left in the game. An errant pitchout from Tom Wilson put the ball on the ground, and Jacksonville recovered it.

Word of Acree's harsh methods spread to other boys, especially linemen. Nevertheless, he expected eleven starters to come back and play on a new Tiger Field in 1961.

But Acree especially wanted Tom Wilson to return for his senior year.

**Coach Acree with Tom Wilson (foreground), Coach Anderson
(background on the phone) in 1963**

CHAPTER 3   DEDICATED TO THE GAME

"Athletics is not more important than math and English, but they are just as important." Abe Martin, Head Coach, TCU, 1961

Acree had made Tom Wilson the starting quarterback toward the end of the 1960 season. The 140-pound Tiger led the team to their first District 8-AAA championship in a decade. Wilson ran Acree's favorite play, a pass-run option, with showman-like perfection. He threw the football as though it were laser-guided.

Life hit Wilson with an unexpected punch when his father, a traveling soap salesman, slipped away from home one day and never returned. Like Acree, when troubles came, Wilson learned to ask, "What can I do to be better?"

Tom attached to Acree as a boy would to a father. Acree coached him like he was his own son. They formed a lifelong bond. Tom dedicated himself to the game. A teammate described him, "Tom ate, breathed and slept football. He wanted to win as much as Acree."

Corsicana's District 8-AAA win in 1960 greatly renewed football interest in the town. In 1961, the Dads Club sold a whopping 570 season tickets. They upped the number of game programs printed each week by a thousand. After just one year, Coach Jim Acree was popular and recognizable around town. If met on the street by a fan, they congratulated him but likely pressed him with their concern, "Will the Tigers have a good team this year?"

That fan might as well have asked a farmer to predict a crop before its planted. Acree possibly smiled and quipped, "You need to ask the players that question."

In Coach's mind, the boys returning for the 1961 season had a problem. How vital was football to them?

Johnny Coker was 5'10" and weighed 150. Other coaches called him a "skinny runt." But he didn't quit. Acree placed him in the middle of the line, a spot generally held by a big man. Tom Wilson didn't have a car, which furthered his credentials with Acree. He and his date often rode with Coker and his girlfriend in Coker's 1950 Ford. Coker described Acree as a mentor who developed the team's attitude, "Nobody can beat us."

Another returning letterman, Kenwerd Goode, listed at 5'11" and 168 pounds, claimed, "Football was my god. I loved it. I never missed a practice, worked the hardest and did everything Acree asked without question."

Perhaps the best physical specimen on the team, Jon Tewes, stood 5'9", weighed 205 and returned to play defensive noseguard. While interviewing him for this book, he said, "I was dedicated to one thing—football."

When asked about his commitment, Tewes said, "If I got knocked down, I got up, went back in and didn't give up."

George Boyd weighed 130 pounds. He had speed but lacked size. He made up for it in work ethic and grit. His role as a halfback was to run with the football. Often, Acree called on him to plunge directly ahead into a defensive line of larger boys for a few yards to gain a first down.

On Boyd's favorite plays, he swept around the end of the line or caught an optional pitch-out and sprinted to a corner. As a trick play, Acree wanted him sometimes to throw the ball. Boyd worked hours on Tiger

Field to learn to throw on the run using his off-hand. While interviewing him, he proudly recalled helping to build the new Tiger Field in the summer of 1961. "To make the end zone in new Tiger Field special, we moved sod to it from the end zone in old Tiger Field."

Phil Paschal, a senior letterman who played both offense and defense, noted the team's fear and respect for Acree, whom he called a strict, authoritarian. About the boys, he explained, "Our class was close, and we had a lot of team leaders, such as Tom Wilson and George Boyd."

Regarding his commitment, "If Tom wanted to throw passes before school, I was there. If Tom wanted to work more after practice, I stayed and ran routes for him. I felt like I was his 'go-to' receiver in games."

Tears welled up in Paschal's eyes as he named other team leaders who have since passed away. Players such as Larry Heathcote, Johnny Watkins and Danny Gordon. He said, "They were men determined to get it done."

The heartbreaking loss to Jacksonville that ended the 1960 Tiger season ignited a rivalry lasting throughout Jim Acree's tenure in Corsicana. Like using seed from a good cotton crop to make the next, Tiger players seeded a desire to whip the Indians, from one team to the next, season after season, losing only once in eight future matches under Acree—and that loss by only one point.

The bi-district loss to Jacksonville was still on Coach's mind in February 1961 when he reviewed the black and white, 16mm game film with the Methodist men's club. In the clickety-clack noise of the projector, Buddy Ward, the author's dad and club president heard Acree summarize his thoughts about the Tiger football prospects in the coming season, "We have a group of boys this year who are determined and who want to play."

Returning were eleven starters from the 1960 team, but Acree needed boys with a passion for the game to replace seniors such as Dub

Garlington, Don Fuller and Steve Baggs. They graduated in May 1961, but because of their small size, colleges, like those in the Southwest Conference, didn't offer them scholarships. They went on to play football at Corsicana's Navarro Junior College, which at the time had a reputation of being an extension of Corsicana High School. Their dreams of football glory ended on Tiger Field.

Speaking to the Methodist men, Acree didn't consider player size the most important characteristic. He commented, "It's gratifying to see a 'small' boy play because of their tremendous desire and dedication to the game."

Boys with those attributes were self-motivated and wouldn't quit. Acree only needed to teach them how to succeed, and he did that through hard work. If a boy screwed up, small or large, Acree made him lug a blocking dummy to the top of the bleachers.

A winning fervor stirred Corsicana parents to encourage their boys, big or small, to play the game. In late February 1961, Drane junior high coaches, Hugh Harkrider and Lloyd Nichols, opened spring drills with a noticeably large number of tryouts: seventy-two.

Coaches Paul Slaughter and Jesse Cummings at Collins Jr High experienced similar enthusiasm with a turnout of fifty-four boys. The author's year-older brother, Dickey Ward, was one of them. The author was in the eighth grade and, at age 13, had no interest in playing football. Instead, he hoped to find a job and earn money to buy a car the following year when he planned to get a driver's license.

Pooling the ninth graders from the junior highs, Acree, Anderson, Miller, Hay and McLeod drilled fifty-one ninth-grade boys who would enter high school in the fall. After one week, that number fell to thirty-two. By August, less than twenty of those boys joined the A-team or B-team. It didn't take ninth-graders long to gauge their commitment to football under Acree. More than half of the players quit as they transitioned from junior high to high school.

* * *

Considering the work hours Acree demanded, the same could be said for assistant coaches. After a year at Drane, Hugh Harkrider resigned in the summer to take a position as a head coach of a Class B school in Moody, Texas. Acree promoted his assistant, Lloyd Nichols, to Drane's new head coach. However, acting as if he had foreknowledge of the coming season's ending opponent, the Gainesville native opted to take a post as a high school assistant in Grapevine, Texas, a AA school.

Coaches come and go. Perhaps no one expected Acree's assistants to hang around very long. But many winced when Raymond Anderson resigned in July to coach track at Houston Smiley. Like a throttle on a racing engine, Anderson had been able to moderate Acree's demanding nature. The two began coaching together at Bonham in 1954. Anderson's soft-spoken but firm voice gained respect in Acree's ear. For example, Acree seemed oblivious when the clock ticked past the end of a scheduled practice time, "Okay, men. Let's run it just one more time."

But conscious of a commitment to the boys, Anderson would interject, "No, Coach, we can't do that."

Acree's practice face might have morphed from a look of game-like intensity to disbelief as if he were a farmer startled by a lightning bolt. He glanced at the watch on his left wrist and then yielded to Anderson. He gathered the boys around him for a few brief remarks about the practice before dismissing them. "Men, we did some good work today but are still not in shape."

If not for Anderson, every practice might have dragged on well into darkness. But by two-a-days in August 1961, the beloved assistant was two-hundred miles away in Houston.

Few men were as good as Raymond Anderson in applying the skills of a coach. He had a brilliant football mind and understood how to win. But he was also a caring man who loved boys and had their best interests in mind. To replace him, Acree sought a man trained by Anderson in Bonham.

Jerry Moore was an All-State receiver at Bonham when Anderson and Acree were assistants to M.B. Nelson. Moore matriculated to Baylor University, became team captain and was a star player. After graduation, he failed to earn a roster spot with the Dallas Cowboys, but he loved football and wanted to stay in the game. Shaping the lives of young men mattered to him. After midnight, Acree telephoned Moore in his Dallas hotel room. He invited Moore and his wife Margaret to Corsicana to interview. Jerry Moore became Coach Moore the next day, responsible for Tiger receivers.

Moore might have regretted the decision once he reported for work that summer. Acree declared himself the de facto supervisor for moving old Tiger Field stadium lighting, bleachers and fencing to the new field location. Acree had gardener-like care for the new field's turf development. He assigned Moore the 2 AM shift to move the water sprinklers on the new field. Planted from seed, the growing turf needed nighttime watering to establish it by the start of the season in September. Waking at 2 AM and driving out to the field, Moore thought about the depths to which he had plunged. After all the effort to achieve the heights of a college degree and football stardom, Acree had reduced Moore to a maintenance worker.

When it came to teamwork, Acree saw no job as too small. Before the fencing was in place, a few local boys decided to drive their cars onto the newly planted grass of Tiger Field and make figure eights. They were unaware that Acree slept in the field house and kept watch with a shotgun. They rolled in one night off Highway 31 and Acree climbed off his mat, grabbed the gun and raced outside to confront the pranksters.

He fired the shotgun into the air and yelled a few choice words. The cars sped off. That ended any thoughts of vandalism before Acree secured access to the field with a chain-link fence.

* * *

Twenty-one lettermen from the 1960 District Championship team returned to play in the fall of 1961. A dozen or so members of the former B-team returned. Among the twenty newly minted sophomores from junior high were Jim Hagle, Gary Roman, Joe Smith, Jim Wood, Johnny Nelson, Donnie Denbow, David Robinson, John Stover, Robert Graham and Sam Cooper. In two years, these boys would become celebrities.

Melding the new sophomores into the returning boys yielded a fifty-six-member squad at the start of two-a-day practices. The total team size had dropped year-over-year by five players. Next year it would drop by ten. More than a few former players attributed the team size reductions to the loss of Raymond Anderson and his moderating influence on Acree.

But attrition also occurred through accidents. The team lost Lynn Cooper for the season due to an injured toe that resulted from a shotgun blast. Unrelated, Acree didn't rank Robert Graham as an A-team possibility, coming up from Drane, because of a prank with a shotgun that went awry (see Chapter 5 of this book). To sort the boys into teams during pre-season scrimmages, Acree ranked them by position. He posted the rankings on a bulletin board in the new Field House to promote competition. He sorted quarterbacks on play calling, moving the ball and squad leadership. He judged running backs on who could best churn out three or four yards slamming into a defense of larger opponents. In short-yardage situations, he liked to hear a running back say, "Give me the ball, Coach, and I'll get you a first down."

Aside from their graded performance in scrimmages, Acree resolved competition between linemen using a "board drill." He placed a 2"x6"x6' board on the ground between two linemen who faced each other as they straddled the board. Acree picked the participating players.

The goal was for one boy to clear the other player off the board. The boys hated the drill. Their noses were so close to the ground in four-point stances that they could smell the turf. At the shrill of Acree's whistle, they launched across the board and slammed into each other, sometimes butting heads, but often the quicker boy plowed underneath the slower one. Acree yelled, "Drive! Drive!"

"Keep your head down!"

"Drive them feet!"

"Move him! Move him!"

And when it was over, the chests of both boys heaved and they wiped the sweat from their brows. Acree would blow his whistle and say, "Okay, men, let's go again. Ready."

Slightly less fearful of smashing into one another, the boys hustled back to re-take their positions at each end of the board. Often, the boy in better condition prevailed. Acree would blow his whistle again. The players exploded toward one another, moving faster than their on-looking friends could imagine.

Thinking of nothing but forcing the other man off the board, they collided as helmets and pads clapped together. Their legs churned; cleated shoes dug into the turf. They pushed, strained and clutched the grass with bloodied fingers to stay low and hold their ground. If one dropped to his knees, his opponent quickly bulldozed him aside. The boys grunted and groaned but uttered not a curse word. Their onlooking teammates cheered and congratulated the winner with a pat on the back. The loser got a pat on the butt, too.

Acree reduced football to boxing. To win, he said to the boys, "Beat the man in front of you."

Waco High

Players practicing against friends daily can lead to a comfort zone, a place with no fear. But the 1961 season started by pitting Corsicana against a large, AAAA class school, Waco High, whom they had not defeated in almost a decade. The Waco Bengals outweighed the Corsicana team by fifteen to eighteen pounds per man.

Even though it was the inaugural game on the new Tiger Field, no one picked Corsicana to win over Waco. They had superior numbers. Acree said, "Waco will play thirty-three players. We will play twenty-two."

Player conditioning was critical since more than half of the Tigers played both ways. Their mental toughness mattered, too. Acree practiced them that week at game-speed, challenging the boys emotionally, yelling, "You get out of it what you put into it."

Enduring full-pad contact, the defensive linemen worked on escaping double-team blocks against larger men and doing it play after play, down after down. Smaller boys fought bigger ones on the board drill to develop their courage. The boys ignored bruises, scrapes and bloody cuts and out-of-joint fingers. They told themselves to "shake it off" if they were hurting. At the close of each practice, Acree put them through more "wind sprints" than Coach Anderson would have allowed.

On game night, school officials spoke before an overflow crowd of more than 5,000, thanking those responsible for building the new stadium. Acree's tireless efforts were unmentioned, but one speaker had a crystal ball, "Corsicana last won a state championship in 1932, and with new Tiger Field, it won't be the last."

The band marched and played, but the Tigers paid little attention to the dedication ceremony. Their focus was on an opponent they considered ripe for the picking on the bright-green field, which they had helped to establish. The game started and the record book for the season opened. How good were the 1961 Tigers?

Tom Wilson handed off to Ole Olsen and Billy Nelson on offense to run the ball. Then he threw it to George Boyd. As needed, Billy Nelson punted perfect snaps by the center, Ken Goode. On defense, Johnny Coker scrambled to recover a Waco fumble. George Boyd intercepted a Waco pass. Circus-like, he tipped a Wilson pass to Danny Gordon. Johnny Watkins blocked to open a gap for Ole Olsen to run through. George Boyd scored the first touchdown on new Tiger Field. He had scored the last one on old Tiger Field. For the extra point try, Ken Goode snapped a spiral to the holder, Tim Flanagan. He had a good placement, but kicker Jim Barnabee missed the goalposts. Later, on defense, Danny Gordon raced in to recover a Waco fumble. The Tigers only put 6 points on the board, but so did Waco High. An exciting first game on new Tiger Field ended in a tie, 6-6.

According to Acree, "The team seemed to be elated over a tie."

Fans thought tying Waco was a moral victory. Waco had a superior team. Tying an old enemy put the Tigers on a course for a good season. They made a few mistakes but took the fight to a larger group of boys and didn't quit.

Notably, a hundred or so season ticket holders from the prior year had not renewed. They believed the team could be better. Coach Acree also agreed. For example, he saw poor tackling and failures to react correctly in situations where the boys had drilled. After the game, he said, "Physically, we are okay, but if we can just get with it mentally."

Palestine

The boys needed to demonstrate the importance of football in every single game they played. They had to prove themselves against Palestine in the second week. As though size mattered to him, Acree pointed out to others, "The Wildcats outweighed the Tigers in the backfield."

If that was not enough motivation, the prior year's Tigers had defeated Palestine, which only infuriated their current bunch—including their coach, Luke Thornton. Acree identified with the Tigers, "I feel they'll go after us with everything."

The game site was in Palestine, and the coaches needed to improve communication between the 'spotters roost' and the sideline. Acree persuaded the Dads Club to buy a war surplus walkie-talkie handset.

Meanwhile, school officials hoped to develop improved parking at the new Tiger Field, mainly to reduce the entrance and exit congestion to its large, unmarked lot. Others complained about flaws in the public address system, which needed to be "ironed out" as if they were only a wrinkle in a cotton shirt.

John Tewes kicked off barefooted to Palestine. The Tigers quickly fell seven points behind when the Wildcats returned it for a touchdown. The score did not dishearten the boys. Tiger blockers created openings that Ole Olsen, Billy Nelson and George Boyd sped through for huge gains, and then Boyd scored. Jim Barnabee's kick tied the game. Tom Wilson nailed Billy Nelson for a significant gain, and then Olsen moved the ball into kicking range. Jim Barnabee kept his head down and kicked a field goal to put the Tigers in the lead, 10-7. A Tiger fumble proved costly, giving Palestine another quick touchdown. Behind 10-14, Tom Wilson passed to Danny Gordon and then to Billy Nelson to put the goal line within reach of Ole Olsen. He carried the ball into the end zone, and Jim Barnabee's kick was good, making the score 17-14.

The Tigers battled back-and-forth with the Wildcats. Both wanted to win. Ole Olsen scored again to make it 23-14. Danny Gordon intercepted a Wildcat aerial attempt. Then Tom Wilson lofted a long pass, and Gordon ran under it, caught it and fell over the goal line. Jim Barnabee's kick made it 30-14. The Wildcats could not move the ball against the stingy Tiger defense, which included Jon Tewes, Johnny Coker and Phil Paschal. The second team saw plenty of action as the Tigers mauled Palestine.

Early in his tenure, Acree was quick to compliment the Tigers. Speaking to the Kiwanians, Acree described them as "A real fine group of boys who work hard and hustle well."

He identified their prevailing attitude: "We may not always win, but we will always be there trying and giving out the best effort."

So how good were the '61 Tigers? Afterward, the newspapers ranked them number three in the state in Class AAA football. Speaking from experience, Acree said, "I know it's human nature to watch your ranking, and I suppose that's part of the fun of playing. But it sure will get you in trouble."

Cleburne

The Tigers traveled the next week to Cleburne to play the Yellow-Jackets, who inspired fear in the toughest of teams. Lurking in the memory of George Boyd was when the Tiger coaches pulled the B-team off the field during a game in Cleburne due to poor refereeing and dirty playing. Known as a rough bunch, the Yellow Jackets in recent seasons had a series of playoff victories, twice making it to the state championship game. The previous year, Corsicana had defeated the Jackets, so Acree competitively reasoned they aimed to get even. The Corsicana defensive line would have to do without the services of starting tackle James Henkel who stepped on a nail that week. The younger boys who knew Henkel's toughness suspected that he pulled it out of his foot and ate it.

The absence of Henkel made a difference. The Tiger defensive line reacted poorly to Cleburne's trap blocking, a situation where a lineman in front of a tackle doesn't come at him when the play starts. The tackle incorrectly reacts by raising up, only to become a standing target for an unseen blocking guard coming fast from the opposite side of the line. A ball carrier can make easy yardage running behind the guard to penetrate the defensive backfield. Aided by a 15-yard penalty for late hitting against Corsicana, Cleburne scored in fourteen plays on its first possession.

The Tigers were not mentally sharp against Cleburne. A deflected ball resulted in an interception of a Tom Wilson pass, but as retribution, George Boyd picked off a Cleburne throw to put the ball back in Corsicana hands. Tom Wilson, Danny Gordon, Ole Olsen, Billy Nelson and Phil Paschal moved the pigskin into scoring territory, but their efforts fell short on downs, and Cleburne again had the ball. Johnny Coker made a saving interception that prevented another Cleburne score.

After the half, Tom Wilson tossed another interception. Cleburne took the ball and marched to the end zone for their second score, aided again by a 15-yard penalty for late hitting. A misdirection play so fooled the Tiger defense that no one came within "20 feet" of the Cleburne ball carrier. A botched handoff ended the next Corsicana drive. After the defense thwarted Cleburne, Tom Wilson fumbled on the next series as he was tackled. He threw another interception to bring the Corsicana turnover count to four interceptions and two fumbles. Two late-hit penalties hurt, too. Cleburne made fewer mistakes. The Tigers lost, 0-14.

After three games in the season, the Tigers had one win, one loss and one tie game. Many doubted they were a good team. The Dads Club was still eighty-five short of the prior year's season-ticket sales.

Jacksonville

Due to poor tackling, missed assignments and late reactions, Acree greeted the Tigers the following week with hard contact work to prepare for the hated Jacksonville Indians. Heavy rain fell ahead of the game.

To Acree, it was a grudge match and he wanted Tiger Field to be in good condition. He postponed the B-team game scheduled on Thursday night, saying, "Time is needed to drain off the water, and the grass is not rooted well enough to take the punishment."

Acree reviewed the film of Jacksonville's last game against Athens. He coached guard Johnny Coker to cut the legs from under a big Indian star lineman. Coker saw his size in the film. As he ran, his powerful knees pumped like pistons. Coker feared a blow to the head just as a boxer might deliver an upper-cut to knock out an opponent. On the screen, he saw an Athen's guard launch himself into the big Jacksonville man's knees. The film didn't show the blood that must have squirted from the guard's nose as a knee snapped against his facemask. In the flickering light off the projector screen, Coker cringed as Acree moved the film back and forth, re-playing the hit.

Perhaps the threat of rain scared away fan support as mostly empty seats witnessed a defensive battle. James Henkel mended to return as a tackle to anchor the Tiger defensive line. He combined with the Tiger defensive ends to stop Jacksonville's favorite plays—sweeps around the ends and slanting runs off the tackles.

Coker winced when fullback Ole Olsen took a hit on the head that knocked him out of the game. Corsicana was unable to run against a fired-up Jacksonville defense. Their big lineman put on a show.

But Acree was a competitor and changed the game plan to throw the ball. It was an opportunity for Tom Wilson to display his passing ability. Wilson completed 11 of 18 throwing attempts. A Wilson pass to Danny Gordon put the ball on the Jacksonville 3-yard line. The game had no score, but Johnny Coker saw his chance. Wilson called the snap, and Coker fired out low and hard toward the big lineman Acree designated. He reacted toward the on-charging Coker. Johnny kept his head down and plowed his shoulder below the knees into the chins of his prey. The man fell to the turf like a tall pine cut at its base. Billy Nelson ran the ball across the goal line. With an extra-point kick by Jim Barnabee, Corsicana defeated Jacksonville, 7-0. Coker celebrated as if he had scored himself.

Irritating Acree, newspapers ranked the Tigers as the number nine team in the state AAA classification. The Tiger defense had improved since its poor showing against Cleburne. The offense demonstrated they could move the ball against a top-rated defense, but ranking them in the top ten stretched even Acree's confidence. He cited the excellent work of linemen John Tewes, James Henkel and Ken Goode. The boys demonstrated with their hustle the secret sauce Acree loved.

Dallas Sunset

But the game against the Dallas Sunset Bisons the following week also tested their commitment. The Bisons were a Class AAAA team, having a larger number of players who generally outweighed the Tigers. Moreover, the scouting report revealed Sunset had a lot of variation in its offense. They ran multiple formations to confuse a defense. As a result, rather than doing padded work outside, Acree stressed mental preparation for the game by putting the Tigers through "skull sessions" on Monday. On Tuesday and Wednesday, they scrimmaged against each other in different formations which the Bison might use on game night. Acree told the Dads Club, "We will be outweighed, but out to win it, just like all the rest."

Ole Olsen returned to play fullback. Ken Goode snapped the ball over the head of Billy Nelson, the punter. Nelson chased it down, turned and kicked the ball on the run. George Boyd sprinted downfield to cover the punt, and a Bison receiver fumbled the ball to Boyd. Behind good blocking, Tom Wilson ran it into the end zone on the next play. Jim Barnabee's extra-point kick was good, and the Tigers led, 7-0.

Two penalties stopped the next Tiger drive. Happy Settle intercepted a Bison throw, but a penalty ruined another potential scoring opportunity. Ken Hamilton recovered a fumble to stop a Bison drive late in the game. Defense won the night.

The skull sessions and work to prepare for multiple offensive sets resulted in alert gameplay by the outmanned Tigers. Corsicana nipped Dallas Sunset, 7-0. The Tiger offense was unimpressive, however, and made discouraging mistakes in the form of penalties. But the team had another win, which delighted Corsicana fans.

Weatherford

With the district games fast approaching, season ticket sales that week closed to within fifty of the previous year's total. The last non-district game pitted the Tigers against Weatherford, a similar team in size to Corsicana, except they had a larger quarterback and an even bigger fullback.

It rained on Monday and Tuesday. Nevertheless, Acree had the boys hit each other with all the speed and power they had, practicing outdoors wearing water-soaked, grimy practice uniforms. They sloshed around in muddy shoes and wet socks, steeling themselves to tackle a bigger backfield on Friday night.

Even though sixth-week report cards were about to be handed out, none of the players thought about how to improve their math and English grades. Johnny Coker stayed after practice with a fellow linebacker, Jim Barnabee, to work with Coach Acree on reacting to the eyes and movement of the quarterback.

The front that brought the rain earlier in the week cooled the night air as Tewes started the game with a barefoot kick. The Kangaroo quarterback gave ground and rolled out on Johnny Coker's side of center. As coached, Coker reacted to drop back and move in a way that followed the quarterback's eyes. Coker intercepted the first pass of the night.

With a tailwind, Tom Wilson struck George Boyd deep on the run, and he scored. Jim Barnabee's kick was good. In the second quarter, as though Acree had flashbacks to his time as a second team member on Bud Wilkinson's Oklahoma Sooners, he substituted the entire second team of Tigers into the game. Tim Flanagan, Jim Hagle and Elic Gregory moved the ball into the end zone. Another good kick by Barnabee put the score at 14-0. James Henkel hustled and fought in a pile to recover a fumble that stopped a Weatherford scoring attempt. However, Weatherford's big quarterback later rushed the ball into the end zone for a score. He followed it with a run for a two-point conversion. The score was 14-8.

The Tigers made two embarrassing blunders. They failed to field the ensuing kickoff as if they didn't know the game's rules. The Kangaroos recovered the live ball in Tiger territory. But they couldn't score. Neither could the Tigers. Then the Tiger center bounced a punt snap to Nelson as the Kangaroos rushed to block his kicking effort. The Tigers escaped their mistakes to win, 14-8. They didn't impress anyone. According to Acree, Weatherford successfully ran its run-pass option play, "the most beautiful play" in football.

Ennis

Despite Corsicana's unimpressive win over Weatherford, the Fort Worth Star-Telegram ranked the Tigers again in the top ten of Class AAA. Corsicana had a 4-1-1 record, while District foe, Mesquite, was unranked with a 5-1 record. Moreover, Mesquite had outscored their opponents in six games, 8.3 points to 1, indicating they were an offensive powerhouse. A weakling in comparison, Corsicana's ratio was 1.5 to 1. In Acree's view, the Tiger offense didn't merit the ranking.

That week, a UIL realignment added Cleburne and Terrell to District 8-AAA, which would take effect the following year. Cleburne had beat the Tigers earlier in the season. Having them added to the district didn't encourage Acree. The UIL also reclassified district opponent Mesquite to AAAA, which the Tigers had yet to play. Acree thought, "To win district, we will have to win against a AAAA team."

Acree feared the Tigers would let a newspaper ranking go to their heads. The first district opponent, Ennis, had an 0-6 record, and the newspapers picked Corsicana to win an easy game. But Coach said, "We don't realize how badly they want to beat us. When you're winning, you forget how important one game can be for a team that hasn't been winning. And the team that wants to win the most can usually do it."

Ole Olson's injury continued to nag him, so Acree promoted halfback Holly Holstein up from the B-team to the varsity. Coach told the Dads Club attendees that week about winless Ennis, "The Lions have some of the best-looking physical specimens you can find."

If he were coaching Ennis, Acree said, "I might pick a time such as this to start a new football season."

He worried that the Tigers would not take Ennis seriously.

To Acree's astonishment, the mother of Jon Tewes took him out of football that week because he got a "C" in English. "Seriously," Tewes said, "It not only caused an uproar at home. The whole town was mad at her."

After the surprise loss of a critical man, Acree coached the boys that week to expect anything. The Tigers worked hard to prepare as though the Lions might be their most formidable opponent of the season. They threw themselves at each other with abandon. Some thought Tewes was lucky, sitting at home, catching up by reading a storybook.

Game night on Tiger Field, Elic Gregory excited the fans by recovering a Lion fumble. George Boyd ran for critical yardage. Then Tom Wilson passed to Billy Nelson. Ole Olsen tried and couldn't move the ball. Tom Wilson optioned left, kept it and ran around the end to put the ball in the end zone. Barnabee's kick was good.

On defense, Wilson recovered a Lion fumble to stop an Ennis march. A stubborn Tiger defense, sans Jon Tewes, halted another Lion drive on downs. The Tigers couldn't advance the ball. Billy Nelson quick-kicked a good snap from Ken Goode to get the Tigers out of poor field position. The Tiger defense held the Lions again. Then George Boyd thrilled the crowd by returning a Lion punt for a touchdown. Barnabee's kick failed.

The second unit, led by Tim Flanagan, brought the crowd to their feet with runs by Jim Hagle and Elic Gregory. Then Vernon Bonnett scored.

Barnabee's kick was good, and the score became 20-0. On their next possession, the Tiger first unit re-entered the game, and Tom Wilson passed to Nelson and Boyd for gains. He then spiraled a beautiful, long strike to Ken Thompson who ran the ball into the end zone. Barnabee's kick made it 27-0. Ennis's late touchdown and two-point conversion resulted in a final game score of 27-8.

Tewes stayed home and didn't see the game. He studied his English book.

Waxahachie

A team gets "high" playing in front of a hometown crowd. Waxahachie's "homecoming" game stoked the Indians to challenge the Tigers. Seeing football as a community effort, Acree encouraged Corsicanans to make the short drive to Waxahachie that week to support the Tigers. "We expect a tremendous effort from Waxahachie," said Acree.

Waxahachie's middle averaged 200 pounds per man. Ole Olsen suffered from a bruised knee and Acree replaced him in the starting lineup with sophomore Jim Hagle. Not wanting his new fullback to shy away from an off-tackle slant, Acree prepared him, "I think they will hit us hard."

After a week of good preparation, Coach Acree expressed confidence in the team, "I believe our boys are ready for them."

All the boys impressed Acree, so he tossed a compliment to encourage his second-string quarterback. "The second unit has been doing a good job in recent games and will see action in this game. Tim Flanagan has been doing a good job handling them."

On game night, Ken Goode said, "Hagle was scared out of his wits."

Perhaps Hagle was fearful of disappointing Acree. Goode, a future minister, sat down and reassured Hagle, telling him how important he was to the team and that he didn't have to be afraid. Hagle, Wilson and Boyd logged first-down runs on the first possession. Wilson passed to Boyd, and on the next down, Boyd ran the ball into the end zone. The

Waxahachie Indians' defense broke through the line and blocked Barnabee's kick. Later, Hagle smashed forward for a first down; Boyd followed with a long run. Then Wilson ran a keeper around the corner to score. Barnabee's kick went wide.

Before the half, Wilson hit Boyd with a pass, then Ken Thompson and Boyd again for a score. Barnabee's kick was good. Happy Settle fielded a punt and gave ground to find an opening, but the Indians tackled him behind the goal line to score a safety. The Indians couldn't move the ball against the stingy Tiger defense. The Tigers won the outing, 19-2.

The Corsicana offense stalled in the second half due to penalties and fumbles, but the defense played well throughout the game. Sales of Dads Club memberships, season tickets and game programs finally exceeded those of the previous year.

An open week followed the Waxahachie game, and Acree eased off practice difficulty, allowing ailing Ole Olsen to recover. Johnny Watkins and Elic Gregory needed the time off, too. They suffered minor injuries in the Waxahachie game.

Athens

After the hiatus, fans were anxious to see the Tigers at full strength against Athens in their third district match.

On game night, lackluster play in the first quarter bored fans, but George Boyd's running brought them to their feet in the second quarter. Likewise, sophomore Johnny Nelson thrilled the crowd with great sideline stepping after catching a zinger from Tom Wilson. Hagle ran it in for a score. Barnabee's kick was wide left. Later, Tom Wilson threaded a tightrope pass to George Boyd and another to Johnny Nelson for gains that enabled Jim Hagle to score again. Once more, Barnabee's kick went wide.

Following a nice Hornet punt that put the Tigers in a hole in the third quarter, Athen's defense dragged Tom Wilson down in the end zone for a safety. After the Tigers punted out, Danny Gordon intercepted an errant Athens pass to put the Tigers in scoring position. Tom Wilson lofted the ball over the Hornet defenders to a streaking George Boyd for the Tigers' third score. Again, Barnabee's kick was wide.

Even though the second unit received ample playing time, they didn't score. The Tigers defeated Athens 18-2.

For the second week in a row, an opponent scored a safety on the Tigers. Coupled with numerous extra point misses by Jim Barnabee, game scores for the season were unusual. A ranked team should have had more convincing point spreads with only one district game remaining. In addition, several defeated opponents outperformed the Tigers in critical game statistics—first downs, yards gained and pass completions. So much for newspaper ranking.

Attendance for the Athens game was smaller than expected for a homecoming match. A light afternoon rain fell on Tiger Field, but did not affect the game. Acree had reminded the boys, "Men, we are representing Corsicana."

Mesquite

Corsicana and Mesquite tied in district wins. Hence, the last game of the season would answer the question of how good a season the Tigers would have. Acree told the Dads about the game, "This is it."

The game outcome would decide who represented District 8-AAA in the playoffs. Ole Olsen, Phil Paschal and Johnny Watkins were ready.

The best running game in the district belonged to Mesquite and their star running back, Charlie Walker. If the Tigers were to repeat as champions, the defense would have to do its job on the Skeeters' home field. But who would step up and deliver plays leading to a win?

Linebacker Johnny Coker had demonstrated his mettle against Jacksonville, so Acree picked the 5'10", 150-pound Tiger to stop Charlie Walker. "Key on Walker. When the ball is snapped, you go hit Walker."

That Friday night, fifty-five hundred fans saw Walker gain only fifteen yards net. The Tiger offense delighted Corsicanans. Led by Elic Gregory, the offense got a break when he recovered a fumbled punt. Runs by Boyd, Wilson and Hagle and a pinpoint throw by Wilson to Boyd, earned the Tigers a touchdown. Sensing a close scoring game, Acree called on Happy Settle to run a "fake extra-point kick" for two points. The Tiger bench leaped and yelled to celebrate the success of the "trick play." Fans went wild when Jim Barnabee later kicked a twenty-eight-yard field goal to ice the game. The Tigers bagged Mesquite, 11-0.

Against Mesquite, the hard-nosed Tiger eleven cemented their reputation as a defense-minded team. Acree characterized them as "Fanatical. They played their best game of the season."

Acree's men were once again District 8-AAA champions in 1961. Two district titles in a row for Corsicana, a first since 1934. The town was on fire for Acree football. A celebratory parade was scheduled for Beaton Street.

Bi-District: Carthage

The Tigers moved into post-season play and made plans to win a playoff game, a feat not accomplished by a Corsicana team in almost three decades. They would play Carthage, winner of District 7-AAA, for the Bi-District Championship. On paper, the two teams were evenly matched, but the sports sections of the newspapers favored Carthage to win.

Corsicanans disagreed, thinking, "they have never lost a game they went at with determination."

After a six-week hiatus, a determined Jon Tewes raised his English grade and rejoined the team. Busloads of students and a long caravan of cars loaded with fans followed the Tiger bus, driven by Lynn Scruggs, to Carthage.

A sellout crowd watched Carthage go after the Tigers. Deep on their end of the field, Ken Goode snapped to Tom Wilson for a surprise quick kick to get the team out of trouble. Carthage couldn't move the ball with Jon Tewes back at noseguard. They punted to put the Tigers back in troubled field position. Starting fullback Jim Hagle and quarterback Tom Wilson traded running the ball for good gains, but the Bulldogs forced Wilson to punt again. The hometown fans sat quietly as the defensive-minded Tigers held Carthage again. They had to kick to George Boyd. After a good return, Boyd and Hagle advanced the ball into Bulldog territory. Hagle fumbled to put Carthage in business, but the Tiger defense did their part to hold off the Bulldogs. Corsicana took over the game at that point.

Wilson and Hagle traded runs, and Happy Settle faked a sweep and stunned Carthage with a deep throw to Phil Paschal who caught it and fell near the goal line. From there, Hagle banged his way into the end zone, and Jim Barnabee's kick was good.

The defense held Carthage again, putting the ball back into the hands of Tom Wilson, George Boyd and Jim Hagle. The three advanced the ball until Hagle ran it into the end zone. The Bulldogs blocked Barnabee's kick, leaving the Tigers ahead, 13-0.

After the half, Carthage scored against the Tiger defense but failed in its attempt for two extra points. On the next Tiger possession, Hagle staged the best run of the night, a long one, plowing through Bulldogs to put the ball into scoring territory. Acree wanted the big fullback to score and it took three more tries before Hagle plunged into the end zone for the third Tiger touchdown.

The Tigers outscored the Bulldogs on the strength of Hagle's running combined with that of George Boyd and Tom Wilson. Blocking by Johnny Watkins, James Henkel, Johnny Coker and Jim Barnabee opened the holes.

Corsicana's defensive front, led by Jon Tewes, James Henkel, Johnny Watkins, Johnny Coker and linebacker Tom Tillery stymied the Bulldog running game. Tewes also worked at the center position on the second team, which didn't score. The Tigers defeated Carthage, 19-6.

District 8-AAA coaches voted Tom Wilson and Jon Tewes as unanimous choices for All-District players in 1961. Other teammates selected as All-District by the coaches included Danny Gordon, Johnny Watkins, George Boyd, Phil Paschal, Johnny Coker, James Henkel, Elic Gregory and Happy Settle. Another five boys received honorable mention awards.

Corsicana had its first playoff victory in twenty-seven years. Football fever swept the town. Acree was a happy Coach.

Quarter-Finals: Gainesville

The Tigers were high after the wins over Mesquite and Carthage. They bathed in the glory of an eight-game win streak. They sat center stage as a group in a pep rally in the high school gym. Fans overflowed the seating capacity while cheerleaders led yells accompanied by the band playing traditional fight songs and the alma matter. No fan was prouder of the Tigers than Acree, but his mind had already switched off Carthage and turned onto Gainesville, their next playoff opponent.

Gainesville won District 6-AAA and would play against Corsicana. They had a ten-game win streak and an All-State quarterback named Mac White. While the Tigers had mostly close-score wins during the season, the Leopards had blown-out opponents on the strength of Mac White's running and throwing. Moreover, Gainesville had beat Cleburne, a team that had defeated the Tigers early in the season. They outweighed the

Tigers by an average of fourteen pounds. Despite the Tigers' heroic season, the pundits didn't give them much hope.

The two teams agreed to play in P. C. Cobb stadium, which seated 22,000 fans, ample size for fans from both towns. Corsicanans drove to Dallas in record numbers to cheer for their underdogs. Elic Gregory was out with a broken thumb. A nagging leg injury hobbled Ole Olsen. Other than those two, the Tigers prepared for a rugged, helmet-to-helmet effort.

On a windy night, Gainesville quarterback Mac White led the smooth-running Leopards to score first. After that, Tom Wilson guided the Tigers downfield by running himself and handing off to Jim Hagle or Happy Settle. Wilson completed passes to George Boyd and Billy Nelson before Hagle hammered into the end zone to tie the score.

The Leopards rebounded when Mac White tip-toed up the sideline to score again. Corsicana couldn't move the ball, but George Boyd intercepted a Mac White pass on the next Gainesville possession to fire up the Tigers. Wilson threw an arching strike to swift David Robinson who carried it inside the Leopard 20-yard line. The Leopards knocked Phil Paschal unconscious, which ended the game for him. Wilson ran and then passed to Ken Hamilton for a touchdown. Jim Barnabee's kick was good and the Tigers led, 13-12, with 43 seconds left before halftime.

The lead masked mental breakdowns during the drive. Tom Wilson fumbled two exchanges with the center. Did Acree make a mistake and insert Jon Tewes at center as he did in the game with Carthage? Ken Goode claims he never had a fumbled exchange with Wilson. Tewes emphatically denied ever playing center or even playing offense saying, "I only played defense."

Without the game film, we'll never know, but there is no confusion about what happened next. Following the touchdown, Acree called for an onside kick. Tewes poked it, but Gainesville fielded the ball in Tiger territory. The Tiger defense wasn't ready. Mac White ran a keeper deep into scoring territory, then threw a zinger to a halfback out in the flat. He ran untouched into the end zone to score. Mac White swept around a corner for two points to end the half with Gainesville leading, 13-20.

In the second half, the Tigers struggled to move the ball. Mac White ran a sweep and produced a long run for a touchdown, making the score 13-26. That discouraged the Tigers.

Corsicana fumbled the following kickoff, giving Gainesville the ball again in the Tiger end of the field. The Leopards marched for another touchdown to take a 13-32 lead. The Tigers gave up one more touchdown to Gainesville's second unit but blocked the extra-point attempt.

With the score at 13-38, the boys didn't quit. Tom Wilson found George Boyd open for a nice gain. Wilson threw a second strike to Boyd who outran everyone to the end zone. The try for extra points failed, and the game ended at 19-38.

* * *

Gainesville eliminated the Tigers from the playoffs. Looking at the game film with the Dads Club, the ever-competitive Acree said, "They are a fine ball club, but they are not that much better than we are."

It was impossible to cover up the mistakes, the missed tackles and the weakness of the Tiger defense in the second half. As for the players, Acree said, "They gave more than they had many times."

Acree finally answered the question asked all year, "Our kids had a fine season."

Speaking before the Rotary Club, Acree complimented the town, "You took pride in the kids, and when you take pride in a kid, whether it's playing football, playing in the band or whatever he's doing, he strives harder to do a good job."

Like Acree, Tom Wilson enjoyed a football career, coaching after playing at Texas Tech. He became an assistant coach at Texas Tech and later a head coach at Texas A&M University, Palestine High School and Corsicana High School. The game meant everything to him.

Jon Tewes became an All-State and All-American selection, who played college football at the University of Houston. He represented Corsicana in the 1962 All-Star Game in Lubbock. When many boys wanted to avoid military service, Jon Tewes re-upped and spent eight years in Vietnam. He was not a quitter.

Johnny Coker attributed his successful career as a plant manager to the leadership characteristics he learned from Acree. "He built men. He was a good coach. His philosophy was to prepare us for life."

George Boyd was faster than a phone call but lacked size. Even though he was a star on Acree's Tigers, he had no future in football. After graduating from the University of Texas, he worked for the U.S. Treasury Department and became a bank examiner. Boyd said that essential skills learned in football contributed to his success, "Acree taught us discipline and teamwork."

Ken Goode gave his life to ministry and is still preaching the gospel seventy years later in East Texas.

Phil Paschal missed out on a scholarship to Baylor because his grades in English weren't good enough. However, he briefly enjoyed football at Navarro Junior College before finishing his playing days at Howard Payne University. He became a coach, and Acree later hired him as an assistant at Midland Lee. Football under Acree changed him, "If I start something, I finish it."

At the Tiger appreciation banquet, SMU coach Hayden Fry told the 1962 players, "Winning is not the most important thing, but trying to win is."

Acree nodded in agreement.

Looking at the '61 team, he confessed, "I never coached a more courageous group of youngsters. You made us coaches ashamed of ourselves because we underestimated you."

To continue the practice of "showing appreciation" to coaches, the Dads Club collected $1600 from Corsicanans as an award. That amount was up $700 from the prior year but split over nine coaches at the high school and two junior highs.

The Tigers of 1961 delighted their fans. Twenty lettermen graduated the following spring. Only eleven planned to return in 1962. Next year's team would need more boys. Fans were unconcerned as long they had their coach.

Although the specifics were unknown, rumors began circulating that Acree had unsolicited job offers from other towns.

CHAPTER 4 ENTERING FOOTBALL

"As a nation, we got to where we are by three methods: faith in God, Yankee ingenuity, and a sense of competition. Football is a way to learn that great lesson—the one of competition." Claud "Chena" Gilstrap, Athletic Director, Arlington State College, 1962

In late August 1962, a month after the failed launch of the Mariner 1 spacecraft to Venus, I was 14 years old and entering the ninth grade in Corsicana's Collins Junior High. The Mariner guidance system failed causing the rocket to blow up five minutes into its flight. I walked onto the school's practice field to try out for football, knowing only the basic game rules, hoping not to be embarrassed, wanting desperately not to "blow up" like Mariner 1.

The Collins Cougars new head coach, Jack Murray, had been recently promoted by Athletic Director Jim Acree. Murray had been an assistant coach at a crosstown rival, Drane Junior High. At the time, football coaches in Texas hardly expected to call one place home very long. Due to the "Boomer" birth rate, new opportunities cropped up as fast as the state's population growth—24% from 1950 to 1960.

Having rejected offers from other schools, Acree himself appeared to have found a home in Corsicana. He as much as said so to the Dads Club, "Without your support, I do not think we could have had as fine a season as we had. It kinda makes a coach feel like he has a home here."

Acree's arrival in 1960 triggered a soaring rise in the town's enthusiasm for championship football. Under his leadership, the senior-high team had won its District 8-AAA Championship two years in a row. The second title came on the strength of a nine-win, two-loss, one-tie record—the best showing in the town since 1934.

Coach Acree was well-liked by most townspeople and respected by the boys on his teams. Emphasizing player quickness and agility, his game strategy centered on having generally smaller Tigers better prepared physically and mentally than their opponents. Rather than banking on having exceptionally talented players, he sought boys who were passionate about football. Each year, however, his teams had a decreasing number of players. The decrease was not simply due to graduation or injury. His demanding practices cleared out dispassionate boys like a gardener removing weeds from a flower bed.

* * *

American Orange, 1959

I loved playing baseball, a sport Acree disliked. In his competitive mind, it was a soft sport that siphoned off boys who might have otherwise played football. I aged out of Little League, marking the first time I heard the words, "You're too old."

I intended to play Junior Teenage League baseball but quit after a few practices. I had to ride my bike across town to Drane schoolyard to attend practices, but foul-mouthed coach J. B. Hendrix was my main inhibitor. Unaccustomed to hearing cuss words in every utterance, I resigned without notice. I was like my mother who became an escape artist rather than a fighter. Having been raised in the home of an abusive, alcoholic father, she reared her kids with a saying, "Don't cuss, call Gus. He'll cuss for both of us."

Even though I missed playing and being part of a team, she thought it was okay that I walked away from baseball. As if she had a vision of the future, she said, "Don't worry, hun. Everything will work out alright."

I explored alternatives for where I might find my place—somewhere I could succeed as part of a group. The word "might" deserves emphasis. I was a boy who would try something and then abruptly quit it if it didn't suit me. I had also quit Boy Scouts. I quit learning to play a musical instrument. I quit studying art. I'd rather be part of a group than strive as an individual. Playing Little League baseball, I learned that it was easier for me to shine in the accomplishments of a team.

Daddy and Mother were working people and expected me to work if I wanted something such as a car. Work implied a job with a paycheck, not something as haphazard as searching backroads for empty soft drink bottles to resell. I might find fifty cents worth of bottles on a good day, enough money to buy a box of .22 shells. I also tried mowing neighborhood yards without a power mower. Our push mower with circulating blades required continual sharpening, and it was difficult to push through thick St Augustine grass, which the nicer homes had. I pushed the mower to a job site, walking on city streets. But not for long; I found only two or three homes within walking distance that would pay for me to mow their yard. I also tried selling newspapers for the Corsicana Daily Sun. I walked the downtown streets calling out "Paper!" but quit when I realized there was no money in it. Tough boys held all the profitable street corners. It was easier for me to walk away than fight them for a corner.

When I returned my unsold papers to the Daily Sun building, I explained my predicament to the man behind the long counter. Knowing it was the end of my employment, he said, "Son, you need a job with a boss man."

Mother sometimes shopped at Piggly Wiggly grocery store located on Main Street at 7th Avenue. When I was a preteen, I rode my bike to the store and timidly knocked on its double-glass front doors to ask for a job. A man wearing a white apron opened one of the doors and told me to come back when I was taller.

At age 14, in the late spring of 1962, I was near six feet and returned to interview with the manager, Mr. Keith Sleight. He was a gruff, disagreeable man who didn't seem very happy regardless of my height. Acree was one reason for his angst.

Sleight asked me, "Do you play football?"

"No, sir."

"I'll hire you if you won't play football. It seems like every boy I hire these days quits to play football."

"I don't like football. I prefer baseball. I promise I won't play football."

Sleight hired me to sack groceries, move boxes around in the backroom, sort soda bottles for return to a local bottling company, re-price canned goods, sweep and mop floors and do just about any job where he could keep an eye on me.

I learned a lot about myself during my first assignment. When customers returned empty soft drink bottles for cash, employees put them inside large plywood bins in the back of the store. Before the bottling company would accept them, however, they had to be sorted by brand into crates containing twenty-four bottles each. After tying a long white apron around my waist, Mr. Sleight ordered me, "Take all the bottles out of the plywood bins and put them by brand into bottle crates."

I followed his instructions literally and worked methodically. The bins held hundreds, if not thousands, of empty bottles. I organized the empties into collections spread over the floor. Dr Pepper here. RC Cola there. Coke over yonder. The open floor space took on the appearance of a colorful crowd of Lilliputians crammed into the backroom.

Mr. Sleight walked in, took one look and barked, "I ought to fire you."

He shook his head and left out through a swinging door back into the storefront. I proceeded to crate and stack each collection. This last step transformed the working space into a maze of stacked bottle crates of various heights, resembling buildings in a downtown skyline. The Dr Pepper stack was the tallest.

I completed the task but used more time than Mr. Sleight thought necessary. He considered letting me go at that point, saying, "You're not worth 0.25 cents an hour."

When I worked in the front of the store, I sacked groceries and interacted with the other employees. The checkers accepted me. I was friendly with customers. But one senior manager, Mr. James Marriott, informed me, "I'm gonna get you fired."

With his chin in the air, Mr. Marriott turned and strutted to the back room to talk to Mr. Sleight. I had only learned his name, but a friendly lady checker, Carol Inman, privately said, "Marriott doesn't like you."

I asked, "Why?"

"You don't laugh at his jokes."

"I don't understand his jokes."

She advised, "Laugh when he laughs."

Carol said a good word for me with Mr. Sleight, who decided not to fire me, but advised, "Show Marriott more respect."

From then on, I fake laughed when Mr. Marriott said anything with a smile. I also treated him like a boss by responding immediately to his requests and showing him that I respected his authority.

None of that was necessary with Ed Staubing, the butcher. When he smiled, he had a long knife in his hand. Reddish-brown blood stains covered his white apron. He once demonstrated drinking blood. Like other employees, he wore a white, short-sleeved shirt under his apron. His big chest and arms bulged underneath. He bulled his way around the meat counter, arranging the display just so, but he flashed a toothy smile when customers asked questions. Beneath the rough exterior was a good man who became a friend.

After a few weeks of working to prove myself, Mr. Sleight delighted me by increasing my salary to fifty cents an hour. I loved working at the "Pig" that summer. Aside from my usual tasks, I helped complete the occasional delivery of a truckload of watermelons. Another employee, Ronnie Martin, a fine man, pitched watermelons down from the truck to open armed boys including Ronnie Odom, Nathan Weaver and me. We stacked them along the walkway in the front of the store. On a hot day, assistant manager, Roy Martin, allowed us to break open a melon in the backroom and eat the juicy heart out of it.

The backroom was a place for socializing while working. We ate lunch there while sitting on large sacks of Imperial Sugar. We jawed about major league baseball or argued about important topics—for example, would power washing your car (which was new at the time) take off the paint? On Thursdays, we teamed up to unload a delivery truck at the backdoor. We also took turns looking through a peephole used to spy on shoplifters. A manager like Mr. Marriott or Roy Martin trailed a shoplifter out the front doors and confronted them. Typically, the manager asked them not to return to the store. Once, a man ran off and Marriott hollered at me, "Get him, Ronnie. Go get him."

I ran and followed the man down 6th Ave, across Beaton Street to Commerce, where he ripped off his shirt and disappeared into a crowd. Trailing behind, Marriott was impressed with how fast I could run while wearing a full-length apron.

The backroom also had a large walk-in freezer for storing frozen foods. We sat in it on a hot day to cool off. But we once used it to play a practical joke on Weaver, a prankster himself who made a habit of arriving at the last minute for his shift and changing into a white shirt he left on a hanger. Once, we soaked Weaver's shirt in water and hung it in the freezer until it froze solid. Moments before his arrival, we placed it back on the nail where Weaver kept it. As expected, he danced in at the exact time his shift was supposed to start, but due to a frozen shirt, he could not immediately change and had to report late for work. Later, someone hid Limburger cheese in Weaver's car, a '57 Mercury. It sat in a hot parking lot and smelled awful by the end of the day. Weaver was mad, but no one ratted out the perp, so Weaver never learned that summer who pulled the prank.

Staubing had a chest freezer for holding date-expired meat that was unsold. On occasion, Ed allowed us to buy steaks from that freezer at a reduced price. Thinking it was no match for the hot flame of a charcoal grill, I didn't mind a little bluish-green color on my choice. On Saturdays after work, Mr. Marriott sometimes invited all of us over to grill meat in his backyard. When gathered around a cooker, the small number of employees at Piggly Wiggly was a bit like a family. I enjoyed the camaraderie and fit in with the other employees. It was okay to be myself and not have to pretend I was smart.

* * *

That summer of 1962, I also earned my driver's license with Coach Slaughter as my driver's ed teacher. I took the test in my step-grandfather's 1957 Chevy. With the windows down, I drove on 7th Avenue wearing a big smile and swiveled my head to see who noticed.

Rita Marriott, the daughter of Mr. Marriott, flirted with me one evening as I left the backyard gathering. She jumped into the front seat and grabbed the keys out of the ignition. She held them behind her back, grinning, and said, "Kiss me, and you can have the keys."

I slid across the front bench seat up next to her, wrapped my arms around her tiny waist and acted as if I was going to kiss her. I snatched the keys out of her hands. "You're a big tease," I said.

She was no more than 12 years old, mischievous and red-headed like my two sisters, Janet Kaye and Kathey Sue. I moved back under the steering wheel, and she scooted up next to me, squirming, making a faux effort to regain the keys. Giggling, she said, "Try me."

At that point in my life, I had not yet experienced a first kiss. Even though she tempted me, I didn't know what to do. Parked in Mr. Marriott's driveway, I feared he would fire me if he caught me kissing his daughter. I started the engine and promised her I would one day. That got her out of the car, but I never followed through.

The summer waned and I hoped to continue working at the Pig when school started. Since I wasn't involved in sports and wanted to buy a car, I proposed a deal to Mr. Sleight: let me work all day on Saturdays and after school for a couple of hours on weekdays. I enjoyed the work as well as socializing with the other employees. Earning a regular paycheck was rewarding, too. Mr. Sleight promised to increase my salary to seventy-five cents an hour once school started.

I found a home, I thought.

* * *

The last Saturday in August, just before closing time, after a long day, Coach Murray and his assistant, Jesse Cummings, looking for me, pulled open the double glass doors to enter Piggly Wiggly. I was wearing a white apron and sweeping the front of the store with a dry-dust mop. Nathan Weaver worked the shift with me. He whistled "Zip-a-dee-doo-dah," sprinkling a reddish, oil-based compound on the floors as he pranced around the empty storefront.

Under neon lights, the coaches watched as I swept the linoleum tile, methodically cleaning along the counter edges, dusting corners by the soda machines and wiping spaces between the basket wheels of the telescoping shopping carts which lined the windowed storefront.

Moving out of my way, both men hopped up to sit on top of the double-row of steel-framed shopping carts. They wiggled to adjust their bottoms to a less aggravating position and settled into what would be a longer conversation than they intended. They watched to see if I would miss a spot. That's what coaches do, look for mistakes, or in Cummings' case, look for something to gripe about. At least that's what I thought they were doing. I didn't know Murray.

Jack Murray reached out to shake hands; Jesse Cummings followed. Murray was a big man stuffed inside a t-shirt with a stomach that lapped over his pants at the waist. He had puffed, fleshy hands but delivered a firm handshake. Cummings looked trim with tan, weathered skin like he spent a lot of time outdoors on a golf course. I didn't know he was a former track star, inducted later into the Fannin County Sports Hall of Fame. Murray smiled, "What are they paying sackers to sweep floors on Saturday nights?"

"Fifty cents an hour, but in September, it goes to seventy-five cents," I proudly exclaimed.

I hadn't seen Cummings since school dismissed for the summer. Murray replied, "We need a better offer, don't we?"

They were there to talk me into trying out for football.

They watched as I worked to pick up a pile of dry dust, darkened by the dirt put down from the day's foot traffic. They were looking at a boy hungry to earn money and happy to have a job. I anticipated a disagreeable conversation and wanted them just to go away. I hadn't seen anything good come from personal confrontation. I wished I could disappear like "The Incredible Shrinking Man."

Working the dust mop, I remembered my last exchange the previous spring with Cummings in eighth-grade P.E. class. He embarrassed me in front of all the other boys. After fumbling a dribble, missing a shot and fouling on a rebound, Cummings grabbed the basketball out of my hands, locked eyes with me, jerked his head toward the gym's back door and said, "Ward! You're no good at basketball. Get out of here and go try football!"

At that time, Coach Slaughter was outside on the practice field, exercising boys through various drills to see who might be worthy of a football tryout. He was extending his arms and hands back and forth, pointing here and there, then squatting like he was demonstrating how to fend off an invisible attacker. He worked the boys on football moves, which included sideways stepping, running backward, getting up quickly off the ground, throwing their bodies at a tackling dummy and wrapping arms around each other. Chirps of his whistle punctuated the various activities. None of it looked fun to do, certainly nothing as fun as throwing and catching a baseball.

However, that spring, I had watched a friend, Ronnie Ragsdale, play in a pickup football game on a vacant lot at the corner of N. 24th St. and Elmwood Ave. We were both finishing up eight-grade. He made a form-perfect tackle that caught my attention. Rags sprinted as if he were running down a fly ball, then stretched out, put his head in front of the runner and at the same time, wrapped his arms around him. They both fell to the ground like two dominos glued together. I marveled, saying, "He wasn't even wearing a helmet!"

I enthusiastically described the tackle to my brother, Dickey, saying, "It was beautiful! He looked professional."

Dickey was a year older and had played football the previous year at Collins. He explained that Rags had a great pursuit angle and tackled with his shoulder. "The coaches showed him how to do that last fall."

Although I didn't understand exactly what he meant, it sounded as if there were more to the game of football than boys just throwing themselves at each other as part of a human demolition derby.

On a different thought, I was also starting to think of girls differently. "Making tackles like that is a way to get noticed!"

My brother had watched me excel in Little League baseball. I hustled when running the bases and started in right field for the American Oranges under coach Ed Blackburn. I could track down and catch fly balls and quickly throw a ball back into the infield. As a spectator, Dickey once saw me ignore the distraction of kids playing "cup-ball" in foul territory to chase down a fly ball, catch it beside the stands, stop, whirl, triangulate the location of home plate and hurl the ball back over the corner of the bleachers into home plate to prevent a runner from advancing. Ed Blackburn told me later, "That was an 'All-Star' play."

"Play ball!" were my two favorite words. My grandfather's, too. It gave us something to talk about. When I aged up to Junior Teenage League, I didn't formally resign. I used the same M.O. as when I left the Boy Scouts; I just didn't show up again. I told Dickey what I did and he said, "You chickened out."

When I reported to Coach Slaughter outside the gym, his first words were, "Did you just quit basketball?"

"No, sir," I said, trying to think of a credible reason why I walked away from the gym. "I don't have basketball hands."

He got to the point, "You can't go through life quitting when the going gets tough."

My father said something like that after reading a quote from Coach Acree in the newspaper.

I fixed my eyes on the ground, staring at the clover mixed with grass, wondering why the uglier one choked out the prettier one and said, "I want to save money to buy a car. I want to get a job."

I didn't mention that J.B. Hendrix was nothing like Ed Blackburn, a soft-spoken teacher of the game, not a cursing, yelling man who had little care for untalented boys like me. Playing for Hendrix's Tigers was not my choice anyway. Slaughter didn't use swear words. He was more like Blackburn.

Slaughter said, "Know what Acree thinks about boys your age having a car?"

"No, but my dad said I could have a car if I could pay for it. That's why I need a job."

"Acree figures if you choose a car over football, you're 'soft.'"

He emphasized the word 'soft' like it was a cuss word. "Playing football will make you tougher. You've got a lot of growing up to do."

Avoiding eye contact, I mumbled something about being "sorry" and turned toward the rack where I parked my bike. Mentally, I had already walked away because of the embarrassment caused by Cummings. I thought, "I'm not hurting myself as much as 'hard ass' coaches are hurting me."

That Saturday night at Piggly Wiggly, Murray and Cummings watched me wield a dry mop, wearing a dirty apron, making about $20 weekly. I was learning how to keep a boss man happy. I thought slowly and worried about appearing dumb. When I goofed up, Daddy had a saying, "Use your head for something besides a hat rack!"

I wanted my father to be proud, so saying what people expected to hear was a good way to appear bright. But like my mother, I also wanted to avoid conflict. Corsicana was a small town but large enough that I could say whatever, then walk away and seldom, if ever, see an adversary again.

Murray said from his seat on the row of shopping carts, "Look, football is the talk of the town. Shouldn't you be part of that?"

"As I said, Coach, when I interviewed for the job with Mr. Sleight, I told him I would not play football. That's the only way he'd hire me."

I couldn't get away from Murray, so I hoped he'd just give up and leave. Besides, if Mr. Sleight came out of the backroom and realized what they were doing, he would take the broom to them.

Coach Murray shifted his weight and scooted his big rear end over a bit to ease the pain of sitting on the handlebars. He pointed at the dust mop I held, "Look, son, it's going to get lonely teaming up with a broom. You won't find your friends here."

I patted my pocket somewhat conceited, "No, but I've got a little money here."

Murray saw a skinny kid who needed to spend money on hamburgers and milkshakes. Cummings had seen my slender legs in the gym. My parents described Dickey and me as "bean poles." With a grandfather nicknamed "high pockets," they couldn't expect much different.

Trying to find a compromise, I said, "I know about the success of Acree's football Tigers. I could work a year, earn some money and try out next year when I attend high school?"

This encouraged Murray, "True, but would you rather sweep floors with people wearing aprons or play football on Tiger Field under bright lights with friends wearing uniforms?"

I chuckled. Like other boys my age, he knew attracting girls was becoming as important as having a car. Comparatively, few teen girls came into the Pig to buy groceries. Hundreds were in the stands yelling for their favorite boys on the field.

"Look at me. Does this look like football material to you?"

Cummings said, "That's another reason you should start playing at Collins; you'll have some time to fill out." He also knew how ignorant I was about football. "You'll need to learn the game, too."

Murray had done a little homework by talking to my brother and asked, "What do you remember about being on The American Oranges Little League Championship team?"

"Good pitching. Donnie Denbow and Terry Nichols were key players. The team didn't make many errors. Got some timely hits. Mr. Blackburn? Best coach in the League."

"You played, right?"

"My name was in the paper a few times, but mainly, I didn't miss any games."

"Blackburn counted on you," Cummings said.

"Over three years he played me at a lot of different positions. I wasn't good enough to earn a permanent infield spot."

"Did you use an asthma inhaler like you did last year in P.E. class?"

I saw Murray sink an elbow into Cummings' side. Murray said, "Like Coach was saying, 'What was getting beat like?'"

Blackburn gave me a shot at pitching, "I was a terrible pitcher—if that's what you're asking?"

And if that was the wrong answer, I added, "One time, the Blacks beat us 1-0. Real downer. We should've won."

I didn't tell him that I missed the team photo because I was late. I had learned to leave stuff out of a conversation if I thought it would make me look stupid.

Losing felt the same as disappointing my dad. I thought about what it was like to please him—for example, a time when I hit a home run to win a game against the Maroons. I was in the on-deck circle, and dad and his friend were sitting in the ground-level seats next to the wire fence. His friend teased me, "Hit a home run and I'll buy you a Dr Pepper."

I was confident when I stepped into the batter's box. I hit the first pitch from Dan Goodwin over the centerfield fence. When I touched home plate, I saw my dad's face through the wire. He had a broad smile, and his eyes glistened under the field lights. His friend had already disappeared to the concession stand. Daddy had appendicitis when he was my age and couldn't play sports, especially football. But that didn't keep him out of World War II combat in Europe. I liked doing good because it made him proud.

Thinking about winning, I said to Murray, "There was a game with the Greens when we came from behind five runs to tie it 9-9. Charles Robinson smacked a single and drove in the winning run. We beat them 10-9."

I remember the dugout went crazy. We jumped up and down, back slapped each other, patted rearends, hugged the coach and celebrated with a Dr Pepper. Nothing separated us; we were the American Oranges.

Collecting the names of other possible recruits, Murray asked, "Who were your friends on the team?"

"Kenneth Whittaker, for one, a pitcher. One night we both hit doubles and won a game."

"You got a feeling for what it's like to win and compete as part of a team?"

"Yes, sir. But with Coach Acree, the whole town has that feeling."

Murray's enthusiasm notched up and he leaned forward, "Right. But there's always next year. We need to funnel good players up to the next level, to replace those that graduate."

Cummings added, "Or get injured."

Murray and Cummings reported to Acree who had inspired a passion for football over other sports. He didn't take his eyes off me, "Acree has created a pressure cooker. Collins needs to win, too."

Knowing Murray had transferred over from Drane, I asked, "Is that also true for the Panthers?"

"Yep. Acree wants results in all the organized programs, even down to the grade schools. It's something the town wants, too. Everyone believes football develops competitive character and toughness."

Weaver was a character we all knew. We could hear him in the back of the store, whistling. I said, "Hitching a ride to work is tough, too, especially when your friends have their own car."

Murray appealed to my school pride, "Drane and Collins have about the same number of boys coming out for football. You could be the difference that helps Collins win over Drane."

Slow thinking, I started to relate how Murray and Cumming's jobs were on the line, too. They needed more players, ones who would show up. In Little League and Junior Teenage League, coaches were volunteers, but not in football. It was their job. "So, you have a stake in this, too?"

Weaver came to the front to get in on the conversation, "Ward, I'm ready to start mopping."

I said, "Okay, I'll finish sweeping soon."

Murray said, "I know you're trying to close. So am I. Football is making history in Corsicana. Don't you want to be part of that?"

Weaver joked, "Making history alright! Acree had the players on their knees last year, yanking weed after weed out of the grass at new Tiger Field!" Being the expert he was, he added, "I heard Acree gave each player a 5-yard stretch of dirt. They pulled a million weeds."

Cummings said, "Yes, they pulled weeds after practice. Acree made sure they cleared all the weeds before they could take a shower and leave."

Murray, remembering his mission said, "The Collins Cougars play our home games on Tiger Field. It's a great place to make memories that you'll never forget."

Weaver bragged, "I saw the first game played there, from behind the bleachers, kissing Phyllis Curry, while 5,000 people cheered above us."

Weaver was just "the Weave," but I teased him, "That gig ended in a tie, right?"

Cummings affirmed it, "6-6, but the fans got their money's worth. Corsicana's old rivalry with Waco is back."

I remember Dad getting excited about football after the 1960 District Championship. When he and Dickey talked about it at home, he brought up names of great players from the past, such as Maco Stewart, Duane Nutt and Ray Jacobs. I had no idea who these men were. More important to me was Mr. Stuart Beebe who started Little League baseball in Corsicana. Going to Beebe Field in Community Park to socialize with other kids was fun.

Murray steered the conversation back to his plan. "Playing at a new facility is exciting—there's a new field house with on-site dressing rooms, a brand new football field, complete with a new carpet of Bermuda grass. It comes with home-field advantage and sellout crowds. New records. District Championships. It's football heaven!"

It was already clear from sacking groceries that Corsicanans had lofty goals for the Tigers. To be friendly at work, I talked to people about sports. I said to Murray, "A state championship is a high expectation many people have."

Picking up on Murray's comments, Cummings explained the difficulties of old Tiger Field, "Previously, players taped up and dressed out at the high school." He went on, "Then they'd truck over to the old Tiger Field on 4th Ave to practice or play a game. At half-time, players crowded into an old, concrete bathhouse, pulled stickers out of their socks and patched up scrapes from falling on the bald spots of hard black clay or mud if it rained."

Weaver said, "That Acree goes out of his way to make players' lives rough. I heard he worked them like slaves on the new field. You'd have to be a dummy to run up and down those stands carrying a blocking dummy!"

I remarked, "That means you don't want to play football, right?" Weaver laughed.

Selling a vision of glory, Murray said, "The town is proud of its winning team. They're also proud of new facilities to show off to rivals. They hope to beat the braggarts from Ennis, Cleburne, Palestine, Waxahachie and Athens. If you work at it, Ward, you can be part of that. You, too, Weaver."

Our conversation had run too long; they were sore from sitting on the carts, and we still had mopping to do. "Coach, I'll think about it, but I'd have to quit work."

Murray said, "Don't quit. Ask the manager if you can work part time and on Saturdays."

Cummings interjected, "Acree hates quitters." He told the story of a kid named Bob Garlington that Acree put on the A-team the previous year, but Garlington mostly sat on the bench during the season. He asked Acree to move him back down to the B-team, where he had fun playing with his friends, Robert Graham and Joe Smith. Acree called Garlington a "rotten apple in the barrel."

Cummings ended by noting that Acree lettered Garlington as a reserve and not as a varsity member.

Needing to quit the conversation, I thought of something clever: "My friends say you've already got all the players you need."

"We have commitments from thirty or so boys, but we haven't had a practice yet. August workouts are about to start. Our first game is against Garland's Bussey Jr High boys in three weeks. Winning the first game can make or break our season. You might help us win."

I said, "I don't even know how to play football."

Cummings nodded in agreement. Murray replied, "You can learn. Besides, you've got the rest of your life to work."

That statement stirred my emotions. "But Collins is a big school with many boys to choose from."

"But we're here talking to you."

"Why me?"

"Building a winner under Acree's watchful eye is a good opportunity we don't want you to miss."

"We think you may have a hitter's instinct."

"You're confusing baseball and football."

"You know what it takes to win, what it feels like to lose and what it's like for the team to depend on you."

"Coach, you sound like you're on a limb."

"We want players who will commit to the game," said Murray.

Cummings spoke to my love of baseball, "Somebody who has a good eye and won't blink when it's time to lay the wood on a running back."

* * *

Generally, football players were popular in town, even respected, especially if they had a letter jacket. It didn't matter if they were star players or not. Without a football letter jacket, I was a nobody in a town crazy about the sport. Murray's statement about "working the rest of my life" stuck with me, so I decided to try out. Weaver did, too.

After talking to Coach Murray, I reneged on my deal with Mr. Sleight. I would have just walked away and never returned, but I wanted to work Saturdays. I repeated some of the lines Murray had used on me to stop Sleight's tirade. Finally, I asked, "Can I work Saturdays?"

He fired me, saying, "No. That privilege will go to the boy I'll find to replace you."

Even though Weaver and I were the same age and went to the same school, we were opposites. He was handsome and broad-shouldered with an athletic build. He walked with a swagger, and regardless of the situation, he was confident, humorous, sly and appeared to be an expert on all subjects—particularly girls.

He and I had the required doctor's exam needed to clear us for football. But Weaver failed his physical, claiming he had a heart murmur, which disqualified him from trying out. Given Weaver's reputation, I wasn't sure it was true. Telling me the news, Weaver added, "Mr. Sleight bumped my pay when I told him I was not playing football."

"Lucky dog," I thought. As always, Weaver came out ahead.

Before our first practice started in the dressing room, I told Coach Murray that I had talked to Mr. Sleight and added that Weaver got a good deal. As if it didn't matter, he said, "Tighten up your shoulder pads and put on those hip pads. I don't want you to get injured."

What I wanted was for him to notice I had made a sacrifice. "By joining up, I increased Weaver's pay."

He ignored me when another player complained about his socks. They had numerous, ragged holes. Instead, Murray barked, "Hurry up! This isn't the time to worry about holes in your socks. Button up those chin straps."

Murray and Cummings were both outfitted in matching athletic shorts, white collared athletic shirts, black coach's shoes, farmer's ball caps and whistles hanging from a shoestring tied around their necks. They pushed the locker-room door open, blew their whistles and yelled, "Let's go!"

Lined with metal lockers and a concrete floor, I cringed at the piercing echo of the whistle sound bouncing around the cinder block dressing room. I thought, "Ain't no whistles in baseball!"

I noticed a sign on the door saying, "VISITORS," and felt right at home.

* * *

Coming onto the practice field for the first time at Collins to join thirty-five or so eighth and ninth grade boys, I noticed a few dozen sparrows lined up on the crossbars of the goalposts. Unsettled, they flitted around, seeming never to be able to find their place. The birds landed and then jumped to another spot in a few moments. Like them, I didn't know if I was in the right place.

Coach Murray stood at mid-field, eyeing the players, looking jittery and pensive under Acree's pressure to build a winning team and, importantly, groom players for the senior high football program. Only boys willing to endure a tough road should apply for a job under Acree.

Murray began by blowing his whistle and hollering, "Line up ...."

I couldn't hear exactly what he said, the wind was whistling through the earholes in my helmet. I thought, "Baseball helmets don't have holes."

The other players scrambled toward assistant coach Jesse Cummings, standing at the north end of the field. Like one of the sparrows, I jumped to follow the flock.

Murray emphasized the need for grit and determination versus size as keys to success in football. He drilled us on blocking and tackling, mainly where to go when the ball was snapped. Early on, he allowed us to try different positions. Sandlot football had players of various ages. I had learned how to run with the ball and avoid younger kids. I could also catch fly balls, so I asked Murray to let me try fielding punts and run them back.

He gave me an opportunity during a punt-practice drill. I caught the ball and started running back up field. I avoided one or two tacklers covering the punt, but big Phil Pillans jumped on my back as I tried to cut across the field. I collapsed under his weight like a tin can stomped with a heavy boot. He landed on top of me. I landed on the ball. It knocked the air out of me, leaving me gasping for breath. The ground skinned my forearms and bloodied my elbows. It hurt worse than falling off my bike after hitting a patch of gravel and slamming against an asphalt road. I wanted to cry.

Murray shook his head back and forth. Afterward, Cummings slotted me as a defensive end. My job was to tackle ball carriers, so I concentrated on learning how to look good tackling like my friend Ronnie Ragsdale.

Before our first game, Murray put me on the roster. I made the team by just showing up for practice each day. In just two weeks, I became a Cougar football player.

The team had a range of talent, but I remember all of us having fun playing the game. It was exciting even to make a tackle. Just like in baseball, teammates congratulated each other on good plays. Murray coached us according to our involvement in the offense, which was nil for me. Coach Cummings worked with the defense. Our fullback, Bill

Allison, had serious talent. He had the power to run over tacklers and the speed to outrun anyone else. Other boys had grit, a passion for playing and a desire to improve. They included Lynn Odom, Ronnie Ragsdale and Mike Nekuza. A few other boys had speed or size, but Murray and Cummings started the players who hustled the most.

Garland Bussey

I didn't start our first game against Garland Bussey, but I was part of the team, and Murray substituted so that most of us played in the game. Anchored by Phil Pillans, our line outplayed theirs. Allison scored. Dick Henson ran for two extra points. We won 8-0. On the bus ride home, we talked about the boys across the line from us, the plays we made and Allison's running.

Terrell

The following week, the team traveled to Terrell and won 34-14. Murray was pleased with our effort, especially the defense. Donnie Edwards and James Smith were standouts. In addition to Allison and Henson, Mike Nekuza and Melton Michaels scored.

Melton lived a block over from me and we became friends. Aside from football, we had a mutual interest in reading science fiction books together. He also showed me how to drill a hole in a nylon cleat, pass a necklace through it and use it as a gift to a future girlfriend. It didn't dawn on me that I'd one day have a letter jacket to offer a girl.

Football was exciting until we started losing.

Duncanville

The following week, Duncanville beat us, 12-14. Allison scored two touchdowns, but the offensive line didn't block well enough to make the extra points. The Cougars had nine penalties, seven of which were off-side mistakes. I knew that a baseball team couldn't make nine errors and expect to win. Neither could a football team.

Mesquite

The following week we played our first home game on Tiger Field and lost against Mesquite, 8-15. Henson scored, and Greg Hammonds made two points. Despite good defensive games by Lynn Odom and James Smith, my lack of knowledge of the game hurt us. Mesquite lined up to punt, and no one was between the kicker and me. I could have easily blocked the punt. Instead, I called timeout before the center snapped the ball. I ran to the sideline and asked an exasperated Murray, "Is it okay for me to rush the punter?"

It's funny looking back and wondering how I could be so ignorant. I didn't have beginners' luck until the next game.

Highland Park

My name appeared in the newspaper for the first time as a starter the following week. Highland Park came to Tiger Field riding in nineteen chartered buses. A good Cougar punt put them in a hole deep in their territory. Our defense held, and their punter lined up in the end zone. He bobbled the football as he caught the snap from the center. I raced in and tackled him behind the goal line for a safety, earning two points. I didn't know enough to ask for the game ball. Those were the only two points I would ever score in seven years of playing organized football.

On another play, I rushed from my defensive end position toward the ball carrier, but someone knocked my feet out from under me and I fell face down on the turf. Another player fell on top of me, landing on the back of my helmet. The hit drove my face bar into the ground; it cracked and popped up against my nose. It started bleeding like a hose bib turned on full blast. Blood poured down the front of my white jersey when I stood up, making it look like Ed Staubing's apron after a hard day butchering in the meat market.

I left some of myself on the field that day. The paper described me as an "aggressive performer."

The following week, I started to reap the benefits of being a football player when classmates elected me as a homeroom representative to the school council.

Athens

Our district play started against Athens. We demolished the visitors, 36-14, on Tiger Field. Most of the ball carriers on the Cougar offense got in on the scoring. That included Allison, Henson, Nekuza and Hammonds, who had a glorious run of 83 yards to score. Charles Paschal made two extra points, and Jim Johnson had an interception runback for a touchdown.

Cleburne

On the first of November in 1962, the Cougars played their second district game in Cleburne and lost, 0-33. Cleburne was a football town, slightly smaller than Corsicana, but being further west, they played "West Texas style." Coach Murray said, "They kicked us real good," as if we had participated in a rodeo.

Our line couldn't block for our backs to run, and our defense couldn't stop the more experienced Cleburne team. Coach Murray explained, "All of the boys on their team are ninth graders. And they have played together for four years."

On the bus ride home, more than a few Cougars nursed battered and bruised bodies and egos. The Cleburne boys also defeated the Drane Panthers that fall. We figured we'd play the identical Cleburne boys the next three years in high school. We did, and that group never beat us again. Football is like that. Grudges carry over from one year to the next.

Defeated so soundly late in the season as we had been, Murray decided it was a turning point. Either we'd snap back and play to win against Ennis, our next opponent, or we'd give up and play unambitiously for the remainder of the season. Murray and Cummings asked, "What kind of team are you? Quitters or fighters?"

In the Tuesday practice that week, I was excited and ready to hit. Murray played quarterback in a full-speed offense versus defense drill to demonstrate how Ennis would execute a run-pass option. As a defensive end, he told me to hit him regardless of what he did with the ball. I aimed to knock him on the ground and gave no thought to the fact that he outweighed me by at least a hundred pounds. When the ball snapped, no one blocked me by design. Murray raced down the line toward me. Undaunted, I dived headfirst into his legs to cut him down. That's the last thing I remember about the play.

I woke up under a shady tree lying on my back with a wet towel on my head. A manager sat beside me and hollered, "Coach, he's awake now."

Murray jogged over to check on me, and I asked him what happened. He said his knee hit me in the head and knocked me out cold. He asked how I felt, and I told him I had a headache. He sent me to the hospital, where a doctor examined but later dismissed me. I attribute any memory problems I have now to that hit, not old age.

Ennis

The Cougars walloped Ennis 30-0. Melton Michaels had two brilliant long runs for touchdowns. My friend, Lynn Odom, even scored on an extra-point pass play. Allison and Henson scored also.

Waxahachie

Playing in front of a hometown crowd, you could say we were fighters the next week because the Cougars beat Waxahachie, 22-0. Our center snapped the ball on a fake punt to Bill Allison who went through the middle of the line and ran like a pinball bouncing off potential tacklers to score a touchdown. Henson and Nekuza both scored, too.

Drane

Our final game of the season was a rivalry match with Drane. The Cougars had a 5-4 record; the Panthers were 5-2. Both teams were 3-1 in district play.

Rain postponed the game for a week, but on the new date, it rained again, so we played in the mud. The Panthers beat us, 8-22. I learned the names of some great football players that day. Ben and Glenn Smith and Steve Winn. Both teams had good linemen, but Drane's slightly smaller blockers were more effective sloshing in the mire and muck, pushing around the Cougars and opening good holes for their running backs.

* * *

After the season ended, Coach Murray named twenty-three lettermen. The first two he listed were Captains Bill Allison and Phil Pillans. Even though I was third on his list, I don't believe his ordering of the names had any real significance. The key players the paper previously mentioned in game write-ups were Dick Henson, Lynn Odom, Brad Haynie, James Smith, Greg Hammonds, Donnie Edwards, Melton Michaels and Mike Nekuza.

The lettermen received all-white sweaters with a large red letter "C" on them. Wow!

I wore mine proudly that winter, valuing it even more than the blue ribbon I'd won in the school science fair. My solar furnace project demonstrated how focused sun rays could generate tremendous heat. But the letter sweater proved how a boy's determined effort could bond him to a team regardless of his individual ability. Without consciously realizing it, I learned that skills could be developed through consistent effort. My confidence soared.

Continuing to reap the benefits of participating in football, an editorial friend featured me in the December 1962 issue of "The Cougar," a school publication. I was honored in the "Who's Who" section along with classmate Marilyn Mitcham, a petite, perky beauty whose dad ran a hardware store.

Wearing my letter sweater, I met a girl from Drane at Beebe Field. A gossip clip from the same December publication noted, "... Hey Ronnie, we hear you have a cute admirer at Drane."

The celebrity of a football letter sweater paid dividends again when I received a good citizen's award early in 1963. My science fair entry may have helped me earn recognition as "Kiwanian of the month" in March. I remember a man picking me up at Collins and taking me to a luncheon attended by dozens of men from the town. I showed them my blue ribbon while wearing my letter sweater. Coach Acree was a member of the Kiwanis Club. It was my first time to shake his big hand.

Later the owner of Piggly Wiggly, Mr. N. E. Burroughs, dismissed Mr. Sleight. Needing the money, I approached the new manager, Roy Martin, about a job working on weekends. He allowed me to work summers and Saturdays for the next four years at the Pig. I eventually became a checker. The stories that could be told with the characters at that store could make a sitcom that would rival the best Hollywood has ever produced. To the anguish of all his co-workers, Ronnie Martin, Roy's brother, was later killed in Vietnam.

Having a 5-5 record that year, Coach Murray moved on to become head coach in Kerens, Texas.

The same fall I played for the Cougars, the Corsicana Tigers repeated as District Champions. The Tigers rapidly became one of the most feared clubs in the interscholastic league under Acree.

Grateful for Murray and Cummings, I began to learn the game of football. I was still a novice, and I didn't gain any weight.

Despite Acree's reputation, the Cougar team experience gave me the confidence to try out for high school football in 1963 when I entered the tenth grade. I had no idea how I would perform, but that didn't matter.

I knew it would be an honor just to make the team. The odds were not good, though. Roughly 1 in 6 new boys who tried out under Acree made the A-team.

CHAPTER 5 RIGOROUS SIDE OF LIFE

"Young men today need more in the way of teaching than their fathers needed. Because they now have cars, enough money to buy many things, and other refinements and eases, they must be taught the rigorous side of life."
Jim Acree

Entering 1962, Coach Jim Acree awarded varsity letters to thirty-one Tigers on the 1961 quarterfinals team. Sophomore Robert Graham was not one of them. He was not a candidate since he was on the B-team that year. This might have been a letdown for a high achiever like Robert, an Eagle Scout and a star tackle for the Drane Panthers—their biggest player. But life comes with its surprises, as Robert had already discovered.

Robert enjoyed making wisecracks that got his friends laughing, especially his classmates and neighborhood friends, Joe Smith and Stanley Richards. He loved pranking others, too. Early in 1961, the three boys had been out shooting their guns and returned to the Richards' home and were upstairs in Stanley's bedroom. While Stanley cleaned his 410 shotgun, Robert picked up a small balsa wood airplane and fiddled with its rubber-band-driven propeller. Stanley finished his cleaning and excused himself to the bathroom. An idea hit Robert and he whispered to Joe, "Let's reload his gun and trick him into shooting it out the window."

Joe grinned in response, "That's great! That's going to be funny as hell when it goes off."

Working quickly, Robert quietly loaded a shell into the shotgun and placed it back where Stanley had left it.

Stanley emerged from the bathroom, and Robert picked up the model airplane and stepped toward an open window at the back of the bedroom. As he pretended to toss the plane out the window, Robert said to Stanley, "I dare you to shoot it with your shotgun."

Stanley replied, "No, I just cleaned it."

Joe encouraged him by raising his arms and taking aim with an imaginary gun, demonstrating to Stanley, "Just pretend you are shooting a bird when the plane flies out the window."

Robert added, "Use your shotgun to make it look real."

Taking the bait, Stanley grabbed the gun, shouldered it and poked the barrel out the window. Robert Graham prepared to launch the plane but started laughing. Joe's grin stretched across his face as he anticipated the "boom."

But in a twist of fate, Stanley yanked the shotgun back inside and pointed it at Robert, declaring, "I'm going to shoot you, Graham!"

Instead of yelling, "Stop! The gun is loaded," Joe turned and dashed out the bedroom door. Robert followed Joe just as Stanley took aim and pulled the trigger.

"BAM!"

Robert fell to the floor as Stanley watched in horror.

Stanley's younger sibling came running from an adjacent bedroom to see what had happened. The child stumbled over Robert and fell into a bloody mess of a leg. Freaking out, Stanley's sibling jumped up and ran out the door and down the stairs. In front of him, Joe disappeared out the front door.

A housekeeper downstairs heard the blast and raced to the bottom of the stairwell. Seeing the child smeared with blood, she yelled, "He shot the baby! He shot the baby!"

Robert managed to stand up, hobble down the steps and walk home, which was three doors down the street.

In anguish, Stanley pleaded with Robert for forgiveness. But confused at the moment, Robert said nothing in reply.

Dr. Grizzaffi, a local surgeon, removed the shot from Graham's wounded calf.

To further relish Stanley's anguish, Robert and Joe colluded and didn't tell him right away they had reloaded the gun as a joke. Stanley believed that he had somehow left it loaded.

While still a Drane ninth grader, Robert could not participate in spring football. But he decided to come out in the fall of 1961 for football as a sophomore. He played on the B-team. Classmate and friend, Bob Garlington, on the A-team said, "With half his calf shot off, Robert had every right not to play."

* * *

A year later, in August 1962, as a junior in high school, Robert came out for two-a-days. He wore a pad over his calf. He was one of sixty-four boys who reported for a first-day practice session under Acree. That included eleven returning lettermen and four starters from the previous year. Acree's work-hard ethic was not a surprise, saying, "Our early workouts will stress conditioning."

However, Acree sometimes astonished assistants and players with seemingly outrageous demands—an unexpected two-mile run to the Green House, a rainy-day boxing match in the Field House, an excessive number of grass drills or wind sprints after practice.

Acree typically had the team line up in rows, blew his whistle, and had the boys sprint 30 yards downfield. With another whistle blast, he'd have them turn around and run back to him. They raced back and forth until some boys could no longer keep running.

A few might quit by walking off the practice field, ending their season. Other boys who had conditioned themselves better over the summer continued to run. For those who couldn't run but didn't quit, Acree ended wind sprints by saying, "Report to me after practice and we'll run some more."

These moments made sense to Acree, but others had to learn to appreciate his strategy of winning with well-prepared, highly-motivated, well-conditioned boys. Acree's goal was to improve a player and the team, but as if he were a boxer, he wanted to model one of life's knock-down punches, which usually came as a surprise. After pushing boys to their limits, he would encourage players to get back up, learn from what happened and go again. Unfortunately, for some boys, Acree's knock downs became knockouts.

Over ten boys dropped out in 1962 after the first week of two-a-days. Heat and injury affected the boys' desire to play. So did their mothers' maternal instincts.

Fifteen-year-old football player Raul Rodriquez of San Felipe High School in Del Rio, Texas died in August 1962 from a heat stroke. The news of his death alarmed players' parents around the state.

In addition, Mike Kelsey, a lineman for SMU, died of an apparent heat stroke while practicing that August. Another player at the University of Texas, Reggie Grob, suffered a heat stroke that led to kidney failure. His death shocked parents and teammates alike.

Speaking before various groups that August, Acree addressed the fear of getting hurt playing football, saying, "It's not a proper reaction. If we get to the point where we are afraid to venture, where do we go from there?"

113

He reminded parents of other grim facts, "More than four thousand high school students have been killed or injured in automobile accidents in the US in the past year."

"Amid such statistics, chances of injury on the grid field are small."

Acree urged Kiwanians in a speech to unite as men against a "quitters" program sweeping the state. According to him, the number one problem facing Texas football coaches was tenth-grade boys complaining about the discipline needed for football and mothers forcing the boys to quit. Acree implied that repeated championship success in towns such as Dumas in West Texas resulted from parents getting behind their kids and making them stay out for football. He stated, "The duty of all parents is to get young men ready for later life, and playing football is one way to do it."

Parents in Corsicana agreed. Despite the summer heat, the town was fired up about football. Winning inspired boys to try out for the team.

* * *

Assistant Coach Jerry Moore didn't particularly like the idea of a Monday scrimmage scheduled in Henderson, Texas on August 27, 1962. Five days of two-a-day workouts the previous week had left several players injured. The team exhibited overall stress from practicing on a string of 100+ degree days (cramps, vomiting, headaches). Ice breaks were insufficient. Rain was nonexistent.

Early Saturday, Acree had scrimmaged the boys among themselves. He described their status to the press, "We had a rugged first week and all the boys, naturally, are sore. But we covered a lot of ground, and they are making progress in their conditioning."

Moore wanted Acree to consider the extraordinary heat wave gripping Texas at that time and reminded him of the risk to the team of going to

Henderson. Because of travel time, the scrimmage would start two hours later than a regular morning practice.

Previously, Moore had witnessed Coach Raymond Anderson have some success throttling Acree when the two coaches worked together in Bonham, where Moore played high school football. Anderson had found the need to do the same in Corsicana, but he had moved on to Houston Smiley. The chore of keeping watch on Acree fell on Moore.

For example, Moore had to intercede for junior Donnie Denbow who misunderstood the start time for practice and reported late. Denbow was not a quitter. Acree personally ran him in 40-yard sprints until Moore finally said, "Coach, he's had enough now."

Moore approached Acree, the only head coach for whom he had worked and showed him a newspaper article. He said, "Jim, look at this weather forecast for East Texas." Even though he had a football build and a muscular form, Moore looked smallish next to Acree. The big coach filled every inch of his chair behind a standard-sized desk.

Moore reasoned, "Tyler was 107 degrees last week. In the two hours it takes for the bus ride to Henderson, we'll arrive when temps are in the 90s. It'll rise to over a 100 while we scrimmage."

Acree's face took on an expression as if he were contemplating how to control the weather.

Moore handed him a list of injured players. "Also, these boys can't see any action. That means a few starters going both ways will have to work the entire scrimmage without substitutes."

Moore argued that the heat would put an already bruised squad at risk for further attrition. Acree handed the piece to assistant coach Jim Miller, sitting in a chair across from the desk. The players called it "the hot seat." Acree asked, "What do you think, Jim?"

Glad to have a break from Acree's questioning of his scrimmage suggestions, Miller said, "I think we should keep the schedule as it is. They'll enjoy hitting other boys for a change, regardless of the temp."

Miller was a handsome man and well-liked by the players. He worked with the linemen, but like all assistant coaches, he lived under Acree's scrutiny.

Addressing Miller, Moore said, "You have an hour of offense scheduled, then an hour of defense. Most of the same players will work both hours. It'll be 100 degrees by noon."

"But we have a stop planned for lunch," Miller said. "As your article indicates, it's hot everywhere, so what are you suggesting we do?"

Moore replied, "We could cancel the scrimmage, stay here and start practice at 7:30 as usual."

Acree, the mastermind, spoke, "Jerry, Henderson is part of our preparation plan to identify starters for our scrimmage with Duncanville this Friday night."

"It's the Dads Club BBQ, and I want parents to see us looking sharp."

Miller interjected, "It's one thing to practice hitting your friends and another to get knocked down by a sweaty guy you've never met, one who's calling your mother names as you get up off the ground."

Moore replied to Miller, "It's the heat I'm concerned about. The receivers will be dragging as they run their routes, and I'm not sure what we'll learn when it is so hot."

Acree said, "Two-a-days last week separated some of the wheat from the chaff. We need to continue their conditioning to be able to play in situations like this."

Miller suggested, "A real plus for us is to find out who's going to stick it out this season."

Having lost his appeal, a frustrated Moore said, "Sounds like this is a weed 'em out scrimmage."

* * *

The following day, junior tackle Robert Graham took one last pee in the Field House before Moore shooed him out to the bus. Robert was the last player to arrive. Having traveled the previous year to the scrimmage in Henderson as a sophomore, Graham didn't trust Acree to stop for players who needed to pee once they were on the road. Robert almost wet his pants.

Moore hurried to lock the Field House doors and hustled onto the bus. Having already boarded, the players, managers and other coaches waited in the early morning light. The bus was rolling by 7:30 AM. Miller took a head count, and two of the injured players hadn't shown. Acree marked them down in his head as likely no longer on the team.

On the ride over, the boys were quiet. Hagle slept against a window. Others snacked on muffins and bananas. Joe Smith sat toward the back, reading a comic book. Coach Acree sat up front and called quarterback Happy Settle to sit with him. He went over plans for the offense, mostly what play to call given the down and distance or situation. He also worked with the second-string quarterback, Gary Roman.

Robert Graham sat next to Smith and crouched low behind big Sam Cooper who had broken a foot the previous year in the B-team game against Ennis. Cooper wanted to make the A-team this year and letter as a junior.

Robert fiddled with the dial of a small radio he sneaked onto the bus. To impress his friends on the trip, for $3.99, he bought a Lloyd's pocket transistor at K. Wolens, a local department store. It came with an earpiece.

Acree wouldn't want him to have it; but for Robert, it was fun to see what stations he could pick up as the bus rolled along Texas highways 287 and 79 toward Henderson. His friends smiled as they watched him listening with an earpiece and dancing in his seat. Turning the dial, a just-released song, "Breaking Up Is Hard to Do," by Neil Sedaka, brought glee to his face. He mouthed the words and wiggled as though he was performing at a school sock hop. Joe Smith giggled.

Other nearby boys turned their heads to see the big tackle having fun. Weighing more than 190 pounds, some would call Robert hefty. But he was as hard to move mentally as physically. Robert was as stubborn as he was stout.

Daydreaming, Robert enjoyed thinking about playing in a band. A better bus trip for him would have been an outing to Dallas to hear a rock band. He winked and gladly showed his bus mates the small transistor when they asked why he was smiling.

However, Robert was a football tryout, learning Acree's ways, hoping to make the varsity with his friends rather than end up on the B-team again as he did last year. Hearing a riff he liked, he thought, "Playing the guitar is cool." He strummed an air guitar, imagining he was on stage.

Robert liked to chase girls at night on the town's main drag with the car radio up loud and his friends laughing. Furthest from his mind was Acree's team rules. Thinking about finding an easy girl shot excitement through his body. "Smoking a cig is cool," he thought. Corsicana was a "dry town" that prohibited the sale of alcohol. Discovering a friend with a beer to share made his mouth water. Moreover, he thought, "A big boy loves burgers at the Dairy Mart, too."

All seriously fun.

* * *

Players watched the trees go by the half-opened windows and could smell the fumes of bus fuel in the warm air. After an hour or so of jostling, twisting and bumping up and down in an unairconditioned bus, one of the sophomore players was carsick and needed to throw up. Acree had the driver pull over on the Henderson side of Jacksonville, and the boy puked on the side of the road. Looking at the nearby stand of tall pine trees, the driver called the name of their location, "The Piney Woods."

Joe Smith found Robert's eyes and mouthed, "Driving the porcelain bus."

They both laughed. Acree took the opportunity to stand up and talk to the boys. Returning letterman and halfback Elic Gregory sat up and listened as if Acree were about to announce a starting lineup. Joe Smith elbowed Robert Graham to listen. Graham popped out the earpiece.

"Men, it's going to be a hot day, and some of you will want to slow down and take it easy in the heat. Let that be the farthest thought from your mind. It's days like this that we discover what we are capable of."

The smell of vomit wafted in through the open door and windows. Acree glanced toward the boy puking outside the bus. "If you focus on your work, you won't notice the heat."

Acree continued, "Based on today's results, the coaches and I will decide who will start against Duncanville in Friday night's BBQ scrimmage. Loafers will not start. Third string may not play. Today, I expect you to do your best, to compete, even when you are worn out and hot. Your opponent is tired and hot too. Let him be the one to slow down, not you. You keep hitting until a whistle blows."

Coach Moore interjected, "Take salt tablets and drink water, but be careful not to drink too much, or you'll be throwing up too."

Acree added, "We're filming the scrimmage today to show to the Dads Club meeting this Thursday. They want to review how you are doing.

We'll concentrate on the fundamentals—running, blocking and tackling. We'll throw the ball some. You'll make mistakes, but the coaches will help you on the spot. For the rest of the bus ride, I want you to think about how you represent Corsicana today. We have won two district championships. People are looking at us and writing about our chances this season. Show them what Tigers can do. Show them how fast you get up when knocked down. Be hitters, not quitters. The monkey is on our back."

Graham whispered to Smith, "I thought this was just a scrimmage?"

Not one to ignore player remarks, Acree eyed Robert's reaction, "Graham, do you have something to say to the team?"

"Yes, sir! We're going to stuff these Henderson boys into a woodchipper today!" His teammates laughed.

Coach Moore stood up to talk. "We want to get on the field against Henderson as soon as we can, so if you need an ankle or wrist taped, come up here one at a time and a manager will take care of it. We'll do knees in the locker room once we arrive in Henderson."

Miller rose to face the boys, "The managers will help us get set up. You unload your equipment and follow me into the dressing room to suit out. We will take the field as a unit, so don't lollygag and keep everybody waiting. I expect you linemen to lead the way. That includes you, Graham. You too, Cooper. You're big, but don't be slow."

When the sophomore completed his spewing and reboarded the bus, Acree closed, "Regardless of the external conditions, you need to make up your mind before you step on the field. Are you going to fight to win a varsity position or not?"

Acree needed Robert's size, but more than that, he wanted Robert's desire and determination. He needed Robert to commit to football. For that to happen, a transformation was required. If anything, Robert and Acree were opposites.

Robert was impulsive and undisciplined. Though outgoing and smart, he sometimes acted as if he were the "class clown." As a sophomore lineman on the B-team, the going was easy for him. He relied on his superior size and more or less had fun with his friends. He played as he had learned football on vacant lots. Boys designed plays by scratching in the dirt or saying, "go here, look quick, go long." Blocking an opponent simply meant impeding their progress. He used his size to get in their way. Hitting was a last resort. When he tackled, he was likely to say something that made others laugh, "Call my sister for a date. She's looking for a softie like you."

Robert loved attention, but not the kind Acree delivered. Acree expected discipline, organized play and game preparation according to a system. He didn't let Robert get away with his antics to entertain his teammates. Robert had to be where he was supposed to be at a specified moment, to execute according to Acree's plan, to block how Acree designated, to tackle as Acree demanded, and in Robert's mind, to play as if he were Acree playing, not himself. Last year Robert had fun the way he liked to play the game, so Acree left him on the B-team.

The bus arrived at the Henderson field, and the commotion of disembarkation began. Following Miller, the boys hustled into the locker room and put on their uniforms. The temperature had not dropped below ninety degrees during the night. When the Tigers arrived, it was already in the mid-nineties.

Robert was a big boy and putting on his uniform with high-top cleated shoes made him feel invincible. A pad covered the scarred calf muscle on his leg. His pants were stretchy and fit snug around his legs and waist.

The thigh and knee pads bulged to look like large humps on the trunks of pine trees. He imagined himself as a bulldozer, capable of pushing any opponent out of the way. His lineman's shoulder pads gave him the appearance of a battering ram compared to the smaller boys. He liked not wearing a cup to protect his crotch like a baseball player. Sissies, he supposed. Robert also thought wearing a helmet made him look goofy. It interfered with sporting sunglasses on a hot, sunny day like this one.

Robert realized Acree was a big man, too. He wondered if Acree had worn the same sized pants when he was a boy. Then again, he thought, maybe these pants have the ghost of Gary Whistler in them? Everyone knows Whistler quit because of Acree. Whether he would be like Acree or like Whistler, Robert didn't wonder. He thought about Robert making the other boys laugh.

His socks didn't have holes in them. Neither was his jock strap all stretched out. If there was a problem, he'd tell Acree. He'd make sure the boss knew. Acree was just a man wearing a whistle. Robert was not frightened by him.

* * *

Acree's speech got Robert thinking about how he had endured two-a-day practices the previous week. His thoughts jumped quickly to recalling a typical day of practice. Start early; the sun is barely up. Calisthenics, monkey bars, parallel bars, shiver buckets, palm blisters on the raised pads below the base of each finger. Repeat. Thank God for a line of boys at a drill. A place to wait before the agony resumed. Grass drills, drop into all fours for thirty yards, crab-backward thirty yards, butt-roll when the whistle blows for thirty yards, wind-sprints thirty yards, repeat ten times. Tired. Sweaty. Stop for a moment waiting in line—hands on hips. Repeat. He bent over at the waist. His hands were on his knees. Repeat.

After the morning workout, Acree gives a chalk talk. As if slashing and dashing with Zorro's sword, Robert thought, Acree strokes the chalk against the slate, making V's for defense, O's for the offense. He numbers the gaps along the line, names the formations, creates numbered plays and shows how and where to block, the type of block and where to run or throw the ball. Lots of details for each position. The snap of the ball sets the team in motion, and like clockwork, they advance together. Each play moves the team toward the goal line like a minute hand advances an hour.

Acree mashes hard to mark a "seal block," and his chalk crumbles. He calls out Robert for nodding off during the talk. Acree is always yelling, not laughing and never having fun. Why does he take football so seriously? It's just a game.

At 5 PM, suit out again in full pads. Calisthenics, jumping up and down, stretching, bending, running in place, big boy's body is sore. Very hot. Hitting drills, ten minutes here, one-on-one tackling, ten minutes there, one-on-one blocking, always running, big boy sweats. Wait in line, breathing hard, sweat running into eyes. Repeat. Drills for linemen, ten-minute offense vs. defense, big boy stinks. Jersey thoroughly wet with sweat. More waiting in line. Repeat. Team drills. Run formations and play against friends. Full-speed blocking and tackling. Bleeding. Hitting. Waiting. Sweating. Repeating. Acree yells, "That's no good. Run it again, men." Or "One more time, same song." Robert doesn't hear any music. Dry mouth, no water to drink, big boy exhausted. Acree says we need to get fit but Robert thinks, it's a sorry kind of fit.

* * *

It was a hot day at the scrimmage, starting at 10 AM. Usually, at this time, they would end a two-a-day morning practice. Not today. They were just about to start the hitting. Robert knew he would stink nasty when they returned from Henderson. After a shower, he planned to cruise 7th Avenue. He loved the sweet smell of DQ ice cream mixed with cooking fried hamburger meat. The aromas are good when Acree is not around, he thought.

Teachers like Acree annoy Robert. Always telling him how to do something, then when he does it, telling him how he does it wrong. Look at Hagle. His muscles are showing big after Acree demonstrated how to lift weights. Hagle followed Acree's instructions over the summer, and now, it's a different Hagle riding on the bus saying, "I hope to solidify my position as starting fullback today."

However, old Hagle still likes to have fun when Acree is not looking. Robert remains unchanged after his B-team experience. Soft look, "sweet boy," according to the girls.

Robert thinks to himself. Acree says times are changing—TV, mass marketing and products to make life easier, but he is behind the times. He wants to keep life hard, Robert reasons. He wants players prepared to face difficulty, experience hardship in practice and triumph over it. Acree says, "Keep going when the going gets tough." Silly idea. This is the '60s. American Bandstand. Motown. The Beach Boys. Bikinis. Forget football. Playing tennis or throwing the shot is easier. No hitting. No bleeding. Lots of smiling, wearing sunglasses, too.

Coming out of the locker room with the team, Robert saw that a cinder-covered track encircled the football field. A crowd had gathered in the stadium to watch the scrimmage. The team bunched up before running together across the track onto the field. As they moved passed the stands, Hagle heard a voice in the crowd, "Y'all be quiet... Here comes Corsicana! Here comes the Tigers!" Excitement shot through Hagle when he heard the proclamation. He picked up his pace and held himself more erect. He was proud of the team and Corsicana. Robert jogged to a spot near the back of the formation to start warm-up calisthenics. He was warm enough already. It was 98 degrees.

Robert heard a coach's whistle blow. The scrimmage started. The Henderson boys hit the Tigers hard. Robert thought about the tackles he saw. Helmet in the chest, wrap 'em up, drive 'em to the ground kind of hard. He could hear helmets and pads pop together with a whack like the cracking sound a coach's paddle makes when it slaps against a big boy's butt.

Like dogs shaking off water after a bath, sweat drops scattered in the sunlight when the boys collided. Amid the thuds and grunts of bodies slamming together, coaches' whistles stopped the play. No referees attended the scrimmage. The coaches point out infractions and teach corrections on the spot. The Tigers were on offense for one hour. They made lots of mistakes. They were on defense for another hour but didn't make as many blunders. Acree is not surprised. In football, the defense usually improves faster than the offense.

The hitting and heat exhaust a few starters, as Moore expects. Acree makes substitutions for anyone bruised up and needing attention from the managers.

Acree inserts Graham as an offensive tackle in place of Ray Stroube and calls a play to run the fullback off-tackle over Robert's position. When the huddle breaks, Robert thinks, "This is good!"

But the Henderson defensive tackle swings a padded forearm like a shortened baseball bat and delivers a blow to Graham's face, stands him up and drives him back into Hagle who has nowhere to run the ball. Acree leans into the next huddle and tells Graham, "Fire out, and let me see you hit that Henderson tackle."

Acree calls a play to the other side, where Sam Cooper substitutes for James Henkel. Cooper launches into the Henderson player and drives him out of the hole, but on the opposite side of the line, Graham's knees fall to the ground, missing his block. The man over Robert races from the backside to tackle the Corsicana runner from behind at the line of scrimmage. Graham walks back to the huddle. Miller notices and admonishes him. "Hustle, Graham. Hustle."

Trying to teach Robert, Acree leans into the huddle and says, "Graham, you can't loaf on the backside when the play is not coming your way."

Acree calls a play-action pass, and Happy Settle fakes to the fullback Hagle who drives forward into the line. Graham imagines cutting the legs out from under the defender in front of him, but the Henderson boy is agile and steps over Robert, who ends up lying on the ground. The tackler rushes in and jumps into Settle's face just as the quarterback tries to throw the ball. Acree gets upset with Graham and grabs him by the facemask. Another reason to hate a helmet. Acree yells like Robert is deaf, "You have to learn the fundamentals!"

He sends Robert back to the sideline for reflection. Robert imagines giving Acree the finger with both hands.

Noon came, and the boys had a lite lunch in the school cafeteria. Hagle didn't eat much for fear of throwing up during the afternoon scrimmage. Robert filled his plate up. A big man doesn't like to be hungry. He saw the other players watching him. It was his size, he figured, and the fact he was smiling. A big man needs to show off how much he can eat.

While Robert is eating, Coach Miller comes by and tells him that he has too much food. He imagines eating the whole plate as the coaches watch. That'll show them! Acree also tells Robert what to eat and what not to eat, saying his stomach won't digest it. Robert speaks to himself, "I know my stomach. I can even eat a DQ hamburger right before practice. No problem."

Acree tells all the players to finish eating and hustle into a room so he can give a chalk talk. Robert thought, "What is a man if he can't decide his own way?"

Acree's low talking at the blackboard and swashbuckling V's and O's describing play design makes Robert drowsy. Crowded into a small room, Acree said, "We got a good look at some people in the morning scrimmage." Robert thinks, "No one is having fun except Acree."

After resting to allow their food to settle, Acree sends the boys back onto the field for a one-hour second-team scrimmage. It pleases Robert that he plays better against the Henderson second-team. The player across from him is skinny but quick. He doesn't wait for Robert to shove him out of the way. Robert misses a stunt move by the boy across from him. Acree explains to Robert how to "read it." Miller gripes at Robert because his jersey is not tucked in. Robert walks back to the huddle, and Acree says, "Hustle back, Graham!" Robert thinks, "My friends aren't hustling, but they just look like it to please Acree."

It's hotter in the afternoon than in the morning. It's one hundred degrees hot. No breeze blows. Nobody seems to mind except Robert, who imagines he is hustling up a big sweat. Robert is sure that he is beating up on the small second-team players. Acree likes small, quick players who are always eager, always in a hustle to please him. They don't put their hands on their hips or bend over with their hands on their knees. They are not so hot to Robert. Acree sends Graham to the sideline for more reflection. Just standing around in the hot sun makes Robert more miserable.

Robert thinks to himself, Acree's methods stink. None of these small players will get write-ups in the paper. They can't block. Besides, if he wants to, he can surprise Acree by slimming down anytime he chooses, but he likes being a big man. When he gets back in there, he'll show those little fellows what he can do. He can slap them on the helmet, push them in the back or discourage them with a good saying like, "You're not so hot, boy!"

But back on the field later, they move too quick to hear Robert over his fast breathing. He thinks, "They are acting like the heat doesn't bother them like they're trying to win. Don't they know it's just a scrimmage?"

When Acree gets mad, he shows it. Robert imagines coaches are always angry. Always watching. Always yelling. Always correcting. Robert would rather imagine being at home watching cartoons. TV programming is new and exciting to him. So is air-conditioning. He likes horsing around with his friends like they were The Three Stooges. It's fun to act goofy like Icky Twerp or Soupy Sales. Waiting on the sidelines and watching the coaches is no fun. There is no place to sit down.

Robert notices Acree's determination to work on a day like today. To sweat and stink, helping boys to learn a game. See how he admonishes big and tall Sam Cooper to get in a balanced, four-point stance. To tell him to keep going even though his injured knee hurts. Acree couldn't just go have a beer with Sam. He wouldn't sit at the lake with him and smoke a cigarette. No, Acree wants to strengthen Cooper, to make him like Hagle. To improve his technique like John Stover who used to run like he was tip-toeing. Acree must stay up late working on his plans for yelling the next day. And next year, graduation comes and sweeps away all his hard work. He sweats and stinks all over again with a new set of boys. He searches the tryouts for a good ball-handler, teaches him to pitch it here, throw it there and look like he's someplace he's not, as if his eyes go opposite his feet. No trouble. Acree finds a way to keep going. Two district championships in a row. Give him some credit. The town admires him. Players are getting scholarships to play major college football. That's something. Winning makes for good stories in the paper. Winning gives the town celebrity. Winning turns the district rivals green with jealousy.

Coaches couldn't help some players. Robert heard about Gary Whistler, but he didn't know what happened. He's sure Acree was the problem. Whistler left the team upset, like he was one of his dad's junk-yard dogs. Then he muzzled himself and didn't bark out the trouble to warn future boys. No matter, now. Robert knew what Gary must have known. The practice uniforms are the same even though the boys inside of them are new. The pads are all the same with the same old stink. Same old helmets fit the same-sized heads, no matter if the insides are different. Same shoes. Same practice field. Same scrimmage with Henderson. Everything is set for a repeat season. Acree has done something, but it's all the same to a boy who is different like Robert.

* * *

Boys entered the bus as they leaked out of the clammy locker room feeling wet and sloppy, hoping to dry out once the bus starts moving. Like relief from a good bowel movement, the scrimmage is over and best forgotten. They put their stinky equipment away on the racks above the seats. Good riddance.

Robert boarded and looked for his favorite seat, one in the back left corner. He didn't want to climb the steps into the bus after the coaches. They might see him moving slowly. His shoulders and ankles ached. His elbows and knees were skinned. His mangled fingers were swollen and stiff. He saved a seat for Joe Smith to see if he hurt like Robert and if he was the same Smith or a different Smith.

Hagle got on and looked like he had baled hay all day and then stacked it in a barn.

Logically, Robert agreed with Acree's way but would never say so. The way of a blocker staying on his feet to defeat an opponent rushing to tackle the quarterback. He agreed that setting the gap between players was a good technique, not just an accident. He agreed that he should keep his feet moving, ready to improvise if the defense called a stunt. Or if he was on defense, running through blockers to get to the ball carrier or Acree's way of sacrificing his body, hurdling it into oncoming blockers to stop a sweep. Ignore rib cage pain. A manager would tape it up.

Robert agreed in principle that Acree was right about formations, plays, blocking and tackling and all the various football elements required to have a championship-caliber team. All the conditioning. All the preparation. Successful teams had a common purpose—the goal of winning. The players all worked together, win or lose. They all did the same calisthenics, monkey bars, grass drills and wind sprints.

But sameness like this was ridiculous to Robert. He was his own person—an independent boy. Life for him was enjoying each day. Every moment was something new to laugh at. He didn't want to disappear into sameness as if he were lying exhausted on a field with a bunch of other exhausted players. He wanted to fertilize and grow who he was, do what made him a big, fun boy—a boy who experienced life like water, always flowing downhill, never uphill.

Once all the boys were aboard, the coaches climbed on the bus. Their faces spoke the scrimmage results as though they had just lost a regular-season game. Acree said, "We had a pretty good scrimmage. The defense is ahead of the offense, which made the normal number of mistakes."

Acree added, "We need a lot more work."

Miller and Moore concerned themselves with the bruised players and encouraged the boys to rest on the ride back to Corsicana. Moore was relieved that no one succumbed to the heat.

Without looking at the film, Acree knew the minuses had canceled the pluses. The scrimmage was over, but the players needed more repetition to function together as a team. Even the most basic game elements required more work. Needed repetition when the players were tired. Needed repetition until they would do it right, if only by muscle memory.

He wanted players to break the huddle in unison, clapping their hands together at the same moment. Opponents needed to hear it as one sound, signifying Tiger unity. Opponents needed to know they faced a team, not an individual. From the huddle, he wanted the Tigers to charge up to the line of scrimmage to assume their positions and to look eager, like they were ready to engage—not sloppy, like each man doing his own thing, walking as though he were taking a stroll toward the TV set to change the dial.

Linemen needed to all adopt the same start position, hands on knees, heads up, in a straight line, straight as a ruler could make them. Acree wanted them to look sharp. When the quarterback cried "Ready!" they should rise up in unison and then drop simultaneously into their four-point stance, not slouching and slumping sluggishly. They should rise crisp-like as though they were one body moving in agreement, heads coming up and bodies lowering as one. When they hear "Set!" Acree wanted the players to remain motionless until the quarterback called the snap count, "Hut one!" or "Hut two!", whatever he signaled in the huddle. In unison, they should fire off to attack the opponent's line and advance together like the front teeth of a tiger chomping a gaping hole in the underbelly of its prey.

Acree sat on the bus contemplating the short time window to get the team ready to face Waco in three weeks. He thought of the players who had dedicated themselves to the team. The players the team could count on to do their part if they were behind in a game—the players who would become starters. Once assembled, the starting lineup needed time to develop as a unit.

He thought of the detailed steps to prepare for the Duncanville scrimmage in four days, the Sherman scrimmage the following week, and the Waco game the week after. The team needed repetition, he thought, to get the players to line up correctly according to the formation called in the huddle, repetitions to execute their called-play assignments correctly, repetitions to read and improvise in any given situation, repetitions to use the most effective blocking technique, repetitions to work as a team until they would not make silly mistakes, especially when they were exhausted, not daydreaming when they were behind. All that repetition takes time, but it would be worth it if they worked hard.

Acree thought, "The boys passionate about the game will put their heads down and work to get the job done. Those players will experience digging themselves out of a hole in practice and learn to keep working in a game when it's not going their way."

Robert was playing with his radio in the back of the bus. No use trying to talk to a different Hagle, he thought. It's a relief to be riding back home. A relief to know there is no more sweating today. The boys had put in a full day.

On a normal two-a-day, they would have a break during the day, but today, travel ate up that precious time. Two hours over to Henderson. Two hours back. Riding home, their thoughts turned to their evening plans. Plans to see their girlfriends. Plans to eat with their families. Plans to watch TV. Plans to drive their cars around town with friends.

Collectively, the boys chattered. They told each other what happened in the scrimmage. Enthusiastically, they retold big plays. Long runs. Recalled some tackles. Who got a big hit then jumped back up, ready to go again. Some told of taking an elbow into their facemask. Cut eyebrows. Bleeding chins from helmet pops. Some spoke of going the wrong way and Acree yelling at them. Others spoke of how tough Hagle ran. They shared what they would forget to tell their dads. They relaxed. They had put in a full day of work and were ready to let loose.

Robert liked the chatter. The sounds bounced around the bus like billiard balls clattering as they scattered from a break. He laughed as he told others what happened on plays when he dropped to his knees. At times, he listened to his transistor radio. The time for the ride home passed unnoticed.

* * *

Daylight savings time was not practiced in the USA until 1966. Nighttime was approaching as the bus rolled to a stop behind the Field House; the driver flipped on the interior bus lights, and Acree stood up to face the players. He addressed them and started by saying, "Men."

Robert instantly wondered, "What did he mean by saying, 'men'?"

Did Acree expect Robert to be a "man" like himself—someone who endeavored to outwork his opponents and someone who led others to anticipate and prepare for situations in order to help them have a better chance of winning? Robert liked being called a man, even though he wasn't exactly sure what Acree meant.

Every eye in the bus was fixed on Acree, as if the players were antelopes watching a lion staring at them. Some boys expected Acree to tell them what time to be at practice the next day. Robert expected Acree to single him out as having done an excellent job. Others were sure he was about to tell them what to expect against Duncanville.

Instead, he informed them, "Today, we started our second week of two-a-days. It's 6 PM. An hour later than the time we usually start our second practice in two-a-days. You had a spirited ride home on the bus and are rested.

Our second workout for today starts in 30 minutes. We need to see the ball under the field lights since this Friday night we scrimmage against Duncanville. Take your gear and get suited up." He walked off the bus with the other coaches.

Hagle had a look of horror on his face. Robert wanted to jump off the bus like a man and tackle Acree. He wanted to surprise him good, hit him hard, incapacitate his big body and wallop his whacky head. Good thing Robert was at the back of the bus; otherwise, he might have ended up in the clink, he thought.

Looking into each other's faces but not talking, the players took their sweaty, stinky gear into the Field House and changed into it. They taped up their wrists, ankles and knees. They saw each other looking sad and miserable and spoke only necessary words. "This is crazy!"

They passed through the north door of the Field House and jogged onto Tiger Field. The coaches had flipped on the bright lights and were waiting for them. The players lined up in the end zone and started calisthenics.

Robert didn't say anything to anyone. Once the others had left the locker room, he handed his stinky uniform and pads over to the manager in the equipment room. He went out the back door, walked to his car and started the motor. Before driving off, he looked at himself in the review mirror. The smile on his face surprised him. He was delighted about the man he was.

Jim Miller, Jim Acree, Jerry Moore, Jerry Matthews, Paul Slaughter, 1962

After the surprise workout on Tiger Field, Robert's decision to quit caused a stir at home. So much so that he later appealed to Acree to rejoin the team. Coach allowed him to return, but according to Coach Moore, he had to run 100 miles as penitence. Acree stipulated that Robert had to have a teammate witness and validate every mile.

Robert was in the B-team photograph in 1962. Acree later moved him to the A-team but did not letter him after the season ended telling the press, "Robert didn't get in enough playing time."

Other players besides Robert Graham left the team. A good running back, Elic Gregory, lettered in 1961, came out for football in 1962 but resigned from the team after the Henderson scrimmage.

The following week, David Robinson tore a ligament in his right knee in the Duncanville scrimmage that ended his season. He had surgery at Waco's Hillcrest Hospital. Donnie Denbow resigned from the team because he had repaired a knee injury in Waco. Sam Cooper suffered a severe shoulder separation, which required surgery. Jack Shivers missed the season because of rheumatic fever. The team lost Robert Pimentel during the second week of two-a-days due to a "tough ankle sprain."

The 1962 varsity team ended up having only twenty-four players. Twenty-two other boys became B-team players. After starting with sixty-four tryouts, the Tigers lost eighteen boys. By comparison, the 1960 team had a drop of just seven boys. The 1961 team lost ten boys.

That October, during the Cuban Missile Crisis, mushrooming support for the Tigers in Corsicana eclipsed even the fear of an atomic bomb. District opponents dreaded playing the Tigers. The 1962 Bengals achieved an eight-win, three-loss season and won the District Championship for the third time under Acree. That string of titles hadn't happened in Corsicana for twenty-eight years. It would be another twenty-two years before another Tiger team repeated it.

As for practicing under the lights following a hard day of scrimmage, Jim Wood and Sam Cooper supposedly chose to play college football at SMU because their football field didn't have field lights.

Quarterback Happy Settle signed a four-year scholarship to play football at Oklahoma State. James Henkel accepted a scholarship and became a star player at Texas Tech.

Writing about the Tiger's success under Acree, a Sports Editor for the Corsicana Daily Sun, Talmadge Canant said, "About the only way to

135

improve on the Tiger's success would be for them to win a state championship. And that's asking quite a lot."

Reading it, Acree likely recalled that Superintendent Dana Williams had hired him to do precisely that.

Robert Graham proudly wearing his letter jacket after the 1963 State Championship (photo used with permission)

CHAPTER 6 BUILDING AN A-TEAM

"The strength of the pack is the wolf, and the strength of the wolf is the pack." The Law of the Wolves by Rudyard Kipling

Assistant Coach Jim Miller had differences with Jim Acree and departed Corsicana in May 1963 for a coaching position in Jacksonville, Texas. He had worked with Tiger linemen for three seasons, two of which ended in heartbreaking losses to the Jacksonville Indians. Whatever the reason, Miller took a job with an Acree archenemy to serve as a head scout against Corsicana.

Interviewing with the press, Acree sent Miller off with perfunctory "good job" remarks, and simultaneously announced, "I'm in the market for a coach now."

Tragic and sad events in life may end fortuitously. In April 1963, Mrs. O. E. Bounds died of a heart attack. Her husband and Superintendent of Corsicana Schools, Oscar Bounds, asked Jim Acree to serve as a pallbearer. Bounds also requested Acree's former assistant, Raymond Anderson, help at the funeral. Anderson had departed Corsicana two years earlier for a coaching position in Houston. After putting Mrs. Bounds to rest, Acree and Anderson, who had worked together in Bonham and Corsicana, likely talked shop.

In a mere three weeks after Miller's resignation, Anderson again became an assistant coach in Corsicana. Acree also named Anderson as Assistant Athletic Director. He was an experienced, administrative-minded teacher and a good football coach. His administrative duties included supervising the junior high schools, but Acree gave him coaching responsibility for the Tiger backfield and the track team. Jerry Moore coached the receivers and was responsible for the baseball program. Acree assumed Miller's role and coached the Tiger linemen. The high school football staff included B-team coaches Jerry Matthews (also head basketball coach) and Paul Slaughter. As steadfast friends, Acree, Anderson and Moore were together for the third time in their young careers. Together, they chased the dream of winning a state football championship in Texas.

Football in Texas was growing. The UIL reported that 936 football teams would compete for state titles in 1963. Among the 126 AAA schools, Dumas was the reigning champion with two-consecutive state titles and a twelve-game win streak. In Corsicana, Acree had three consecutive District 8-AAA titles. Press pundits predicted the Tigers to win a District 8-AAA title again but picked the Graham Steers to beat Dumas and win the AAA State Championship.

In 1963, Acree had only twelve returning lettermen from the previous year's District Champion team. Just six of them were seniors. Acree equated experience with winning. "We won't have many seniors, and younger boys make their share of mistakes, and mistakes hurt you."

Speaking to a civic group about the '63 Tigers, he concluded, "A five and five season wouldn't be a bad ending for us."

Stating publicly what he believed about the upcoming team didn't imply that Acree resigned himself to such a result. On the contrary, it meant he would double his efforts to prove himself wrong.

Winning championships was so normal to Jim Acree that conceivably it became part of his identity. He had a collection of letter jackets and trophies to prove it. He was a basketball State Champion in 1944, an All-State football player in 1946, a Sugar Bowl Champion as a member of the Oklahoma Sooners in 1948 and an Orange Bowl Champion in 1954. As a boxer, he pounded his way into the Oklahoma City Golden Gloves heavyweight championship in 1949 and won the Amateur Athletic Union (AAU) heavyweight title in 1953.

As part of a high school coaching team, he had eight consecutive district championships in AA and AAA football. But his teams didn't make it very deep into the playoffs, often losing in the bi-district (first) round. In '63, winning a state championship appeared to be an "elusive butterfly."

But Jim Acree was determined if he was anything. No matter how unlikely it might have seemed, a state championship was always in his thoughts. After losing the bi-district game to Jacksonville in 1962, he told the Dads Club, "We have our eyes on the future and hope that someday Corsicana might be up in the running for a state championship."

That July, he commuted four-hour roundtrip daily to East Texas State College to complete continuing education requirements as a teacher. At the same time, he also prepared for the start of the '63 season. His hardwork methods gave him confidence. He rejected offers to coach elsewhere and instead called Corsicana "home." But to be truly home, he wanted to win a state championship.

In his mind, he needed a team of experienced, senior players to win. Except for 1932, Corsicana had come up short, always lacking senior talent in critical positions. However, having roughnecked in Texas and Oklahoma oil fields, Acree understood the value of a pipeline.

To assemble a team each year, his strategy was to deploy experienced players. Seniors first, then juniors he had coached as sophomores. Then juniors up from the B-team. Following were sophomores from the two junior highs, but very few boys coming out of junior high met his requirements for experience, talent and maturity.

Acree also poached talent from other teams: basketball, baseball and track. Urging parents to get their boys to come out for football, he tirelessly promoted the game as a speaker in civic clubs and church gatherings.

Acree encouraged boys regardless of size, speed, ball handling or blocking and tackling abilities to play football. He looked for courage, teamwork and leadership. He planned to develop his men in all these areas if they stayed out and played. Players with different abilities were needed to fill all eleven positions on the field. Working with the available boys in 1963, Acree had to identify each player's talent and put the boys into the correct team positions that maximized the potential for winning. Acree excelled in this regard and exercised his prerogative season-by-season, game-by-game and often, play-by-play. In his own words, he had underestimated the '62 team, saying, "With a few adjustments, they might have made it further into the playoffs." He didn't want to repeat that mistake in 1963.

With Miller gone, Acree had the responsibility of coaching the Tiger linemen. The only returning, starting senior linemen were guards Jim Wood and end Johnny Nelson. Both were two-year lettermen. Acree had nightmares that no one could replace James Henkel and Rey Stroube; both experienced tackles lost to graduation. Could he rely on Sam Cooper and Robert Graham? Both were seniors, but neither lettered their junior year. Sam was injury prone and recovering from shoulder surgery. Robert was coming out of Acree's doghouse. Initially, Acree thought he would use talent from the B-team, stating, "Success will depend on how young linemen come along."

After considering the size of seniors Cooper and Graham, Acree decided not to gamble on the smaller B-team boys. He must have also applied a long-held football adage, "a good big man is better than a good little man."

The team had other problem areas. In the spring track meet that year, no Corsicana boy finished in the top three of the 100-yard dash or 220-yard race. However, District foe Cleburne won all three positions in both events. The Tiger's fastest boy, David Robinson, had lost his junior year experience due to a knee injury suffered during a pre-season scrimmage. Acree worried publicly, "We will lack speed in the backfield,"

As Head Coach, Acree challenged Coach Anderson to consider the returning players and come up with a backfield. He sent Coach Moore to recruit Donnie Denbow back to football. Denbow was a talented senior, who missed his junior year due to knee surgery. Acree badly needed linemen, but Denbow returned at an end position and became a receiver, rather than a tackle, the position he played in junior high and on the B-team when he was a sophomore. In addition to his size, Donnie was an exceptional baseball player with outstanding catching ability and deceptive speed.

Looking at the returning backfield roster with Anderson, the two men made vital decisions. They moved senior tailback Joe Smith to the offensive line and made him a guard. At 160 pounds, he lacked size, but he made up for it in quickness and agility. Likewise, they moved backup fullback Don Ivie to a defensive tackle position. He was an aggressive player, who gained in size and speed as he matured into a man. Both boys were intelligent and capable of learning completely new roles in a short period before the season started.

Regarding needing smart players, Acree noted, "We expect to be running 100 different plays with different blocking assignments. You can't be dumb and do things a football player must do these days."

"The game is no longer a choice between brains and brawn."

Acree assigned B-team coaches Paul Slaughter and Jerry Matthews to analyze the sophomores coming from the junior high programs and identify two or three mature boys who had already decided they wanted to excel in football. The coaches selected Bill Allison from Collins and the Smith twins, Ben and Glen, from Drane. All three were good athletes with the football maturity Acree was looking for. Allison would become a backup fullback on offense and backup noseguard on defense. Ben was a savvy ball hawk with enough speed to play in the defensive backfield. Glen had ample quarterback experience in junior high and would be a backup quarterback on the varsity and a starting quarterback on the B-team.

In some ways, finding players is a game of numbers. A coach can assemble the talent needed to make a good team given enough boys. However, boys moving from junior high to high school tended to quit football. Acree used his marketing skills to bolster parental support to encourage their boys to stay out for football: "The football program aims to build character, not just emphasize winning."

By character, he meant discipline. "We believe in working hard and building character. With air conditioning, it's difficult to get young players to work hard enough to get in proper physical condition. It is not until they are tired that the process of improvement begins."

The coaches also agreed to meet with parents at the Field house to help them understand the football program. They briefed mothers on what to expect from the rigorous training of two-a-days, which is known in football as a process for separating the "men" from the boys. Despite their efforts, horror stories regarding blisters obtained swinging from monkey bars circulated in the hallways and discouraged many boys from trying out.

To help reduce attrition, the coaches decided to eliminate the annual Henderson scrimmage and schedule only one external preseason scrimmage in Bryan, Texas, a AAAA school. Acree tasked Paul Slaughter and Jerry Matthews to scout the Broncos once they started their workouts. Even if it was just a scrimmage, he didn't want to be surprised in front of a hometown crowd.

Acree obtained UIL approval for the boys to eat together during two-a-days in the school cafeteria if they paid for their meals. His scheme invited tryouts who passed their preseason physical exams, to work on Tiger Field daily and earn a future meal. As could be expected from Acree, to warm up for the job of pulling weeds, he had them run to the Green House and back for conditioning. When rested and wearing shorts and t-shirts, the mile out and back was no problem for most boys. That would change when two-a-days started, and they were sent to the Green House and back wearing full pads after a two-hour practice session. Running to the Green House became a symbol of pain and punishment.

Anderson's administrative ability ensured that all coaches understood the changes in UIL rules that year. Because of their stringent enforcement, Acree stipulated that Corsicana would observe the UIL rules to the letter.

Despite all the planning in the run-up to the start of two-a-days, Acree was still gloomy and predicted that only "blood, sweat and tears" awaited the Tiger team on the field that season.

* * *

Two-a-day practices started on August 19, 1963, and fifty-seven boys showed up for the first 8-10 AM workout. The senior lettermen returning from the '62 team included Jim Hagle, Marc Maxwell, Johnny Nelson, Gary Roman, Joe Smith and Jim Wood. Returning juniors who lettered as sophomores in 1962, included Bruce Butler, Jerry Anderson, Don Ivie, Bill Henson, Rankin Koch and Chick Whistler. Other talented B-team players from 1962 joined the 1963 team. This included seniors John Stover and Mark Dawson and juniors Ron Cottar, Roger Goldesberry, Ricky Libal, Ronnie Rhoads, Stan Rosen, Nicky Sanders, Jerry Sheets and Danny Wilcox. Importantly, however, no letterman was returning as a center.

The center is a critical member of a football team. Mastering snapping the football and blocking in the next instant is akin to earning a black belt in Jiu-Jitsu skills. A center can't just zone out. He must attend to the quarterback's signal calling, either verbal or a hand signal. In the moments before the snap, a center must recognize stunts, plan his blocking maneuver and correctly manipulate the ball to avoid causing his teammates to jump offsides.

Moreover, the center must master the art of accurately "long snapping" the football to a punter. Disaster results if the ball dribbles along the ground or flies over the punter's head. After injuring a knee, Acree played center at OU and in the Army, so he understood the importance of the position. He knew he could train the right boy, but who had the smarts?

After playing on the B-team in 1962, senior John Stover returned for two-a-day practices in 1963. Arguably, he and junior Stan Rosen were two of the most intelligent players on the team. If you knew them only through the classroom, one carried a lawbook, the other a slide rule. At the time, neither boy had remarkable athletic ability. But Acree's job was to coach them to snap the ball as a center, not run with the football. If the team needed a runner, the ball would go to big Jim Hagle, a highly experienced senior fullback.

* * *

That year, I was a fifteen-year-old boy trying out for football. I worked at Piggly Wiggly that summer and planned to enter the tenth grade at Corsicana High School. My first organized football year was the previous year when I played at Collins Jr High. I had met Jim Acree earlier that year at a Kiwanis Club meeting, but I didn't know him. As a big-small town, Corsicana was like that. A name was known, but not the person. It's generally worse when two football teams play; the opposing players rarely know the names of the boys on the other side of the line. This applied to a boy's knowledge of coaches, too. In his playing days at

Abilene Christian College, Paul Slaughter was a big man and a lineman. I had no idea at the time that he grew up in Corsicana. I knew nothing about his family.

I was inexperienced, but Acree was known as a winner, and I wanted to see if I could make the A-team. Doing so would impress my dad who loved football but could never play it because of a medical issue when he was a boy. Acree required us to pre-qualify by passing a doctor's physical and running a mile in less than six minutes. Even though I had to use an asthma inhaler, I had no problem qualifying.

At Collins, the coach put me down as a defensive end, and I played enough to know the essential game elements—e.g., tackle the ball carrier. I discovered that organized football was precise and planned compared to sandlot football, a game of throwing, catching or running for fun played with neighborhood friends.

As a Cougar football player, my name was in the town newspaper only once. I tackled a ball carrier in the end zone for a safety. Some boys my age regularly saw their names in the paper, especially quarterbacks, running backs and receivers. Reading the sports page, I learned names like Glen Smith, Steve Winn, Brad Haynie and Travis Hair. At Collins, the coaches put the most talented players on offense, thinking, "if we can't score, we can't win."

If it is good enough, the defense can hold an opponent to a tie. Coaches said a game ending in a tie was like "kissing your sister." I thought I understood their meaning since I had kissed a girl at a school dance that spring, but I wasn't sure since I had never kissed either of my sisters.

As the first two-a-day workout started on Monday, Assistant Coach Jerry Moore yelled for the receivers to join him in front of a backstop situated on the practice field. With hopes of seeing my name in the paper, I envisioned catching the ball and gloriously running to the end zone.

Acree hailed the linemen and linebackers to follow him. He was the type of man who put fear into boys like me. He was all business. There was nothing friendly about him. Coach Moore focused on results too, but his voice resonated with an instructive tone like he would answer a question if I were brave enough to ask one. Acree talked directly like a boss, calling us "men" as though we were soldiers prepping for combat. I became anxious just hearing him methodically describe how a play's design would eliminate enemy players and open an easy path for a running back. "If you execute the way it's designed, we'll score a touchdown."

I understood that football teams had a glory hierarchy, somewhat like the military. I knew from war movies that the privates did the grunt work, and the generals got the fame. In a similar scheme, football had interior linemen, such as guards and tackles, but the quarterbacks, fullbacks, halfbacks, flankers and ends were the ones who got their names in the paper.

Acree wanted players who outhustled their opponents or, better yet, knocked them to the ground. He wanted players who would tackle without blinking and wrap up a ball carrier as though hamstringing a horse. And after hitting, jump back up, ready to go again. He looked for boys who loved to hit.

Coach Moore stood about fifteen yards away from a designated spot in front of a net stretched between the goalposts. A player put his back to Moore who signaled when to turn around and face him. Moore threw the football to the player. The goal was to catch the ball, return it to Moore and rejoin the back of the line. Moore said, "React to the football."

The drill seemed simple, like playing catch in baseball. The trouble was I failed to snag a single football. It was like playing catch with your eyes shut until the last second before the ball arrived. Every time I turned around, he had already thrown the football, which sailed right by me.

When I put my eyes on it, the ball flew by like a bullet, out to the left, right or over my head. I grazed it several times, making it wobble into the net. In a raspy voice, Moore hollered for all the boys to hear, "If you can touch it, you can catch it!"

Seniors Johnny Nelson and Donnie Denbow had no trouble catching all the footballs thrown when their turn came. Moore complimented them, "That's it! Go to the football!"

"Good job. Tuck it as soon as you catch it."

Moore's drill made sense to me, but as a "slow thinker," I couldn't react fast enough with the quick actions needed to grab the ball. At Piggly Wiggly, I could catch watermelons tossed down from a truck, but I couldn't catch Moore's footballs. If he had thrown it to me instead of out to the side or above me, I would have caught it. I didn't have "all thumbs," but I moved in slow motion while the football zoomed by at full speed. Like bursting a dropped watermelon on a hot parking lot, I ruined my career as a receiver.

After missing my fifth attempt, I hustled toward the back of the line with my head down. Moore pointed, not knowing my name, "You, go over to Coach Acree and work with the linemen."

I accepted Moore's verdict and trotted off without looking at the other players. Moore's judgment was a letdown for me. It represented a failure on the first day, on the first drill. And in front of all the other players, too. It cut as bad as Cummings telling me I wasn't good enough to play basketball at Collins. I thought about quitting on the spot, but I had already attracted enough attention. Besides, Acree was looking at me as I jogged over to his area of the practice field.

I dreaded telling Acree what had happened, "I can't catch a football." I'm sure he didn't know my name, but he didn't ask. As though he had a private messaging system with Moore, he barked, "Get in line and let's see if you can hit."

I became a football lineman, fighting an obscure existence, dirtying up my uniform from head to toe every practice, looking and smelling like I had crawled the length of the field on my belly.

After "knocking heads" with many boys whose names we were still trying to learn, we cleaned up in the Field House. Acree gathered us into the weight room; only there were no weights in it. Instead, folding metal chairs faced a chalkboard and we had a "skull session."

* * *

Acree mesmerized us with "Split-T" formations, play designs, trap blocks, cross blocks, reach blocks, counter motions, reverse runs, options and receiver routes. Unbelievably, he also expected us to remember his scribbles on the board. The boys who had previously "lettered" under Acree knew much of what he taught. They had experience and understood what to do.

Simple things mattered to Acree. For example, he was particular about appearing sharp in a huddle or at the line of scrimmage. The center set the location of the huddle, holding one hand in the air. Acree wanted the team to form a perfect oval around him, players leaning in, bent at the waist. No one could stand erect. Only the quarterback talked. He called a formation, a play and a snap count. Good quarterbacks looked the other players in the eye as if they were saying, "Coming your way. Get ready."

When the quarterback said, "Ready? Break," we clapped in unison and hustled to the line of scrimmage to arrange ourselves in the correct formation, not "sloppy-like," but straight and streamlined like the fins on a new Chevy. When the quarterback called the snap count, Acree instructed the linemen to "fire-out" or move fast like a car peeling rubber off a start line.

With the speed and force of a mortar shell, the right halfback might explode out of his stance toward a designated gap on the right side. He shaped his arms as a receptacle for the football. The quarterback's job was to insert the ball in the "breadbasket" of the halfback just as he reached the line.

The idea of the play was to catch the defense flatfooted or "napping," as Acree used to say. The back could be past the line and running free in the secondary, gaining yardage before the defense could say, "Monkey's Uncle." Every play had a strategy behind it. All the hitting, pushing, shoving and falling to the ground masked the cunning finesse of proper play execution.

Acree explained the defense too, and the conditions where we expected the offense to run or pass, short-yardage situations like the goal line or the design of special team plays (punting, kick-offs, field goals, extra points). These were altogether different elements he wanted us to learn, contributing to how he defined "experienced."

It was essential for us to work together as a team. We had to depend on each other's moves, much like marching band members hang on the correct steps and right notes of their mates. However, a surprise element can occur in football. An opponent may come crashing into the backfield and disrupt the expected flow, cause a fumble and bring an unexpected end to a play. The fans would cheer, and the boy might get his name in the paper.

Acree talked for about an hour, then expected us to perform the plays that afternoon in practice. I couldn't even reach out to touch a football flying by my head. How would I master all these formations, play designs and blocking assignments? Learning my duties at Piggly Wiggly grocery store was far simpler than mastering Acree's football playbook.

Football was surprisingly complex, but I felt a satisfying sense of having a strategy, a belief that a play's design would work if I did my part. Of course, I thought only of doing my part. I didn't ask the guy next to me how he felt about his job. I was still trying to learn his name.

After the "chalk talk," Acree released us to go home and have lunch, rest and return for the afternoon skull session and practice. He asked us to be suited up and ready to go at 4 PM, when it supposedly "cooled off a bit." That hour in August in Texas is the hottest part of the day. As a gridiron, the stripes on a practice field resembled a hot grill, ready for frying meat. In addition to the formations and plays, Acree drilled us in the afternoon on football basics: one-on-one blocking and one-on-one tackling. The other coaches worked with the receivers and backs in different areas of the practice field. The linemen could see the ball handlers off in the distance, and we were jealous, thinking they had an easier time of it. Privately, the linemen characterized the backs and receivers as softies. Their practice uniforms were not nearly as filthy as ours. They hadn't spent enough time on the ground. And they didn't have Acree standing over them shaking his head.

* * *

Acree brought us all together for conditioning drills—in other words, torture. He planned to "run us 'til we dropped." Thirty-yard wind sprints first. We moved to all fours and raced like monkeys up and down the field. He had us face up and crab walk backward. We hurried up and down the field as if we were avoiding the vultures that circled overhead. Back on all fours, we butt rolled, and with every whistle, we rolled a different direction, first right then left. The "grass drills" ended practice sessions.

After practice, we shed our nasty uniforms and cleaned up while the managers, Gene Garrett and Johnny Elmore, washed our gear. At 7:15 PM, Acree assembled us again in the high school cafeteria for supper. At my table, I was the subject of a joke that first evening meal. When I asked someone to pass the salt and pepper, I heard, "Here, Ward, catch this. Oops! Never mind."

We worked out together, hit each other like enemies and then ate together as if we were friends. The experienced boys already knew each other. Generally, boys tried to fit in or go unnoticed. Unstated at the time, I look back and see that Acree wanted us to bond as a team, but as a boy, I had only a vague idea of the meaning of the word "team."

Sophomores, like me, merged in from two junior highs. We hardly knew each other's names if that. Seniors somehow knew the names of sophomores that were good players in junior high. Upper-level students chased down and initiated a few incoming sophomores by giving them unique haircuts, such as a Mohawk or a burr.

As two-a-days days progressed, I slept well, but occasionally, I had nightmares from the practice sessions. In one dream, I ran but couldn't escape Acree. No matter how fast I was, he was right behind me, reaching his big hands out to grab my facemask. Exhausted, like a fish on a hook, Acree held me, explaining what I did wrong.

I dreamed I had to block Jim Wood or tackle Jim Hagle in an open field. Wood's hammering forearm dropped me helplessly to my knees. Hagle's powerful legs churned through the tissue paper weak strength of my arms. I pictured these three with dread and sensed they would always haunt me with their looming presence. Fifty-plus years later, I was not wrong.

Acree divided the boys into an A-team (varsity) and a B-team (junior varsity). Players with serious talent and previous experience went onto the A-team, which numbered thirty-one or thirty-two, boys depending on the placement of sophomore Glen Smith, who was the quarterback on the B-team but kept a clipboard play-log for Acree on the A-team.

A-team members became objects of interest in the town, while the B-team players were not even popular within the school student body. Through the newspaper, A-team member names became well known.

Weighing about 150 pounds and lacking any notable talent (experience, size, speed, smarts or ball-handling skill), Acree put me on the B-team. Chalking it up as a failure, I considered quitting. My brother Dickey was also on the B-team, and we rode together to practice in an old '52 Ford. He said, "If you quit, I'll quit, too."

After lunch, we discussed quitting while resting on a bed in front of a window unit blowing cool, moist air on us. "I can make money after school, working at Piggly Wiggly."

Dickey eventually wanted to join the Marine Corps, "Sticking it out will help me get ready for boot camp when I'm old enough."

"I can't get to work after school if you take the car to practice."

We decided to stay out for (not quit) the B-team. However, a few other boys decided to quit. The B-team dwindled to twenty-one players, and we didn't have enough boys to scrimmage against ourselves.

Football is a competitive sport played between two teams from different schools, likely from different towns. To simulate this at the end of the first week of two-a-days, Acree split the A-team into roughly three teams and had them scrimmage against each other on Saturday. The boys were impressive and hustled, which pleased Acree. However, his critical eye could see that the players needed improvement. As though he were a hammer working on bent nails, he said, "Once they get straightened out, they'll do well."

After the second week of two-a-days, on August 30, 1963, the Dads Club held their annual BBQ dinner. Fans paid a dollar per plate for their first look at the 1963 Tigers. Acree created two scrimmage squads, blue and gold (white) teams. Referees were employed to call the imitation game to help train boys for actual game conditions.

The names of the players of both squads made it into the newspaper. The "starting lineup" would emerge from the competition between the two groups. Making varsity was a glorious step but becoming a "starter" for a position was even more so because it designated the best player on the team (not already assigned to another position). Starters received more playing time than "substitutes." Tiger "reserves" saw little playing time but had a tradition of standing on the sideline, ready for Acree's call to enter the game at any moment.

The two A-team squads impressed the crowd as well as the press. Comparing them to Tigers from the previous year, sports editor Talmadge Canant wrote, "We predict that before long most of these youngsters will make you forget what you saw a year ago."

For Acree, the intrasquad scrimmage had demonstrated how much work the A-team offense needed. They struggled to move the ball against the other squad's defense. Running all those formations, play designs and assignments without mistakes was challenging even for the best, most experienced players.

* * *

After two-a-days, Acree set expectations for a typical work week of game preparation by practicing in full pads on Monday, Tuesday and Wednesday, shorts, t-shirts and helmets on Thursdays and game uniforms on Friday nights. He prepared the varsity to scrimmage Bryan High School on Friday, September 6, 1963.

Acree briefed the Dads Club on the offensive starters for the Bryan scrimmage. The key men were quarterback Gary Roman, fullback Jim Hagle, halfbacks Chick Whistler, Ronnie Rhoads and David Robinson, ends Johnny Nelson and Donnie Denbow, center John Stover, guards Jim Wood and Joe Smith and tackles Sam Cooper and Robert Graham. All these men were seniors except for Whistler and Rhoads. Eight were returning lettermen.

Leaders come in various forms. I observed who I thought to be the leadership core: Wood, Denbow, Nelson and Stover. They were the quiet types who did what Acree said before he even had to say it. I knew Denbow as a teammate on the American Orange Little League team. He was years more mature than any of the other boys. I never saw him waste time or even make a joke.

Although mature, Nelson would occasionally crack a smile. Johnny and I worked together when he was a checker at Piggly Wiggly grocery store.

Like a minister, Jim Wood had a powerful presence, except he doled out judgment with a forearm rather than words. All the linemen knew to shut up and listen when Jim spoke, which he seldom did.

Stover, I knew from Collins Jr High. He was a ninth-grader when I was a seventh-grader. I happened to be in the class his mother taught. He visited her class one day, and I made a wisecrack to impress my friends. He came looking for me after school and intended to give me a good thrashing. However, he displayed control by only putting a warning finger in my face. I knew he could beat the crap out of me if he wanted to. He had buddies, too. Linemen huddled around Stover wherever he raised his arm.

Gary Roman was co-captain with Jim Wood. Acree recognized their leadership skills. Roman could throw and run. Off the field, he had a winsome personality. Having good looks, it seemed like all the girls wanted to date him.

Hagle, Whistler and Cooper were also leaders, but they were athletically talented, gregarious types that led by example on the field. Hagle and Whistler always had a smile and stood out in a crowd—one by his size and power, the other by his efficient, machine-like play execution. Sam Cooper was tall and powerful. He laughed and talked with a sound that came from deep inside him. I suspected he had a lot going on in his head that made it out only in the matter-of-fact look in his eyes.

Robinson and Graham were jovial leaders of a different sort. They did their job when Acree was looking. Otherwise, rumors circulated in the hallways that they had a good time off the field. Following their leadership was not a good idea.

Generally, the starters were lettermen who played for Acree the prior year or had enough experience to know what he expected. To win games, the team counted on Roman, Hagle, Denbow, Nelson, Rhoads, Whistler and Robinson for scoring. As for the defense to prevent the other team from scoring, the names were essentially the same as the starting eleven with a few exceptions because most of the starters played "both ways." Playing both offense and defense required superior conditioning, which Acree exacted with the skill of a drill sergeant.

In what Acree called an "Oklahoma 5-2," the defensive starters included inside linebackers Jim Wood and junior letterman Bruce Butler. The junior nose man was a first-year Cody Sherrard, a quick, 5'3" 145-pound aggressive scrapper who chewed tobacco. If Cody didn't spit in the center's eye, he relied on cunning and quickness to slip past him. Like a weasel finding his way into a chicken coop, he could disrupt backfield play before it hatched.

Sam Cooper and Robert Graham were defensive tackles, but junior Don Ivie competed with Graham to start on defense. I could see the sparkle in Ivie's eyes as he practiced. His sly smirk betrayed his intent to win Acree's approval somehow. He was quick as a wild boar and loved to hit. He tracked down ball carriers like a compass needle finds north. Ivie started as a defensive tackle by the third game of the season.

Donnie Denbow anchored one end position. Senior Marc Maxwell and junior Bill Henson competed for the other end.

Roman and Hagle were the defensive cornerbacks. Deep backs or "safeties" were Rankin Koch and Chick Whistler. Often, Hagle played up on the line, in a position Acree called a "monster back." The other defensive backs followed Hagle and "rotated" into the strong side of an opponent's offensive formation.

Starters on defense had a knack for tackling a ball carrier, akin to that of a fly swatter's skill for eliminating a pest. Communicating what he valued most in the defense, Acree characterized them, saying, "They all do the job well—good effort and hard-hitting, and we have no complaints in this department."

As a field goal and extra point kicker, "specialist" Rickey Libal was also in the main group. The team depended on him. He wore a funny shoe that had a square toe. Occasionally, Bill Henson kicked in his place. Kickers, like quarterbacks, needed self-assurance. The core group consumed the most playing time on offense, defense and special teams. I learned all their names but as a sophomore, I didn't know much about their lives.

* * *

The Tigers scrimmaged the Bryan High School Broncos on September 6, 1963. The teams wore unnumbered practice jerseys and kept no scores. Acree laddered the A-team into three separate groups, first, second and third teams. Each unit saw action against the Broncos. The hundreds of fans in the Tiger stands didn't need numbers to recognize Jim Hagle's powerful running form, the darting speed of Chick Whistler and Ronnie Rhoads and Gary Roman pass completions to Donnie Denbow for first downs.

Hustle and hard hitting mattered on defense, and even without jersey numbers, fans quickly spotted "first-team" standouts Cody Sherrard at noseguard and tackles Don Ivie and Sam Cooper. Second team highlighters included Holly Holstein, Bill Allison and Rankin Koch. Acree used Glen Smith from the B-team to quarterback the "third" varsity team. He led the Tigers on a sustained drive but failed to cross the goal line. The scrimmage ended in a draw.

* * *

Slaughter coached the linemen on the B-team. As he did the other boys, he taught me how to block and tackle. To block, he said, "Get underneath the defensive player and force him to stand up." "Always drive your feet to push him in one direction or another." "Keep in contact with him. Don't let him slip off to the side."

He gathered his lumbering form and squatted in his stance to demonstrate, "Feel him sliding, and don't let him get around you." Slaughter's voice was encouraging. "That's it. Keep your position."

I hated the one-on-one drills, but they were necessary. If I were to play, it wouldn't be because of my size, speed and power. My "technique" would be the difference. Slaughter trained me to stay on my feet rather than launch my body into empty air and land sprawling on the grass. He illustrated with his big body how to shift my body around and keep the opponent in front of me. He showed me how to flare my elbows to increase my width or to throw a boney elbow to pop an opponent. Delivered to the helmet, it would "ring his bell."

He put his big hands on my shoulders and pushed to show me how to block without holding. "Close those fists, so you don't grab a jersey," he said with a voice of experience. "Now, fire out and meet him on his side of the line."

I did what he told me to do. I blocked against Larry McLaurin and felt his body give way under my legs' pushing, driving force. The thought occurred to me that McLaurin might have been loafing, but I had confidence I could move him if needed.

Agility was important. When my knees dropped to the ground, Slaughter would yell, "Quick! Get on those feet and keep moving!"

When I fired out, if I shut my eyes and missed an opponent, he said, "Look where you're going. Blocking is not like kissing your girlfriend. He's moving, too."

At 150, I couldn't block as well as Jimmy Pillans, 160, or David Porch, 165, so I didn't start on offense as a guard. I didn't count it as a failure because I started on defense. I was gaining experience and felt part of the B-team.

On defense, Coach Slaughter put me down as an inside linebacker. Jimmy Prater already occupied the defensive end position. As a linebacker, Slaughter taught me to "take on" the blocker or to "shed him" and "keep moving." Fast reaction time was necessary. "Get off on the ball." He taught me to "read a key," for example, to "watch the fullback and move the direction he goes." He ran drills for us to react to the motion of the quarterback—front out or reverse out. When pursuing a running back, "watch the numbers on his jersey, not his arms and legs."

He told me, "Stay put if you see cross motion, and forearm the guard."

Teaching me to tackle, "Put your head in front." He'd say, "Don't just hit the ball carrier; put your arms around him and grab hold. Wrap him up!"

We'd do drill after drill and then drill some more, practicing our technique. Sometimes one-on-one. Occasionally, two-on-one to learn about "double-teaming." Other times, five-on-five. But the mantra was always, "Let me see you hit!" "Let's hustle!" "Come on, Ward! Get with it."

One time, a foot or a knee hit me in my man parts—I didn't see it coming. It left me with a deep ache, a sick, empty feeling, like something way down low was knocked way up high where it didn't belong. I imagined a musket ball jammed high-up in a long, empty barrel. I lay on my back with my knees pointed toward the sky. I wanted to roll over and puke, but Coach Slaughter raised my waist off the ground and bounced my butt back and forth. He did this a few times, and even though I told him I was dying, he assured me I'd be okay.

Scrapes and bruises became so common that I didn't even bother to complain. My geometry teacher, Miss Mammie Moore, grimaced when she saw the blisters on my hands. She noted a boil where my helmet liner snugged up against my forehead, "You should see a doctor about that."

Sometimes a finger would "jam" when poked end-first into a hard helmet or shoulder pad. It might ache, and Coach Slaughter would pull out on it to make it feel better. I soon learned how to "pull out the knuckle" myself. It was scary to look down at my hand and see the end of a finger pointing in a different direction than it should. It hurt but dealing with such troubles as minor problems became part of changing from a boy into a man. About as fast as I absorbed the intricacies of football, my body was transforming. My weight changed very little, but my muscles became hard. Calluses formed on my hands, elbows and feet and more than a few scars marked my forehead. I'm reminded of this almost daily when I shave and I see two white scars from "helmet pops" under my chin.

As a defensive linebacker, Coach Slaughter showed me how to "stunt" with a tackle. How to "step up" and unexpectedly "shoot" through a gap. I liked surprising the offense that way. Generally, it led to a clean tackle or a fumble, but that depended on the play called by the offense. As Slaughter advised, it was not wise for me to always play aggressively, but rather, "Keep them guessing."

I liked hearing Slaughter say, "Good hit, Ward!" It was reassuring and built my confidence as a linebacker. Even though I was not very big, he said, "You have football speed." I wasn't sure what he meant, but I understood it must be a good thing. I liked to please him. But as a sophomore, pleasing Acree was near impossible.

Slaughter dutifully built players. Acree was building a team to play a ten-game schedule with five non-district opponents—Waco, Palestine, John Tyler, Jacksonville, Bishop Dunne in Dallas, and five district opponents—Ennis, Waxahachie, Cleburne, Athens and Terrell. Because of three straight District 8-AAA championships, fans expected at least that from the '63 Tigers. Acree was not one to give false hopes. After three weeks of work, he worried about the offense. "We're way behind."

Acree's concern about being behind wasn't logical since UIL rules permitted AAA teams to begin workouts a week earlier than AAAA schools. However, having yet to win a game against Waco since coming to Corsicana, a one-week advantage didn't give him cause for optimism. The first game of the '63 season was scheduled on Friday, September 13, and Acree was superstitious. The Tigers had not beaten the Waco Bengals in thirteen years, including the three years he had been at Corsicana. He spoke to the Dads Club on Monday evening before the Friday game on the thirteenth, saying, "We'll make lots of mistakes out there, but I feel like the boys will hustle for us. If they do, we'll be in the ball game. If not, we might be embarrassed."

Acree taught the team a few new plays that week and resorted to his proven methods—repetitive drills, extended practice sessions and topping off each day with conditioning exercises that would take the hustle out of even the most dedicated Tigers.

Waco

On game night, students sat on the west side with the bands and adults cheering from the east side. The Waco coach, Wayne Gardner, predicted the winner would score five touchdowns. He was correct. Jim Hagle tallied three himself; one was set up when Johnny Nelson almost scored after catching a pass from Gary Roman. After a second Hagle score, Roman ran in for a two-point conversion. Then Ronnie Rhoads caught another Roman pass for a touchdown. After that, second-string quarterback Rankin Koch tossed a scoring pass to David Robinson, speeding behind a Waco defender. Robinson ran for a spectacular touchdown that put the crowd on its feet. His perseverance and talent paid off.

Ricky Libal kicked four extra points. Defensive standouts included Don Ivie, Sam Cooper, Donnie Denbow, Jim Hagle and Rankin Koch. Notably, Acree played all thirty-one A-team members in the game. Like the whole of his being, he wanted the entire team to experience the joy of winning over Waco. He believed that if a boy worked out all week, he deserved a chance to play, even if only for a few downs. He was building a team of winners, not just a few stars who would get their names in the paper. Corsicana fans stormed the middle of the field when the game ended and celebrated the end of a thirteen-year drought.

The 36-6 win over Waco, the first in over a decade, must have triggered hope in Acree, an optimism that lurked beneath the surface, one too daring to predict. He was superstitious and wore a blue shirt during the game, just like the late Johnny Pierce, the last coach to take the Corsicana Tigers to a state championship. Acree's coach at OU, Bud Wilkinson, was superstitious, too. Whatever he did leading up to a victory, he repeated it the next week, hoping for a similar result. Acree did the same.

Acree also noted the number of penalties the Tigers received—thirteen. He would take steps to correct the mistakes, but he stopped worrying about not having a center. John Stover made no errors in the game, not even after snapping the ball six times for punts. The lynchpin was set. The team had a center.

* * *

Like life, I find it strange how football teams work. No one would compare Stover's talent to that of Hagle's. Yet, as perfect as Hagle was at the fullback position, Stover was at the center position. He made up for what he lacked in speed and weight in smarts and a subtle understanding of the game—all taught to him by Acree. He was the right talent, at the right time with the right coach. Acree made the difference in Stover's journey to become a man. His obsession with player preparation (mental and physical) pushed Stover to improve each week and excel despite his lighter weight, ordinary strength and average speed. Under Acree, Stover was on a short-term journey to become the most improved player on the team.

As a champion at OU, Acree had experienced the benefits of reviewing the game film to correct mistakes, so he prepared the varsity for their game with Palestine, the second opponent, by addressing the thirteen Tiger mistakes logged against Waco. He showed the players the Waco game film and just like in practice, he employed repetition. He'd point out a player's mistake, rewind it and then point out another mistake. He'd back it up again, play it and then perhaps compliment some player. At times his comments were encouraging or instructive, "Way to stay home, Wood" or "Great pursuit angle, Ivie." "String him out, here, Henson. Don't let him get outside." "Sherrard, pursue down the line when you pop through like that." Once the season started, the team spent almost as much time in the film room as it did on the practice field.

Palestine

The right combination of desire, perseverance and talent is unbeatable. On September 20, 1963, Palestine had two future All-State players on the field, Bill Bradley and David Dickey, but Sam Cooper "laid the wood on Dickey," caused a fumble and hustled to recover the ball. Following the turnover, Gary Roman threw a touchdown to Johnny Nelson.

John Stover giggled on the sideline when the Palestine center snapped the ball over his punter's head. This put the Wildcats in a poor field position. Jim Hagle intercepted a Bradley pass, which led to the second Tiger touchdown by Hagle. Ricky Libal kicked the extra points, and the Tigers led 14-0 at the half.

Don Ivie, Ron Cottar, Cody Sherrard and Jim Wood played outstanding defense, allowing Bradley to score only once. Gary Roman sneaked in another touchdown and later passed to Donnie Denbow for the Tigers' final touchdown. Palestine blocked Libal's last extra point try, but importantly, Corsicana had only four penalties in the game. They defeated the Wildcats, 27-7. That and the fact that the Tigers completed nine of eleven passes delighted Acree. Smiling afterward, he exclaimed, "the offense is starting to jell."

Acree liked "crisp execution." Seeing the offense work like an engine firing on all cylinders was inspiring. Moreover, Palestine was a traditional, difficult opponent. Defeating them handily served as a benchmark. Watching the Tiger offense progress in two weeks from being "way behind" to purring like a healthy tiger must have heartened Acree's desire for another championship season. He wore his blue shirt again.

* * *

For competitive experience, coaches scheduled B-team games against the B-teams in other towns. The playbook for the B-team offense and defense mirrored that of the A-team, but since we were primarily inexperienced sophomores, we had trouble executing the system. Coaches Paul Slaughter and Jerry Matthews took their cues from Acree on what he expected from us. It was possible for an individual to "move up" to the A-team, but they had to stand out in some needed position or demonstrate a knack for the game with a "hit-'em-hard" attitude. Our starting B-team quarterback, Glen Smith, permanently joined the A-team after the B-Team's schedule of eight games ended.

Matthews announced the starters for the B-team season-opening game against Palestine B-team. I wasn't one of the offensive players named. The two teams played on Saturday morning instead of the regular Thursday night. Palestine requested the schedule change following UIL rules, which permitted every boy to play only one game per week—either A-team or B-team. The schedule change made some Wildcat B-team players available for the varsity game against Corsicana, in case they were needed.

In announcing the starting line-up, Matthews said, "Most of the boys are having a little trouble adjusting to the system."

He meant that we couldn't remember the plays. In the scramble from the huddle up to the line of scrimmage, a lot goes through the mind of a boy, all of which affects his execution. For one, the disposition of the face of the unknown boy on the other side of the line can be a scary sight. See an angry, nameless face, and you might forget the snap count, the designated play or worse, your blocking assignment. Was I supposed to fire out or pass block? Was this a trap play, or am I supposed to block down? All the action happens in real-time; getting it right was like trying to catch a football flying by my head. Boys like me frequently messed up. Our minds and our bodies were developing, but not necessarily at the same rate. I played in that first game as a linebacker, where I had a chance to hone my hitting skill. Matthews yelled, "Ward, go to the ball!"

We won the game 24-12 primarily on great running by speedster Steve Winn and the throwing of quarterback Glen Smith. From Drane Jr High, Steve was a delight to get to know. He had a sense of humor and smarts to match his speed. His girlfriend and I attended the same church, so I connected with him. Glen was also from Drane. He was friendly, unpretentious and laughed easily. After the game, his name ended up in the newspaper. Assuming he's done something good, every boy likes to see his name in the paper.

* * *

The following Thursday, September 26, 1963, the B-team came together to defeat Duncanville on a muddy field, 14-0. Again, Steve Winn and Glen Smith did the scoring, but significantly, the defensive team formed a wall such that Duncanville never saw the rain-soaked grass on the Tiger end of the field. The newspaper cited the "workhorse" defensive efforts of Phil Pillans, Gary Schutte, David Poarch and Ronnie Ward. Slaughter's persistence in coaching paid off.

164

As an inside linebacker, I had an outstanding game. One play stands out in my memory. The night sky was black, and the lightly falling rain glistened under the field lights. Our uniforms, which started white, turned muddy brown after a few plays. Their quarterback pitched the ball to the fullback as he attempted a "sweep" to my side of the field. Our tackle on my side, Phil Pillans, blasted inside and caved in their line. I ran behind Phil, passed a blocker to my left, and arrived heads-up on the ball carrier just as he started to turn up field. Our end, Jimmy Prater, behind me, took on blocks from their end and tailback, so it was just me and their fullback alone on the edge. I didn't wait for him to turn toward me. I kept running at him like a heat-seeking missile. On reaching him, I aimed my head in front and launched my body, eyes wide open, toward his jersey number. When we collided, I wrapped my arms around him, and my momentum drove him to the ground. It was a clean hit. Slapping against each other sounded like popping a wet towel. He toppled over as if his shoelaces were tied together. I might have heard my brother yell "timber!"

Afterward, Slaughter and Matthews both praised me. They said, "You jelled as a player."

I would not have succeeded if Coach Slaughter had not helped me grow to confidently execute my position. My dad was proud. He beamed afterward as if I had hit a home run to win a baseball game.

There was no film of the B-team game against Duncanville but had there been I would have worn out a few projector bulbs re-watching the game. In hindsight, it was a small thing, but it was one where I made several plays that caused Slaughter and Matthews to brag about me to Acree during their review of the game with him.

Coach Slaughter later told me he learned a valuable lesson in my case. Don't "talk up" a B-team player to Acree! The following week, Acree moved me to the A-team and gave me jersey #41. I proudly wore it for the next three years. I never played B-team football again. I was just beginning to know some of the boys from Drane. Now that I was on the A-team and a Corsicana Tiger, I sat in meetings with a new set of boys, whom Acree called men, most of whom were like gods to me.

John Tyler

The following Friday night against John Tyler, a formidable AAAA opponent, Jim Hagle scored four touchdowns. We thrashed the Lions, 28-0. Hagle's touchdowns included a 90-yard opening kickoff return. After crossing the 50-yard line, he went untouched to pay dirt. Nothing short of 6'3", weighing 190 pounds with 10.2 speed (in the 100), Hagle had All-State power. John Tyler had allowed only 21 points in their previous two matches.

Acree must have thought of his All-State career at Maud watching Hagle run. As a high school receiver with a similar physique to Hagle, Acree caught 105 passes (15 in one game), scored 85 points and gained 1,478 yards. Likely, mentoring Hagle awakened in Acree the feelings of being a state champion, especially after the Dallas News polls ranked Corsicana that week as the number three football team in the State (in Class AAA).

Jacksonville

The next game, against Jacksonville, was a grudge match. Acree readied us for the game as though we were attending a street fight. The experienced players knew what to expect—hard hitting, aggressive football and last-minute Jacksonville heroics. The Indians looked sloppy but were always a formidable opponent.

A stomach bug plagued many of the players during the week. Bruce Butler started at guard in place of Joe Smith. On October 4, 1963, a standing-room-only crowd at Tiger Field watched Hagle carry the ball 22 times for 146 yards—yielding an average of 6.6 yards per carry. Yet, he failed to score in the game. I watched the Tiger defense from the sideline. They were superb. The opposing quarterback, a powerful runner, had a zero-yard rushing average on four carries. Bruce Butler recovered a Jacksonville fumble that set up the lone Tiger touchdown. Quarterback Gary Roman shined. He completed 10 of 13 passes to Johnny Nelson and Donnie Denbow. Our passing yardage almost equaled rushing yards gained. On a short run, Ronnie Rhoads scored the only Tiger touchdown.

Driving the ball on one series, fourteen plays, our offense worked like a new lawn mower cutting tough weeds. Ricky Libal booted two field goals and an extra point that made the six-point difference in the game. Our defense thwarted the Indians the entire contest, and only a last-second 62-yard touchdown pass put the Indians on the board. Jacksonville lost, 13-7. Former Coach Miller must have been disappointed. His inside knowledge didn't lead to a Jacksonville victory.

Despite the close score, Acree knew the Tigers dominated the game. Like a boxing champion, the team had hit Jacksonville with a one-two punch, running and passing. The more formidable Tiger defense delivered a knockout blow.

* * *

I would not have learned linebacking by watching Jim Hagle run. Instead, I became a student of Jim Wood and Bruce Butler, our starting linebackers. Acree's full-pad workouts included a drill where the first-string defensive line and linebackers faced the second-string offense who play-acted like the upcoming opponent's offense. Today it's called seven-on-seven.

Acree stood behind the linebackers and gave hand signals to each position on the dummy offense. Then he signaled the quarterback to start the play, "Down. Set. Hut one!" The offense ran the play Acree had indicated, and the defense reacted full-speed against it. Acree used this to prepare the Tiger defensive interior to stop anticipated offensive plays—e.g., a wing set running back with a pulling guard executing a counter play out of an "I formation." He used it to train the defense against multiple formations, different plays with backfield motions, cross blocking, traps and block-downs from an upcoming opponent.

In skull sessions, Acree diagrammed selected opponent plays, telling us what to watch for and how blocking might occur. To see it for real, he showed us a film clip of the opponent running the play in a previous game. Afterward, we'd go to the practice field and repeatedly defend against it.

I loved to watch Wood and Butler work. Both were quick, aggressive and powerful. Butler was a bit taller and had a rangy build. Before the snap, he'd often get "happy feet," as though he were anticipating where the ball would go. He was already moving mentally when the ball snapped. He was a silent type, and like a killer tiger in a jungle, he wanted to ambush running backs.

When the opportunity presented itself, he tackled ball carriers viciously, often "running through" smaller boys. One moment, a back was upright, running north, and in the next, they were lying on the ground with their head pointed south. Butler pushed off them and jumped up, ready for the next play. The ball carrier might be dazed as though they had run full-speed into an invisible steel pipe hanging over the field. Butler carried his body with a defiant look but played as a team member, ensuring he did his part on every down. Once, he crouched low in his stance and voiced, "I'm tired from lack of sleep." Moments later, the ball snapped; Butler charged at the blocking guard like a bull, exploded into him and butted him back on his rear into the backfield. Players on the drill squad shuddered and hoped Acree would not send them against Butler on the next play.

Acree delighted in coaching Butler. Watching him, a thin smile cracked around the whistle in his mouth as though he were watching a film of himself playing linebacker in Maud. Butler played hard, but his unpredictability made him even more fun to watch. Most of the players were downright scared of him. Acree had worked the hard life of an oil field roughneck, so he identified with Butler's dad who worked in an oil field. Although I spent years playing with Bruce in high school and later in college, I think I barely scratched the surface of what went on inside of him.

Watching Butler was like enjoying a boxing match ringside, but Jim Wood had a very different style and was possibly more effective as a linebacker. Like Butler, he was mostly silent, occasionally barking out one or two-word adjustments to the noseguard or tackle as he read a formation. His position stance looked solid like a tree planted in rock. To read an offensive set, Wood glared into the fullback's eyes or interpreted the look on a quarterback's face. When the ball snapped, a guard would spend himself against Wood like a car crashing into a big oak tree. A center might try to "cut him off," and Wood would simply step over him. An end might try to block down on Jim, but he met a powerful forearm in the process. Wood was quick mentally and physically. "Bruce, it's coming your way."

Wood played low and hard. Reacting to the ball snap, he'd move fast through the gap between the center and the guard, speeding past both and chasing a ball carrier from the backside. Catching him, he looked like a tiger pulling its prey down from behind to complete its kill. I would have never understood the game by just watching the football pass between the ball handlers like a fan. Observing Butler and Wood, whom I admired, made me want to emulate them. Unfortunately, I didn't have the physical talent of either one of them.

Most of the time, I just watched drills. On occasion, if all the juniors had already had a go, Acree would substitute me as a guard. I was little more than a nuisance trying to block either linebacker. If time allowed, he sometimes tried me in place of Wood. The guard blocking me might be Joe Smith, an offensive starter who didn't play defense. He was short but fast, like a running back. When the ball snapped, he was on me like a wasp that I couldn't swat. My forearm sailed above his head. By the time I read the keys, he had tied me up, and a running back blew past like a flying football, untouched.

After a play was over, Joe cracked his characteristic smile as if he had pranked me. It was disheartening, and I was sure he did the same to real opponents in game situations. Later in the Field House, I approached Wood (while he was sitting on the potty); I told him my frustration. He offered instruction, "You have to react, not think."

The formations, keys and play-action were like several footballs flying by my head, and I needed to put my body into motion without having to reason first. As a 15-year-old boy, easily distracted, I lost focus as he spoke. Even the different bathroom habits of the A-team puzzled me.

After I made the A-team, Daddy regularly attended the Dads Club meetings for the film reviews. He'd come home and tell me what Acree said. Having never played football, he sometimes asked me questions about certain plays or the other boys. Acting as if I were an expert, I gave descriptive answers to him while trying to emulate Acree, whom I could hear in my head. "The guard is blocking down on the nose man and the center is pulling to block the linebacker. It's a cross-block." Daddy would nod his head in agreement.

Different boys had different reasons for participating in football as an extracurricular activity. I wanted to become part of the team. Other A-team players like Nicky Sanders and Jerry Sheets enjoyed important roles, knowing Acree valued their consistent presence as experienced substitutes and capable practice foes against the starters. He could count on them as part of the puzzle he was putting together. "Our club is improving—it's got to for the coming game and for what's ahead."

Acree looked down the schedule and knew the team needed players such as Jerry Anderson and Ron Cottar at tackle positions. They were aggressive linemen who wanted in the game. Both aimed to make their mark; most of all, they wanted to hit somebody. Stan Rosen was a substitute center for John Stover. The two were very similar. Perhaps John was slightly more mature as a senior, and that's why Acree had so much confidence in him. Lonnie Elmore was another senior lineman, but it was his first year playing organized football. I saw in his face the same inexperience and lack of confidence I saw in myself. When Acree substituted us to play, the starters had already won the game. It was better if "the play went to the other side." That way, we didn't look so bad on film.

Riding on the A-team bus made me sleepy, so I napped. Pranksters like Joe Smith and Bill Henson decided to initiate me as a new sophomore. Smith put shaving cream on my hand and tickled my nose. I rubbed the shaving cream all over my face, which startled me into consciousness. As I woke, I could see the faces of almost everyone laughing, especially Smith. He was particularly proud of having successfully teased me. As I came to know him, I started to think Smith lived for moments like that. I suppose that's the purpose of initiation, to humble the initiate. I desperately wanted to fit in and be part of the team. No matter what older players said, I believed them.

Bishop Dunne

Few substitutes played in the Jacksonville game since it was close, and the Indians were known for last-minute comebacks. The opposite was true for our next match on October 18, 1963 against Bishop Dunne of Dallas. It was a new team that had no seniors. Coming off an open date, the Tigers were completely healthy—and prepared. We beat the Falcons, 34-0. Our second string, as well as substitutes like me, played much of the game. For me, playing in a game was like going to the state fair and riding the rides. I equated the idea of belonging with the experience of playing. When I played, I could join in with the other boys as we told stories about the game.

"Did you see Hagle's punt? I can't believe it! Sixty-seven yards!"

"See my block on Roman's run back?" "I cut their guy down to the ground!"

"One more block, and Roman would have gone all the way!"

Playing with a little nip in the air at 8 PM made the game more exciting. We scored touchdowns quickly as though we were collecting Halloween candy while Trick-or-Treating. Gary Roman scored early on a 42-yard run, following good "downfield" blocking. Hagle ran across another score in the first quarter. Ricky Libal made the extra points. The second-team quarterback, Rankin Koch, ran in the next score, and Libal's kick was good.

Leading 21-0 at the half, the starters scored quickly at the beginning of the third quarter. The reserves played the remainder of the game. Cody Sherrard and Bill Allison carried the ball for good gains, and Holly Holstein scored the fifth Tiger touchdown. Acree practiced some razzle-dazzle and had Rankin Koch, the holder for Libal, fake an extra point, but Koch's run failed to make it into the end zone. Only the names of offensive players made it into the paper. Dunne scored zero points, but the paper did not print even one defensive player's name. But we all got to play in the game, which meant we grew experience-wise together.

Getting hurt is seldom on a player's mind until an injury occurs. Bill Allison injured his right wrist in the Bishop Dunne game. Acree had it x-rayed at the hospital. Fortunately, he was fine. However, a Falcon center, Mike Young, suffered a broken lower right leg in the first quarter, and an ambulance carried him off to Memorial Hospital. Playing is all fun until someone gets hurt. Injury in football equates to a loss.

Having no injuries, the Tigers were undefeated and untied after five non-district games. Our 5-0 record put us in a select set of unbeaten, untied teams from around the state.

Jovial Dads Club member, Mr. John Nelson, built solid like a propane tank, shoved open the Field House door after the Bishop Dunne game and greeted the players with a giant smile saying, "The best is yet to be in '63!" The players all smiled. I was happy to be on the A-team, but I had yet to contribute anything meaningful. I had helped beat the Duncanville B-team, but how do you become part of a team without some significant individual contribution? I didn't enter an A-team game until the starters had already decided the outcome. The A-team photo published that week in the newspaper excluded me since I joined after the photo was taken. This underscored my sense of estrangement. Having moved up from the B-team, I was a tag-along.

I started to feel cheated out of playing regularly on the B-team, helping to win games with my friends from Collins. I finally understood what Cummings had said about Bob Garlington. But Bob was brave enough to talk to Acree. The last thing I wanted was a confrontation with Acree. Regardless, I had no idea how to talk through my feelings of being peripheral. I would rather quit.

The week of the Bishop Dunne game, the UIL announced a realignment of Corsicana to a AAAA school. Future district opponents would be from larger cities: Waco, Austin, Temple, Killeen, Bryan and Cleburne. The change wouldn't take effect until the following year.

Having a 5-0 non-district record, Acree characterized our upcoming district games as warfare. Each opponent wanted to be the one to "knock off" the Tigers. Up first, the Ennis Lions believed it was their year to settle a score with Acree. Suddenly, 1963 became a do-or-die year if Acree was going to win a AAA State Championship. He would need all the help his blue shirt could deliver.

CHAPTER 7 RIGHT PLACE AND TIME

"They do me wrong who say I come no more
When once I knock and fail to find you in;
For every day I stand outside your door
And bid you wake, and rise to fight and win."
Opportunity by Walter Malone

Rosemary Acree laundered her husband's blue shirt and hung it on a line to dry in the backyard. To Jim Acree, wearing it on game days was magical. The 1963 season started with five wins and no losses.

She went about her business, but so did a neighborhood dog that must have smelled the scent of a primitive challenge that remained in the shirt's threads. The mutt jumped up and tore it off the clothesline. Growling and shaking the shirt in its mouth like vanquished prey, the dog fled the scene, dragging Acree's lucky charm under its paws to who-knows-where.

Acree came home from work, and Rosemary gave him the bad news. "The blue shirt was torn off the clothesline by a dog."

Without hesitating, he demanded, "You go and find that shirt!"

"Shoot the dog if you have to."

A search party scoured the neighborhood for the remains of the charmed shirt. They found it abandoned in a ditch. Rosemary mended the rips and tears with a needle and thread and rewashed it. Stitched here and there, it appeared as though Dr. Frankenstein had used it as a pattern for the flesh of his monster.

Never seen again was the lucky dog. Jim Acree wore his mended blue shirt to the next Tiger game.

Ennis

Corsicana faced Ennis as its first District 8-AAA challenger in 1963. Having a 5-0 non-district record, the press ranked Corsicana #1 and Ennis #2, who had a 4-1 record. The Lions had last defeated the Tigers back in 1957. In 1963, they had an "open" date before the Corsicana game and worked two weeks to prepare for the Tigers. It was their last district shot at Acree who was moving to Class AAAA in 1964.

The Lions' offense featured a powerful single-wing attack, where their big quarterback turned into a blocking guard after he pitched the ball to a running back. Having an extra blocker on the corner created a manpower advantage that would overwhelm our defense. Acree claimed, "Ennis will be a real, real tough opponent."

Friday night, October 25th, 1963, Acree had his Tigers "ready to play." Ennis expected a "fullback attack" from Jim Hagle. Acree knew the Lions would set up defensively to stop Hagle's running, so he and Jerry Moore devised a play that worked as follows: Take end Donnie Denbow and split him out wide on the left side of the offense. On the opposite end, flex out Johnny Nelson to make a slot for a halfback or bring him in tight and put the halfback outside as a wingback. Either way, the offense's right side appears "strong" to the defense. To account for the imbalance, Ennis was coached to "rotate" its secondary into the strong side of the Tiger formation. That left one man to cover Denbow on the "weak" side.

In this situation, Moore taught Roman and Denbow to use a hand signal to call a new play at the line of scrimmage. If the defensive man out wide covering Denbow lined up seven yards or more off the line of scrimmage, Roman pretended to adjust his helmet by moving his facemask up and down. Denbow would spy the signal and change the play. No other offensive player needed to know about the change.

When John Stover hiked the ball, Roman rose and threw it immediately to Denbow. Because he didn't have to wait for the receiver to run a route, Roman tossed a "quick pass" to Denbow. This put the big, fast end away from the main body of players in open space running with the football. Given the room he had to maneuver, many defensive backs could not tackle the swivel-hipped receiver one-on-one. In football terms, Acree created a "mismatch." Corsicana started its scoring when Denbow ran 56 yards for a touchdown after catching a quick pass.

Acree wasn't through surprising Ennis. He called for an onside kick on the ensuing kickoff, which caught the Lions flat-footed. Denbow, in on the kicking team, raced downfield to scoop up the free football and scampered 60 yards untouched for another touchdown.

Big Jimmy Acree from Maud had his way that night. In the second quarter, he set up Ennis again by running Hagle repeatedly into the middle. As usual, he split Denbow out each time. Ennis eventually changed its defensive formation to stop Hagle, leaving a single man wide to cover Denbow. Roman wiggled his face mask and hit Denbow again with a quick pass.

As if Acree had backed up the game film and run a replay, Donnie raced 56-yards again for his third touchdown of the night.

The Lion's single-wing offense was ineffective against the Tiger defense. Acree put in the reserves when the game score reached 35-0. In boxing terms, he had scored a technical knockout, but the referee didn't stop the fight. Ennis scored against the second-string Tigers and followed with an onside kick attempt. Acree inserted Donnie Denbow on the receiving team. The kick dribbled on the ground and Denbow fielded it on the run and returned it for his fourth touchdown of the night.

The Tigers continued to score against the discouraged Lions. The happiest reserve of the night was third-string, senior halfback Mark Dawson. Acree inserted Dawson on a short and goal situation. Mark ran the ball into the end zone, and the Tiger bench erupted joyfully as if he had scored a winning touchdown in a close game. Dawson practically levitated as he sprinted back to the Tiger sideline. He jumped into the arms of his teammates. They hoisted him on their shoulders and paraded as though he'd single-handedly won the game. He bragged afterward, "I hold a record. A halfback that scored every time I carried the football." He only carried it one time that season.

* * *

Another boy's name made it into the newspaper. Ennis attempted a last-minute desperation pass, "which Ronnie Ward intercepted." The ball came right to me. I wrapped my arms around it and trapped it against my body like I was catching a watermelon at Piggly Wiggly. I fell to the ground as time expired.

That night, a well-prepared Tiger team destroyed the Lions on Tiger Field, 56-8. Later, when the team reviewed the game film, Acree complimented Dawson for his score. Regarding my interception, he let the film roll by and said, "Even a blind sow finds an acorn every now and then."

In the flickering light of the projector, I saw the other players and coaches laugh at his remark. Like my initiation on the bus by Joe Smith, I laughed with them. At that point, I had no idea what Acree thought of me, but in my 15-year-old mind, I had made a football play that contributed to a win. Dawson had a record touchdown per carry that night. I established a personal record of a single interception that season.

I had a date after the game and got home too tired to talk. My dad volunteered to take me out for breakfast the following morning.

Early Saturday, over bacon and eggs in the restaurant of the American Club Motel on West Hwy 31, Dad commented, "Acree wants to win a state championship."

I said, "Yes, he mentions the playoffs sometimes when we take a break on one knee during practice."

Sipping his coffee, he congratulated me on the interception.

Grinning, I replied, "Thank you. My competitive nature kicked in when I saw that ball in the air. No way was I going to miss it."

Locking eyes with me, he said, "You were in a position to make a play and you did."

When Acree saw Denbow catching and running that night, he likely thought of his performance in 1946 as he led the Maud Tigers over their District opponent, the Bowlegs Bisons. Big Jim Acree, a star receiver, scored the game-winning touchdown and was a major factor in setting up Maud's other scores with pass catches and long runs. Maud's Tigers won the game, 20-13. Acree was an All-State end in 1946. Donnie Denbow became an All-State end in 1963. Like Acree, he was the right talent at the right time for the Corsicana Tigers. He made a difference when his opportunity came.

* * *

Unlike college coaches who recruit talent from many places, high school coaches work with local boys who volunteer to play. Acree shaped the '63 team into an offensive powerhouse. We outscored non-District opponents 137 to 32. We overwhelmed our first District opponent, Ennis, 56-8.

At the season's midpoint, there were only 46 unbeaten, untied teams in the state, regardless of UIL classification. Ranked number one in Class AAA, the Dumas Demons held back-to-back State Championships and a 16-game winning streak. Fans started to believe that for Corsicana to win a state championship, it would have to go through Dumas.

But first, it had to get by the remaining District 8-AAA opponents, Waxahachie, Cleburne, Athens and Terrell. These teams longed to knock

Corsicana out of the unbeaten ranks. The opposing district coaches gunned for Acree. Not one had defeated him since his arrival in Corsicana.

Coaches use different means to motivate their players. Acree's primary method was to prepare us so thoroughly going into a game that we had the confidence of Muhammad Ali entering a boxing ring. He told the team, "We've got to rise to the occasion."

Football was changing from a game of a hard-charging fullback that made "three yards in a cloud of dust" to including a passing attack with receivers split away from the main formation. In 1960, the Tigers featured W.R. Garlington and Don Fuller primarily running the ball. In 1961, along with Olsen and Hagle's running, Tom Wilson's throwing success to George Boyd led the '61 team to the quarterfinals. However, the Tigers ended the '61 season with the smallest point margin of any other quarterfinalist team. The '62 team was a do-over featuring the running attack of Jim Hagle and Happy Settle occasionally throwing the ball. But in '63, the combination of Donnie Denbow and Gary Roman created a legitimate passing game, and even more so with other experienced receivers, Johnny Nelson, David Robinson, Chick Whistler and Ronnie Rhoads. Coupled with the powerful running attack by Hagle, the Tigers had a scoring machine that delighted fans and filled opponent scouts with dread.

Waxahachie

Coach Jerry Moore and Donnie Denbow's diligence turned the tricky timing quick-pass into something as dependable as a handoff against the second district opponent Waxahachie on November 1, 1963. Moore, a star receiver himself, worked every opportunity after practices and on weekends throwing footballs to Denbow and the other receivers. Denbow caught so many balls in practice that he developed callused fingertips.

A cold front arrived in North Texas with November, and on a clear night, under a full moon, high school girls bundled up in the stands with their big, teased up hair and watched Jim Hagle score a touchdown set-up by a 46-yard catch/run by end Donnie Denbow.

Following that score, Hagle picked off an Indian pass and returned it 49 yards for another touchdown.

Gary Roman scored on the ground in the second quarter after a drive featuring several catches by Denbow.

In the third period, Roman dropped back and launched it deep to Denbow who scored again on a 63-yard pass/run play.

In addition to Ricky Libal's extra-point kicks, sophomore Bill Allison scored twice.

All these names made it into the newspaper. The Tigers scored 40 points to Waxahachie's 7. Another lopsided victory. The Indians didn't score until the fourth quarter against the reserves. They could complete only 6 of 22 pass attempts, while the Tigers made 9 of 14 for 249 yards passing.

Wearing his favorite shirt, Acree smiled on the bus ride back to Corsicana. With a 7-0 record, the Tigers were one of only 33 remaining unbeaten, untied teams across the state. That week, polls ranked Dumas, Graham and Corsicana as the top AAA teams. The thrill of a state championship run was no longer unthinkable. Corsicana's optimistic fans began to ask, "How many miles is it to Dumas?"

Like affluent kids expecting a present at Thanksgiving, Tiger fans in barber chairs, grocery-store checkout lines and the Cotton Mill reasoned that the Tigers had the 8-AAA District in the bag. Their speculation stretched forward to who their bi-district opponent might be. "Palestine?"

Acree refused to participate in general assumptions. Instead, he put his head down and worked us to prepare for Cleburne, the third district opponent that year.

Cleburne

The scouting report from Coaches Slaughter and Matthews on Cleburne said, "The Yellow Jackets are big, fast, hard hitting and tough."

Acree zeroed in on the word "tough." He predicted a difficult game, saying, "We hope to win it with a score of 7-6."

Resorting to his superstitions, "What worked before will work again," Acree practiced the team on Monday, Tuesday and Wednesday in full pads as he had all season. He focused on the running game, full-speed blocking and tackling and ended workouts with lung-busting conditioning drills. The weather was cooler, but we began to wonder what Acree might do if we lost on Friday night. Woe set in when the Corsicana B-team lost on Thursday night to the Cleburne B-team, 7-6.

On November 8th, 1963, anxiety fell on us like the rain falling on Yellow-Jacket stadium in Cleburne. Every player had knots in his belly. It was a muddy game, played with a slick football, which limited passing— so limiting that Roman attempted only three passes that night and did not complete a single one.

Cleburne had scouted Denbow and double-teamed him. That meant one less man inside to try and tackle Jim Hagle and running back Ronnie Rhoads. Two Tiger drives, deep into Cleburne territory, ended in fumbles. "Mistakes," as Acree called them. Carrying a muddy ball was akin to eating fried rice with metal chopsticks.

After a scoreless first quarter, David Robinson bobbled a punt, and a Yellow Jacket recovered it at the Tiger 1-yard line. Our defensive eleven attacked the Yellow Jackets who appeared sluggish as if they were nesting in cold weather. Wood, Butler, Ivie and Cooper forced Cleburne to turn the ball over on downs at the Tiger 3-yard line.

The starting offense seized their moment. They marched 97 yards in a sixteen-play drive to make the score 7-0 at halftime. In the locker room, Acree urged us to keep fighting. Saying, "You know what to do," he reinforced the team's confidence. The linemen said, "Coach, we can block these guys. Let's run it down their throats."

A tense, scoreless third period ensued. The struggle reduced the center of the field to a sloppy pigsty. I watched as the teams pushed each other back and forth like they were playing an odd game of "Tug-of-War." No grass remained in the middle of the field.

Standing on the sideline, wearing a clean uniform, I could hear the cheerleaders, "Push 'em back! Push 'em back! Way back!" Hagle fielded a punt and worked as if he were a charging bull, corralled and looking for a way of escape. He raced toward the middle a few steps, then popped right onto the outside grass near the Tiger sideline. He was running directly at me with muddy Yellow Jackets flying after him. Suddenly, he planted his powerful right leg to cut up the field to seize an opening.

Under the glow of the field lights, I saw his cleated foot act like a shovel working against the turf as it cut underneath, bunching up the grass, exposing a long gash of wet, black soil. Foot planted, Hagle pushed forward through several tacklers, knocking them away as if he were a bulldozer forcing big rocks aside to clear a path ahead.

Watching just yards away, I felt power oozing from his Acree-like frame. He churned up field several yards before succumbing to a gang tackle. Acree was standing immediately to my right. As I turned my head to follow Hagle, my eyes caught Acree focusing on Hagle's running. Unconsciously, Acree stiffened his neck, shoulders and arms and set his legs in a bent-knee stance to brace as though he anticipated contact. Wearing only a blue, short-sleeve shirt, his powerful arm muscles tensed and rippled as he faintly popped an elbow forward to shed a tackler like he was carrying the ball himself. Looking back at the mental image, I can see the champion in Acree mimicking Hagle's every move. It was one All-State player watching another All-State player in action.

Late in the fourth quarter, Hagle punted a whopping 62 yards in the rain. Center John Stover raced down and fell on it at the 1-yard line. This put Cleburne in a deep hole. They had to punt and the exchange left the Tigers in a good field position. After a mistake-less, multi-play, 44-yard march of machine-like execution, Gary Roman scored the second Tiger touchdown. With two minutes left in the game, David Robinson made an interception, redeeming himself. Our offense drove the ball for the final score of the game. Hagle did the honors and it ended 21-0.

The Tigers ground out 302 yards, with Hagle doing the main running. Corsicana dominated the game at the line of scrimmage. Acree played very few substitutes because of the close score. Afterward, he commended the team for its unity and noted the senior leadership. Notably, we proved we could play in the mud if forced to. Fans screamed, "Way to go, Tigers!"

That same Friday night, Graham lost by "one measly point" to Brownwood, 13-14, and dropped in the rankings to number nine. Corsicana moved up to the number two spot behind Dumas in Class AAA. We faced a do-or-die situation against Athens in week nine of the season.

Athens

Athens and Corsicana both had 3-0 District 8-AAA records, and whoever won the game between us would enter the state playoff race. The other teams in the district had already been eliminated. The players focused on the game the way tournament golfers bare down to make a putt that determines the prize winner. The season was on the line.

On November 15, 1963, nearby Lake Navarro Mills flooded with water from the recent damming of Richland Creek. Likewise, Corsicana fans filled Tiger Field in a sellout crowd of about 5,000 to watch the Athens/Corsicana game. Members of the Dads Club formed a welcoming line on the field to greet the Tigers as they eagerly flowed out of the Field House to enter the gridiron. I passed by my dad and he vigorously clapped and grinned wide like I was the only player receiving shoulder slaps and hearing shouts of "Go get 'em, Tigers!"

The press favored Corsicana, 27-20. After a 54-yard drive, Gary Roman initiated the scoring. With the help of a line of blockers, Jim Hagle returned an Athen's punt 80 yards for another touchdown. In addition to the extra points, Ricky Libal booted a field goal. With good downfield blocking, David Robinson finalized the first half with a spectacular 46-yard touchdown run.

In the third period, Roman passed to Nelson for a touchdown. Then, as if Acree were dousing the Hornets with kerosene, he called on Hagle to score again in the fourth period. Libal's missed kick made the score, 37-0. Substitutes like me got into the game at that point, which ended with a Corsicana win, 37-7.

The Tigers were in the playoffs again for the fourth straight year. The win thrilled Acree. Luke Thornton, head coach of the Palestine Wildcats and winners of District 7-AAA, met impromptu with Acree after the Corsicana/Athens game. Thornton and his staff attended and were on hand to scout the Hornets and the Tigers. Acree allowed him to speak to us inside our dressing room at the Field House.

I'm sure the wily Thornton wanted a close-up view of the boys destined to play in two weeks against his Wildcats for the Bi-District Championship. I don't recall anything he said, but Acree didn't allow him to distract us. Immediately, Acree's admonitions turned us toward

Terrell, not Palestine. Acree repeatedly reminded us, "We play one game at a time."

Terrell

The Terrell game was meaningless since Corsicana had already wrapped up the District Championship. Nevertheless, Acree pleaded, "You just don't understand how badly Terrell wants to beat us."

To put a loss on the Corsicana record would make their season, one that "Terrell would never forget."

Their season became unforgettable for different reasons, but as a reward for the win over Athens, Acree replaced the scheduled full-pad workout on Monday with a meeting to review the game film of Terrell's surprising victory over a tough Cleburne team, 21-20.

He gave an ominous description of Terrell's Wing-T power running game which they also used to beat Waxahachie, 35-0. He mentioned that Corsicana last had an unbeaten season in 1949. Regarding the depth of Terrell's desire to upset us, Acree employed the exact words he learned from Bud Wilkinson, "Our opponent is working 'till after dark!'"

Success can bring overconfidence, and with an unbeaten, untied record, opportunities for distraction were abundant. For example, in recognition of the team's achievement, Corsicana Mayor Herbert Johnson proclaimed Friday, November 22, 1963, as "Tiger Day." His declaration acknowledged the "fame brought to the City." Fan enthusiasm was so high that even players' mothers attended Acree's briefing at the Dads Club. He pointed out our problems in the Athens film and explained, "A good team doesn't make mistakes." From his Oklahoma experience, he added, "Mistakes will haunt you."

On Tuesday and Wednesday, Acree worked us in full pads. The weatherman forecasted a wet night in Terrell. He expected a low-scoring match. The press picked Corsicana to win, 21-6.

Unexpectedly, Terrell canceled the B-team game arranged for Thursday, claiming a scheduling issue. We speculated they wanted to combine the B-team players with their A-team and "platoon" against us, wear us down, and overcome us with persistent pressure from rested replacements.

In a light workout on Thursday, the players told stories about "crazy people" living in Terrell. As a stress buster, the idea of kidding each other about an opponent took hold.

Tragic events on Friday cemented memories of what happened on November 22. Most everyone remembers where they were when Lee Harvey Oswald shot President John F. Kennedy while riding in an open limousine on the streets of Dallas. I was in Miss Helen Bonner's history class when she informed her students. Administrators and teachers scrambled to make new plans. Some people stayed glued to their TVs, watching news coverage of the tragedy.

Top of mind for Acree was fear that Terrell would cancel our game. Tiger B-team star, Steve Winn, recounted the story of hurriedly driving Acree out to pick up the team bus. He said, "Acree rushed to gather the Tigers onto the bus and start the drive to Terrell, believing officials wouldn't cancel the game if they were on their way."

Riding up to Terrell, Acree stood on the bus, faced us, and held onto a silver pole for balance. As if he had a personal relationship with the President, he said, "President Kennedy would have wanted us to play this game." Knowing Acree, I think he wanted to get us to Terrell and force them to play or forfeit rather than reschedule the game.

Friday night was dark, cold and windy. The bands didn't play in honor of the dead President. Runs by Rhoads set up Jim Hagle's first score on Corsicana's first possession. Pass catches and runs by Chick Whistler set up Hagle's second touchdown on Corsicana's second possession.

Rankin Koch's interception and runback put the Tigers in scoring position on our third possession. Gary Roman threw a bullet against the wind to Johnny Nelson who scampered into the end zone. On the Tiger's fourth possession, Roman, Hagle, Rhoads, Robinson and Chick Whistler all gained rushing yardage in a drive that ended with Whistler scoring his first touchdown of the year. Despite the mood in the stadium, we teased him for "Picking a fine night to show off."

On our fifth possession, passes by Roman to Denbow and Nelson, and runs by Hagle and Whistler put the ball in scoring position. Roman carried it over the line. Ricky Libal succeeded in four of his five extra-point kicks. At halftime, the Tigers led, 34-0.

In the second half, Ronnie Rhoads scored. Sophomore reserves Bill Allison and Ben Smith scored. Our ability to score on every possession demoralized Terrell, but they put together two scoring drives against our second-stringers with two extra points on each one. Corsicana mauled Terrell, 53-16.

We hurried off the field and into the dressing room to cheer when the game ended. Even though my name wouldn't be in the newspaper, my uniform was dirty. I thought of it as a badge of honor.

That week, the newspaper ran a photo of Acree, Moore and Anderson in the dressing room at Terrell. Standing in front of a blackboard with "53-16" written in large numerals, all three were smiling. The caption read, "Victory Grins."

On Friday, I felt overlooked again when local businesses ran a full-page ad in the paper congratulating the team on a District Championship and a 10-0 record. An individual picture of each team member wearing a white shirt and tie was included. Because of lopsided victories, I was getting in some playing time, but the ad omitted a picture of me. I didn't say anything to Acree. I didn't say anything to anyone.

Bi-District Game: Palestine

Palestine won District 7-AAA, and the Tigers would face them in a bi-district playoff game on Friday, November 29, 1963. By convention, the game would be played in Palestine since they came to Corsicana for our second season game. The Tigers had won that match, 27-7.

The B-team season ended, and Acree worked with Matthews and Slaughter to identify fourteen boys to designate as a "suicide squad." They were asked to learn Palestine's offense and run it against the A-team defense. Acree quickly assessed Palestine's main threat, quarterback Bill Bradley. He asked Coach Matthews to quarterback the suicide squad. Matthews dressed out in full pads that week and was surprisingly good. He pranced around the practice field like an actor playing a part, and we called him "Hud," after the Paul Newman movie of the same name. He was primarily a basketball coach but devoted himself to football that fall.

Matthews was sleek and fast and could throw the football. His antics enlivened our workouts and helped lift the spirits of suicide squad members. He motivated them to do their best against the A-team. When asked about the effectiveness of the squad's efforts against the A-team, my friend Lynn Odom said, "They generally kill us."

Coach Matthews was everything but humble. Despite hearing his voice, "Go easy on me!" I wasn't alone in wanting a shot at him when he ran a play. Even Butler chimed in, "If he comes my way, Acree's going to need to call an ambulance."

As named in the paper, the suicide squad consisted of ends—Pat Ellington, Lynn Odom, Travis Hair; tackles—Phil Pillans, Larry McLaurin and Nicky Georges; guards—Jimmy Pillans and Henry Henkel; centers—Don Robertson and John Hogan; tailbacks—Steve Winn and Wayne Thedford; fullbacks—Brad Haynie and Jimmy Prater; and wingback—Gary Schutte.

Acree's idea was to embody the Palestine players, formations and plays so that the A-team could work physically against what they saw on film and visualized in skull sessions. The main impetus, however, was to stop Bradley. Acree's trick helped the defense focus on stopping the Wildcat's primary weapon.

With good plans for offense and defense, Acree concentrated on preparing us for special team plays, kickoffs, punt returns, fake field goals, goal-line offense and extra-point tries.

November 29 was a cold night, and like the other players on the sideline, I had a Tiger-blue cape wrapped around my shoulders to keep warm. Acree wore the same short-sleeve blue shirt, tie and dark brown pants with no coat.

We stood on the sideline and watched Jim Hagle take the opening kickoff back for an 80-yard touchdown. We jumped and hollered, and in the excitement, all our capes fell to the ground. Every one of us wanted in the game. After a sustained drive Corsicana scored again in the first quarter. At the half, the score was 14-0.

In the third quarter, Bill Bradley intercepted a pass by Roman and returned it for a touchdown. It was the type of mistake that Acree warned us about. In the fourth quarter, Roman made up for his boo-boo by scoring a touchdown himself. Bradley countered with a touchdown pass to David Dickey, their All-State fullback.

The score was 21-14 when Acree called my name to go into the game. I threw off my cape and eagerly stood beside him, waiting for orders on what to do. The urge that spurred him to send me in must have passed. I never entered the game.

Very few subs played that night. A demonstration of leadership occurred when the senior boys took over after the last Palestine score. The Tiger offense "controlled the ball" by marching, soldier-like, from our 25-yard line down to the Wildcat 11-yard line. Acree called multiple running plays—left, right and up-the-middle before the game clock finally expired. The final score was 21-14.

Quarterfinals: McKinney

We earned a playoff spot in the quarterfinals just as the Tigers two years earlier did. Surely, Acree thought back to 1961 and the heartbreaking loss to Gainesville. What would he do differently this time? We woke on Saturday morning to read that we'd be facing the McKinney Lions.

Contingents from Corsicana and McKinney met to negotiate a neutral site for the game. Acree led the Tiger delegation, and they settled on a Saturday game in Dallas at Forrester Field. The stadium could accommodate the large crowd expected.

Acree exchanged game films, giving McKinney our Ennis and Cleburne games. I don't know why he picked those two films, but he had a reason. Ennis was a blowout game for us, and McKinney would see mostly substitutes like me playing. This conveyed as little information about our starters as possible. Cleburne was a mud game where our passing was unused. This film would tend to hide the arm of Gary Roman and the route running of Donnie Denbow and Johnny Nelson.

Acree pored over the McKinney film, strategizing with the other coaches on how to stop their offense. He was still scratching his head at gametime.

Since it was a Saturday game, Acree could have released us to spend Friday night at home in our own beds. Instead, he wanted us to stay together as a team, perhaps as he had experienced in college at OU.

Before the quarterfinal's game with Gainesville in 1961, Acree took the Tigers to a hotel in Dallas. The Tigers had lost then, so in '63, he decided on a more rugged plan. He had us spend the night in the Field House. We slept on mats scattered around on the cold concrete floor in its various rooms.

Somehow, I ended up in the "weight room" on a mat next to Donnie Denbow. When the lights went out, a few of us continued our banter, and Denbow quickly shut it down. Poking me on the arm, he sounded, "Shhhh!"

During the night, a scorpion crawled on my forehead and woke me. Not knowing what it was, I sleepily brushed it off with my hand, but it stung me. I sat up yelling and slapping at it, trying to kill it. Denbow's reaction was altogether different. As if it were no big deal, he said, "Lay down and go back to sleep."

Preparing us, Acree said that the McKinney Lions had a methodical ground attack. Proving it after the opening kickoff, they marched into the wind on a twenty-one-play drive to score first.

Our offense couldn't get rolling against their tough defensive, so Hagle punted. Their offense continued to mix up plays that stumped our defense. They marched again into our end of the field, but Bruce Butler came to the rescue. He snagged an interception, and the momentum change sparked our team.

Roman faked to Hagle off tackle and kept it around the left end to score. Libal's kick tied the game, 7-7. On the next series, Sam Cooper tackled a Lion runner in the backfield, and the wind carried the sound of the hit. "Whack!"

McKinney lined up to punt, and their center snapped the ball over the punter's head. Acree scrambled into action to tell Roman what plays to call. Our offense took over on the Lions' 6-yard line, and Hagle scored in two tries. Libal's kick was good, making it 14-7.

McKinney started another drive into the wind, but Sam Cooper smothered a Lion ball carrier behind the line again and the half ended. No further scoring happened in the game. Both teams had drives that sputtered. Rankin Koch ended one Lion drive at the Tiger 1-yard line with an excellent tackle. Hagle ended another McKinney drive with an interception. Sam Cooper came through more than once. He stopped another McKinney drive and recovered his second fumble.

McKinney was a case study of how mistakes can cause an excellent team to lose. Two interceptions, two lost fumbles and a snap over the punter's head cost them the game.

As a coach, Acree constantly reminded us to play sharp and avoid mistakes. "A blocked kick can kill us."

Looking at the film, McKinney almost blocked a punt by Hagle. Had they been successful, the game could have had a different outcome.

We had a quarterfinals victory and advanced to the semifinal game against Graham who had beat Dumas 13-0 that day. The question, "How far was it to Dumas?" was no longer relevant. Corsicana fans attended Acree's post-game film review in record numbers and asked questions about Graham's football team for the first time.

After the win over McKinney, a full-page ad appeared in the Corsicana Daily Sun congratulating the team. Along with the other players, it included a bust photo of me wearing a white shirt and tie. Mother saved a copy of the paper. She kept articles about all the games that year. Our winning affected even her. She wore a large "streamer" pinned to her dress and came to the games with Daddy.

After the McKinney game, I saw a change come over Acree. He knew we were not ready to play against McKinney. Even I was tired after the game and didn't even play. When I got home after the bus trip back from Dallas, my dad wanted to talk, but I said, "I had a bad night's sleep on a concrete floor. I'm going to bed."

Acree didn't want to disappoint the town by making a mistake that would get us beat. For example, inserting an inexperienced player like me into a game could be fatal. I might miss a block or a tackle that a tired, experienced player would make. From that point forward, Acree relied only on players with the most game experience, regardless of their classification. I didn't play another down the rest of the season.

As disappointing as it was, the narrow margins in our playoff games justified his cautiousness. But I wasn't just along for the ride; I wanted to play. I accepted Acree's decision without saying anything, even to my dad. Unlike Moore's earlier decision not to consider me as a receiver, I felt prepared to play as a linebacker. I had practiced like every other boy, made every meeting and put on my uniform, but I didn't play. I wasn't the only boy who didn't play. Acree didn't explain to us his reasoning. He left us to work through our disappointment on our own.

I retreated the next week into my junior high hobby of reading science fiction novels, where laser guns drilled holes in aliens; only in my case, I imagined the enemies were unknown players on the other team. My superhero of choice became Green Lantern, and I wished for a power ring to help me get into a game.

Semifinal Game: Graham

The semifinal game with Graham was on Saturday, December 14, 1963, in Arlington's Memorial Stadium. Whether from conservatism or common sense to get out of the rain, Acree had us practice on Tuesday inside the gym. We wore helmets, shoulder pads, shorts and tennis shoes. We hit each other, but there were no knockdowns to the hardwood floor.

The gym workout prepared us mentally—who and what, when and where for specific game situations. I sensed Acree wanted us outside where we could hit each other as hard as possible. He said, "West Texas teams downplay Central Texas football as weak. Graham thinks we play two-handed touch football."

On Wednesday, we did practice outside in bitterly cold weather. To stay warm, we wore gray sweat suits underneath our pads. In my mind's eye, I can still see the sweat-top hoods flapping behind teammates' helmets as we worked on plays Acree designed to use against Graham. The suicide squad enacted their offense. On one series, Acree inserted me as a fullback in his seven-on-seven drill. I got a taste of why he needed "fresh meat."

We were supposedly working at half speed. I took the hand-off and moved through the line toward Jim Wood. I was just about to make a move and go around him when his forearm sent shudders through my body. My legs buckled, and I ended up on my knees, dropping to the ground in front of him. It looked as though I had assumed a praying position. A few boys laughed, saying, "Let's send these Graham boys to the prayer altar."

The Graham team featured P.D. ("Pay Dirt") Shabay as quarterback and E.A. ("Elite Athlete") Gresham as the center. Both were All-State players. They were childhood friends and decided it would be cool to use initials instead of their names at a young age. I've written a detailed description of the Graham game as an Appendix, so I'll only summarize it here.

Before writing, I called P.D. Shabay to discuss the game and our coaches. Much like I think of Jim Acree, he described how Roy Curry, his coach, silently lives in his head. "I'm still doing what Curry wanted me to do."

About two-a-days, he said, "Curry held the water hose while each of us took a drink. He looked for boys who wouldn't quit."

In talking about the game between us, I thought of Acree's "good team" definition when Shabay reflected, "The Steers were a good team, but Corsicana got the break it needed to win."

He took no blame for a key penalty; instead, "Corsicana got the break it needed." During film reviews, Acree had preached to us, "Good teams don't make mistakes that get them beat." P.D. was the cornerback who got the pass-interference call as he tackled Donnie Denbow running a pass route while the ball was in the air.

From Graham's perspective, the "controversial call" allowed the Corsicana drive to continue, and we won the game in the last minute. Shabay said some of the Graham players still haven't gotten over the loss, especially middle linebacker Boomer Davis, who was ejected after throwing a punch at John Stover covering a punt.

P.D. lamented their loss, saying, "We were not over confident, but we were disappointed to lose the game. It's part of life."

Even though Donnie Denbow outplayed him one-on-one several times, he complimented only Jim Hagle, saying, "He was the best player we ever faced."

He thought Corsicana was a good opponent—"a challenge." "We would have to play our best to beat Corsicana."

He recounted his hip pointer injury during the Dumas game and how the T.C.U. trainer, Elmer Brown, "got him ready to play" against the Tigers.

On game day, Acree wasn't sidetracked by the pregame rumors of injured Graham players that might not see action against the Tigers. All of the Steers showed up to play in Arlington's Memorial Stadium. So did our seniors. Jim Hagle made numerous critical runs for first downs. End Donnie Denbow proved he was an All-State player with several amazing catch/run combinations. He made them against Shabay, another All-State player.

Acree's worst nightmare came true in the third quarter, with the game tied at 6-6. Roman threw an interception. Shabay tipped the ball into the hands of another Steer who returned it 68 yards up the sideline for a touchdown. Graham led over the Tigers, 6-13.

Early in the fourth quarter, the Tiger offense was rolling, but Acree needed to rest Hagle and Roman. He inserted sophomore Bill Allison in as fullback and junior Rankin Koch as the quarterback. Bill never controlled a pitch from Rankin and fumbled. Graham recovered it at their 29-yard line. Midway through that last quarter, another Tiger drive ended when Roman again threw an interception. At one point, Acree helped Hagle limp off the field with an ailing knee. Thinking the game was lost, some Corsicana fans began to leave the stadium.

Graham started a new drive with a great field position on the 50-yard line. Our defense stopped the Steers after three downs, but on their punt attempt, Cody Sherrard jumped into action before the ball was snapped and drew an offside penalty. They got the ball back with a first down at the Tiger 39-yard line. They ripped off another first down at the Tiger's 25-yard line in two plays. Mistakes disheartened our bench, but not Acree. Gathering the defense, he said, "Men, if you'll dig down deep, you can win this game."

What happened next was nothing short of a state champion effort. Wood was playing despite an ankle injury. Their fullback powered into the middle. Butler and Wood stopped him for no gain. Twice more, Steers ran into the teeth of the Tiger middle and had only 5 yards to show for it. With the clock at 3 minutes and change, on fourth down, needing five, they tried to sweep right, but "limping" Jim Wood pursued down the line and tackled the ball carrier from behind for a loss.

When Acree reviewed Wood's play at linebacker, it must have been like watching a film of himself linebacking in Maud. "The Oak" Jim Wood made timely tackles that stopped Graham when the game was on the line.

The Tigers took over on our own 23 with 3:03 on the clock. Gary Roman threw unbelievably accurate passes to Denbow when it counted. And Hagle powered through the Graham defense to make critical first downs and then score. Roman made a final two-point run that sealed the win at 14-13. Every senior that played made outstanding contributions, including Johnny Nelson, Sam Cooper, Robert Graham, Marc Maxwell and Joe Smith.

Corsicana's mayor designated the following week as "Champion Week." Corsicana was the only undefeated/untied team in the state (in any classification).

State Championship Game: Pharr-San Juan-Alamo

After some jousting between the coaches, the AAA title match was set to take place on Saturday, December 21, 1963, between the Tigers and Pharr-San Juan-Alamo Bears (PSJA) in Victoria, Texas, at Patti Welder Stadium. The PSJA Bears were preseason favorites to repeat as finalists because they had been finalists the prior year against the Dumas Demons in Ft. Worth's Amon Carter Stadium. Feeling tricked by Dumas into playing up in West Texas, the Bears preferred a smaller venue, south, closer to their fan base.

In the meeting, Acree became upset at the condescending attitude of the PSJA representatives. There was no customary exchange of previous game films between the coaches. Knowing Acree wanted their film, a PSJA representative invited him to Pharr to review their game against La Marque. Given an eight-hour drive between the two competitors, the invitation was insincere and taunting.

After losing the semifinal game to PSJA, La Marque filed a complaint with the University Interscholastic League (UIL) that Pharr had a nearby Port Arthur coach scout the La Marque workouts before their semifinal contest. Although the UIL dismissed the complaint, Acree saw an opportunity for a deal and sent a private plane and pilot to La Marque to negotiate to obtain the La Marque film of their game with PSJA.

Acree had the team engaged in a light workout Monday in sweat suits as a small, single-engine plane buzzed over the practice field. The wing of the plane waved a signal from the pilot that he had the film. Despite the engine noise, I'm sure the pilot could hear our loud cheer from the ground.

As was customary, the Dads Club viewed the film of the Graham game on Monday night. The screening was notable because Halsey Settle had shot the game in color—a first. It was also noteworthy that Coach Moore did the briefing, not Acree.

Acree holed up in his office and studied the La Marque/PSJA film. He looked for a way to surprise the Bears. He resented their treatment of him as an inexperienced newbie when they decided on a game location. Unaware of their blunder, Pharr had awakened in Acree the fight of a state champion. He worked long into the night, thinking of how he might deliver the football equivalent of a surprise left hook to the Pharr coach.

The two teams had no common opponents, and although we were from the same state, we knew little to nothing about each other. Rumors abounded all week. The La Marque coach called the Bears "Scrappers." They heard Corsicana was known as "Oil City," so Acree said, "They want to beat the tar out of us!"

In our boyish way, knowing they lived in far South Texas, we lined up across from the suicide squad and laughingly yelled, "I'm going to knock you into a taco barrel!"

The suicide squad that week worked to mimic the Bear defense. Playing an aggressive, pursuing gang-tackling style, they were challenging to score against. Corsicana had a high-scoring offense, so Acree, the game strategist, looked for a weakness to exploit.

Having lost the title match the previous year, Pharr wanted to win badly. Acree figured that an aggressive, attacking defense could be fooled by a play that starts as something it's not.

Back in game five, against Bishop Dunne of Dallas, Acree tried a fake field goal, but it failed. For the PSJA game, he drilled the field goal team, especially Rankin Koch, the holder and second-string quarterback, on how to take a snap, and instead of setting the ball up for a kick, rise and move left, outside to throw the ball to Jim Hagle who lined up as a blocking back on the left edge. Ricky Libal, the kicker, would block the defender coming in from Hagle's position.

Knowing the Tiger offense would have a tough time moving the ball, Acree also had Hagle practice punting the ball. He practiced kicking so many times that his foot went numb.

"Dragging Beaton" took on a new meaning to high school kids when the entire town lined Beaton Street in Corsicana early Friday as the Tiger "Blue Goose" bus rolled slowly through town to start its journey south to Victoria, Texas. It made it one hour to Bremond, Texas, before breaking down, which infuriated Acree. Corsicana sent a yellow school bus to take the Tigers the remaining distance to Victoria. We checked into the Continental Inn and Restaurant and had a light workout, supper and a skull session before going to bed.

Victoria's weather was cloudy, cold and wet at game time. The match turned into a defensive contest played on a muddy field. Six Pharr game possessions ended by punts, two by interceptions, two by fumbles, two by turnovers on downs and one when the clock ran out at the half.

One Corsicana possession ended by scoring on a great trick play, another when a field-goal kick failed, seven by Hagle punts, none by interceptions, one on a fumble, two ended by turnovers on downs and the last one when the clock ran out. The seven Hagle punts averaged 41 yards to Pharr's 25 yards. With his punting, Jim Hagle kept the Bears in a hole the entire game.

The Bears' offense never crossed the Tiger 20-yard line, nor were they ever close enough to attempt a field-goal kick. We won the game, 7-0.

Our only score came in the second period, when Sam Cooper tackled a Bear runner, causing him to fumble. Sam recovered it to give the Tigers great field position. However, the Pharr defense stopped Corsicana at the 17-yard line. Acree had the Tigers set up for a field goal but called a fake kick. After a perfect snap by Stover, Rankin Koch stood up, took a couple of steps to his left and lobbed the ball to Jim Hagle who was wide open in the flat. Eleven Bear jock straps fell to the ground as Hagle jogged across the goal line untouched.

Corsicana had two other scoring opportunities. In the middle of the fourth quarter, Bruce Butler recovered a fumble at the Bear 29, but the offense could not advance the ball. Another long field-goal try by Libal on third down was short. On the next PSJA drive, Hagle intercepted a pass and returned it to their 1-yard line. I cheered the loudest on the sideline, hoping the offense would score. Acree might let me play if they did. However, we could not put the ball into the end zone.

When the title game ended, Corsicana fans rushed onto the field. Back in the crowded dressing room, out of the cold, we celebrated becoming state champions. There was not a sad face in the bunch.

* * *

The journey to becoming a state champion was a once-in-a-lifetime experience for the team. Coach Acree was back on familiar turf, smiling big for the camera like he was glad to be home after a long journey.

What happened that season became a part of every team member. It changed who I was, maybe even how I appeared. In high school that spring, I carried myself more confidently, knowing that somehow, if I worked hard, I could eventually do whatever I set as a goal.

It's sobering to realize that a single man, like Acree, could have such a profound impact on all our lives. He purposed to make us state champions in football because coaching boys to be their best was his calling. Had he been a physicist, a doctor or an engineer, he would have somehow gathered boys around him and turned them into the best any of those disciplines had to offer. He would have transformed their lives to become like him, a champion.

As I look at the dressing room pictures taken by O.E. Scarborough, I see boys, coaches, parents and fans celebrating. Without their helmets and pads, the players look like boys, not the men they were on the field. Nevertheless, they were men in the mind of Jim Acree. It's fitting that I

Bottom: Robert Graham, Jim Wood, John Stover, Joe Smith, Sam Cooper
Top: Donnie Denbow, Gary Roman, Cody Sherrard, Jim Hagle, Ronnie
Rhoads, Johnny Nelson, Chick Whistler

don't appear in a single photograph. I was grafted onto the A-team after it was already established. I might doubt that I was on the team if I didn't have a letter jacket and a few other items as proof. No one has ever questioned it, but I look at my trinkets and remind myself that I was part of a magical season.

For all his hardness, I realized that Acree cared for me even though I was inconsequential. He must have sensed my disappointment. He came over to my locker as I changed clothes. He shook my hand, smiled and apologized for not playing me. He declared his intentions, "If we could have only scored when we were down on the 1-yard line, I would have put you in the game."

A football field is a "gridiron" where boys line up next to one another, and coaches like Acree, Moore, Anderson, Slaughter and Matthews transform them into a team, and in our case, not just another team, but a team of state champions. We could climb no higher rung.

Bill Henson yelled, "Let's sing!"

Acree led in belting out, "When the Roll is Called up Yonder, When the Roll is Called up Yonder, When the Roll is Called up Yonder, I'll be there."

Although my voice didn't matter much, I sang just as loud as the other boys.

Back as a state champion, Acree was home, and like him, I was "just tickled to be part of it."

After high school, Hagle, Denbow, Wood and Cooper attended SMU on a football scholarship. Roman played his college football at Texas Tech. Robert Graham played briefly at Navarro Jr. College in Corsicana. The football careers of the other seniors on the '63 team ended appropriately in a town named Victoria.

Acree after the win over PSJA

Despite everything I know about Acree, I realize that he will always remain a mystery in many ways. He moved through our lives with the force of a hurricane that brought discipline instead of chaos, growth not destruction and achievement rather than ruin. Only a state champion could orchestrate all the machinery required for the Tigers to win that year.

As of this writing, Corsicana has never won another football state championship.

CHAPTER 8 BOXING DREAD

"Maco Stewart asked me privately to influence Acree to stop making the players box. Nothing was wrong with it, but it appeared barbaric to outsiders." Assistant Coach Jerry Moore

In 1954 my father, Buddy Ward, moved our family to a house on the corner of 12th Ave and South 31st Street in Corsicana. Located at the edge of town on the south side of the east-west railroad tracks, it was in a scrappy, tough-guy neighborhood or at least that is how I saw it.

Buddy was smart, musically talented, funny and loving. But he had a quick temper and didn't tolerate stupidity. He was not quite 6' in height with a slender build, and he wouldn't take "lip" from anyone. Raised on the south side of 7th Ave, he came from a broken home of four boys and, like his own father, made a living as an iron worker at Oil City Iron Works.

Having served as a WWII combat rifleman, Buddy was familiar with violence. He fought in France, Belgium and the Rhineland but seldom talked about the horrors he saw in the Army. The aftermath of a battle was too revolting to consciously consider.

Once, however, he described the terror of the enemy shelling his company while they were in foxholes located in a forest; he told about the whistle that incoming shells made as they split trees and exploded upon hitting the ground. He said he'd heard men scream and cry, praying for the bombing to stop. And then silence came.

A period of waiting followed the shelling. Apprehension spiked at the sound of the clackity-clank advance of German tanks moving through the forest. Fear increased when small arms fire signaled German soldiers accompanying the tanks. Dread surrounded him. Hand-to-hand combat was a possibility.

Dickey, his firstborn son, was about to turn nine years old. He was taller than most boys his age. Like our mother, he was a gentle person and shied away from conflict. I was his seven-year-old little brother. I didn't have the muscle for battle either. Besides, I had Dickey to look after me.

Eating supper one night, Buddy saw markings of rough treatment on Dickey's face and found through conversation that a neighborhood boy was bullying him. Buddy said to Dickey, "Next time he bothers you, I'll give you a quarter to whip his ass." And then he added, "But if you don't fight back after he beats you up, I'm going to whip you with my belt!"

We dreaded the thought of a belt-whipping from Buddy. Each lick had the sting of a scorpion. Over the next few days, we were careful to watch out for our tormentor. We hid when we saw him. Soon, however, our watchfulness waned.

One day, we played on the swing set in the backyard. Dickey stood beside the seesaw, watching me attempt a daredevil feat. We didn't see the bully as he snuck up behind Dickey. I reached a thrilling height and bailed out of the swing. I landed on my feet and turned around to get Dickey's approval. Instead, terror filled my eyes. It was too late to yell.

The bully clenched his right fist and threw a looping punch, striking Dickey on the back of the head. I froze as I watched my brother lurch forward, stumble and land face down on the black dirt surrounding the swing set. Before I could move, the bully was on top of Dickey with his knees straddling Dickey's back. He delivered blows to Dickey's head and the side of his face.

I burst out crying and heard the screen door slap against the house behind me. I turned to see Buddy yanking his leather belt from his trousers while bounding off the wooden porch to run toward Dickey and the bully.

The two fighters struggled against each other on the ground. I saw mother enter the doorway and unthinkingly extend her arm to catch the screen door as its long spring pulled it back toward the opening. She clenched her teeth and shook her head, as if she were biting into a piece of tough jerky.

Buddy stood over the two boys, yelling, "Dickey, I'll give you a quarter to whip him!"

The two boys managed to rise to their feet. Still pushing and shoving, Dickey backed away toward the porch as the bully hurled insults.

Dickey turned to run, and the bully ran after him, hitting and slapping him from behind. Buddy yelled louder, "Dickey, I'll whip you with this belt if you don't fight back!"

Mother held the door open for Dickey, but the bully jumped on his back just as he entered the house. The two wrestled to the floor in our tiny kitchen. Dickey rolled over and used his long legs to kick at the bully and push him away. Trying to escape, Dickey scrambled on all fours through a doorway into the adjoining dining room.

The bully followed and wrestled him down onto the wood floor and sat on top of him, whaling away with his fists.

Trying to escape, Dickey arched up and pushed the bully off the top of him and then rolled over to sit on the bully. Dickey's knees straddled his foe, and he used his weight to pin him to the floor. Mother would have ended the fight there, but Buddy yelled, "Hit him. Hit him. Hit him!"

Dickey started to punch the bully, landing one blow after another on his face. Blood gushed from the bully's nose, and his cheeks and forehead turned red like a bad sunburn. Mother cried out, "That's enough!"

I bawled and rubbed my eyes. Buddy started putting his belt back through his pant loops. Mother pulled Dickey off the bully, and the two boys stood up. The bully turned and ran through the kitchen and out the back door. The screen door slapped against the house.

Dickey was sobbing and shaking. His face was scratched and bleeding. His shirt collar was turned up on one side, and his shirt tail flapped outside his jeans. Buddy took a quarter out of his pocket and shoved it into Dickey's hand. The bully never bothered Dickey again.

The episode was unforgettable, and I hated the thought of ever forcibly having to fight another boy.

* * *

On the other hand, Jim Acree embraced fighting while still in high school. Stepping into a boxing ring excited every limb in his stout, muscled body. To him, boxing reduced human competition to an enjoyable one-on-one struggle. Undaunted, he relished the opportunity to test his cunning and skill against another boy, presumably equally motivated.

Boxing was popular in Oklahoma, where Golden Gloves started in 1936. Indians in Oklahoma excelled in the sport, and Acree's Coach George Tallchief in Maud, Oklahoma encouraged him to fight. Just as Acree began lacing his mitts up for the first time, an estimated 20,000 people attended the Golden Gloves tournament in Oklahoma City in 1946.

Acree seized the opportunity to shine as a fighter when boxing's popularity swept the state. In 1949, boxers from 49 Oklahoma communities participated in the Golden Gloves tournament. That year, Chicago hosted the national tournament and the Oklahoma squad won the Golden Gloves team title. Acree stood out in team sports. As a boxer, he excelled as an individual.

Coming off an AAU heavyweight championship in 1953, Acree fought his way to the Oklahoma Golden Gloves title fight again in 1954 but lost. In the spring of that year, graduation from Oklahoma University ended his boxing career. But not his love of boxing.

ONE of the football players who dot this year's Golden Gloves lineup is Jim Acree, Maud, a freshman end at the University of Oklahoma who'll box for the Oklahoma City district novice team in the state tournament here next week. Acree is a light-heavyweight.

Sports

THE DAILY OKLAHOMAN

Acree's genetics and early life experiences turned him into a superior fighter. His large, tall frame with long arms and big hands allowed him to battle the greatest of ring adversaries—heavyweights. His competitive nature welcomed the sight of a cheering, ringside crowd as he confidently focused on the challenge of defeating another boy in front of him. He gave thought to each foe and considered what strategy would work best to his advantage.

Acree was a quick, crafty and determined fighter. As a strategy mastermind, he danced his feet, moved in and out and jabbed at an opponent while looking for an opening to land a roundhouse punch or an unexpected left hook.

Rather than back away, Acree fearlessly advanced closer to an opponent's body despite skin-splitting jabs to the face or numbing blows to his arms. As defensive weapons protecting his body, his hairy forearms acted like tough shields covered in hide, not skin.

His conditioning was such that in a few seconds, he could rapidly punch an opponent's gut and render him breathless, no longer able to fight. His left hook was a surprise if he fooled a foe into thinking he was right-handed. When his hook landed, it had the force of a head butt from a charging bull. Acree grinned when the referee raised his outstretched arm in a show of victory. He relished being a boxing champion.

As a football linebacker, Acree had a reputation for hard hitting. Likewise, as a boxer, he delivered a powerful blow that might knock an opponent out cold. Once, an Oklahoma coaching assistant jumped in to stop a fight between Acree and another player. An Acree punch landed on the coach's jaw just as he stepped between the fighters. The punch coldcocked the coach.

Another time, Acree applied his boxing skills outside the ring to knock a man off his feet. While at Bonham, he refereed basketball games to make extra money. A fan approached him from behind and called him an SOB after a close game. The fan made the mistake of grabbing Acree's shoulder from behind. In one motion, Acree turned and delivered a left hook that knocked the fan out cold. Later, the fan apologized to Acree for his part in causing the fight.

* * *

Acree went on to excel in coaching football players, but just as he mixed football and boxing in college, he did so in Corsicana. However, times changed in the 60s, and he had little luck in turning the hearts of boys to love boxing as much as he did. Packed full of determination, that didn't keep Acree from trying.

When Acree forced two boys to square off, the nature of the fighters determined the scrappiness of the bout. No boy wanted to look weak in front of his peers, and having little training, most simply fought without technique as if they were in a street fight. In that sense, many found it disgusting and feared boxing like a beat down from a town bully.

If Acree picked two determined, formidable combatants, each had an objective to hurt or injure the other in a way that would end the fight. The goal was to remove an opponent's will or ability to box. In some cases, bloodying a nose or closing an eye with constant jabs did the job. Or, while defending himself, the muscles in a boy's arms might receive so many punches they would no longer function. A fighter who couldn't hold up his arms couldn't defend himself, so he would give up. Others refused to continue fighting after receiving blows to the head or a punch to the body that was too painful to keep going. A fighter could signal defeat by turning his gloves out and saying, "No more."

The worst scenario happened when Acree picked a hard-nosed, experienced fighter to box a boy who didn't want to fight. Such a boy might have lacked confidence, feared pain or knew he would fail in front of his friends. The sight of Acree's boxing gloves terrorized such boys.

Acree would send losing fighters to the Green House. In his way of thinking, the long run gave a boy time to relive a match and find the courage to overcome his fear the next time he boxed.

Some boxers had a tremendous pain threshold. Acree himself once returned to fight another round after having a jaw broken in the ring.

Other players succumbed to technical knockouts. That is, they experienced numerous head blows, or maybe just one, that fogged their brain function so that motor control failed. No longer able to stand, they collapsed to the floor. Alternatively, they staggered aimlessly about the ring before Acree stopped the fight.

A countdown was used to officially determine technical knockouts. Acree acted as a referee, but I don't recall him ever using a ten count to stop a match.

Acree knocked out an opponent in 1949 when he put Gail McGhee to "sleep." However, players seeing a friend lying unconscious on the floor only heightened their anxiety about fighting in the ring.

Boxing is mainly about hitting and hitting repeatedly and either taking a punch or delivering a blow. The word 'hit' was a four-letter word to many boys, but hearing "leather pop" brought a look of joy to Acree's face.

The players dreaded Acree forcing them to box. A hit to the face diminished bravery in most of us. Even the thought of an unexpected punch to the gut could cause us to tense up. Many boys didn't want to fight the way Acree forced us to. Wanting us to go all out, I remember him yelling, "Get after it!"

* * *

Reclassified to a AAAA school, Acree needed a greater number of tough, larger boys willing to fight. To increase the size and strength of players in the off-season, he organized weight room drills and included them as part of the regular physical education (P.E.) class. He also emphasized proper diet. He warned us against eating at the local Dairy Queen, saying, "Your stomach can digest shoe leather before it can break down the lettuce in one of those hamburgers."

Dickey was beginning to fill out his 6' 5" frame, but I failed to gain weight. Acree arranged for my parents and me to consult with a local dietician at the hospital. She advised me to drink extra milkshakes and sprinkle wheat-germ oil on my food at mealtime. My dad tried shaming me into eating larger portions saying, "Even the old lady next door eats more than you do!"

I didn't gain weight, but Acree had more significant problems. UIL rules restricted the rigor of spring training to three weeks. How could he sustain or increase player toughness and confidence during the long months of "off-season"?

Boxing met Acree's need. He believed its requirement for hitting increased our confidence and forced us to stay in good condition to fight. Boxing was a proxy for football to toughen boys to fight their way out of adversity, maybe to come from behind in a game.

Under Acree, the seniors of the '63 championship team had all boxed one another. They came from behind to defeat Graham. Down 6-13 with three minutes left in the game, they staged an almost impossible comeback to win, 14-13. In Acree's mind, boxing had toughened them individually to become a more determined team.

Gary Roman, who led the comeback as the team's quarterback, was a fighter. He loved to box. He previously had bloodied Bruce Butler's nose and knocked out the front teeth of teammate David Robinson.

Jim Wood, a co-captain with Roman, boxed ferociously. Teammate Marc Maxwell said of fighting Wood, "We headbutted each other and knocked ourselves to the floor."

"Acree rushed in to wipe the dust from our gloves and restarted the fight."

"Wood hit me in the chin and scored a standing knockout."

Marc said he staggered on his feet and mumbled even though he was out cold. Acree jumped in to stop Wood from further pummeling him.

In Acree's mind, boxing was a perfect replacement sport for football during the ice-cold months of January and February. Boys could continue slugging it out when tired or hurting. The previous winter, he took James Henkel, Bruce Butler and Ron Cottar to the Golden Gloves tournament in the Dallas Memorial Auditorium. Henkel almost made it to the finals but lost on a close decision. An opponent eliminated Butler in his first match. Cottar won a bout with a technical knockout but was knocked out in the next round. Rumors spread that Cottar didn't wake up until the foursome reached Ennis on the drive home.

Marc Maxwell recalled an incident when player conditioning became a factor. Acree selected my brother Dickey to fight Larry McLaurin. In a three-minute round, the two boys launched a non-stop volley of rapid punching at each other. They were so energetically flinging the heavy gloves that, after a few minutes, both became exhausted. With their chests heaving and red-faced, neither could manage to raise an arm to swing another punch. Their friends laughed when the two boys leaned against each other, propping each other up and gasping for breath. Acree ended their match after the first round. He sent both of them to the Green House, telling them to improve their conditioning.

* * *

Acree had the Tigers fight in the Field House, where the players came each day after school. The Field House was a rectangular, one-story structure made of cinderblock with long, straight walls. A red-brick façade of Corsicana's Whiteselle Cherry Reds covered the outside, and Tiger blue painted the inside.

Players fought in a box of a room with a blackboard hung on its north wall. Acree usually used it for skull sessions, but it contained his instructions for the day in the off season. The boxing room included weight-lifting stations, which Acree had the Tigers remove into an adjacent visitor's dressing room on boxing days. The south wall had high, push-out windows usually opened for ventilation. The floor was concrete gray and sloped slightly for drainage. A high center separated it into two parts, each half having a water drain centrally located. Hosing the floor down on occasion gave it a cold-slab appearance like the floor in the meat market at Piggly Wiggly when we swept out the sawdust and washed the blood off of the concrete.

When thirty boys crowded into the boxing room, they bumped shoulders. It was small for its purpose, but more so when they formed into a circle to make a boxing ring. On boxing days, it had a gym smell. Added to that was the wet, rusty smell of blood.

The boys, 15 to 18 years old, were mainly cold and nervous when Acree had us box each other. We were anxious about any area designated as hitting ground. Memories of the "board drill" still circulated among the linemen. All the boys were acquainted with Acree's one-on-one football drills in an area not much larger than a dining room table. He laid two blocking dummies on the ground, parallel to each other. He lined up two boys facing one another between the dummies and designated one as a blocker and the other a defender. Acree instructed the blocker to fire out and hit the defender, pump his feet and push the defender backward, out from between the two dummies. Acree used cliches such as, "If the going gets tough, the tough get going!"

Pointing at the ground, he instructed the defender, "This spot is your spot. I want you to grab roots, growl and be there when the smoke clears."

At his signal, the two boys unleashed on each other. The defender wielded a padded forearm. The blocker launched underneath and rammed his helmet into the other boy's chest. Dirt and grass flew from churning feet. Their bodies strained against one another. Vision turned into a blur. Pads and helmets cracked as their bodies smashed together. The boys growled and groaned like enraged bulls until Acree blew his whistle to stop their effort. They automatically looked to Acree for affirmation. But often they'd hear, "Run it again, men! Same song, same verse!"

Once more, the boys would fling their exhausted bodies at each other with all the power they could muster. Blood mixed with sweat. Specks of debris in their eyes masked tears of pain. Eventually the hitting stopped, and he moved on to the next pair of boys.

The boxing room evoked a different kind of dread, a primitive fear. We were dressed only in light t-shirts, shorts and soccer shoes, so we had no helmets or facemasks. We had no artificial protection. No pads.

The ceiling light was dim, and a winter storm approaching might darken the sky outside the high windows on the back wall. Outdoors, the wind whistled and splattered raindrops against the glass. Lightning flashes and rumbles of thunder evoked thoughts of horror movies. The closed, heavy, metal doors in the boxing room kept out the weather but combined with the blue cinder-block walls, they gave the appearance of an inescapable prison. It was small with no sense of personal space. Boys bunched into a ring. Like a dungeon below ground, the room smothered any hope of rescue. It became a place of punishment. A sacrifice to a boxing god happened in the center ring, and most of us dreaded the thought of appearing on the altar before Acree.

Had we known in advance, some of the boys would have skipped P.E. class that day and claimed their car broke down on the drive out to the Field House. Other boys who hated running, would volunteer to run to the Green House. Acree likely agreed, but they would have to box first. Running to the Green House was his punishment for any show of weakness—failing to traverse the parallel bars, falling while hand walking the parallel bars or losing a match in the boxing room.

* * *

Boxing became a monster in the converted weight room. Our heart rates doubled at the thought of it; some panicked and feigned injury to escape. Grim-faced boys became quiet. The blackboard might as well have had a personal note scribbled on it, "You are a chicken. Everyone in the room sees you trying to hide. Acree calls you a man, but you are a coward."

The Field House became a haunted place. The boys recalled stories of previous fights. Stories where the ghosts of former Tigers cried out in pain with cut eyes and bloody noses. No one ever forgot the horror of hearing that James Henkel laid a boy out in a single blow, his eyes ticking back and forth like the pendulum in a coo-coo clock.

Tales circulated of Tigers screaming, as blood ran out their nostrils and into their mouths. They spit teeth, sputtered whimpering noises and cried in front of their peers. The boxing room made even the strongest of the boys feel like they were hog-tied and strapped into the front seat of a convertible plunging over a cliff into the Grand Canyon.

No matter how many times the boys crowded into the boxing room, we dreaded it, never felt any comfort or consolation in it and never welcomed it. Every day in the boxing room was a sorry day.

Even today, walking into a weight room, I get a chill. I react by imagining it converted into a boxing room. I glance around its walls and make sure there is a quick-exit door. The spit in my mouth turns dry. My head swivels in search of a place where I can loiter. The clinking noises of the weights on the bars rattle like chains around my ankles. I jump at the thud of a weight falling on the floor. Instinctively I search the room for the presence of Acree's looming figure.

Early in the winter of '64, the weather outside was cold and wet. Lightning occasionally flashed across the bluish-black sky. I parked on the gravel lot near the Field House and talked with teammate Ronnie Ragsdale as we walked toward the Field House. "Weather looks like Acree will have us boxing today."

We were both linebackers on defense. Rags was smarter, so Acree slotted him as a center on offense. He replied, "I'd rather do my hitting on the field."

Gesturing with my thumb back toward the yellow grass covering the practice field behind us, I said, "Me, too. I'm not afraid out there, but with boxing, it's a different story."

We discussed a plan in case Acree picked us to fight against one another, "I'll lean in and you can hit the top of the head."

"Sounds good. That way, we won't flatten our noses or split a lip and bleed."

"No surprise upper cuts either."

In the boxing room, our buddies crept around like caged rats looking for a way to escape. Everyone knew their turn was coming. Like sheep going to slaughter, some thought it was better to go early and get it over with. A boy knocked senseless wouldn't have to suffer the anxiety of watching his friends bloody each other's noses.

Like worms writhing in a fishing can, the boys wiggled nervously as they waited for Acree to enter the boxing room. A glance at the floor followed by a step back concealed an attempt to hide in the crowd. The boys tried not to make eye contact with each other. The fear generated sweat that saturated our t-shirts. No one wanted to hear stories later from their friends of how fearful they looked. Who would want a girlfriend to listen to a buddy telling her that her date made muffled clucking noises in the boxing room?

Acree entered the room and closed the door behind him. The room became smaller with him inside. He waded through the ring of boys into the open space left in the center. He might as well have been a large ice-breaker ship moving through the stiff boys and breaking them up like frozen sea.

He wore his standard coaches' outfit: a ball cap, a polo shirt, shorts, coaches' shoes and athletic socks, but he carried a stopwatch and two pairs of sixteen-ounce boxing gloves. The players hated the sight of those things.

* * *

Each boy looked at Acree with fear-filled eyes as he pulled a 3x5 card from his shirt pocket. Smiling like he was standing in a donut shop making a selection, Acree put the card back in his pocket and moved as if he had all eternity to pick out two fighters. His eyes investigated each face. No one wanted to make eye contact with him. Boys started to pray, "Lord, please don't let him pick me."

Acree's face in the boxing room differed from his game face on the sideline. Serious as always, it seemed to carry a hint of glee like he was standing ringside to watch a Golden Gloves match. The passage of time slowed as his eyes searched from boy to boy, his large body turning to miss no one.

If his gaze fixed on a boy, the boy would look away, pause and then look back to see if Acree was still peering at him. The boy felt a sense of relief when Acree's eyes moved on to the next boy.

Acree looked for a face to match a name, like a teacher scanning a classroom for a volunteer, but no one raised their hand in this case. Acree settled on Jim Wood, a senior linebacker with forearms like Popeye's. Quickly, he turned back to those already passed over and picked Bill Allison, a sophomore fullback. The other boys in the room relaxed. Each breathed a momentary sigh of relief.

Modern "face-saver" headguards weren't available, so Acree only needed to help Allison and Wood lace on the boxing gloves. Lacing gloves was tricky, but Acree did it quickly like he was tying his shoes.

The gloves were big and bulky and made our hands feel swollen. They turned fists into the size of cantaloupes. After tightening them up by pulling with their teeth, Allison and Wood slammed their bulky fists together to test what it might feel like to smash into a soft face.

Both boys had muscular builds, powerful necks and matching arms and legs. Wood was not heavier but a bit taller and sported a haircut as if he were about to enter the Marine Corps. The younger Allison behaved like a clown and joked around to release his tension. However, he was the only one laughing out loud at his jibes. He should have concentrated on his jabs.

Acree positioned the boys in the center of the boxing room and they touched their gloves together. He held up the stopwatch and said, "Men, this is not a boxing match; it's a fight!" He stepped back, said "Go!" and started the stopwatch.

Wood attacked Allison like Lon Chaney's *The Wolf Man* going after a helpless villager who wandered into a dark alley. The donut hole trapped Allison like his back was against a wall. Wood leaned forward into his prey and alternately hurled left and right punches at Allison's head and body. Each blow came with a thud sounding like a wooden bat slamming into a canvas-blocking dummy. Allison's head jumped forward and backward as Wood hit him. He squealed a call to surrender that sounded like a needle skipping across a vinyl record.

Wood punched fast as if he were attacking a speed punching bag. He hit Allison multiple times before Allison's knees buckled, and he dropped to the floor. Every boy's face expressed his worst fear. Nobody counted the punches. They came too quickly. To stop Wood's flurry, Acree blew his whistle. He put his big left arm between the two boxers, and the action ceased. Allison staggered to his feet, and Acree helped him as he fiddled to unlace the mitts. With his face red and battered, he wobbled and exclaimed what everyone else already knew, "He whipped my ass!"

To motivate boys to fight, Acree reminded them that losers had to run to the Green House.

Strapping and unstrapping the one-size-fits-all gloves mercifully consumed time. Still, during that period, the dread that hung over the room became another moment of terror as Acree glanced at his 3x5 card and resumed scanning the boys for two more fighters.

As though he wanted to set an example, Acree had Bruce Butler and Ron Cottar battle each other next. It was a prolonged fight—maybe two, three-minute rounds. Both fighters danced around jabbing at each other, swaying as if trying to charm the other into a momentary lapse of concentration and then struck with the quickness of a rattlesnake.

Butler's quiet demeanor, but long reach and fierce punches, made the players gasp when he connected. "Whap!"

Each boy witnessed a display of power they hoped they would never experience personally.

Cottar was more compact but muscular and tenacious. He fought like a badger and kept advancing into Butler no matter how many times he was hit. He analyzed Butler who didn't seem to fear a blow to the face.

Butler and Cottar boxed as if they understood the sport like Acree did. They boxed for the challenge and individual glory that came with winning.

Other boys watching prayed for the time in the boxing room to expire.

* * *

Dreaming that the assistant coaches had dismissed the players, boys Acree had skipped over fled like escapees through the nearest door. They raced like ants spilling out of a mound going in different directions—any direction other than the one Acree used. Fear swept over them that he might change his mind. They made their way to the back gate and gladly ran the slab to the Green House.

The boys who won their fight moved slowly to show off their bruised faces, scraped arms and cut chins. These served as temporary marks of survival. Often boxers reached out to their teammates to discuss the fight. They didn't want to hit each other, but they had no choice. They whispered, "No telling what he would do if I didn't hit you."

"He's crazy, man."

What would he do behind closed doors in the boxing room if he would kick our tail on a practice field for loafing?

As the losers made their way to the Green House, the winners transferred the weights back into the boxing room. Each boy had a release of anxiety. "I'm glad it's over."

The weight room was a joy to see again. To some, the relief was like a divine gift. They sighed, as if they had narrowly avoided a high-speed collision at an intersection. That feeling didn't last long, however.

The boys unconsciously started rocking back and forth, bouncing on their feet. Angst fell on them again when they stopped fantasizing and realized Acree was searching for a particular face again. But whose face?

* * *

Each boy was terrified and hoped that Acree would pass over him that day. No one was sure of his criteria. If he was doing it to help the boys, it was unclear to them how it helped. There was no explanation, no teaching as there was in football. He aimed to expose a primal reaction—who would fight for survival?

But why Acree picked the fighters he picked, no one knew. Why did he match friend against friend? Why would he pit a skilled boxer against a novice? Was he looking for natural boxing talent? We fretted, wondering if he remembered who boxed the last time we entered the boxing room.

We had all these questions. But without any answers, our fear raged as the matches continued. A few seniors thought Acree wasn't mean-spirited but only acting out his love of boxing like a Spaniard takes friends to a bullfight. It was an experience he wanted to share with them.

220

To most of us, however, it was like inviting us to wait inside a dark theater for an attack from the *Creature from the Black Lagoon*. Boxing erupted in the middle of the circle like *The Thing from an Alien World* exploded through a door and slashed through frozen researchers at the North Pole.

Acree scanned the terrified faces with no discernable logic or reason. He settled his gaze on Ronnie Ragsdale, then he paused. Was he waiting for Ragsdale to react, to perhaps try and bolt out of a door? Ragsdale looked from side to side. Was he waiting for Ragsdale to voluntarily step forward, entranced by Acree's gaze as if it were a tractor beam slowly drawing him into the ring?

Ragsdale's fears kicked in. Would Acree make him fight Cottar? Would he choose Butler? Instead, Acree jerked his head, turning his gaze to Lynn Odom and me. He called each of us into the ring. Ragsdale relaxed.

Odom and I were friends. I was a bit taller with greater reach. Odom was tougher, however. He applied himself to Acree's weight training and developed a stocky, muscular body. Acree strapped on our gloves and centered us in the ring. He started the match. As Odom looked for an opportunity to strike, I moved toward him, taking a single step. At that moment, I was dead center in the boxing room, and Odom perched on the flooring, slanted slightly downhill. As he stepped back and dropped his arms to peer over his gloves, I stepped toward him and flung a punch at his gloves just as he lowered them. My roundhouse connected with Odom's unguarded face. His feet tangled, and the lucky punch sent him stumbling backward. The circle parted, and there was a collective gasp as Odom fell to the floor on his right side. To him, the blow felt sharp as if he had run into the corner of an open cabinet door. Instinctively, he touched his red forehead with the big glove to assess the damage. His eyes narrowed to focus on me. Friends or not, he could see nothing but a head he wanted to bash.

Never taking his eyes off me, Odom quickly jumped up. Acree rushed over and wiped off Odom's gloves that had touched the floor. He then stepped back out of the way. Odom rushed toward me, head down, swinging away. I didn't want to fight, so I defended myself while saying to Odom that my punch was an accident. Neither Acree nor Odom would have any of it.

Odom delivered a flurry of punches. I persisted in blocking them. Soon, Acree yelled at me, "Hit back! This is a fight! Don't just block his punches and back away!"

The fight continued with Odom trying to regain his pride, while I backed around the circle to save my friendship. Our three minutes expired, and Acree stopped the fight. Both of our faces were red hot like burners on a stovetop. He declared it a draw and ordered us both to run to the Green House.

Acree unlaced the gloves and started his scan for another pair of boys.

Ragsdale was standing at the back of the circle near the east door. He tensed up again. At that moment, Coach Anderson opened it to come inside. Ragsdale lurched toward it to slip out while it cracked open. But he couldn't make it before Anderson pulled the door shut behind him.

Ragsdale thought, "What if Acree saw me trying to get away?"

The horror of personal, one-on-one fighting froze Ragsdale's mind. Fear of hit after hit to the head will do that.

Acree sensed the boys were afraid, but he resumed scanning. A pattern emerged of him regularly picking matches for Wood, Butler and Cottar, as though he wanted to use them to test the courage of the other boys. The boxing monster spoke to Ragsdale, "Acree's not strange. You are."

Ragsdale thought, "Why does he want to scare us by waiting until the last minute to select fighters for the next match?"

Boxing suggested, "Perhaps he has a tournament in mind?"

Ragsdale expressed his dread, "I hope he picks someone else!"

Ragsdale knew Acree would eventually search for him. The butterflies in his gut told him his time was near.

Panicked, he quickly devised a new avoidance strategy. He waited until the last minute to invoke it. Lurking behind the other boys, he knew Acree's eye would pick up cross-motion; after all, he was a former linebacker.

Ragsdale decided to travel clockwise just ahead of Acree's scan. If he could take advantage of Acree's fixations, he might be able to stay in front of the scan and go unnoticed.

Boxing tormented Ragsdale, "It's not going to be pretty when I get you in that ring! Ha! Ha! Ha!"

Several matches came and went. Ragsdale's strategy was working. Acree picked me again. "Damn!"

He paired me with Bobby Heard, a tackle who outweighed me by at least forty pounds. As Acree laced up our gloves, I imagined Dickey having to fight the bully. Acree was like a Buddy Ward, standing there with his belt drawn.

Bobby had a hard face like that of a statue. We were about the same height, but he was much more substantial. His round form hid the power of his unseen muscles. If he connected a fist on my jaw, I'd be down for ten counts. Acree started the fight, and I moved in and out, bouncing on my feet, ready to go in whatever direction necessary to avoid a punch from Bobby. I punched opportunistically but half-heartedly and didn't leave a mark on Bobby. I didn't want to hit him accidentally like I did Odom and make him mad. I backed away quickly as needed. That saved me from Bobby, but Acree sent me to the Green House.

After my match, the tension in Rags' face created lines on his forehead. I was out as a potential boxing partner. Acree would not pick me to fight a third time.

Rags resumed moving one step at a time at the back of the ring, circling in the direction of Acree's scan. He made sure that he never looked at Acree's face. Falling under Acree's gaze would freeze him motionless and ruin any chance of escaping.

Acree called on Bruce Butler. He punched like a jackhammer. Acree paired him with Bill Allison who was still recovering from the earlier match with Wood. Acree showed Allison how to hold up his forearms and block punches, but it took just one advance from Butler to dispatch Bill.

Butler's ending punch flew between Allison's raised forearms like a Bruce Lee karate chop going through balsa wood. It landed on Allison's nose and knocked him backward, arms flailing, into the circle, which parted to let him fall to the floor. Luckily, Allison made use of the toilet before entering the boxing room. Otherwise, his statement as he got up would have been confirmed. "He knocked the shit out of me!"

Acree followed the part in the ring to help Allison up from the floor and remove the boxing gloves. As they came off, he turned to the center of the ring at the very moment Ragsdale decided to continue his lurking maneuver around the backside.

With a soft chuckle, Acree called "Cottar" a Golden Gloves fighter. Hearing Acree snicker, goosebumps raised on the back of Ragsdale's neck. Eyes fixed on each other, Acree motioned Rags to the center ring.

CHAPTER 9   CLASS AAAA COMPETITION

"Man is by nature competitive, and athletics teach a boy to compete fiercely,
yet within the framework of the rules." Jim Acree

Acree's popularity soared at the start of 1964. His accolades after winning a state championship buried any issues over having the players box each other.

The Balfour company, which sponsored the Texas High School Coaches Association's Hall of Honor banquet, named Acree their 1963 Coach of the Year. Acree received write-in votes in the Texas Sports Writers balloting for high school football Coach of the Year. The Dallas Coach of the Year Clinic selected him to conduct a teaching session on "Opening up the Offense."

The THSCA Board of Directors invited Acree to join their ranks – very fitting since Johnny Pierce, the former Corsicana coach, who led the Tigers to their only other state championship in 1932, co-founded the organization in 1930. The Association grew from its three founding members to 28 coaches at its first meeting in 1933 and increased to 4,200 in 1964. Acree wore a suit and tie and served on the Board for three years.

The THSCA South Regions balloted to honor Acree by selecting him and his staff to coach the South team in the annual North-South All-Star game, scheduled in Ft. Worth, August 1964. He spoke at numerous civic meetings in Corsicana, and his name appeared regularly in articles in various publications such as Texas Coach and newspapers such as the Ft. Worth Star-Telegram, Dallas Times Herald and the Corsicana Daily Sun.

Acree, his assistant coaches and their wives were guests of honor at the Chamber of Commerce banquet in January 1964. When the emcee introduced the honorees, the audience of around 500 Corsicanans stood and "wildly applauded."

At another heavily attended public banquet called "Tiger Night," put on by the Dads Club, School Board President Maco Stewart presented a $3,200 appreciation award to Acree and his staff. The amount tripled that given when the practice started after Acree's first District Championship in 1960. Giving appreciation awards to coaches was common practice in Texas at the time.

The UIL updated its athletic rules yearly. Its regulatory grip on Texas football steadily tightened as membership grew to almost a thousand schools in 1964. The organization wanted to protect the amateur status of school competitions. They wanted coaches to be teachers, not professional football coaches. They wanted players not to receive anything not offered to all students.

Acree asked the UIL for permission to take the '63 team to the Cotton Bowl to see the University of Texas play the Naval Academy. They approved his request. I don't know what the tickets cost to see the Cotton Bowl in January, 1964 or who paid for them, but I'll never forget sitting with the State Championship team to watch future Cowboy star Roger Staubach play. It was undoubtedly a benefit not offered to every student.

* * *

A football truism says, "Experienced coaches should identify leadership in a team and fix any issues before it costs them a game, or a championship."

Acree met with his team of assistant coaches in the coach's suite at the high school. He thanked them for their efforts to win a state championship. Coach Moore expressed the staff's opinion, "Coach, we appreciate your leadership, too."

Humbled, Acree listened as Coach Anderson jibed him, "Our job wouldn't be half as difficult if we didn't first have to vote you down on what to do next."

All the assistants chuckled, including Matthews and Slaughter. With an authoritarian style in place, assistant coaches seldom overruled Acree.

Coach Slaughter said, "The real credit for the championship goes to the talent we had on the team. Hagle, Denbow and Roman were exceptional players."

But knowing that coaching also makes a difference, Coach Matthews said, "Yes, but Coach called that fake field goal against Pharr to win the State Championship game."

All the assistant coaches nodded in agreement. Acree said, "Thank you, men. Talent, preparation and a team who overcame adversity won the championship."

Not far from Acree's mind was the requirement to build a new team for the 1964 season that could compete in Class AAAA. "But let's not forget, we have a new set of District opponents who want to knock us off our pedestal."

The staff agreed, and Acree got down to business, "Our goal is to win District. Let's review the seniors and identify the leaders."

* * *

In 1947, the UIL ended championship dominance caused by large cities with a single high school by creating multiple classifications based on school size. Texas was growing in the 60s, and as larger towns increased in population from the post-war baby boom, new high schools popped up as fast as shopping malls. Larger cities divided their eligible boys into multiple competing schools, which further leveled the competition. For example, by 1964, Waco had grown to about 97,000 citizens. To Waco High, it added two new high schools, Waco University and Waco Richfield, to make three segregated high schools. This reduced enrollment at Waco High possibly explains why Corsicana, which had a population of only 19,000, was able to defeat Waco in 1963 after a thirteen-year hiatus.

Corsicana's reclassification to AAAA came in the middle of the '63 season. Not to make the realignment a distraction, Acree initially downplayed it. Referring to opponents such as Waco and John Tyler, (another traditional AAAA ranked opponent), he said, "We've been playing some of these teams all along and have done pretty well."

In keeping with his competitive personality, Acree secretly relished the opportunity for novel competition. Winning four straight years over District 8-AAA opponents had become too predictable. Moreover, a few opposing coaches complained that Acree overworked his players. The rub came because Acree played to win, not just engage in extracurricular activity.

Dads like my father argued that winning consistently at the AAAA level would become difficult for Corsicana, "Larger schools have access to more talent."

Acree agreed, but his competitive nature didn't see that as a big issue. "These AAAA people put their britches on the same way anybody else does—one leg at a time. They are just as human as we are."

"They may have a few more people to work with, and injuries might hurt us worse than they would some of the larger schools, but we'll play with them, as long as they just use eleven players at a time."

Dad said, "There wouldn't be multiple UIL classifications if larger schools didn't have a competitive edge."

Segregated school systems were only at the beginning stages of integration and did not factor into Corsicana's re-classification in 1964 (e.g., the first all-black school, San Antonio Wheatley, didn't compete in the UIL until 1966). However, desegregation laws at the time permitted students to attend their high school of choice in Corsicana. Feasibly, Acree could have recruited Negro players from Corsicana's all-black Jackson High School to attend Corsicana High School, but he did not take advantage of that opportunity. San Antonio Brackenridge did, however, and Warren McVey lit up the scoreboard with forty-six touchdowns in 1963. As a comparison, Jim Hagle had half that number with twenty-three scores.

Acree believed player dedication, discipline and desire served as trump cards over talent. "Men, you can accomplish anything in your life if you want to badly enough. If you have enough pride, desire and determination, you can be successful at whatever you choose to do."

In his mind, if the players had a will to win, the "difference" was one of preparation; teams could enjoy success if they hustled on the practice field and outworked their opponents. His Tigers won games over more talented teams many times. One sportswriter noted the widespread respect Acree enjoyed, "His clubs are among the most feared in interscholastic circles."

Acree expressed his core ideology, "If our boys come out for football, and stay out, and play, and if they pay the price, they can compete in any category of football."

* * *

However, UIL rules limited the preparation time of Acree's "pay the price" philosophy. Rules constrained his ability to condition players in ways he deemed necessary. Acree thought nothing of practices running late, which made him vulnerable to accusations of overworking the boys. UIL rules pinched his "run it one more time" ethic between specifying when practices could start and how long they could last. That limited his savage use of repetition. He had to either settle for team unpreparedness or face punishment for a UIL rule violation. Jealous coaches he defeated would likely be the first in line to complain about his methods.

A growing UIL rulebook trapped Acree in a maze of intricate dos and don'ts. To illustrate, a player could only suit up for one game weekly, either on the A-team or the B-team. However, if Acree wanted to improve a quarterback on the B-team like Glen Smith by allowing him to also suit up on the A-team and keep a clipboard log of play calls, he violated a UIL rule. Glen could do the job in street clothes, but since he was part of the team, Acree wanted him to wear a uniform.

A competitor like Acree might trade off impersonal UIL rules for an opportunity to help a player or help the team win. He wanted to see boys do their best, but purists in a changing culture didn't see it that way. A rule is a rule. They could defend every jot and tittle of an increasingly complicated set of instructions by claiming a moral high ground, "Player safety matters most."

Had Corsicana remained a AAA school for the '64-65 seasons, some believe Acree would have had a dynasty of state championships. If he thought this way, he never let it be known publicly.

Objectively, in 1964, Corsicana went from the top rung of the UIL enrollment ladder in Class AAA to the bottom rung in Class AAAA. For example, Waco Richfield, a relatively new high school in Waco, had more than 1,600 students enrolled. Corsicana High School's hovered around 750. Richfield was twice the size of CHS. Corsicana fielded thirty-four players, whereas Richfield suited up closer to fifty boys. AAAA schools like San Antonio Lee had over 2,700 students in attendance, almost four times that of CHS.

The UIL drew enrollment lines to ensure good competition and to please its members. Misclassifying a school too low could lead to a string of championships. Misclassifying too high might lead to consistent losses. Misclassification, either way, led to unhappy members. Corsicana fell into no-man's land. It was enormous compared to some AAA schools but small compared to larger AAAA schools.

Greater enrollments allowed large AAAA schools to ratchet up the available player talent. Speed, open field running ability and pass receiving achieved new scoring levels in class AAAA. For example, Linus Baer of San Antonio Lee and Warren McVey of San Antonio Brackenridge were AAAA running backs who scored eighty touchdowns between them in 1963. By comparison, Jim Hagle, Donnie Denbow and Gary Roman scored only forty touchdowns in 1963. Acree's high-powered offense did not win a playoff game by more than seven points—and that was after "Opening Up the Offense."

With an increased emphasis on the passing game, AAAA quarterback requirements also intensified. Quick decision making, options play execution, pocket passing and throwing accuracy became keys to success. Gary Roman was second only to P.D. Shabay of Graham in completion percentage, but AAAA quarterbacks like Inez Perez of Corpus Christi Miller put the ball in the air 50% more often than Roman. The quarterback, in most cases, was the most versatile player on the team. His running ability became less of a requirement as an emphasis on passing increased.

Acree had a system for grooming quarterbacks. Looking backward, in '62, he replaced Tom Wilson with a combined Happy Settle and Gary Roman. If he called a run play, Settle typically took the snap. But on pass plays, Roman took over because he threw the ball more accurately. In '63, Roman's ability to run and throw earned him starting honors as a quarterback. Backup Rankin Koch threw only twelve times in '63. Third-string quarterback, sophomore Glen Smith, didn't get A-team throwing opportunities.

* * *

As coach of the South All-Star team, Acree waited for Warren McVey, Linus Bear and Inez Perez to report for practice before the game. His philosophy of winning by preparing experienced players versus relying on raw talent surfaced in a press interview, "I'm just like the old Missouri mule; they'll have to show me what they can do during our practice sessions."

To compete in AAAA football, he needed to grow team size. Except for '62, the size of his AAA teams remained relatively constant—30 in 1960, 33 in 1961, 24 in 1962 and 33 in 1963. Acree had worked out the details, "Where we have 15 or 16 boys, the other teams will have 24 or 25."

For the '64 team, he speculated, "We will have to depend more on sophomores this year than we have in the past." However, looking forward, only three sophomores lettered in 1964. He lacked confidence in the offense, "We'll have to rely more on defense to help win games."

Given Acree's coaching philosophy, he wanted the returning seniors to step up and fill the leadership gap left by the departure of Wood, Roman, Hagle, Denbow and Cooper.

A whopping number of fifty-two high school tryouts came out for spring football in February 1964. This encouraged Acree. He started our afternoon drills in the rain, saying, "If we can keep enthusiasm and participation like this, we can play football at any level!"

That number remained the same throughout the three weeks of spring training allowed by the UIL. Tryouts didn't include incoming sophomores who were still in junior high and not allowed to practice according to UIL rules. Returning were fifteen junior lettermen who would become seniors. This was two times the number of returning senior lettermen on the '63 team. However, natural cliques formed among the seniors. I'm sure there were members in each subgroup who disliked some boys in the other groups. The '63 seniors didn't have cliques.

Four sophomore lettermen returned and would become juniors. I was one of the returning sophomores. The other thirty-three boys included most of the twenty-one players from the previous B-team and a dozen new tryouts.

Senior tackle Don Ivie hated participating in spring training. As a returning starter, he didn't have to prove himself, but to help the team, he worked as though he did. The same went for end Bill Henson. As linemen, they hustled and set an example for younger players like me. Always the first in line for a drill or the first one back from a run to the Green House, slotback Billy Frank "Chick" Whistler was a leader too.

Not all the coaches were thrilled by the turnout. Coach Matthews' main priority was basketball. The playoff run into late December delayed his use of Hagle, Roman and Koch on the basketball team. The early start of football in February further strained Matthews's need for players and created additional friction with Acree. Moore and Anderson had similar issues coaching baseball and track but resigned themselves to Acree's priority on football.

When boys came out for football, Acree stressed that commitment and hard work would be required to attain anything worthwhile. He rejected tryouts who wouldn't follow his team rules: keep a curfew, don't drink alcohol and don't smoke. Acree went after senior slotback and noseguard Cody Sherrard for chewing tobacco. He threatened, "You'll never touch the football again."

He had us stop drinking Dr Pepper before practice because it made our sides ache. Coach Slaughter lectured us on taking time for regular morning visits to the bathroom. Acree emphasized a need to take care of our bodies. Recalling Loy, he warned us, "You're tempted to, but don't drink. It can destroy your life."

If we developed the sniffles, Coach Anderson gave us chewable vitamin C tablets (I loved the taste). If we complained of a sore throat, Coach Anderson sprayed Chloraseptic on the back of our throats (I appreciated the soothing feeling).

Once a player was "on the team," Acree expected a focus on football— not girls, cars, music, movies or other sports. We joked as teenage boys that if girls came to mind, Acree wanted us to think of a football as having lipstick around the laces and ends covered in bra cups.

No one loved football more than Jim Acree. He was always scribbling play designs on napkins and thinking about play execution. It was told that his wife Rosemary once stood in front of a mirror and used lipstick to draw a football play on her body. When Coach came home late that evening, she met him at the door and opened her housecoat to reveal what she thought might get his interest. He looked at her intently and said, "You have the linebacker in the wrong place."

Although the season was six months away, Acree worked us in full pads that spring and expected the linemen to hit hard, as if the season had already begun. In March, he held the Blue and Gold (White) game. I was a guard and linebacker on the Blue team. Acree named senior Ricky Libal as the quarterback. Libal was the B-team quarterback his sophomore year, as was alternate Blue team quarterback Glen Smith. I expected Acree to name Glen as the quarterback.

Libal was an outstanding placekicker, but the previous season, the three quarterbacks were Roman, Koch and Smith. Given Acree's preference for experience, Glen should have been his choice for quarterback of the Blue team, but Acree picked Libal.

Glen was a winning B-team quarterback. He threw a pretty pass, and his winsome personality contributed to his popularity among the other players. He had fun playing and was someone who could unexpectedly turn around a ballgame. Why Acree passed over Glen is unknown. When

I asked Glen about this, he only offered a boy's perspective, "Acree didn't like me."

Glen may have felt that way, but many times during the season, Acree started him as a halfback and receiver. Glen made numerous pass catches and made many excellent runs. He scored several touchdowns. Glen had Acree's blessing as a player, but not as a quarterback. I think this was a mistake by Acree. A year later, we had words about it. All I got was a kick in the butt and a verbal reminder of who was in charge.

Specialist players, like kickers, can sometimes appear as loners who seek isolation to focus mentally on their craft. Acree expected a lot from seniors. I suppose he wanted to incorporate Libal into a role where he could have a greater opportunity for team leadership.

Libal threw an interception on his first pass attempt in the Blue-Gold scrimmage. It was not a good night for the Blue team even though we had the majority of the returning seniors, including Chick Whistler, Ronnie Rhoads, Bill Henson, Jerry Anderson and Stan Rosen. We managed only 21 yards passing and 125 yards of penalties. We lost, 0-22.

Juniors on the White team upstaged the Blue team seniors. Bill Allison scored two touchdowns, and Steve Winn made a fantastic runback of an interception.

A single spring game didn't define the team but it did inform the coach. Rankin Koch effectively replaced Roman at quarterback. Koch planned to become a minister. He would have to prove to the other seniors that he could do his part when "the going got tough."

Acree was unsettled about Hagle's replacement. He vacillated between Ben Smith and Bill Allison well into the season. There was no one to replace Denbow.

Graduation erased the entire '63 starting offensive line. Except for Don Ivie, Bruce Butler and Bill Henson, the returning senior linemen had little playing experience. Nevertheless, Stan Rosen was a shoo-in for the center, Don Ivie was one of the tackles, Bruce Butler had one of the guard slots, Bill Henson had one of the end positions and Dan Wilcox the other end. Acree didn't decide who would fill the remaining tackle and guard positions until two-a-days in August.

Acree wanted seniors to step up and prove he could count on them when game action started, but there were no obvious replacements for talented tackles like Sam Cooper and Robert Graham. Seniors Jerry Anderson and Ron Cottar had an opportunity, but Acree was in a predicament, "We are going to miss all those big, strong people."

* * *

In a backdoor way of complimenting the individual talent on the '63 team, Acree identified a success requirement for the '64 Tigers saying, "They'll have to be a better team."

Years later, while working in the computer industry, a manager asked me, "What is a team?" Thinking back on my football experience, I said, "We each do our part, and we score a touchdown." But he asked, "Who do you trust to do their part?"

He gave an analogy of a team as a wheel with spokes. As the wheel rotates, the whole load rests on each spoke when its time comes. His analogy made me think of how the '63 Tigers trusted Jim Hagle to make a first down in short-yardage situations. The whole stadium could be keying on Hagle. Still, he would gain the yards needed. Or if we were in a third and long and required a great throw and catch, Gary Roman and Donnie Denbow did their part.

In '63, when the Tigers were behind the Graham Steers 6-13 with less than 4 minutes left in the game, and it was fourth and five on our 20-yard line, the team counted on Sam Cooper and Jim Wood to stop Graham. They did. When the Tigers needed a two-point conversion, Acree called on Gary Roman to get the ball across the goal line. He did. When the outcome of the game fell onto the shoulders of the '63 seniors at critical moments, we could trust them to do their part. All of them were team players who demonstrated outstanding leadership.

In '64, it wasn't just player size that was changing; team leadership was too. Acree had a new crop of seniors who needed to prove they would rise to the challenge and play their best when they were tired, bruised or behind. According to him, they needed a sincere desire to win and a willingness to pay a greater price for victory over an entirely new set of district opponents.

Beyond Acree's struggle to build a team, he also had to produce a fall schedule. It was complicated by the championship win and the switch in classification to a new district. Non-conference foes wanted to play Corsicana because of its winning record. This attracted fans, which meant more significant gate receipts. The opposite was true for scheduling B-team games. The insular Waco schools and Corsicana's AAAA status limited potential opponents.

The size of the new 13-AAAA District (twelve teams with two six-team "zones") didn't permit the Tigers to have an open date during its ten-game schedule. If we won our zone, we'd have to play an extra game to win District. There was no room for an open date unless Acree eliminated a non-district foe like Ennis and played a nine-game regular-season schedule. Given his dislike for open dates, that didn't happen.

Not having an open date would prove to be costly.

* * *

After football that spring, my friends worked in the weight room and played other sports. I worked at Piggly Wiggly, unloaded delivery trucks and stayed in shape by running to the Green House after half-hearted sessions in the weight room. I hated that room. The clinking and clanking inside it reminded me too much of boxing.

Dickey quit school and Mother signed the papers for him to join the Marine Corps at age 17. He had dyslexia and struggled to read. Not recognized in those days, he was a special needs kid who thought of school as a "prison."

With Dickey gone, I had our old jalopy Ford to myself. Dutifully, I kept Acree's curfew and didn't drink or smoke, but I can say without a doubt that when I looked at my girlfriend, I saw nothing that resembled a football. Not smoking and drinking was easy for me because she did neither.

At Acree's urging, the school district recognized the need for lighting improvements at Tiger Field, including a new scoreboard. The upgrade cost was huge—$7,000—about the list price of two brand-new Chevy Impala hardtops with 387 engines and 4-barrel carburetors. Two 110' tubular light towers were erected thanks to Fred Allison and the Dads Club. A new scoreboard was also purchased. Winning a state championship came with some benefits.

* * *

When Acree took charge of the South All-Stars in August, he had a team of incredible talent: at quarterback, Inez Perez of Corpus Christi Miller, with Linus Baer of San Antonio Lee and Warren McVey of San Antonio Brackenridge as running backs. He had a set of quick, big, strong linemen that averaged 213 pounds, and several had All-State designations, including Jack Herrington from Austin.

Odds makers favored the South's explosive offense over the North. Acree and his assistant coaches Moore, Anderson and Slaughter had only a week to teach twenty-eight heralded players how not to make mistakes as a team.

The North team, coached by Charlie Qualles from McKinney, whom Corsicana defeated in the 1963 quarterfinals game, had Jim Hagle. As a trade, Acree offered Qualles any of the South's running backs for Hagle, but Qualles declined.

Before a record crowd in Amon Carter Stadium, Acree lost his first game since 1962, 14-28. According to him, the South's stellar athletes played only "18 minutes of good football." Acree's methods were ineffective on a squad of players who were born exceptional. They made too many mistakes. Coach Slaughter said, "We didn't have a quarterback."

He underscored his point by saying, "With two All-State running backs behind him, Inez Perez, weighing 145 pounds, called a quarterback sneak on the goal line. He didn't score."

Linus Bear, a University of Texas recruit, left the game in the first quarter after blowing out a knee. It's said that Acree's Oklahoma teammate, and the UT head coach, Daryl Royal, held Acree responsible. No Acree Tiger ever received a scholarship offer to UT.

Acree didn't lose any sleep over the loss. Jim Hagle, an SMU recruit, was the star of the winning North team. As team captain, he played almost every down in the game and demonstrated exceptional team leadership. His running, tackling and punting delighted fans on offense and defense. By association with Hagle, Acree won even though he lost the game. By all accounts, Hagle became a man under Acree's leadership.

* * *

After a disappointing Tiger spring scrimmage and seeing the All-Star talent in August, Acree was not optimistic about our chances in the new district. He confessed, "In a poll of the coaches, I picked Waco Richfield to win our zone and Corsicana to finish third behind Cleburne."

He justified his vote against the '64 Tigers, saying, "We lack experience and depth." Acree seemed to convolute talent and experience. Why discount our experience when we had twice as many returning seniors as we did in '63?

He thought the obvious, "We don't have the equivalent talent of Sam Cooper, Jim Wood, Johnny Nelson, Jim Hagle, Donnie Denbow and Gary Roman." Or he meant we didn't have the same senior leadership we had in the championship season. He could see the need for a close-knit group of seniors that could act as spokes in a team wheel and do their part to meet challenges that inevitably arise in a football season.

As Corsicana baked under a hot August sun, a neighbor who farmed his land said to Acree, "I hope your football season doesn't end up like my cotton crop."

The August sun wilted players as well as crops. Seventy-six boys reported for two-a-days. Acree quickly divided the tryouts into forty-one A-team players and thirty-five B-teamers. When team photos were snapped, those numbers dwindled to thirty-four and twenty-seven, respectively. I was thrilled that he put me on the A-team again but earning a starting position as a junior was only a dream.

Acree had two weeks to condition us for a scrimmage against Sherman and another week to prepare us to play Bonham in our first game. It disappointed him that our first four practice days had to be non-contact workouts according to UIL rules. We dressed in t-shirts, shorts and soccer shoes and ran through the motion of football play execution. Supposedly, the purpose was to allow boys' feet time to adapt to new shoes and to get in shape. Player safety was the new mantra around the League.

To develop toughness, Acree had us swing along a twenty-foot length of sunbaked, steel monkey bars and hand walk equally long, hot parallel bars. We quickly developed multiple blisters on our palms and fingers. If a boy could not traverse the bars without touching the ground, Acree sent him to the Green House after three chances. Coach Moore ran with such boys so they wouldn't have to make the journey alone. Turning boys into men required mentors, like Moore, to successfully make the transition.

Just as we dreaded boxing and monkey bars, we dreaded grass drills. Picture a row of boys running on hands and feet for thirty yards. The blisters on our palms popped and filled with dirt and bits of grass. After crossing the yard marker, we turned around and came back the same distance crab walking, which consisted of moving backward as fast as possible on our hands and feet with our tummies facing the sun. Big boys struggled not to drag their bottoms on the ground.

Each trip of thirty yards became a race to impress Acree. Every boy hoped that Acree would take notice of their hustle. We'd look up when we crossed the finish line to see who'd outdone who. Acree treated all of us the same. Linemen mixed with running backs and ends.

Acree had us do butt rolls as part of grass drills. In a horizontal line, we moved as fast as possible on all fours, and then on hearing Acree's whistle, we'd roll right on our butt and come up to face forward in an all-fours position. We'd continue covering ground until he blew his whistle again. Then we'd butt roll to the left. Other times, we ran backward or just sprinted thirty yards or he mixed up the drills – all fours, crab walks, butt rolls and sprints.

Grass drills exhausted players to the point of collapse. The number we did depended on how pleased Acree was with our conditioning. If we were energetic, enthusiastic and enraptured with football, we executed them until Coach Anderson stepped in to say, "That's all we have time for today, Coach."

If Acree was unhappy, we watched the sun set behind the mesquite trees to the west of the practice field.

During one set of grass drills, a classmate beat me on one of the thirty-yard trips. As we rejoined the back of our respective lines, he stepped in front of me and said, "I'm better than you."

He was joking, but his comment made me realize I was loafing, not giving it my best. He became an incentive for me to work harder. The next time we reached the start point, I jumped into my four-point stance. Acree called out, "All fours," and blew his whistle.

I shot forward like a monkey poked with an invisible electric prod and covered thirty yards fast enough to impress even Tarzan. That classmate never beat me again on the practice field. However, I conceded the weight room to him. He developed muscles on top of muscles as if he wanted to look like Johnny Weissmuller, the athletic actor who played Tarzan in the movies.

My classmate and I were friends off the field, but as two linemen vying for a starting position, we competed when it came to football. On the other hand, Steve Winn, our speedy running back, and I were in English class together. He always performed very well on writing assignments. I admired his skill, but I never tried to compete with him as a writer. Inspired by Acree, however, the practice field was a different kind of classroom.

Steve ran a fast 9.7-hundred-yard dash, which was impossible for me to beat. However, in 30-yard grass drills, I always tried to best Steve and sometimes did. Desire and determination mattered. Maybe quickness off the line was a factor or focus. We never vied for the same football position, but our desire to impress Acree caused us to compete for his attention on grass drills.

Our lack of "time to prepare" for our first opponent Bonham, a AAA school, stressed Acree. Having formerly coached there, he was convinced they were "out to get him."

UIL rules allowed Bonham to start practicing a week ahead of Corsicana, which he saw as spotting them an advantage. The four initial days of our practice had to be without pads, which put us further behind in his mind. He concluded, "Our problem right now is that Bonham has 10 to 16 days (of workout time) on us. We are just way behind."

On the practice field or in a game, Acree hated being behind. He had only twelve workout days in full pads to prepare us to play a AAA team. We worked out under the new lights at Tiger Field on Monday night. He planned to show the film of the All-Star game to the Dads Club but didn't because of a "late practice."

Acree was anxious about the game and so were the fans. Based on Acree's cynicism, some predicted a loss. Maco Stewart acknowledged that we might lose the season opener but said, "The Tigers won't embarrass us."

Undoubtedly, Acree felt that UIL rules limited his ability to get the Tigers ready to play. There weren't enough hours in the day. "The biggest problem is," Acree concluded, "we are not in shape."

I don't think he was referring to our conditioning. After a light practice Thursday in shorts and t-shirts, Acree said we made too many mistakes. As a result, he did not name the eleven starters on offense, which was his habit. Instead, he listed two players contending as a starter for each position.

As a junior guard playing behind a senior, I was thrilled to be named a potential starter. Possibly, he sensed some entitlement and wanted to put a quick end to it. But did Acree's indecisiveness impact the confidence of the seniors who were the de facto team leaders?

Acree convened his regular Thursday night team meeting in the band hall at the high school. After reviewing film, play assignments and down and distance situations, he dismissed the team, but he asked the potential starters to remain behind. For the first time, I received a pregame vitamin shot.

Coach Anderson helped Acree as he poked a hypodermic needle into the top of a small bottle and upended it. He extracted a measured amount of red liquid into the syringe. He thumped the syringe and said it was "Vitamin B, which will give you energy."

With his right hand, he pushed up the sleeve of my white t-shirt and jabbed the needle into the exposed shoulder. After the injection, I left the room. I joined other boys outside the door rubbing their shoulders. I hated shots. But I didn't know to escape during the interval between dismissing the team and setting up the worktable. Two former players told me they refused to take the shots. But most of the boys accepted it as a jab of honor, akin to participating in a secret ritual of an elite club.

Were the vitamins the same as dope? No, and I know the difference. Years later, dressing out for a college game, a player next to me "popped an upper" before a game. His eyes changed. Usually reserved, the pill caused him to play in a reckless, give-his-body-up style. I asked him when he started the habit and he said, "High School."

According to the Corsicana Daily Sun, other Texas high schools offered vitamins to players, but contrary to some rumors, Coach Acree never gave us dope or anything detrimental. He thought our bodies were sacred.

Acree also had a ritual of putting honey on our pregame meal at the Corsican Motel and Restaurant on Business 75. Everyone ate the same food—a plate of sliced roast beef with baked potato, green beans and rolls. Players and coaches sat four at a table in the large restaurant. As the wait staff served our food, Coach Acree personally went from table to table, scooping honey out of a large jar on top of each player's food. We loved it! The players practically licked their plates clean, consuming even the skins on the potatoes.

Bonham

In a come-from-behind win, we opened the '64 season by beating Bonham 21-14. They fumbled twice in their territory, gifting Ricky Libal two easy field goals. Then they scored on a short pass. Our offense could not move the ball. After a Bonham runner crisscrossed the field on a lengthy run, they scored again. Our defensive teamwork reminded me of the Keystone Cops. We trailed at halftime, 6-14.

I don't remember what Acree said in the Field House to fire us up as a team, but we came back determined to win. Players did what they had to do. Senior Chick Whistler and junior Ben Smith made excellent runs on two drives, and Rankin Koch did the scoring on quarterback sneaks. Koch also threw passes for good gains to senior Ronnie Rhoads and junior Glen Smith. The game ended with an interception by Glen.

In reviewing the film afterward, Acree criticized our lack of team play on defense and the need for us to learn basic blocking techniques on offense. Players who tackled poorly or missed blocking assignments saw their shortcomings played out on the projector screen. One player told me, "He always talked about taking pride in yourself and not letting your teammates or school down."

Fort Worth Carter Riverside

The following week we worked to fix our mistakes, improve our technique and work together as a team. "Focus" and "hustle" became watchwords in practice—focus on wrapping up a ball carrier when we hit him, then continuing to hustle after first contact when blocking or hurrying downfield to get a block or make a tackle from the backside.

Against Fort Worth Carter Riverside, our second opponent, Acree still felt unsettled with the team makeup. He shuffled the starting lineup right up until game time. Carter Riverside was a true AAAA team with linemen bigger than ours (average 200 vs. 172 pounds).

Juniors Ben and Glen Smith scored touchdowns, and junior fullback Bill Allison did most of our running. Rankin Koch completed eight of fourteen pass attempts, and Ricky Libal delivered a flawless kicking game. We fought better as a team but huffed and puffed against a larger opponent to win a close game, 17-7.

I wasn't a starter but managed to log a lot of playing time. A picture by O.E. Scarborough of Ronnie Rhoads and me making a defensive play appeared in the newspaper. The caption described us as two reasons why Carter Riverside completed only one of eleven pass attempts. Notably, most of the names called out in the newspaper were juniors, not seniors.

After the Riverside game, Acree complained about our lack of conditioning. UIL limits on practice time annoyed him, "Men, we need to get in two hours of work this afternoon in an hour and a half."

Coach Anderson, "That's right, Coach, an hour and a half."

After an hour and a half, Acree would look at his watch during a team drill and say, "Let's do that one more time, men."

After several more repetitions with slight variations, "We can't end on that. Run it again. Same song, same dance."

An hour and a half stretched into two hours.

John Tyler

Our third opponent was John Tyler, a traditional AAAA enemy. While we whipped Carter Riverside, they had smeared Dallas Adamson, 61-12. The town buzz was about defending a sixteen-game winning streak. Instead, we focused on how to stop John Tyler's fierce scoring engine. Ranked ninth in the state, the press favored the Lions to win the game. Defensive back and senior Roger Goldesberry could not play because of a leg injury. However, it allowed sophomore Mike Nekuza to play as a punt returner and defensive back.

Acree continued to juggle the list of starters. This included choosing between senior tackles Ron Cottar and Jerry Anderson, slotbacks Cody Sherrard and Chick Whistler and ends Bill Henson and Dan Wilcox. Glen Smith started as a halfback or split end. Ben Smith started at fullback instead of Bill Allison. Acree warned the Dads Club about a possible loss saying, "The team hasn't jelled."

Acree looked for consistency in team play. For example, on defense he wanted defensive backs to communicate with each other to establish coverage based on the opponent's offensive formation and the game situation. By not working together, an opponent might get an easy touchdown.

Acree wanted offensive linemen to coordinate last-second blocking adjustments based on the play called and the defensive formation presented by the opponent. This required a quick assessment of the defensive positions as we lined up, accompanied by very few communication words between adjacent linemen to clarify who had who.

I was surprised when Acree named me as a starter. In his mind, I must have "beat out" the senior who had worked as the starter in the position since two-a-days began six weeks earlier. I worked well with senior tackle Don Ivie who lived life with the same intensity as he played football—adrenaline filled excitement. Some players said he liked to party.

My dad walked a bouncy step when I told him the news after the team's Thursday night pregame meeting. I rubbed a spot on my shoulder, as we talked, but didn't tell him about the vitamin shot. He said, "I'm proud of you. You're growing up."

On Friday night, John Tyler did not score in the first half due to two interceptions—one was by senior Bruce Butler and the other by sophomore Mike Nekuza. The Lions managed a touchdown in the fourth quarter to take the lead, 0-7. Senior Chick Whistler returned the ensuing kickoff to our 31-yard line and then made a spectacular catch and run for a touchdown. No doubt Chick rose to the challenge and proved he was a leader. The score was 6-7.

More than six minutes remained in the game. Fearing we might not score again, Acree's "play to win" mindset decided to go for two extra points. Tyler had limited us to a meager thirty-five total rushing yards, but Acree called for Allison to run a slow-developing sweep to our right to get the two extra points. Allison didn't make it and we lost our first game in seventeen outings by a score of 6-7.

On the Sunday afternoon following the loss to John Tyler, Coach Acree gathered the Tigers in the Flame Room at the Lone Star Gas Company to review the game film (note: to thwart "extra effort" coaches like Acree, the UIL later banned the showing of game film to players on Sunday afternoons). Assistant Coach Jerry Moore flipped off the overhead lights, and the room went dark except for the projector splashing a blueish-white light off the screen.

The flickering light briefly reminded me of going to the Navarro Drive-In theater across from Tiger Field on Highway 31. Contrary to the film we were about to see, trips to the Drive-In with a date were pleasant. Against the hum and clickety-clacking film projector, Acree showed us our mistakes, back and forth, over and over. He explained how we could have won the game.

The failed two-point play, already etched in my memory, deserved extra attention. Acree described what the film showed. I blocked down on a man in the gap between center, Stan Rosen and me. That opened a hole for their linebacker to come through our line and jump on fullback Allison's back.

Acree calmly pointed out that Rosen, a senior, and I should have communicated and changed the blocking. Stan should have reach-blocked the defender in the gap and I should have released onto the linebacker. That would have kept him off Allison. Acree turned his head and spoke directly to me about the missed assignment. "It's hard to cross the goal line carrying a 200-pound linebacker on your back."

Even today, I rerun that play in my mind and dream of a do-over. The film review helped us see how mistakes hurt us overall. As a senior, perhaps Stan should have signaled a blocking adjustment to me. He didn't.

Maybe the play Acree called was a mistake? It was a slow-developing sweep. The Tyler linebacker keyed on Allison. A play with a better chance at scoring might have been faking a slant play-off tackle and Koch keeping the ball around the corner. That play had worked with Roman in the Graham game the previous year. Acree didn't make that call. We had to learn a life lesson—how to deal with a loss.

Other mistakes riddled the game. We had 12 penalties that cost us 132 yards. As a team, we were aggressive players who didn't let up until the whistle blew. That led to penalties for late hits. I never felt we played "dirty" like a few teams who pinched, slugged and poked when the referees were not looking.

However, referees tossed fellow linebacker and guard Bruce Butler out of the game for fighting. He was great in the boxing room, but it was unsportsmanlike conduct on the field. As a senior, it was a poor example. Acree attributed it to a lack of self-control and said, "We want our boys to be 'gentlemen tough,' not just tough for the sake of being tough."

Bruce's raw talent produced inspiring examples of hitting. Once, he narrowly missed hitting me as he flew by to deliver a crunching tackle on a receiver. Afterward, I remember saying a prayer to express gratitude that he didn't accidentally hit me.

No one admired Bruce more than I did, but he had a defiant air about him, spoke very few words and played at an emotional high that few could emulate. His striking good looks attracted girls, but most of us were just glad that we wore the same uniform as he did.

In Acree's way of thinking, we were not a good ball club. We were inconsistent and made too many mistakes. Acting out of our emotions created mental errors during a game which, according to Acree, effectively "undid hours and hours of preparation."

Jacksonville

Acree started me again both ways in our next game against Jacksonville. The Indians were always a tough team; we had to come from behind in the fourth quarter to win, 9 to 8.

Running the ball 27 times for 173 yards, junior Bill Allison proved himself as the rightful successor to Jim Hagle. We were behind 3-8 in the fourth quarter when senior Rankin Koch pulled the offense together to produce a twenty-one-play, mistake-free drive that led to the winning touchdown. He did what champions do. Koch threw passes to seniors Cody Sherrard and Chick Whistler to set up Allison's touchdown run. Senior Ricky Libal missed the extra point, so the final score ended like that of a baseball game. Nothing like the high scoring offense of 1963.

Ennis

In our last non-conference game of the season, we beat Ennis 28-3. The heroes of the game were junior Bill Allison and senior Ricky Libal. Acree was happy because we played better as a team and made fewer mistakes. Through Bill's workhorse running and three touchdowns, Acree's "fullback offense" returned.

Moreover, we hustled downfield to make blocks, which helped runs by Allison, Ben Smith and senior Ronnie Rhoads. Although I did nothing notable, my name made it into the newspaper.

Cleburne

Acree was a football mastermind. Just as quarterbacks and receivers work on timing pass routes, Acree had the linemen arrange blocks so that holes opened at precise moments. Preparing for our first District game against Cleburne, he studied the film and noticed that the Yellow Jacket's defensive lineman over my position (left guard) tended to line up on my outside (my left). This meant Don Ivie (our left tackle) could "reach block" him on a play designed to the other side and thus free me to release inside and go after their middle linebacker, Danny Elam.

Acree's idea was for me to block Elam in such a way as to drive him "out of the hole." The play was "22 dive right," a simple halfback plunge into the two-hole on the right side, opposite where I lined up. It sounds complicated, but Rankin Koch would simply front out from the snap and stick the ball into the carrying cradle of our speeding halfback, Ronnie Rhoads. If executed correctly, Rhoads could "hit the hole" running right at Danny Elam. But just as Elam prepared to make a tackle, I would come from the backside and knock him out of the way. From Rhoads' perspective, Elam would simply disappear as if he were part of a magic act. In the blink of an eye, Rhoads would be past the line of scrimmage, past the linebacker and running free in the secondary.

Sitting in the film room, concocting the play, I watched Danny Elam and imagined him to be a beast of a linebacker who would tackle Rhoads so fiercely that he might knock out his teeth. Gloating, he would stick a bloody tongue through the slots and taunt Rhoads, lying on the turf, groaning in pain. Ronnie had a hip pointer, which was extremely painful. I wanted to do my best to block Elam out of the way.

Acree assured me that Elam's first step would be to his left. All I had to do was knock him in the direction he was going anyway and move him past the hole. To further prepare, Acree had us run the play during a scrimmage in practice. I worked out a signal with Don Ivie to tell him he needed to "reach block" the man lined up on me.

When Friday night came, with our formations and play called, the Cleburne lineman across from me got into his 4-point stance. Just as the film predicted, he lined up on my left shoulder. I hollered to Ivie, our code phrase, "I'm going!" When the ball snapped, I darted toward Elam.

Ivie successfully blocked the linemen I abandoned. Simultaneously, our right guard, Bruce Butler, and center Stan Rosen double-teamed the lineman over Bruce out of the two-hole. Acree was right; Elam stepped left as Rankin Koch moved right.

When I hit Elam, it was like pushing a Volkswagen in neutral downhill. He slid past the "point of attack" and a hole opened. Rhoads squirted through into the secondary to make a nice gain. After the whistle, we patted each other on the rear and huddled up for the next play. Seniors Rhoads, Whistler, Sherrard and Koch played an exceptional game. So did Bill Allison.

The game film captured my block on Danny Elam, but town photographer O. E. Scarborough took a perfect still photo just as Rhoads hit the hole. It captured the surprise on Danny Elam's face, the mistake-free blocking and Rhoads running untouched. My name and the photo appeared in the school paper, Jungle Beast Journal, after we beat Cleburne, 35-22.

Mr. Scarborough graduated from Navarro Junior College in Corsicana, and he and his wife owned a photography studio in town. O. E. photographed just about every social event in Corsicana, including almost all sports activities. His collection of negatives spanned three decades. When he passed away, his wife closed the studio and eventually moved to Tyler to live with their son. In 2007, I tracked down his phone number and called her. I was driving, talking on my cell phone like a wheeler-dealer, ready to pay thousands of dollars to acquire his negatives. Ms. Scarborough sounded resentful over the phone, "People only wanted to pay me 25¢ here and 25¢ there."

I apologized and asked her to name a price and sell me the whole collection. She said bitterly, "I lit a fire in a 55-gallon barrel in the backyard and burned every negative."

I pulled the car over onto the shoulder and stopped. After hanging up, I took a few moments to blot the tears off my cheeks. It was as if she had informed me of the death of a loved one.

Waco High

Our offense was in glorious form against Cleburne. The following week against Waco High, our second District opponent, even the defense was ready. We beat them for the second year in a row, this time 20-0.

Waco couldn't handle junior Bill Allison's running, nor could they hold back the Tiger defensive linemen – seniors Jerry Anderson, Cody Sherrard and Don Ivie. Corsicana outrushed Waco, 321 yards to 91. Allison carried the ball 21 times for 156 yards. It was as if we were watching Jim Hagle being reborn, only more compact, with pinball-like moves; Bill was hard to "wrap up."

We once witnessed a tackler hitting Bill low, around the knees, and Allison rolled over the back of the tackler in a summersault and landed on his feet. His forward momentum set his direction, and once his feet touched the turf, Bill started running again. Even Acree was amazed as he backed up the film and played it over. I never saw Acree grin as wide as he did when he watched Allison make the "summersault" run.

I started both ways against Waco and had a good game. The team seemed to jell. We performed so well that fans felt sure we would become District 13-AAAA champions.

After the Friday-night win against Waco High, some of us gathered at Tiger Field on Saturday afternoon to play touch football. Acree encouraged us by saying, "Running around on Saturday will help work out the soreness and keep you from tightening up."

It was a beautiful fall day, and as a lineman, I played my rightful position, quarterback. Rolling right, I planted my right foot so I could turn and throw back across the field. I gasped in pain. Planting my foot, I twisted my right knee and tore a meniscus. It was excruciating. Someone ran to get Coach Anderson who was in the Field House. He applied a "cold pack" to retard the swelling. Coach Acree drove me to Dallas to see Dr. Stonie Ray Cotton, a surgeon who said I needed surgery but permitted me to continue playing until the end of the season. He added, "It will be painful," which was not a consideration for Acree.

Coach Anderson worked out a scheme to temporarily "put the meniscus tear back in place" by rotating my ankle while holding my lower leg and twisting my knee (sounds painful, but it worked). He had also performed the same magic the previous season on Jim Hagle's knee. Anderson taped my knee in a way that used pressure to help keep the tear in place and gave me the confidence I needed to run on it. Though hobbled, I was able to play the following week against Bryan.

He frequently "adjusted" and taped my knee many times the remainder of the season (even coming over to my house if needed). If I was in a game, I'd limp over to the sideline, lay on my back and relax my leg. Anderson would hold my calf in his left hand and push my knee toward my chest to "open the joint." He'd rotate my foot, left and right, back and forth, and have me straighten my leg. After a few such adjustments, he would re-tape it, and I'd be back in the game. As he was for many others, Anderson was instrumental in my journey under Acree.

Bryan

In the game film against Bryan, I could see how I favored my knee. Still, I appreciated that Acree demonstrated his loyalty to players by continuing to play us even though injured. Most would rather play with pain than stand on the sideline. He thought that was part of becoming a man.

As we traveled to Bryan to play the Broncos for our third District game, the Blue Goose broke down in just about the same place on Highway 14 where it went kaput the previous year (on the way to Victoria for the State Championship game). Even with a rebuilt engine, the bus was unreliable.

Acree got mad at it as if it were a player who loafed. He kicked it and yelled at it, but it wouldn't spring to life. Some say he struck matches and tossed them at the engine, hoping it would light on fire and burn up. A nearby town, Bremond, lent us a yellow bus to complete the trip. A few fans had also followed the team bus in private cars. They ferried Coach Anderson on to Bryan along with several players who needed extra time to get ready to play.

Senior end Danny Wilcox recovered a fumble in the game to set up a touchdown pass from Koch to Glen Smith. Ricky Libal made a clutch field goal to make the score 10-7 at the half. To score again, Rhoads, Whistler and Allison contributed to a drive that Koch finished with a touchdown pass in the end zone to senior Bill Henson. We defeated Bryan, 17-7.

To the delight of Tiger fans, that same night, Waco High defeated Waco Richfield, the team Acree had picked to win our zone. We assumed a one-game lead in our zone by defeating Bryan, but Acree was not pleased with the news. We had defeated Waco High, and he worried we might relax, thinking we had already won the zone championship. He said, "Don't think Waco High has won the zone for us."

The team needed a break from the grind without an "open date" in our schedule. We overnighted in Bryan and attended the Aggie/Razorback game on Saturday. As awesome as the crowd was in Kyle Field, Texas A&M lost to Arkansas, 17-0.

Coming home from Bryan, Acree surprised us again with an overnight stay at Hilltop Lakes Resort. As boys, we had great fun riding horses and bicycles (in my case) and swimming and fishing the next day. Exploring the large resort and forgetting about football was refreshing, if only for a day. The coaches were able to relax also. It was the right thing to do for the team. However, the UIL might have been concerned about who paid for the opportunity offered only to the football team.

Waco University

We easily beat Waco University the next week, 41-14, but we played inconsistently. This troubled Acree. At times we looked good driving the football, but three penalties stalled three drives, and we had to settle for field goals by Ricky Libal. We also botched hand-offs and turned the ball over, fumbling twice. Worst of all, we attempted a quick kick, but an errant punt snap by senior Stan Rosen gave University a touchdown when they fell on the loose ball in our end zone.

Acree continued to juggle the lineup in search of a team. He inserted the second-team backfield in the second quarter. Exciting runs by Rankin Koch, Chick Whistler, Ronnie Rhoads and Bill Allison and a fantastic catch by Glen Smith offset our mistakes to help us win the game. But we were not playing well like the championship Tigers from the year before. In describing our performance to the press, Acree used the word "spasmodic."

In hindsight, the trip to Hilltop Lakes might have been a mistake.

Waco Richfield

The zone title came down to our final game against Waco Richfield—the team Acree had picked to win it at the start of the season. Although they had lost a zone game, they would advance if they defeated us. After three grueling full-pad workout days that week, Acree described the team. "Mentally, they're just not sharp."

Nevertheless, the press put us in the top-ten AAAA ball clubs that week. We were living on the brand of the '63 Tigers, an 8-1 record and Acree's reputation. The press had not watched our recent game films and seen our Jekyll and Hyde nature. As he had done the week before, Acree started me on defense, but he started senior Nicky Sanders on offense due to my knee troubles.

Acree never failed to do all he could to get us ready to play, but what players do on the field decides the outcome of a game.

On their first possession, senior Bill Henson's tackle stopped Richfield. Suffering from a painful hip-pointer, Ronnie Rhoads fumbled on our first possession. Our defense stopped the Rams again and they punted. Unbelievably, we failed to field the ball and let it roll dead at our 6" line. It was a terrible mistake. The offense could not move the ball, so we punted, putting Richfield in good field position.

Penalties helped them move the ball half the distance to the goal line. They scored, and we were behind, 0-7.

Good teams fight back, however. On our next possession, Rhoads, Whistler and Allison, led by Koch, evened the score with only four minutes left in the half. It's as if we had remembered Acree's lectures on teamwork and his reminders of how hard we had worked to get to where we were.

On their next series, our confidence popped like a balloon when defensive back Rankin Koch misread a play-action pass after they put a back in motion. Rankin came up to take on the fake run and allowed Richfield to complete a pass to the man in motion, wide open behind him. It was an easy touchdown. The score was 7-14 at the half.

Our situation at halftime was almost identical to that in the Bonham game, our first game of the season. We trailed Bonham, 6-14 at the half but came back to overcome the deficit and win 21-14. But they were a AAA team. After the half in Waco, we didn't come out of the locker room ready to meet the challenge. In Acree's parlance, "We were not sharp."

We started the second half driving the ball, but a mistake in the backfield left it lying on the ground. Richfield recovered it. Our defense rose to stop them, however.

On our next series, the Richfield defense pressured Koch, who underthrew our receiver, resulting in an interception. Richfield scored and, with a two-point conversion, led 7-22.

Behind, Acree inserted Ricky Libal at quarterback. Richfield intercepted Libal's first pass. Our rising frustration swallowed our focus and preparation.

Our defense got the ball back for us, and Acree re-inserted Koch at quarterback. After driving the ball into scoring territory, an error in the backfield resulted in another fumble.

Even so, our defense stopped them, but when we took possession, Koch threw another interception. Deflated and emotionally drained, we allowed Richfield to score again. It was 7-29.

Acree re-inserted Libal in place of Koch. Good runs by Allison, Rhoads and a stellar catch by Glen Smith scored a final touchdown. A two-point conversion made it 15-29, and the game ended.

Richfield intercepted four Tiger passes and recovered multiple fumbles in an otherwise statistically even match. They didn't out-rush us, out-pass us or out-punt us. We had almost the same number of first downs and nearly the same yards lost in penalties.

The spokes in the Richfield team wheel did their part. They made key plays when they had to. The spokes in our team wheel broke under pressure.

Record-wise, we tied Richfield as Co-Zone champions but having defeated us, they represented the Zone in another game to decide the District champion. Our season ended with eight wins and two losses.

As a junior, I had suited up twenty-four times under Acree. It was my first bus ride home after a loss. The team was sad and silent. The trip lasted a little over an hour, but our regrets turned each minute into an eon. Thankfully, the Blue Goose didn't break down.

* * *

In writing this chapter, I talked to many seniors on the team about our disappointing game against Richfield.

One player said, "It was a low point in my playing experience. I still have its bitter taste in my mouth."

Another said, "It was a sad way to end my high school career. I had a sick feeling."

A few thought we were outcoached, saying, "They were prepared and stopped us cold."

But the game statistics tell a different story. We were evenly matched except for our mistakes.

Another senior said, "Their defensive alignments were not what we expected."

This is common in games, and we made adjustments during the game. For example, at halftime Anderson discussed with the defensive backs the fake play that tripped up Rankin Koch. We didn't fall for the same play again in the second half.

One player wrote me, "The game plan wasn't right. We had the same old playbook."

In reviewing game descriptions, our receivers were open when interceptions were thrown. Our runners were able to make significant yardage. We did have several penalties for late hits and made turnovers that killed good drives. We didn't plan to make mistakes, but we did. That's the way life is. We hope and pray that crap doesn't happen, but it does.

Most players I interviewed for this book expressed positive regard for Coach Acree, but several seniors on the '64 team declined to be interviewed. One said, "You wouldn't like what I have to say about Acree or my sophomore, junior and senior years as a football player under him."

The '64 seniors were not a close-knit group of leaders like we had on the '63 team. They failed to unite against Richfield and demonstrate a focused effort to win. We let each other down. Mistakes were our undoing. But why were there so many boneheaded moves? Had Acree overworked the team or the coaching staff? He hinted at this possibility. "Hindsight is always better than foresight, but I think we were just tired."

Some players cited that our reclassification from AAA to AAAA created a talent gap. The statistics don't support that conclusion. Several '64 seniors received D1 scholarships, including Bill Henson and Bruce Butler (SMU), Don Ivie and Ronnie Rhoads (TTU) and Ricky Libal (UofH). Stan Rosen walked on at Air Force Academy and earned a position on the team. Chick Whistler played at NE Louisiana State.

The press accepted the '64 season disappointment as a "rebuilding year." That explanation neglects the talent we had. Several seniors were named All-Zone or All-District players. Bill Allison was a future All-State player. However, Acree needed to rebuild the leadership of the '63 team, but that didn't happen. Perhaps Acree's juggling of the starting lineup robbed confidence from the seniors?

Not one to wallow in a loss, Acree didn't break out a "crying towel." He thought the Tigers had a "good season."

Going 8-2 with a co-zone title, he was right about Corsicana's ability to compete in Class AAAA. Except for penalties and punting, the Tigers outshined our AAAA competition in every category—more yards gained (passing and rushing), more first downs and fewer turnovers. Acree complimented the '64 Tigers, saying, "They worked as hard as any club we ever had."

Notably, in a post-season speech after the '65 season, Acree complimented the senior leadership on the '63 and '65 teams but omitted the '64 seniors. As an experienced coach, Acree had a seasoned view of what makes a good team. Publicly, he would agree with a summary advanced by one player, "We won as a team, and we lost as a team."

Was anyone other than the players disappointed by the '64 season? Not the Dads Club. They handed out the annual coaches' appreciation gifts as always. The fans were proud of the team, too. The yearly Tiger Loyalty Banquet sold out. In a gala ceremony, Don Ivie and Ronnie Rhoads received the lineman and back of the year awards.

But whoever selected the letter jackets that year was disappointed. Compared to the high-quality jackets of the '63 and '65 seasons, the '64 jackets were cheaply made, like white elephant gifts. The chemical smell of the fake-leather sleeves was nauseous; their pale-yellow color was disgusting. Even though mine had a "C" with two-letter bars, it stayed in the closet. Yellow was not my color. I didn't dare let my girlfriend wear it. Eventually, the stitching disintegrated, and the jacket fell apart. I removed the "C" and tossed the remains in the trash.

Acree had not won a District Championship for the first time in his coaching career. That next August, in '65, he sat alone in his office at the Field House and contemplated how to build a new team from the returning seniors—boys like me, juniors on the '64 squad.

He would have to do it without his experienced team of assistant coaches. After the end of the 64-65 school year, Raymond Anderson resigned from coaching to become a full-time school administrator. Jerry Moore resigned to take a college coaching position at SMU. Jerry Matthews left to coach basketball in Corpus Christi.

Acree couldn't leave; his oldest daughter Susan's senior year was 65-66. He had opportunities to go elsewhere but turned them down.

To sort out the troubles in his mind, he put on his green rain slicker and tied the laces on his running shoes. He headed out the back door and started a run to the Green House.

1963-64 Coaches Raymond Anderson, Paul Slaughter, Jerry
Matthews, Jerry Moore, and Jim Acree (seated)

After a victory in 1965. Jimmy Prater (bent over), Gary Schutte (37),
Ronnie Ragsdale, Ronnie Ward (41), Gary Buchanan (32)

CHAPTER 10 RUN TO THE GREEN HOUSE

"If you can fill the unforgiving minute
With sixty seconds' worth of distance run,
Yours is the Earth and everything that's in it,
And—which is more—you'll be a Man, my son!"
If— by Rudyard Kipling

Exhausted, feeling gritty and sweaty in my football practice uniform, I come off one knee to start a slow jog toward the Green House. The team just finished a full-pad, two-hour, two-a-day workout under a hot August sun.

I catch a whiff like that from a bag of rotten onions on the produce aisle at Piggly Wiggly. We angle across the practice field toward the back gate. Our bodies need a drink. A teaspoon of water would taste sweet, but only a lake could quench our thirst.

Partly to simplify breathing, our open mouths resemble the cracks in the dried ground that passes under our feet. They express the surprise of another seemingly endless demand from Coach Jim Acree.

We had gathered around him, thinking it was the end of practice, but after a brief critique of what he considered a dismal practice, he noted our lack of conditioning, then finished by commanding us, "Run to the Green House."

A trip to the Green House meant I was still two miles away from a drink, a shower, clean clothes, food and a date. We were boys who came to play football, but Acree wanted men toughened physically and mentally to win games. As a senior beginning my third year playing for Acree, his demands no longer shocked me. I just thought he was crazy.

As the team moved across the wilted grass of the practice field, we formed a javelin-shaped line that aimed toward the southern opening in the perimeter fence. Beyond it was West Park Row, a one-lane concrete slab traveling west toward the sun.

Acree's face displays his disappointment as he drives the school's surplus jeep across the rocky parking lot to the exit gate. He leaves stunned boys in his wake. Like the team's sour mood, the dust from the road curls up with the jeep's exhaust smoke to foul the hot, dry air. We need more work to get ready for the upcoming season. Acree isn't happy to end our practice. He makes sure we aren't satisfied either.

To conserve air for the next stride, we talk very little among ourselves, but most of us whisper short expletives in the direction of the jeep.

Writing this almost six decades later, I realize Acree was the coaching equivalent of a horticulturalist attempting to graft us into his root system. If successful, we'd take on his competitive nature to win and grow a desire to outwork an opponent. The fruit would be our transformation into men who would become winners, regardless of what obstacle life put in front of us. If not successful, he didn't give up. He redoubled his efforts and pressed further until boys either quit or became examples of endurance.

Acree was dictatorial and brutal, forcing us to endure endless, painful experiences, mostly football-related such as excessive running, contact drills, boxing, grass drills and monkey bars. Rather than causing us to quit, he hoped to toughen us to fight through adversity, which inevitably happens in football and in life. Some boys did resign the team, but not everyone who endured Acree escaped with positive regard for Coach.

As I ran toward the slab to become a man like Acree, he taught me that I could improve myself through dogged, personal effort. I learned that surviving his ways could change a boy into a champion or embitter a soul. For the latter type, wisdom for a successful life would have to come from elsewhere.

I am just one example. Some boys look back on Acree and reject the man and his methods. Implicitly, they also condemn Corsicana's collective tolerance of him and his desire to win. The town wanted boys to become men in the community. But only the players have a deep, experiential understanding of Acree's effect on our lives.

As our grumbling subsides, we plunge into our thoughts. To establish a rhythm, I silently count my steps, "1, 2, ..., 39, 40, 1, 2, ...". Like enumerating lashes from a whip, I reset the count at "40." I time my footfalls to set a pace with a clock ticking in my head, "..., 8, 9, 10, ..." Two years of running under Acree have conditioned me to know the level of effort he expects. "Do your best. Give all you've got."

Without rain, the August sun bakes the black soil into a dry crust and turns green grass into a yellow-brown straw. The heat extracts the energy of even the wind. The hot air is motionless except for shimmering particles of dust floating in the sunlight. Strides of the boys in front of me kick more debris into the haze.

Some of the boys have an Acree-level desire and take off like jackrabbits. I think of Marc Maxwell, a senior on the '63 team. In thought, I see him jump out ahead in a group run to the Green House and race to be the first to finish. Maxwell wanted to please the coaches, particularly Acree. He hoped for a reward of more playing time in a game or even a cherished starting position.

I move across the field, and grasshoppers occasionally take flight in a taunting fashion, skipping ahead a few yards as if to say, "Catch me if you can."

Their scattering flights remind me of a youthful, disorganized style of pick-up football on a vacant lot with neighborhood kids. A gaggle of grade-school buddies, choosing sides, picking out goal lines, agreeing on simple rules—three completions make a first down, no running the ball—funny remembrances of friends in an unruly huddle, reporting "I can beat him," with a leader hurriedly making plans for a play, drawing assignments in the dirt, knowing a sure touchdown would happen, laughing when it did, bantering as we celebrated, drinking from a water hose when we ended the fun.

I lick my lips but feel only crusty dirt set in dried spittle. The actual game of football is for men. It's not ad hoc, but coached, timed, measured and played before crowds. Record books keep scores. The men in the town brag about their team. Fathers beam with pride when their sons win. Mothers tell stories about their boys' achievements. Wins matter in Corsicana.

I think, "How fast I went from a t-shirt and cutoffs on a vacant lot to a helmet, pads and cleated shoes on a striped field, playing under bright lights, people cheering, bands playing and cameras rolling."

Changing from kid to a boy happens quickly like that of switching from street clothes into a padded uniform. The transformation from a boy to man, though, is slow, requiring a seemingly endless number of strides, one after another, on a run not marked by distance but by achievements and failures. In football, it's a good block, a missed tackle, a good run. But the making, maturing and erosion of dreams to become a man is damn hard under Jim Acree.

Stirring the drifting dust from his jeep as I approach the gate, I pace with linebacker Ronnie Ragsdale. Friends from youth and running side-by-side now, we both come under the examining glare of a new coach, Don Ross who replaced Raymond Anderson. Acree dropped Ross off to open the gate and then proctor it. His instructions were, "Make sure all the boys pass through onto the slab and turn toward the Green House."

Coach Ross was more like Coach Anderson – not driven like Acree.

* * *

The high shrubbery near the roadside obscures Acree's jeep, which rolls west on the slab into heat waves shimmering off the pavement. Like the wild shrubs that line the slab, Acree was a big man, 6'-3", 215 pounds. His exterior prevents us from making sense of why he has us running to the Green House. We understand the need to get in shape, but not with the overbearing intensity he deems necessary to achieve it.

Fearing punishment, we yield to his authority and follow his rules. After all, we want to play football. Why he drives us to the point of quitting is anyone's guess. Running nearby, Ragsdale speaks, "The only thing on his mind is winning."

A dozen boys dropped out the first week of two-a-days. "Why don't we quit, too?", I replied.

"Don't know. Too dumb, I guess."

"He says we've invested a lot."

"What's one more trip to the Green House?"

Ross saw two linebackers, matched in height and weight—both starters, quick to read offensive sets, but neither with remarkable talent. To him, we were "coach's players." Two boys who worked hard in practice and hustled on drills but were not playmakers. Our glory belonged with that of the team, not in individual stories.

I pass through the gate first and look right, down to the bend in the road. Acree's jeep is already out of sight. I inhale the lingering exhaust from the jeep. I cough, then wheeze, and think, "Ross will let me go back to the Field House and use my asthma inhaler."

Anderson would too. That's the difference between Acree and the other coaches. They say yes. He says no. And Acree would add a kick in the rear for asking.

Thinking, "Get this over with. Going to the Green House and back is the goal."

I run, ignoring a stab of pain in my chest. The struggle last season of playing with the pain of an injured knee taught me not to quit because of a bit of pain. "Breathe shallow until I get out of this."

A different person now and a senior under Acree, I am determined to defend my position as a starter. That role will pass soon enough to another player after I graduate.

Ross butts into the conversation in my head, "Ward. Pick it up!"

Off the grassy field that had tugged at my steps, my pace quickens on the slab, "1, 2, 3, ..." I scold myself, "Slow down. Slow down!"

I remember what my dad said about running a quarter mile when I tried out for the track team, "Don't start like a house on fire and burn down!"

I seldom think of my dad without also thinking of my granddad. He questioned me about trying different sports in junior high and then choosing football. He thought it was a mistake. His generation preferred boxing and baseball.

Football was king in Corsicana. I quit baseball, got a job and worked to earn money to buy a car, but now Acree, the crazy man, wanted me to run everywhere.

Acree likes running. The dads in the booster club like Acree. He wins football games. The town wants winners. Acree calls us men. Men outdo their opponents. They study the game, fix their mistakes, look for an edge and play to win. If choosing sides, Corsicana would want to be on the men's team. The boys' team would lose.

Ross prods us, "You're supposed to be leaders!" His booming voice pierced the earholes in the other helmets that passed through the gate at that moment, reminding every player of what Acree expected. "Hustle! Don't settle for second place."

Wanting to please him, "Yes, sir, Coach!" then to myself, "..., 10, 11, 12."

Passing through the gate, the team moves like a snake around a corner, curving, bunching up and thrusting forward. With a turn of the head, I catch sight of two teammates coming up from the B-team. They seldom play. I wonder, why do they stay? Why are they doing this damn run to the Green House?

Surely their parents understand the hell Acree puts them through? Did they make a pact with each other? Do they stay to support another friend?

Maybe they stay because they are not on game film for Acree to criticize and embarrass in front of the rest of us? If Acree thinks a boy has more to give, he demands it like a ransom from further intimidation. His unreasonable requirements are humiliating as they were for Nicky Georges. Too big and not strong enough to hand walk the parallel bars without touching his feet, Acree sent him to the Green House.

Ross yells, "Move over to the shoulder," and the line of boys obeys. First, our cleats were on the concrete slab, "click-click-click," which turned to "crunch-crunch-crunch" as we moved onto the dirt-packed gravel, patchy grass and clumps of weeds. I step carefully to avoid twisting an ankle. Ragsdale trails behind me. The line of boys, again in single file, stretches the length of a football field.

Out of Ross' earshot, I ask, "Worried about us getting run over?"

Ragsdale hears the sarcasm and replies, "Always."

Suspecting Acree has some scheme in mind, I ask, "What gives? Why run wearing full pads?"

Ever logical, Ragsdale replies, "And why wear helmets?"

Joking, I say, "So we can butt heads with the jeep at the turnaround?"

"More likely, grab us by the facemask," says Ragsdale, "and pound a fist on the top of our heads."

I add, "Bottom fisted like a sledgehammer!"

Acree supposed football sense was like a spike that could be driven into our heads. He wouldn't miss an opportunity to pound it deeper. Worried, I think, "What is the surprise that crazy-ass has for us at the jeep?"

After 200 yards, the road bends right. Cars had cut the corner, dropped a wheel off the slab, pushed mud, dirt and pebbles into a knoll, and changed the shoulder into a treacherous rut next to a mound. Anxious, not wanting to stumble or fall, I look down and place my footfalls to avoid the blackness of the rut. Shadows of players running in front of me dance on the ground.

My eye picks out the round, dark shadow of a player's helmeted head. "Dark hair is attractive," I think.

Rags' sister, a brunette, has a pretty smile. A memory of her plays like a movie in my head. She starts to move and talk. I forget I'm running.

She inspects the framing of an apartment building under construction on the lot where neighborhood boys once played touch football. Walking the concrete slab, she weaves effortlessly in and out of the wall studs, her body just developing and her eyes sparkling. She smiles, flirting-like. I watch as she runs off toward home giggling—too young, not a woman. The movie stops playing as if the film breaks, but it's Acree interjecting himself into my thoughts.

"Acree calls us men, but I'm not a man," I think. My girlfriend comes to mind, not a football. She has dark hair. She listens and doesn't blab. We have fun together, but a different kind of fun than Acree football. I have no idea how to become a man playing for Acree. It's just a word.

Ahead, a narrow, one-lane bridge carried the slab over a small creek. Acree stopped the jeep at the bridge and looked back up the slab. Which boys have the lead in the run? The leaders set an example for the slackers. Others are satisfied to limit themselves.

Acree had said as much in his pre-season letter to the players. "The difference between being GOOD and being GREAT is a matter of extra effort."

He liked hustle to see which boys did that extra bit. Now was the time for doing, Acree believed. "It's always easier to TALK about doing things. It's much more difficult to WORK to accomplish your objectives."

Acree had learned the benefit of running from Tallchief. It was the trait of a warrior. A heart that decides to run longer than its adversary results in exceptionalism. He runs us as though we can prove we'll outlast a foe in the waning moments of a game. And then he'll run us more to be sure. To win against larger AAAA opponents will exhaust our store of energy. Acree must enable some hidden desire for us to win. He can count on the runners, especially those who were like him—exceptional.

Noting the seniors leading the line of boys, Acree cranks the jeep and motors further west toward the turnaround point. Liberty Road intersects the slab and on the southeast corner sits a one-story house, painted green. Whoever named it "Liberty" was a sadist. Only another notch on the road to being a man. There was no freedom in reaching it.

* * *

Acree left assistant Coach Slaughter at the bridge, "Ensure no player tries to hide under it and rejoin others on the return leg." Bill Allison once tried to hide and got caught. His was not the first attempt to cheat Acree and suffer for it.

Slaughter was a big man, but he hardly ever raised his voice, never bullied us or used force, but instead patiently taught us, believing steady encouragement would triumph. He shouted at the linebacker pair as we crossed the bridge, "Keep it up, men."

"Always, Coach!"

Recalling having tattled on me, Slaughter barks, "Do it right, Ward."

I reply, "Yes, sir!"

I recall the terrible day I wore school-issued athletic socks to Slaughter's government class. I was issued a pair of socks without holes at the previous day's practice, a rare prize. The temptation was too great. I kept them after the workout to wear the next day, not thinking it would set a bad example of using school property for personal benefit. A man wouldn't do that.

When I arrived at the Field House for the afternoon session, Slaughter had already briefed Acree on my poor example. With forty-plus boys in various stages of undressing and dressing in front of their lockers, Acree stepped out of the coach's office into the dressing room naked and loudly berated me. My locker was directly across from his office door. Acree condemned me and warned me never to do such a thing again.

The room fell quiet. All the boys were as still as rabbits that heard a predator's call. Acree enumerated my punishments, which came like claps of thunder. I lowered my head in shame, my eyes falling; my gaze passed from Acree's angry red face down to his hairy chest, then to his slight gut, and then his words were suddenly silenced, replaced in my thoughts by the image of Acree's male nakedness.

Even growing up in a home with six people and one bathroom, I had only once caught a glimpse of my father, uncovered, coming out of the shower. Like this incident, and brief as it was, it too seized my mind, locked it in curiosity and amazement, and I wondered about my future manliness; was that my destiny, too?

Disciplinary actions by Acree were beyond harsh, but like a father, he cared for each boy, and as such, each formed their own opinion, some hating him, others loving him, most respecting him. Acree was a winner, and a winner attracts followers, even if his torture tools included unbearably painful public reprimands. Acree had kicked me physically, but I was not a squaw man. I would not quit. He had changed me. More profound than my yearning to become a man, I also wanted to be a winner.

Beyond the bridge, about a quarter-mile, the shoulder of the slab both flattened and widened and sloped up to a hump in the slab. On cresting it, Acree would come into view, again sitting in the jeep waiting and watching. The line of boys lengthens and separates—the boys' group by their desire, talent, camaraderie and grit.

The natural runners take the lead, and the reluctant plodders lag. Out of Acree's sight, a few interspersed running with walking.

Boys bunched like clusters of grapes whose muscadine vines spread along the fence line and through the low bushes on each side of the slab. Disturbed by the runners, the cicadas chirp a song in high decibels matching the summer temperature.

The infrequent cedar, oak and Mexican Buckeye provide shade only along the fence, not on the slab, the shoulder or the runners. Occasionally, a resident from a house next to the slab ventures into their backyard, into the afternoon heat, maybe to unclip dry clothes hanging on a line and look up to watch the boys as we pass. I imagined them thinking, "Running in this heat? What fools must they be!"

The sun broils us from above, and its reflection off the slab bakes us from below. Parched, sore and sapped, relief could only come through my legs.

I need to complete the run. My goal is to get off the slab. The thought of making it to the hump pushes me forward like a newborn turtle racing across an open beach to make it to safety.

Back at the gate, Coach Ross watched the last of the boys slowly disappear around the bend in the slab. As Anderson did, I hoped he would counterbalance Acree's punitive methods. He gave us three salt tablets and a cup of water before practice.

Acree approved "ice breaks" to help hydrate us, but Jimmy Prater learned not to hide ice in his socks. Acree spotted the telltale bumps in the sock tubing covering chunks of ice around Prater's ankles, so he commanded Prater to run laps around the practice field. Prater ran until he vomited. Coach Ross didn't speak up—maybe because of his newness or perhaps he didn't know what was happening?

No one goes against Acree, but Coach Anderson or Coach Moore would have interceded on Prater's behalf. Anderson's experience in the Navy taught him how to speak to authority, but he was gone now, sitting in some air-conditioned office in the school administration building, oblivious to the torture Acree inflicted. Anderson had learned how to dampen Acree's methods yet still have us ready to fight on the playing field to win even when exhausted.

A few dads were scattered along the fence around the practice field, watching the workout. They didn't object either. Like Acree, their focus was on winning. No one questioned Acree for pushing us so hard, practicing us so long and conditioning us to near collapse. He was teaching us to outlast an opponent, but inadvertently, they showed us how to excuse a man preoccupied with winning.

Acree acted like a Texas cowboy, single-handedly breaking a herd of wild mustangs so that he could trust them to deliver at the goal line.

Times were radical, however. Kennedy had been assassinated. The sexual revolution was underway. Vietnam was heating up. The space race intensified against communist Russia. Boys had cars and were going to college in large numbers. Acree said, "As a country, we will regret raising a generation of 'soft' men."

I didn't see any soft boys on the slab. I saw a cluster of runners ahead, cresting the hump, some sophomores from their size and gate; others I recognize only by the size of their hearts. Acree loves to see boys hustle with hearts pounding in their chests, and see players trying and pushing to get better. I think, "We'll see who lasts, who walks with his hands on his hips, who puts two hands on his knees, who stoops then staggers."

My brother Dickey had dropped out and would never experience what it was to become a winner—Acree's way. After joining the Marine Corps, he said, "Boot camp was easier than two-a-days under Acree."

Coaches love players who expend themselves in training as if they were in a game—those who eat, sleep and watch a game film as if winning football games was their purpose in life. As a sophomore, I was on the B-team and had a good game as a linebacker on a muddy field against Duncanville. On Slaughter's good report, Acree moved me to the varsity the following week. Acree's quick action taught Slaughter not to brag on his players, at least not to Acree.

I loved the A-team prestige, the pep rallies, riding the Blue Goose, warming up on the field under the night lights, the crowd gathering, the band playing, the cheerleaders jumping, the thrill of the playoff game series, the glory of a state championship, a celebratory dinner with champagne and wearing a fine-quality letter jacket.

Winning casts a spell on boys, charms them to give their hearts and bodies up, captures them like the excitement of a beautiful girl and teases them with the possibility of further validation that they are men. Quitters would never know its effect under Acree. Neither would boys with attitudes soured by his methods.

Climbing to the hump, I want to satisfy the urges that push me forward, to complete a practice under a hot sun, to finish a run to the Green House or to become a man. Desires that I do not understand drive me.

Should I focus like Acree, always striving to win? Should I become like Anderson, a caring man, or Slaughter, a gentle man or be like my father, who walked prouder than ever, having a Marine as a son and another starting on an Acree team?

A senior carries the burden of leading. I guarded my words, became introspective and saw the coming season as my last chance to win another championship, after which I would graduate and pass into the unknown, a place where seniors scattered, perhaps never to see each another again.

An internal clock sounds an alarm, lost in thoughts about disappearing and the possibility of further conquest in Corsicana. Going up the slight incline toward the hump, my pace slows. Reacting, my heart thumps faster, and my steps quicken, "1, 2, 3, ..." I push to top the hump.

At the crest, I look back and see the last of the boys in the long string walking across the bridge. I also see a heavy tackle saving up to make it to the turnaround. I hope Acree doesn't see him walking.

Ahead, the slab has a slight dip where a shimmering pool appears under the hot sun as if it were water, and blue like the sky, sparkling and inviting. But there's no water.

It is a mirage; I think of how my girlfriend's eyes sparkle. I first saw her at Beebe Field, where Jr. High boys went to flirt with girls. She soon wore my letter sweater, earned while playing 9th-grade football at Collins. Unlike my redheaded sisters and bleached-blond mother, she was a brunette. Proudly my steady now for two years, I upgraded the sweater to a state championship jacket.

I run past a classmate's house that backs up to the slab. We hardly know one another. She was captivating when wearing a buttoned blouse.

Excitement surges within, filling me with an urge to reach the oasis. "...,7, 8, 9, ..."

Such fantasies frustrate me. Chase them, and they prove to be just that, unreal. One tip proved false on a date that lasted but 30 minutes. Never again would I listen to gossip from other boys.

Boys exaggerated and likely lied. For a man, a relationship must be physical, but she must also share conversation, laughter, music and dance. Dancing close with her to "Moon River" set my dreams in motion; surely, their slow, steady, rhythmic steps would lead to me being a man someday.

The seniors of the '63 season were men now. They were off pursuing their dreams, and only their reputations linger—the "cherry picker," the "heartbreaker" and the "crazy one." I was still a boy fantasizing, but in a short time, my football nickname "spear" would become only a memory.

After passing the mirage, I see Acree 200 yards ahead sitting in the open-top jeep at the turnaround. The lead runners are circling it to start their run back.

I imagine the slab as a narrow road leading to becoming a man like Acree. Every boy must run it himself if he wants to be such a man. But I think, "If I had a new Oldsmobile 442 rather than an old Ford, I could impress my friends."

With such a car, Jeff Walker attracted friends. He came out for football but quit.

I had seen David Niven in *Bedtime Story* and aspired to have a sophisticated appearance, well-shined shoes, refined manners and an ability to speak French. I thought, "A man could live with such misery."

* * *

Acting like progress markers, I imagine the expansion joints in the slab as tick marks on a giant yardstick measuring my progress step-by-step, getting closer to Acree, toward becoming a man, but further from Ross and Slaughter.

To me, they are strong and trustworthy men, liked by others. Becoming like them is appealing, but how to do it is a mystery.

I now make out other players' faces on the return run. I see the blank looks behind their facemasks. To cope, they retreat into their imaginations, too.

To encourage them as they pass, I yell, "Way to go! Hang in there!"

Wanting to make a good impression as I approach Acree, I tighten my waist and straighten my back. A good running form hides my fear. I don't want him yelling at me if I appear to struggle while running. Acree would think I am out of shape, or loafing. A kick in the butt would follow.

I want his approval. I want to please him. I look up the gentle incline to see him in the jeep and tell myself, "Look good."

As I reach the jeep, I lock eyes with Acree, whose head rotates to follow my steps to circle the jeep. I hope he can see the determination on my face. I want him to see my desire. I wish he could see how angry I am.

Earlier, during practice, we were scrimmaging each other. Acree called a reverse play where I pulled from my right-side guard position to block the offside tackle. The play design was a reverse, such that the ball carrier would run through the open hole in the line behind me if I moved the defensive tackle out of the hole.

My assignment was to hit a sturdy sophomore tackle, David Derryberry. As a boy with a short barrel-like body, David had solid legs shaped like 12-inch diameter steel pipes driven into the ground. Knocking him away from the hole would require a tremendous hit.

The first time Acree ran the play, I improvised and thought I could smother Derryberry. By collapsing over him, I prevented him from touching the passing running back. But that was not what Acree wanted. Returning to the huddle, I looked into his eyes and immediately knew he was not pleased. "Run it again, men."

Acree wanted me to hit him, not finesse him. The second time, I went low on David, hoping to knock his legs out from under him. Instead, I banged against him as if I had run into two adjacent fire hydrants. Derryberry didn't move. I collapsed down to the ground in the hole. The running back had nowhere to go. Immediately, I heard, "Run it again, men!"

The third time, I aimed my helmet at Derryberry's mid-section, which he defended with a padded elbow. He sought to please Acree, too. I exploded into David, but my feet left the ground too early; I couldn't maintain a steady pushing power. I failed to move him. Dazed and tired, I heard Acree say, "Drive them feet, Ward! Run it again, men!"

The fourth time, I was angry and looked down, not wanting anyone to see my tears. It hurt like hell to hit Derryberry. As a senior, everyone could see that I couldn't block him. It was humiliating. However, Acree conditioned me not to give up.

When the snap came, I rotated left, quick-like, from a four-point stance, stayed low in perfect form and raced full-speed down the line toward Derryberry. Knowing I was coming, he squatted and crouched near the ground like a German tank, dug in, waiting for the arrival of an incoming artillery shell.

Moments before reaching Derryberry, I gathered my arms and coiled my body, tensed my muscles, and with all the momentum I could muster, I launched my weight at David to knock him away from the hole. I continued pumping my feet and moved him out of the way like a man pushing a stalled car in neutral off the road. The back sailed through the opening.

Without looking at Acree, I stood tall and returned to the huddle. With a slight grin, Acree looked at me, "I knew you could hit. I wanted you to know it, too."

At the turnaround, making my way around the jeep, Acree inspired confidence, "You can do it, Ward! Get going, Ragsdale. Keep your heads up, men."

The Green House faced north. It had a wooden front porch that wrapped around to the east side. A bay window with a high, gabled roof protruded from a front-facing room on its west side. The protrusion and a low roof shielded the porch from the sun. A single tree shaded the backyard. Its shiplap siding sagged. Its green paint peeled off, giving it an old, weathered look. The covered windows in the front slumped. The house looked like it was crouching to defend itself against the sun.

Having two red brick chimneys, the high-ridged roof baked in the heat like the boys in front of it running on the slab. No one ever seemed to be at home. Perhaps its occupants fled down Liberty Road to find a cooler place in the countryside?

Green House, Google Maps, "Streetview," digital images, January 2022 (http://maps.google.com)https://goo.gl/maps/1BvRTJBY5R8kdLTt8)

Gone were all the greats of the '63 championship team. They, too, had seen the Green House from the slab. They were boys who became men and proved it by winning a series of close playoff games. Players such as Jim Wood had seen the slump of the Green House on a hot August day. He modeled a linebacker and guard for me. I assumed the positions he'd played. I thought, "I would like to be remembered like Jim."

Never a showoff, Wood stood cross-legged, hands-on-hips, elbows out, game-faced, with penetrating eyes that glared at opponents. He was stout as an oak, spoke few words, but smiled often. He laughed when amused and delivered a forearm blow that stopped blockers dead still. It seemed that he was always prepared to win.

Heading back toward the dip with a tired look, I struggle to maintain a good running form, keep my back straight, head up and not stumble. I think, "This damn helmet is heavy."

I get Ragsdale's attention and say, "Acree wants us to run with helmets on to strengthen our neck muscles."

He replies, "Or learn to view the world from inside a helmet."

At the thought of having decoded Acree, I crack a brief smile. It's delightful to put reason to his madness. Winning validated his ways to improve and make boys stronger—ways that made him proud as a man— ways to rise above the rest—ways to win and make the town proud— ways that infuriated some boys.

The sun burns on my back and saps my desire to keep running back toward the hump. What would I rather do? Give in to the weakness I feel in my legs, sit in the shade of a tree and go to sleep? That's not what Acree would do. He'd focus on the next step. Take one after another. Challenge himself to continue running.

I look up to the hump and see what must be the last of the boys coming over it to make their way to the Green House. Runners litter the slab traveling in each direction. Occasionally, we nod to each other, but generally, we avoid eye contact. No one wants to peer into someone else's misery.

As the heavier boys continue to move toward Acree, the sound of the heaviness in their footfalls drums a steady march toward their becoming men. The scratch of their cleats grabbing for purchase, the swish of nylon-covered thighs rubbing together, and the short breaths became rhythmic with each stride, one step after another. Combined, they give the sound of drudgery in motion.

I pass a driveway, then another. Suddenly, I become conscious of the sound of a car coming from behind me on the slab. I can see boys ahead scurrying to give way; the driver slows and passes through the scatter but then guns the engine, creating a cloud of exhaust. We suck down a foul-tasting gulp of air, losing precious breaths. Coughing adds to the song of drudgery. In a whisper, Ragsdale asks, "What would Acree do?"

I reply, "Run down the car and make the driver's life miserable."

We both chuckle.

As a running buddy, Ragsdale encourages me, "Keep going, man. We don't lack much."

Having good friends made life bearable under Acree.

I didn't let go of the thought of Acree in the jeep. We called him "Coach Acree" but could have easily called him "Lord Jim." Always controlling, he had a massive presence. He was the centerpiece of Corsicana's fanatic football focus. He had silenced the surrounding devils, Palestine, Athens, Tyler, Ennis, Waxahachie, Cleburne and Waco.

The man, Acree, dominated a conversation as if he were a charging linebacker delivering judgment on a puny, unfortunate ball carrier, destined to pay the price for expressing a boy's opinion. I had talked to him about making senior Glen Smith the team's quarterback instead of

282

Acree's choice of junior Mike Nekuza. He scolded and reminded me that he was in charge of the team.

Acree leveled the players and humbled anyone who thought he had a better idea. There was no room for jealousy on the team or petty affairs. What mattered was an attitude of playing to win as a team. As unreasonable as I thought Acree was, I respected him and sometimes wished I was like him, but I was not exceptional like that man.

Acree taught football like a parent teaching a child to play a game, showing a player how to do it, watching him do it, pointing out his mistakes and making him do it repeatedly. And doing it until he could react without making mistakes. Until he could perform it even though he was exhausted. Until he could play to win.

At times, I was grateful for Coach Acree. He drove me to Dallas Methodist Hospital for knee surgery (my parents worked and couldn't take off). When I woke on the hospital bed, he stood over me as I puked green bile. Groggy and disoriented, I mumbled, "Coach, I need to pee."

The small bathroom was across the room from my hospital bed, located on the far wall. Acree threw back the white sheet to uncover me and, in full Acree mode said "Well get up and go pee."

I pointed at my knee, "But Coach, my leg is in a cast."

He retorted, "If you want to pee, you will have to walk yourself to the commode."

Groggy, wanting to puke, with a bladder about to burst, I somehow climbed off the bed and hobbled over to the bathroom. I was in such a stupor that I peed my hospital gown a bit. I limped back to the bed and managed to climb into it. Acree said, "See, you can do what you have to do."

I cross back over the hump and see the bridge below with Slaughter waiting beside it. Tired, I shorten my steps, straighten again to be more upright and feel as if I'm running in place with the small physical steps. My feet are fiery hot inside my shoes. I think, "I have to get off this slab."

Successive expansion joints that cross the slab change to become mini-finish lines. I strive to run from joint to joint. I count the number of strides between them—20, 21, 19, 20 or was it 18?

I approach the bridge, and I admire Slaughter, a man who steadily performs his job, not so ambitious as to create conflicts with other men, but resourceful, always helpful, not trying to impress but making a difference doing what he must do.

Unlike him, I could not be a patient teacher. Instead, I need to follow a mentor who will inspire me to improve, someone who will not tolerate a slacker and challenge me to achieve and excel, a man like Acree. I grunt, "Almost done, Coach!"

"You men are doing fine," observes Slaughter. "Go on and finish up."

The lead runners round the bend toward the gate. I feel the gentle climb away from the bridge and remind myself, "I enjoy being a boy and playing football. Going on dates. Working at Piggly Wiggly."

What kind of man would fit inside of me? My dad wants a smart man. Slaughter wants an honest, hardworking, good man. Acree wants an exceptional man.

I think of my girlfriend and just want to be a man.

The glare off the slab is as white as a welder's arc. I squint to see ahead clearly. Salty sweat covers my face and my eyes sting. I can't wipe them because of the helmet. I told myself, "Acree knew that and wants us to feel the sting."

I consider yanking the helmet off, but more than anything, I want to reach the finish line. I continue to try to please Acree, but what kind of man will I become?

I run the curve around the bend, and Ross comes into view at the gate. A cloudless, blue sky stretched across the pavement like a banner across a finish line. Ross barks loud, "Run hard through the finish. Don't loaf!"

Every stride becomes a struggle, but as Acree's boys we keep running. We find something inside ourselves that pushes us ahead faster, but my thoughts jumble like loose marbles in a drawer. I want to finish. I expect to. I hope to win, but unlike Acree, I know I'm not special. Ross yells, "Run! Run through the finish! Don't let up!"

I pass back through the gate with Ragsdale beside me to finish the run. We collapse into a slow jog toward the Field House. Like manhood, it's not too far away.

We didn't understand what we accomplished on the run except for completing another demand. Perhaps in crossing the finish line, we became a little more like the men Acree wanted us to be. We started with an ounce more boy in us, but Acree had replaced it with a bit more of a man by the finish.

Prepared to win, we believed we would win, so we played the game to win and never quit.

He intended to turn us into players on a local stage, but after graduation, we could play anywhere in life. Running to the Green House under Acree achieved that much.

I wasn't there to see the last of the boys make the turnaround. Rumors of Acree's actions against the walkers are legendary. Did he follow them back in the jeep, prodding them like cattle, honking his horn, humiliating them, or was it true that upon their return, he had them run the bleachers in the stadium, lap the cinder track or do a few more grass drills? Whether we liked him or not, he challenged all of us to become men.

CHAPTER 11   CLASS AAAA PLAYOFF TALENT

"The ability of a team to become a champion is based on very few simple fundamentals. These are 1. More will to win than your opponent. 2. Better physical condition than your opponent. 3. Be physically tougher than your opponent. 4. Execute the fundamentals of football – blocking, tackling and running – better than your opponent. 5. Make fewer errors than your opponent."

Jim Acree, Off-season letter to players before 1965 season

The 1965 football season had many firsts. We made the playoffs as a AAAA team, a first in Acree's career and Corsicana history. Winning a AAAA District championship was also a first for the thirty-three boys on the team.

We earned a spot in one of the state's AAAA quarterfinal games without losing or tying in twelve straight games. Only eight AAAA teams remained from the 126 that started the '65 season. The press ranked us the number four team in the state.

At halftime in the quarterfinal game, however, we trailed behind San Antonio Lee 14-20.

Our coaches covered offensive and defensive play adjustments, then Acree and his assistants left us alone in the locker room at UT Memorial Stadium. Going out the door, Acree turned and said, "Don't come out unless you make up your minds to win the game."

286

Usually, the coaches came out of the locker room with the team. But the situation was not normal. Most of the players were silent in the oversized room. A few boys focused on the problem and spoke encouraging words. Others shook their heads and stared at the floor in disbelief that we were losing.

My friend and defensive tackle, Lynn Odom, whispered to me, "Ronnie, I can't beat the guy in front of me."

Acree had said, "All you have to do is beat the man across from you."

As defensive captain, I called our defensive formations, but I didn't know how to help Odom. I said, "Lynn, we have no one tougher than you. Go out there and knock him on his butt."

We lost track of time. In what seemed like the brief period to buckle a chin strap, an angry referee shoved open the locker room door and aggressively waved for us to follow him. He yelled, "Get out to the field or you'll forfeit the game!"

We rose, put on our helmets and walked out of the locker room. We ran to the sideline where Acree waited for us. He was clapping his big hands and wearing his blue shirt. We had no idea how the game would end, but he did.

Acree leaving us in the dressing room was a mistake. Exceeding the half-time period by a reasonable amount, the referees penalized us 15 yards for being late to take the field at the start of the second half.

Acree football was about winning, but supposedly football mirrors life. If that's the case, losses are bound to happen. If an Acree football team is losing at halftime, it's possible for setbacks in life to happen—for example, the ending of a long-term relationship with a girlfriend. Notably, seniors like me would soon graduate and enter life's playoffs.

In the football playoffs, we faced the crème-de-la-crème of AAAA talent. We had grit and some talent. San Antonio Lee had determination and loads more talent. Twenty-five of the San Antonio Lee players went on to play college football. At most, a half-dozen '65 Tigers ended up playing any amount of college ball.

Like wringing water out of a washcloth, Acree squeezed results out of the boys he had. He prepared us to fight to win. But he didn't prepare us to lose. He hoped we would never have to learn that lesson on his watch.

Losing a football game can be woefully disappointing but losing the structure and routine life offers after high school can be devastating.

Perhaps men like Acree can put losses behind them and quickly move on to the following year, but boys in the game take it personally. I had confidence and some wisdom, but not enough.

All-State fullback Jim Hagle said, "The '63 Tigers had the hardness of tempered steel." By comparison, the '64 Tigers were of plastic and cracked with a hard knock from Waco Richfield. But what's the story of the '65 Tigers?

Acree set our dream on fire in a humid, rainy spring training that year. He instilled in us the hope of becoming state champions. Being a state champion was the "up yonder" in the song we sang, "When the Roll is called up Yonder."

Given the loss at the end of the '64 season, the press designated 1965 as a "rebuilding" year. But as teenage boys, Acree asked us what we wanted as seniors. We told him we wanted to play championship-level football. Acree decided on a junior quarterback, Mike Nekuza, over senior Glen Smith. The rest of us had to fight for the right to wear the Blue and Gold.

Acree did not miss an opportunity to spontaneously test the limits of our commitment. During spring workouts, I was in a circle of boys doing the "shiver bucket" drill supervised by Acree. We circled and faced one another as we each pushed and pulled, horizontally, out and back to our chests, a steel bar connecting two buckets filled with broken concrete.

Coaches Moore and Anderson watched over separate groups of boys working nearby on the monkey bars and isometric stations.

Ever mindful of his presence, I could sense Acree walking behind me and momentarily ducking into the Field House to ensure no one was hiding inside. Admittedly, we were laughing and joking between grunts, and I was not giving my all to shoving the buckets. Without warning, I felt a kick in the butt that lifted me off the ground.

The surprised look on my face mixed with pain. Acree had reappeared behind me. He yelled at me to stop loafing and admonished me as a senior to show some leadership. I started shoving the buckets as fast as I could. Of course I was embarrassed, but becoming a senior didn't automatically make a boy a leader, especially like the leaders on the '63 State Championship team.

Talmadge Canant, the sports editor at the Daily Sun, described me that spring as "a tough, scrappy youngster" who came onto the A-team in the middle of the '63 season and "logged all kinds of time in the remainder of the season as an offensive guard and defensive linebacker."

I don't remember playing that much. In reading Canant's work, it was a stock phrase he applied when summarizing gossip about a player overheard in a Dads Club meeting. Perhaps he thought I was tough because I didn't wear arm or elbow pads, which earned me a good reputation among the other linemen. He added that I was "a mainstay" in the '64 season. In the '65 season, Canant channeled Acree, "the Tigers will depend on him again this fall."

I didn't know Mr. Canant personally, so he likely heard those comments from Acree directly as he reviewed a film of a spring scrimmage in a Dads Club meeting. During a film review, Acree narrated the action and highlighted the good and bad plays and the performance of the boys who made them.

Acree also shared his expectation of the coming season, "We may get beat some this fall, but I don't think we are going to be embarrassed."

The dream of repeating as a state champion rested on our toughest boys, tackles Phil Pillans, Don Robertson and Lynn Odom, who were also seniors. All three possessed a defensive linemen's ambition: "lay a good lick on a ball carrier."

Acree also emphasized to Mr. Canant the importance of junior tackles Bobby Heard and Terry Chandler. He understood linemen to be intelligent, aggressive boys who loved to wallop opponents on every play.

He also knew the pride of being a lineman, "Anyone can carry the football. It ain't heavy."

As Acree did in '63, he first sought to create an offensive line. Linemen were like plow horses working deep in the 'back forty.' We labored in obscurity during the Blue-White scrimmage that spring. The usual focus was on the ball handlers: Mike Nekuza, Glen and Ben Smith, Bill Allison and Steve Winn. The quarterback of the Blue team, Glen Smith, played exceptionally well in the first half, but Nekuza, the quarterback of the White team, had a tremendous second half. Whites won, 28-14.

Glen had a slashing, cutting style of running that aimed to fake out a tackler. Nekuza was taller and his running probably reminded Acree of Gary Roman's sweeping strides that propelled him around tacklers. He could also punt, and Acree liked to quick kick, which would be easier to disguise with Mike as a quarterback.

I preferred Glen, a classmate who could see the field and had fun calling plays as if he intended to win in each situation. Personality-wise, Glen was ferromagnetic and attracted other players. Mike was a great athlete who could be shaped like cast iron. He did what Acree wanted.

Glen had no control over Acree's choice. A quarterback sets the attitude of a team. That year, the Tigers were like Mike, quiet, businesslike and methodical, but by the quarterfinals game, predictable on defense. Taken together, we were wrought iron and delivered on the promise of some good football, but we were not steel, the stuff from which the '63 team turned dreams into reality.

Coach Moore was not my position coach, but we developed a relationship because of his teasing manner. After showering and wrapped in a towel, I walked toward my dressing area, and he approached from the opposite direction. He stopped and pointed to a grated drain on the concrete floor saying, "Ward, don't step on that drain." Then he said, "You might fall through the slots since you are so skinny." We laughed. He had nicknamed me "spear." It was his way of reminding me to gain weight.

Coaches nicknamed boys, but the reverse was also true. Compared to Acree, Coach Edwards was small and almost frail-looking. His coach's outfit was too large. If rain fell during practice, Edwards' water-soaked clothing collapsed onto his body, revealing his skeletal frame. He appeared skinny, like a rain-soaked rat whose fur was wet. He wasn't my position coach, but some boys called him "rat." That fall, it became "rat-fink" because of his allegiance to Acree. He informed Acree if he caught us doing anything for which Acree would disapprove. In hindsight, Edwards was a good coach, a team man who did his job and went on in later years to become a great head coach at Duncanville.

We had nicknames for Acree too, but no one dared breathe them aloud.

* * *

The Bonham Warriors were of interest to Corsicana because they were our opening opponent that fall. In addition, Coach Acree had started his coaching career there. The UIL silenced Bonham's hopes of a state championship that season. The UIL Amateur Rule allowed players to receive a $15 letter jacket. Anything beyond that was "compensation" and grounds for probation.

Bonham players had received a pamphlet from the newly-formed organization, Fellowship of Christian Athletes, valued at 17¢. An anonymous tipster reported "the gift" to the UIL. By allowing the distribution of the "church book" to players, the UIL found Bonham guilty of breaking the Amateur Rule and put the school on probation for three years. Excessively, the UIL punishment further declared Bonham ineligible to compete for their District Championship that year.

The penalty seemed harsh and out of balance with the infraction, but the UIL wanted to make an example of Bonham. The ruling stirred up a controversy about which Acree said, "That may happen to me. But I intend to take every step I can to see it doesn't."

Acree was committed to keeping UIL rules. He was also a director of the Texas High School Football Association and helped organize its August meeting. It made no sense for any coach to knowingly violate UIL rules. Given the UIL's disciplinary powers, too much was at stake. Acree was intelligent, and his livelihood and professional reputation depended on following League rules to the letter.   But his competitive nature demanded that he do no less than standard professional practices at the time. In other words, he did what other coaches were doing.

Acree was not only a busy, committed coach. He was well liked around town and aimed to fit into the community through his involvement in civic organizations and church groups.

He worked to help Tiger boys obtain summer jobs, which were scarce in Corsicana. Fortunately, I was a regular sacker/checker at the Piggly Wiggly grocery store. A few boys could get jobs at the Nipak plant in Kerens. Others worked for the Highway Department.

Acree organized an odd-job crew that did back-breaking work he found around town—mowing, digging graves, hauling hay and maintaining the Miller Hat Company swimming pool. He tended Tiger Field as if it were a private garden. Like a master gardener, he had boys pulling weeds and watering the sod.

One day, he needed dirt for Tiger Field and showed up at my house driving a dump truck. Three other boys were in the back. He told me to hop in and go to Italy, Texas, where he had arranged to have us load the dump truck using shovels.

Stupidly, I used the one short-handled shovel he had. We worked from early morning to late afternoon, tossing dirt into that massive back end. When he dropped me back at my house, I was worn out as if I had run a marathon.

As always, the annual edition of "Texas Football" by Dave Campbell that summer was a must-read magazine. Campbell included Bill Allison on his "Super Team of 1965," but he also named Mike Nekuza, Ben and Glen Smith and Ronnie Ward, saying, "The Tigers aren't big, but they'll hit, and if Coach Jim Acree can find some linemen, it could be a big year."

* * *

Seventy Tigers came out for football in mid-August, but the UIL did not permit coaches to conduct supervised workouts for the first four days. It was up to the seniors, and especially those who had previously lettered, to demonstrate leadership by completing Acree's long list of exercises— calisthenics, running sprints, back peddling, running sideways, high-stepping through a grid of ropes, passing, catching and kicking the football, swinging through monkey bars, hand-walking along parallel bars, straining against the isometric bars, rope climbing and lifting weights.

There was no UIL rule about giving salt tablets to players. The twice-daily workouts in shorts and t-shirts were exhausting. Without supervision by Acree, we created an illusion that the seniors had a leadership role on the team. However, once the coaches took over, our role diminished to out hitting the other boys during a drill and out hustling lower classmen to the next exercise. Under Acree, players had no say in who played where or what we did in practice.

Coach Acree divided the boys into two teams and held a Saturday scrimmage on the second day of padded workouts. He wanted to maximize competition between players for starting positions. And he also wanted to find out who the hitters were.

A hit concussed big man and tackle Phil Pillans, which hospitalized him for observation. The following week, we were happy to see him walking around in shorts and t-shirt, observing the workouts. After a Saturday scrimmage with Sherman, Acree introduced Phil along with the other seniors, noting our "good leadership."

Labor Day, we practiced twice to get ready for the upcoming Friday night trip to Bonham. As expected, Acree named Nekuza the starting quarterback on Wednesday. A few seniors were chatting outside the west end of the Field House after practice that afternoon. "Rat-fink" overheard me say, "Glen Smith should be our starting quarterback." A few minutes later, Acree barreled out of the side door, madder than a husband whose wife had cheated on him. He tore into us verbally and focused on me saying, "I'm the coach of this team, and I determine who plays where. Not you!"

We disbanded and made it to our cars without having to run to the Green House. As though he were still seething, Acree didn't list me as a starter against Bonham, but he didn't list anyone else starting as a guard. I assumed he wanted to send me a message.

Bonham

Despite an outsized UIL penalty for a "church booklet," Bonham was ready to play football. Early in the game, the Warriors were the first to put points on the board when Nekuza fumbled deep in Tiger territory. On our next possession, Mike threw an interception, but we had ten seniors starting on defense that came to the rescue and kept Bonham from capitalizing on the turnover.

Game momentum shifted on our next possession when Acree called a reverse (one of his favorites). Ben Smith sailed for 48 yards up the sidelines. After another first down, Bill Allison passed untouched behind an unnamed guard's block and ran 38 yards for a touchdown. The guard got to his feet and watched Allison run from behind. As if he had scored, he jumped for joy when his friend crossed the goal line. Jimmy Pillans missed the extra-point kick.

The Tigers scored again before the half when Nekuza missed a handoff but made an extraordinary athletic play to run 30 yards for a touchdown. Acree called for a two-point conversion, and Gary Schutte grabbed a high pass from Nekuza. We went into the locker room at the half, ahead 14-7.

The bands marched at halftime, but a new "Blue-Gold Brigade" drilled in the bleachers. Dressed alike, the girls wore white, long-sleeved blouses, white gloves, blue vests, blue skirts and white tennis shoes and performed hand routines in unison. They chanted, "T-I-G-E-R-S!" Many players had girlfriends in the Brigade and received first-hand fan accounts after the game. Part of the player experience of Friday night football was running on the field between two lines of Brigade members. Best of all was to have a particular one waiting to meet you outside the Field House after the game.

After the half, Allison scored for the Tigers, but Jimmy Pillans again missed the extra point try. Nekuza fumbled in the fourth quarter to set up Bonham's second score. Allison scored again for the Tigers, but Nekuza's keeper for a two-point conversion failed. We won 26-14.

Seeing the bright lights of downtown Dallas while riding the Blue Goose on the way home was exciting. We anticipated what the Dallas Times Herald would say about us the next day. Acree praised the team's good attitude and determination. Noting the improvement of Phil Pillans and Lynn Odom, he complimented our "outstanding line play."

Stoking our hopes of making a championship run, he also praised the "leadership of the seniors."

My dad's habit was to take me to breakfast on Saturday mornings at the Continental Inn. Between bites, he said, "The Tigers are a AAAA team," but not thinking we had accomplished much, added, "Bonham is a AAA school on probation."

We had a team, but did we have AAAA-level talent? It would take time to answer that question. However, it was not unreasonable to believe we could improve. We did everything Coach Acree asked us to do, especially Jimmy Pillans. Despite much after-practice work, he didn't progress at making extra point kicks under game conditions. Junior Dick Henson took over the kicking job. Jimmy focused on his role as a starting defensive nose-guard (lined up over the center), where he excelled using his strength, quickness and aggressive line-play. He was a boy made of iron for sure.

If blocking by the offensive line could ratchet up and match the running ability of Bill Allison, Steve Winn, Ben Smith and Mike Nekuza, we had a chance to be a championship team. At least, that's what we told ourselves. Acree started the same group of boys against Fort Worth Carter Riverside the following week.

Fort Worth Carter Riverside

Allison opened with an 83-yard romp to score first, and "Little" Steve Winn matched it on our next possession with an 81-yard sprint for a score. Acree let Glen Smith play quarterback in the fourth quarter, and his throws and runs dazzled the crowd. After the game, Acree praised the offensive line's work for its blocking. He commended the defensive line, too. Carter Riverside didn't make it across midfield until the last minute of the game. We rolled over the AAAA Eagles, 33-0.

John Tyler

John Tyler was a formidable AAAA opponent. Great performances by Steve Winn, Gary Schutte and the Smith twins led our scoring, but I remember the game primarily for our defensive play.

Acree noticed the Lion guards setting larger than expected gaps and told me as a linebacker to "step up in there and shoot through the gap."

Several times, I chased their quarterback, Danny Palmer, around the backfield. He completed a desperation pass on one play that resulted in a touchdown. As he and I jogged beside each other, all eyes were on the scoring end of the field. He back fisted me in the face. Hitting my face mask didn't hurt, but it startled me. I didn't retaliate right away.

Again, our senior-led defense limited them to six points as Palmer tried to sweep around the end for two extra points but failed. Our offense came from behind to take the lead, 14-12. Late in the game, Palmer marched the Lions downfield, and we needed to get the ball out of their hands. Even a field goal could beat us. But if we could stop their drive, we'd win the game.

As linebackers, Acree regularly prepared us to participate in pass defense. After regular practice ended, he turned on the lights of Tiger Field and personally drilled the linebackers in reading a quarterback's opening steps.

We lined up as a pair across from Coach as though he was the quarterback. He held the ball and popped a hand against it to simulate a snap. Sometimes he would tuck it immediately and run up between us to simulate a quarterback sneak. He wanted us to greet him with a forearm, which we did. Bill Allison hit him more vigorously than I did. He admonished me if I didn't hit him hard enough to suit him, "You can hit better than that. Hit me!"

As a seventeen-year-old boy, I learned to take out every bit of frustration and hit him as hard as I could. The hits never phased him. Other times, Coach Acree opened out of his quarterback stance and sprinted down the line. We pursued him but didn't tackle him. Most of the time, he would open and drop back to one side or the other as if he were going to pass. After taking three or four steps, he looked to where he would throw the ball and then throw it. Our goal was to move with his eyes and catch the football. I wished Coach Moore had been there to see me grab the football. As a more experienced senior, Acree couldn't throw it past me as Moore did when I was a sophomore.

If we did the drill wrong, Acree came to our side and showed us how to move. We learned by imitating him. Whatever Acree said was gospel to us. I loved those one-on-one drills with him. The intimacy of him privately teaching us the game made me feel as though he was a mentor sharing his innermost secrets on how to play football.

The Lions were near scoring territory when Palmer opened back on my side and looked where he would throw the ball. I opened outside and dropped back as Acree had taught me. I watched Palmer's eyes. He threw toward an end, running a curl route behind me. I stepped in front of the receiver and caught it as though it were a perfect pass to me. The interception stopped their drive. They never threatened again in the game. We defeated them in 1965 on their home field, the Rose Bowl, 14-12.

The '65 Tigers had to fight to win against the AAAA Lions, who had a much larger squad. But Acree was proud of us, telling the Dads Club, "Tyler substituted nine to eleven boys every time the ball changed hands. The game proved we could play against teams with that large of a bench."

Corsicana was a small AAAA school. The larger AAAA schools fielded squads with separate boys on offense, defense and special teams. The UIL limited the time coaches had to teach, and staff sizes bounded squad sizes to the number of boys they could handle. Larger schools were more likely to have enough talent to make separate teams.

The Tigers didn't have that luxury, so Acree emphasized conditioning. We had to be able to play "both ways." Against John Tyler, seven Tigers from the 1965 team (Bill Allison, Gary Schutte, Don Robertson, Lynn Odom, Ronnie Ward, Ben Smith and Mike Nekuza) played every down, offense, defense and special team.

As boys, we had grown up having fun playing touch football against each other. We especially liked to win. As kids, a game experience left us exhausted as if we had spent a long day at the State Fair, riding rides, trying for a prize on the Midway and seeing fascinating exhibits of what the future may bring.

On the bus ride home, no matter how sore and tired we were, Allison and Haynie got a few of us laughing and celebrating. I sat in the back of the bus, drank a can of chocolate-flavored Nutrament and mentally relived that pass interception against Danny Palmer.

With many of us bruised up from playing the entire game in Tyler, Acree made Monday's practice lighter than usual. Beating a good AAAA team like the Lions made us think we were a good team. We were not exceptional, though, because we were not big. I didn't understand the value of our speed and toughness, but Acree did. Holding off, Tyler proved we could come from behind in a hard-fought game and win. Seeing what we were made of, Acree praised our "determination."

Jacksonville

During his tenure in Corsicana, Coach Acree always respected Jacksonville, our fourth opponent that year. Their coach had a philosophy like his—out-hustle and out-hit an opponent. We prepared as though Corsicana were sending an army to represent it in a war against a neighboring town. 1965 was a "rebuilding year" for them, and we sliced them up in their Tomato Bowl, 31-0.

The Smith boys made touchdowns, as did Allison and Nekuza. As a backup to Dick Henson's field goal and extra points, Acree worked in junior Ronnie Dosser to kick an extra point. Many substitutes enjoyed playing time in the game. Acree used our lead in scoring to try a trick play under game conditions. He substituted Glen Smith in at quarterback to handle the ball. Ben Smith scored on a double reverse. Later, Glen also made a couple of crucial interceptions while on defense. But the star of the game was the Tiger defense. Jacksonville didn't make a first down until the second half.

Records don't win ball games. At 4-0, we started to believe we might be a championship-level team. Players can deceive themselves in many ways into thinking they are better than they are. In the same stadium, the '63 state champions had barely vanquished Jacksonville, 13-7. The '65 team destroyed the Indians. Moreover, we had won four consecutive weeks away from home. But a record meant little to Coach Acree who believed, "You have to play every Friday night, and you're only as good as you play."

Ennis

I don't know if it was part of his weekly shtick or if Acree believed that Ennis, our last scheduled non-district opponent, was good enough to beat us. As though he were angry at us, he put us through hard contact drills that week saying, "we were not really hungry."

Small mistakes while playing Jacksonville riled the perfectionism in Acree. That week, he taught us some finer details of the game, how to recognize changes in the opposing defense and switch our blocking assignments to adjust. Using three days of hard contact drills, he aimed to rid us of any propensity to make the same errors in future games.

Acree was obsessive. He never used the words "good enough." As though we were back in August two-a-days, he prepared us to battle the Ennis Lions like it was the most important game of the season.

Designated as our "homecoming" night and being our first home game, he did not want to be embarrassed in front of an expected overflow crowd. In hindsight, he expected trick plays from Ennis, so he prepared us for about anything they might do. In addition, being homecoming, many of the '63 state champions would be at Tiger Field to watch us play against a traditional enemy.

Just as the '63 team overwhelmed Ennis, 56-8, the '65 Tigers stunned the Lions, 49-0. A "standing room only" crowd watched the game. Glen Smith picked off an Ennis pass to start a drive for our first score, which Bill Allison made. On our next possession, Steve Winn zoomed through a hole created by an unnamed guard to run 76 yards, untouched, for our second score. Behind a wall of Tiger blockers, Mike Nekuza returned a punt for 90 yards to score our third touchdown. Glen Smith came in at quarterback and hit second-stringer Don Jones for a 58-yard touchdown. All of Dick Henson's kicks were good. We led 28-0 at the half.

The Tigers elected cheerleader Billie Sloan as our football sweetheart that night. The Blue-Gold Brigade dedicated its drills to Darelle Green, our senior classmate who came to the game after surgery in Houston. She cheered the Tigers from a hospital bed located on the sideline.

Glen Smith received the Ennis kickoff in the second half and returned it 85 yards for a touchdown. According to Glen, Coach Acree jumped him afterward saying, "What did I tell you to do?"

In some way, Glen's touchdown run displeased Acree. Bewildered, Glen said nothing in response. It's hard to know what might have upset Acree. He saw something he didn't like, and his quick temper kicked into action. I don't think it was the fact that Glen scored, but perhaps he wanted to see us execute methodically, drive the ball and not get an easy touchdown.

The fact that Ennis looked tired and appeared to give up probably disappointed Acree. Mike Nekuza and Melton Michaels completed our scoring against the Lions. Our senior-led defense held an opponent to zero points for the third time that season. The '63 championship team worked that magic only once in non-district play. However, unknown to us, state championship football was courting the Odessa Permian Panthers out in West Texas and their new head coach, Gene Mayfield.

Cleburne

With non-district play out of the way, our first north zone opponent was Cleburne in Yellow Jacket Stadium. The Yellow Jackets had an offense with a point production similar to ours and a defense that was just as stingy. We had a non-district record 5-0. They had a similar record, 4-1. But Acree more than prepared us to play that night, and before a standing-room-only crowd, we defeated the Yellow Jackets 22-0. I continued to think we might be like the '63 team, who had won convincingly there 21-0.

The Cleburne game is very memorable to me for several reasons. They drove the ball to our 1-yard line on their initial series of downs. As defensive captain, I called a "goal-line (61) defense" that put a Tiger in every gap. I dropped into a down position between a guard and a center, and when the ball snapped, I moved quickly through the opening. I ended up between the legs of the ball carrier. He dropped the ball to the ground but recovered it for no gain. We repeated that effort for the next three plays and held them scoreless.

During the game, I picked up an important tip, or key as it's called in football. Cleburne huddled with their backfield facing us, standing behind their linemen who bent over with their hands on their knees, facing their quarterback. The quarterback had his back to us as he called their plays. I watched the faces of their running backs as the quarterback called a play. Invariably, one of the backs would glance to where the ball was going and quickly look away before breaking the huddle. As the game progressed and the key proved reliable, I knew where the ball was going and called a particular stunt on that side of our defense. We were very successful in stopping their running game that evening.

Don Robertson, our largest defensive tackle, was on my side of the line. I called a stunt where he shifted at the last second to a gap between their guard and tackle. I slid to the outside just as the ball snapped and met their big fullback, Gary Butler, head-on at the edge for no gain.

Coach Acree made another memory when Ben Smith suffered an injury in the second half. Ben was down on the field in pain, and Coach Acree ran out to check on him. Acree quickly assessed Ben as having a leg cramp, but instead of taking the time to get Ben to his feet and walk him to the sideline, Acree bent over, picked Ben up and heaved him over his shoulder as if he were a 150-pound sack of potatoes. With Ben riding belly-down on Acree's big shoulder, Coach walked briskly to the sideline, and the game resumed play. Who does that? Only Jim Acree. He was concerned for Ben's condition, but he wanted the gameplay to continue quickly since we had the momentum. Had we been in practice and Ben suffered a debilitating cramp, Coach Acree would have simply yelled at him, "Get up! You're not hurt!"

Glen Smith scored our first touchdown against Cleburne. Nekuza played well, scoring our second touchdown. Steve Winn also scored.

I remember playing every down of the Cleburne game—offense, defense, and special teams. Afterward, exhausted and breathing rapidly, I sat outside the locker room, too tired to go in, undress and clean up. Coach Acree asked a doctor to check on me and the doctor said "He's hyperventilating and suffering from low carbon dioxide. Put a paper sack over his head for a few minutes, his system will stabilize, and he will be fine."

Not having a handy paper sack and wanting to get out of town quickly because of a rowdy crowd, Acree volunteered, "Wouldn't it be faster to drag him over to the bus and set him beside the exhaust pipe?"

The doctor replied, "I said carbon dioxide, not carbon monoxide!"

Acree was a history teacher, not a chemistry major. After leaving the stadium, the Blue Goose twisted and turned down a narrow street. A group of Cleburne teenage fans yelled expletives and "mooned" the bus as it passed. Acree saw them and commanded the driver to stop. He hopped off the bus and gave the Cleburne fans a quick lesson in sportsmanship. We never told him, but several of us dropped our pants and, with backends pressed against the window glass, returned the mooning. He would have killed us had he known it.

The fact that our defense blanked Cleburne went unnoticed in the newspaper, but for the first time I sensed we had a special set of boys on both sides of the ball. Seven of us played both ways. All of us were in top condition, as good as any championship team. Acree told the Dads, "They are in better shape than any team I have had."

Waco High

After the win over Cleburne, the papers ranked us number ten in Class AAAA football. The football scribes loved our imitation of the '63 team and began to make comparisons. That team drummed Waco High, 35-6. We were on a similar roll. In perfect weather for football the following week, we defeated Waco High, 26-7.

Bill Allison scored three touchdowns with no mention in the paper of the contributing blocks by linemen. Steve Winn garnered nearly 200 yards in rushing, having one scoring run of 78 yards. Bill was a workhorse; Steve was a thriller.

Gary Schutte came through with a timely interception that stopped a Waco scoring threat. We had two sustained drives of nine plays each which pleased Coach Acree. No-mistake football was his goal, and we delivered.

Bryan

Hoping to be a contender for the state title, the Bryan Broncos came to town the following Friday night. Sporting a four-game win streak and matching our 2-0 zone record, we studied them on film and visualized how to outplay them. Acree had unleashed a monster. We sat in the film room together and schemed how to block or run stunts against them. Acree warned us not to be overconfident, but we had fun imagining how we could win.

Winners must have confidence, but overconfidence can lead to being "cocky." Acree hated swagger. He didn't train us to think that we'd win or lose. He prepared us to give our best on each down and winning would follow. I can say that I never went into a game confident that we'd win or worried we would lose. Thanks to Coach Acree, I never entered a game where I wasn't ready to play football.

We had no idea who would earn the state title, but Bryan's hope was unmerited. We defeated them 34-3. Reading the write-up in the paper, you'd never know that the Tiger linemen shined. The Broncos scored a field goal on their first possession. We needed only one offensive series against them to adjust to their defensive game plan. After that, we played like a machine; our offense scored like the '63 champions. Allison and Winn made long runs, but we sustained multi-play drives with dive plays, sweeps, counters, reverses and passes. In addition, Nekuza, Schutte, Ronnie Dosser and Melton Michaels all performed well. The team played together as if all the players had a champion's mindset.

The newspaper skipped over mentioning the linemen, but Coach Acree made sure the Dads Club heard the names of the Tiger boys in the trenches. As he reviewed the game film, he highlighted line blocking that made running and throwing the football possible or the defensive moves that kept Bryan out of the end zone. He mentioned Phil Pillans, Don Robertson, Lynn Odom, Ronnie Ward, Dickie Pimentel, Willard

Simmons, Jimmy Pillans, Chuck Butler, Ronnie Ragsdale, David Derryberry, Bill Kent, Frank Dunn and Phil Smith.

Uncharacteristically, Acree exclaimed, "Our kids are doing a great job! We are competing with 745 students in high school against schools with twice that many students."

Acree was amazed and proud of his AAAA football team saying, "[The players] stay late on their own to perfect their skills. We actually think they utilize their time better during the season than they do at other times."

I used my spare time to date my girlfriend, read science fiction books and build a solid-state laser for my science fair project that year. It was an enormous undertaking, and I had started on it that summer. I saved up eighty dollars to buy four large capacitors needed for the power supply. I assembled it at night on an ironing board in my bedroom. I had my uncle James Ward, a research tech at LTV Aerospace in Arlington, Texas, check my wiring. He found and helped me fix a couple of key bugs.

I invited Coach Acree to our house one evening to see my progress. His immense presence filled my small bedroom, a converted single-car garage. I demonstrated how to solder wiring and reviewed my plan with him to cause a ruby crystal to lase. He joked with my dad about not understanding what I was doing. Daddy said, "I hope he doesn't burn down the house."

Waco University

After conquering Bryan, the '65 Tigers moved up in press rankings to number five in the state in Class AAAA football. Being undefeated and having such a stingy defense, we thought we were "hot stuff." As one of only 37 unbeaten teams, we played against Waco University on a dingy, muddy Waco field in our ninth game of the '65 season. The papers picked us to win by four touchdowns. Our defense had matured against

John Tyler and Cleburne, but our offense did so in the Waco University game.

Particularly Bill Allison. He demonstrated his mettle in harsh conditions. We put together an initial 80-yard, 17-play drive to score in our opening possession. The muddy field conditions worked against Steve Winn's speed and Glen Smith's cutting ability; hence, our play calling resembled a fullback offense, "Allison right, Allison left." Like Jim Hagle in '63, Bill made critical fourth-down runs to keep drives alive. When it came time for Allison to do his part, the team could count on him.

A fumble by Nekuza set up the first Trojan touchdown, and a breakdown in our defensive secondary allowed them to make an easy score. Their attempt at a two-point conversion failed, and we held a slim lead at halftime, 7-6.

In the third quarter against the University Trojans, we put together another sustained possession in muddy conditions. Allison slipped through tacklers as if he were a wet, mud-covered razorback. Nekuza ended the drive on a slicing 20-yard run to score. We went ahead, 14-6.

In the third period, University scored again on a 78-yard pass play that featured good blocking on their part and a missed tackle in our secondary. The Trojans tied the game at 14-14 with a two-point conversion. Slipping and sliding in the mud tired both teams, but we forced University to punt late in the fourth quarter. Acting like the '63 Tigers against Graham, our offense put together a mistake-free, sustained drive to go ahead, 21-14.

The most outstanding player of the game was Bill Allison. He carried the ball 30 times and gained 252 yards in the mud. The newspaper account of the match exclaimed the play of several Tiger linemen, Phil Pillans, Don Robertson, David Derryberry, Lynn Odom, Ronnie Ward, Ronnie Ragsdale and Dickie Pimentel, saying, "They paid the price, and because of it, the Tigers are still alive and kicking."

Three sustained drives proved that University's defense could not stop our offense. Twice we proved we could come from behind and win in miserable game conditions. Acree summarized our play, "We were pleased with our offensive efforts, our blocking improved, and our backs ran well."

Texas football is no respecter of rankings. San Angelo, ranked number two, played Odessa Permian, the tenth-ranked AAAA team that week. The Permian Panthers won the game, 8-7.

Waco Richfield

Regardless of our rank as the number five AAAA team, the outcome of our last zone match against Waco Richfield would determine whether we advanced or sat out the rest of the fall season like the '64 Tigers. Acree worried that might be the case, telling the Dads, "I believe our youngsters will be ready. But regardless, you must remember, they have worked hard all year."

Remembering that we had worked hard all year would have been no consolation if we lost to Richfield. We had bought in so thoroughly to Acree's methods that we were like pledges expecting to become members of a fraternity of champions.

Acree prepared us for Richfield, but we didn't go after them out of revenge for what happened in '64. Instead, we burrowed into them and examined their soul as a football team. In a guild of football players, we found them wanting.

That week, I watched their game film so much that I developed a dislike for how a few of their players loafed when a play went to the opposite side of the field. Another of their starters ambled downfield on punts. In my boyish mind, he violated an unwritten pact between players to hustle on the field. Studying him in the film, I made a judgment. He didn't play to win.

Richfield didn't meet my boyish perceptions, and without telling Acree, I decided in the film room that I would personally punish them for dishonoring the game.

Moreover, their star fullback, Hays Moore, had lived in Corsicana before his family moved to Waco. He lived one block over from me, and everyone in town remembered how great a baseball player he was in Little League. He hit home runs not just over the fence but over the light poles.

We'd heard all week how "big" Richfield was and how "big" Hays Moore was. Their size mattered not a stitch to me. In the film room, I envisioned blitzing (driving) lanes between their big, loafing linemen that I could use to seek out Moore and knock him to the ground.

I plotted how to nail a guard who loafed on punts. He always dawdled while going down the sideline in a containment position guarding against a runback. I knew where to find him loafing along the sideline, right in front of the Tiger bench—right in front of Acree.

Wearing Acree's game face, I crossed the white line that Friday night to enter the field of play, and like the rest of my teammates, I was excited but collected, ready to do business. We were "fired up," according to the press.

Our line dominated the big Richfield players. Our offense overpowered their defense. Mike Nekuza fielded a punt and returned it for what appeared to be a touchdown. I splattered a loafing guard in front of the Tiger bench. The players scattered when momentum from my hit carried the Ram skidding on his back out of bounds. Hearing the lick, Acree turned from watching the ball to dodging the Ram sliding by on the ground. Acree's eyes beamed with excitement.

The referees said Nekuza stepped out of bounds at the 30-yard line. Six plays later, Steve Winn skirted through a hole made by our linemen to give us a 6-0 lead in the second quarter.

Richfield could not move the ball. But Ben Smith, Nekuza and Allison ran over the Rams on the next Tiger series. Glen Smith passed to Willard Simmons in the end zone for our second score. At the half, we led 13-0.

Gary Schutte came to play in the second half. He deflated the Rams further by returning an interception 32 yards to give us a 20-0 lead (Henson's kick was good). In the fourth quarter, Gary lined up 63 yards from paydirt, grabbed a long Nekuza pass and ran for a touchdown. He outran the loafing Rams to make the score 26-0 (Henson's kick failed).

Richfield did not have a ground game. Their running backs were like targets in a shooting gallery. One time their quarterback handed the ball to Moore who slanted off-tackle, but I was waiting for him. Their end had blocked down on our tackle, Don Robertson, to clear an opening. To close it, I slid behind Don to get heads up on Moore as he came toward the line of scrimmage. I coiled as if I were a snake waiting to strike. Just as he reached the line of scrimmage, I exploded on him. His size didn't matter. I learned in physics class that force equals mass times acceleration. He was larger, but my acceleration was greater, and just as I had envisioned in the film room, I knocked him to the ground for no gain. I said to him, "Welcome back to Corsicana."

The hit on Hays Moore has always stuck with me because of Acree's comment as he reviewed the game film with the team. I played for Acree for three years, and he always wanted us to improve and get better. He never called me by my given name, so when the film advanced to my tackle on Moore, all he said was, "Ward, good movement and positioning, but you should have filled sooner."

There was no pleasing Acree. I had waited for Moore to come to me instead of going to meet him. Moore weighed over 200 pounds and thought he could run over me. He didn't, but Acree figured I should have tackled him for a loss behind the line instead of no-gain.

The win over Waco Richfield made us zone champions in District 13-AAAA, and the next week, the press notched our rank up to number four in the state in Class AAAA. I asked my dad what he thought about us as a team. He said, "Y'all are really good."

"Do you think we are as good as the '63 team?"

He replied, "You've won your zone playing AAAA football. You may be better than them."

"But do you think we can be champions like them?"

At the Dads Club, Acree said of the team, "They are capable of winning the championship if they decide to."

Acree corrected the town's misunderstanding that we were in the playoffs. We had to win District before we would join the state playoff race. Lose the District game against Austin Travis, and our season would have ended without a championship. Acree preached, "Football is a game of mental preparedness, and the team that is prepared to play the right kind of football is going to win."

By "right kind of football," Coach meant to play a mistake-free, hard-hitting fight to win. Play every down as though the game outcome rested on it. Otherwise, losers will have regrets—plays they want to do over for the rest of their lives.

I was only seventeen in the fall of 1965 and didn't comprehend the destructive nature of regrets and how they can steal future happiness or trap a person in the past. Regrets are sorrowful memories of previous life events that replay in an endless loop and always yield a dissatisfying outcome. They perpetuate the grief of loss. As an older man now, I know them well.

Austin Travis

The Austin Travis Rebels, south zone champions in District 13-AAAA, had a 7-3 season record and played inconsistent football. They had shocked the Austin football world with a surprise win over neighboring powerhouse, Austin McCallum.

To play Travis, Acree practiced us as if we had lost against Richfield. We fumbled four times against the Rams, and he decided to cure the ball carriers of that disorder in one week. He had promised us back in August during two-a-days that he would slack off hard contact work in practice if we made it to the playoffs. In his mind, we weren't in the playoffs, so he had us in full pads, practicing full-speed against each other on Monday, Tuesday and Wednesday.

A boyish sense of injustice raged in my mind. For the first time, I looked at Acree as if he wouldn't do what he said he would do.

But our backfield did what he taught them to do that week. We didn't lose a fumble or throw an interception to Austin Travis. Instead, Don Robertson recovered one of their fumbles, and the Tigers intercepted five Rebel passes. We defeated them 34-12 on Kyle Field in College Station before a cheering crowd of Corsicana fans.

The list of Tiger stars who ended the title dream of Austin Travis included Steve Winn, Bill Allison, Ben and Glen Smith, Mike Nekuza, Gary Schutte and Dick Henson. Glen Smith intercepted three passes and logged a brilliant running game, scoring one touchdown from the quarterback position.

But unmentioned linemen also contributed by making it possible to pull off a 17-play drive of 85 yards for our first score. And on the defensive side, the rush from our linemen forced Austin to throw the ball 35 times.

Fans like the surprise of scoring in a game. In one 62-second stretch, fans saw Steve Winn score, then Travis on a long-pass-run combination, followed by another long touchdown sprint by Steve Winn. Bam, bam, bam! —a wide-open game with lots of thrilling plays.

In defeating Austin Travis, we became District 13-AAAA champions, a first in Corsicana history. In addition to AA and AAA football, Acree also became a AAAA champion for the first time. He was back on familiar turf. Corsicana was a champion again in a new world of AAAA football competitors. The '65 Tigers had an 11-0 record. It was an easy step for everyone at that point to compare us to the '63 team.

Winning the State Championship in '63 elated the town as though it had summited Emory Peak in the Chisos Mountains. Similarly, like we were marching up Guadalupe Peak, the tallest mountain in Texas, winning week after week in '65, we gradually raised our hopes for a AAAA championship. Players, coaches, students and the town experienced small doses of that same high after each win. The excitement around town overflowed as businesses posted signs saying, "Go Tigers!" in store windows. Ads ran in the newspaper congratulating the team.

But fans in Alice, Texas, San Antonio and Odessa were just as proud of their teams.

Typically, playoff games are challenging to win because the opponents are the best of the best. Austin Travis had stumbled into the District title game, so overwhelming them didn't say much about the '65 Tigers. Our two previous come-from-behind wins showed that we had mettle. But were we made of championship playoff material? We would find out playing our bi-district opponent, the Alice Coyotes.

Bi-District: Alice

The game and UIL classification force a form of similarity among Texas football teams, especially those in the playoffs. Game complexity and UIL rules limit the preparation time a coach has with players. If two opposing coaches value conditioning, quickness and agility, variances in their teams may come down to the differences in style and player talents.

The Corsicana Tigers and the Alice Coyotes were very similar teams, but Alice had only two players that started and played both ways; Corsicana had seven. In describing Alice, Corsicana superintendent O.E. Hendricks observed, "In many ways, the clubs will look almost identical."

Playing the bi-district game in University of Texas Memorial Stadium, Glen Smith put us in good field position after a great kickoff return. We scored first on our opening drive of 58 yards in eleven plays.

Linemen worked in the trenches to clear gaps for runners and hold up pass rushers. Nekuza passed to Schutte, Simmons and Ben Smith, and runs by Allison advanced the ball over the goal line. Dick Henson's kick was good.

Alice had its turn next. They drove the ball down to our goal line and threatened to score before I recovered a fumble on the 6-yard line. Our linemen met their running back head-on, and the ball exploded out from behind him like a cork popping out of a bottle. Acree trained, I grabbed the ball as if it were "found money."

Toward the first quarter's end, Alice scored on a pass play and tied the game, 7-7. The similarity between the two teams became obvious by our similar hitting and scoring.

Next, we put together a nine-play drive. Our linemen hurled their bodies against Alice's defenders like axes chopping at sturdy trees. Nekuza passed to Schutte and Simmons, then Allison scored on a 13-yard run. Henson's kick was good.

Gary Schutte and David Derryberry led the Corsicana defense to make plays that forced Alice to turn the ball over on downs inside our territory. From there, the combination of Nekuza, Allison and Winn and our offensive line drove the football to the Alice 4-yard line before an interception ruined a scoring opportunity. That play kept them in the game. Championship caliber teams make such plays to stop opponents.

However, our defensive line forced them to punt. Glen Smith returned it for a touchdown, but a clipping penalty erased his effort. Our mistakes started to hurt us. Nekuza tossed another interception, and Alice gained momentum. We played like we wanted to give away the game, not win it.

Alice started to drive for a score, but the Coyote running back dropped the ball on the ground. Lynn Odom recovered it to end their bid. Our defense kept us in the game. We led at the half, 14-7.

Alice took advantage of a pass-interference call against our defense in the second half to score on its first possession. They tied the game 14-14.

Defensively, Alice made good halftime adjustments, and our offense could not move the ball. Likewise, our defensive line made plays to thwart Coyote's sweeps and reverses.

In the middle of the fourth quarter, Nekuza boomed a punt over the Coyote safety who chased the ball down inside his ten-yard line. He picked it up and started a return run, but a hustling group of Tigers streaked downfield to gang tackle him and knock the ball loose. Ben Smith recovered the fumble at their 6-yard line.

We took over in scoring position, but our offense could not push the ball across the goal line. With fourth and two, Dick Henson kicked a field goal. A cheering Jimmy Pillans outjumped all the other Tigers. We led, 17-14. In an exciting finish, Alice and Corsicana had the ball twice more, but neither team managed to score again.

Two interceptions and three fumbles cost Alice the game. Penalties hurt both teams but were most inopportune for the Tigers. The film review revealed just how scrappy the game was. Either team could have won it.

Our fans noted that the '65 Tigers had a 12-0-0 record at that point and were one of two unbeaten, untied teams left in the AAAA playoffs. Our idols, the '63 Tigers, were the only unbeaten, united team in Texas after they won the State Championship. Acree wasn't into making such comparisons. Instead, he lauded the Alice running back David Keys and moved on, "I hope we can play this next game as well as we played this one."

Quarterfinal Game: San Antonio Lee

Alice was the best team we had played up to that point. Our mistakes and their defense prevented the breakaway scoring we had enjoyed all season. Notably, the excellent performance of their running back was a harbinger of what we could expect in the quarterfinals match against San Antonio Lee.

San Antonio had the state's highest-scoring team. Statistically, Lee's Pat Sheehan more than matched Alice running back David Keys and the Volunteers' linemen were big, strong and quick. Watching them on film was scary.

The bi-district games whittled the top sixteen AAAA teams down to the top eight. Undefeated and untied after twelve games, we had every reason to imagine ourselves to be as good as the '63 State Championship team. Coaches told us if we could beat San Antonio Lee, we might go all the way.

But wearing sweat tops during our last practice, a cold winter rain fell on us on the afternoon before the game on December 2nd. Acree noted that our fingers turned blue. He was pleased with our preparation. He reported no injuries to the press, although my ankle was swollen and bruised after Nekuza stepped on it during the Alice game.

My ankle injury caused Acree to send me to the home office of Dr. Albert Horn for chiropractic treatment. Located only a block from the high school, his two-story house slumped under tall oak trees. Bared of their leaves on a winter's day, the place was dark and scary. The office inside looked like a lab that would make Dr. Frankenstein proud. As a boy trying to become a man, I was glad Acree was not there to see me crying when Dr. Horn twisted my ankle back and forth like he was a safe cracker hoping to find a correct bone combination.

Acree's Oklahoma teammate, Darrel Royal, head coach at UT, had promised to cover the field at Memorial Stadium, so Acree expected us to play on dry turf. Although Lee had superior offensive and defensive statistics, many people thought the game would be a tossup. Some expected a scoring fest. It would come down to who had the ball at the end.

On the game's opening drive, Lee returned an intercepted Nekuza pass for a touchdown. From his nose-guard position, Jimmy Pillans blocked their extra point attempt. Nekuza hit Willard Simmons behind the Lee secondary in our next series with a beautiful pass to score. Henson's kick was good. We led 7-6.

Both defenses stiffened, and after two series, the teams exchanged punts. Their big tackle Jerry Townsend opened a hole on the left side of our defensive line, and Sheehan passed through as if he were a Ferrari leaving a showroom. He ran 61 yards untouched for their second score. After their two-point conversion attempt failed, they led 12-7. For the third time that season, we were behind.

Gary Schutte picked off a Lee pass in the second quarter and returned to their 20-yard line. Winn and Allison worked from there to get the Tigers on the board again to make it 14-12. We had the lead for the second time in the game.

It was short-lived after Sheehan again popped through a hole on the left side of our defense to race 41 yards for a touchdown. Their two-point conversion succeeded, putting them in the lead at the half, 14-20. They had found a weak point in our line. As a player, I thought we needed some sort of halftime adjustment if we were going to stop them in the second half. They were spreading us out and easily running past us like we were spectators.

But Acree thought differently. He said, "Our defensive linemen need to get with it and beat the man in front of them."

And beat them consistently. Those same linemen, playing both ways, needed to do the same on offense. Our 175-pound defensive tackle, Lynn Odom, faced their 210-pound future All-State tackle Jerry Townsend on every down.

After the half, our defense bucked up and stopped Lee on their first possession at the Corsicana 12-yard line. Our next possession ended with an interception of a Nekuza pass, which set up Lee's next score. Their fullback crossed the goal line on a short run. They attempted a two-point conversion which failed. They led, 14-26.

Our next possession went nowhere, but our defense stopped Lee again on downs at the Corsicana 14-yard line. The fourth quarter started with us having the ball on our 16-yard line. Steve Winn raced off right tackle, passed a linebacker, and outran the Lee secondary to the end zone. Henson's kick was good, and we trailed 21-26.

The Tiger defense stopped the Volunteers on downs again at the Tiger 32-yard line but our offense could not make a needed first down. That was our last breath.

Coach Acree decided to punt the ball to Lee with 4:50 remaining in the game. I don't think this was a coaching mistake. We had plenty of time to try and score again if we could get the ball back. But they played ball control afterward and made four consecutive first downs. I regretfully relive those series of downs, thinking I could have called some stunt or defensive formation to force them to punt. That didn't happen.

The clock ran out on the '65 Tigers. And we lost the game.

The loss to Lee was a sad ending to our dream of becoming AAAA state champions. Although Acree felt that we played well enough to win, he said, "We made too many mistakes."

* * *

I accepted the loss because in preparing that week, Acree and I were alone in the film room and he said, "We're going to lose this week."

At the time, I didn't understand how he knew that or why he said it to me. Part of the reason might have been because I limped around on a crushed ankle that quarterback Mike Nekuza had stepped on the previous week while playing Alice. He may have been trying to motivate me. As an experienced coach, Acree could see the difference in the talent of the two teams. Their squad wasn't that much larger than ours in the number of players (41 vs. 33), but five different boys from Lee lined up across from me during the game. Two or three defensive linebackers and offensive guards. Lee had lots of talent.

In researching material for this book, I communicated with Doug Conrey, the center for the Lee Volunteers, in '65. Doug runs a long-snapping school in San Antonio. He wrote back saying the '65 Tigers were "the toughest and MEANEST football team that I ever played against in my eighteen years of competitive football! And Coach Acree was even meaner. In the 4th quarter Bill Allison came in for a series as the nose-guard, and on the first play, he knocked me back into the backfield! What a beast."

Conrey played college ball at Sam Houston. He indicated that twenty-five juniors and seniors on the Lee team went on to play college football or run track.

Corsicana had only two D1 scholarship seniors on the '65 team—Bill Allison (University of Arkansas) and Lynn Odom (Texas A&M). Don Robertson received a scholarship to play at the University of Louisiana in Monroe. Gary Schutte played at Sam Houston State on scholarship. Ronnie Ragsdale and Phil Pillans played at Henderson County Junior College. Steve Winn received a track scholarship at Lamar Tech University. Junior Mike Nekuza played football at SMU on scholarship. I ended up playing at East Texas State University on scholarship.

An estimated 20,000 fans watched Lee defeat the Tigers 21-26 and end our twelve-game win streak. Our defense could not stop Pat Sheehan, who scored two touchdowns on long runs. He had more yards running than Corsicana did as a team. To our credit, we were the only team to score three touchdowns on the Volunteers that year. They were state finalists.

The Permian Panthers proved they owned Friday night lights that season by winning their first AAAA State Championship against San Antonio Lee, 11-6. If we had somehow managed to win over Lee, I don't know if we could have defeated Brazosport and Odessa Permian for the title. I do know this. The '65 Tigers had champion-level desire and determination. Those teams would have needed champion-level talent to beat us.

*　*　*

The '65 Tigers were dream makers that failed to deliver another state title to Corsicana. We were the earliest in what would become a long string of Tiger teams who could win championships but not repeat the '63 state title win.

My laser project won the local science fair that spring, and its success pushed my desire to become a scientist. I placed second in the regional competition held on the Baylor campus. The award included a subscription to Scientific American, a leading scientific publication. The first issue I received contained an article on the workings of computers, which were new at the time. Reading it, I decided I wanted a career in computing. Just as a laser focuses a beam of light, that article helped set the course of my life after high school.

I wanted to go to college but didn't know where. I hoped I would get a D1 scholarship, but I didn't. The loss of football, a significant part of my life, confused me. Neither of my parents had any college experience and offered little advice or direction on what I should do next.

I didn't have the money to attend college on my own, so I accepted a football scholarship to Henderson Country Junior college in Athens, Texas. I was disappointed as if I were put back on the B-team in my boyish mind.

Unexpectedly, Arlington State University offered me a football scholarship. It was a four-year college with an engineering school, too. I signed with them and made a new plan to live in Arlington and work at Six Flags over Texas that summer. I planned to train after work at the University for fall football.

I moved into an apartment with two electrical engineering students attending summer school. They made it clear that I could not play football and major in engineering. All they did was study.

My routine consisted of waking early each morning, eating a fold-over ham sandwich for breakfast, packing a ham and cheese sandwich for lunch, arriving at the park before it opened, working all day, coming home and having another ham and cheese sandwich for supper, reading until I got sleepy (about 10 minutes), sleeping all night and starting over the next day.

When I went to the University's athletic area to work out, I hoped to meet other players. Located in the Metroplex, the University didn't have a sizeable on-campus student population. I never met another athlete working out on campus after work. This disillusioned me, especially given what I had experienced under Acree. We were gung-ho in high school. Where was their commitment in college?

After six weeks, my parents drove up from Corsicana to see how I was progressing in my experiment to live away from home. My mother freaked out when she saw how much weight I had lost, from 175 down to 165. She made me quit my job that night, and my parents followed me back to Corsicana. As if life were a game of Monopoly, I unhappily heard, "Go to jail. Do not pass GO."

Mother wanted me to stay home and enroll at Navarro Junior College. A landmine had earned Dickey a Purple Heart in Vietnam and Dad didn't want me to go to the Army. Embarrassed about returning to live at home, I felt like a failure. I just wanted out of town.

The football coach at the Military Academy arranged to call me, and he explained a possible future at West Point. Still, I needed a year of studying calculus and physics at Quantico, Virginia before I could join the team. I discussed such a plan with my girlfriend and declined the offer. I was too immature; I would have wasted their time.

Instead, having the wisdom of a dodo bird from the isle of Mauritius, I decided to follow my friend Steve Winn to Lamar Tech in Beaumont, Texas. As if I were an acolyte entering a monastery, I resolved to give up football and focus on studying engineering. That first semester, I sat in my room studying calculus and physics, watching other boys play touch football in the common grassy area between dorm buildings.

It took the loneliness of that reality to realize that I missed being part of a team. I studied a semester there before I ran out of savings. I needed a new plan if I was going to avoid Vietnam.

I contacted Coach Moore, but he indicated there wasn't an opportunity for me to play football at SMU.

East Texas State University in Commerce, Texas had a reputation as a "teacher's college," but it was also known as a place for a "Second Chance." For example, Bruce Butler, a star linebacker on the '63 and '64 teams, matriculated to SMU but was kicked out for fighting. He got another opportunity to play at ETSU.

I contacted Butler, and he arranged for me to interview with Head Coach Earnest Hawkins. I contacted Coach Acree and told him of my interest in returning to football. I explained how much I missed the team aspect of the game. When I asked, he agreed to let me borrow two films from the '65 season that East Texas State had requested. He even suggested the

John Tyler and Cleburne games, two of my best efforts. He was very cordial and didn't seem stressed. He was glad to see me finally make up my mind.

When Coach Earnest Hawkins at East Texas State University watched the John Tyler game film, he said, "Looks like you were where you needed to be when you were supposed to be."

He offered me a full scholarship, and I joined the ETSU Lions in the spring of 1967. The school didn't offer a major in engineering, but its math and computer science programs met my ambitions.

Acree would have helped me through this transition from high school if I had asked him. He was leaning on the parallel bars when I last walked out of the Field House.

Going over and talking to him, he said, "You're one of the most dedicated players we've ever coached. You spent more time in the film room than some coaches."

I said, "Thank you, Coach; I learned a lot from you."

We shook hands and parted. The next time I saw him, I played football for ETSU and he was a coach at SMU.

Coach Jackie Edwards (left) and Coach Don Ross (right)

CHAPTER 12 ATTITUDE

"To escape criticism, say nothing, do nothing, be nothing."

Elbert Hubbard, American aphorist publisher

Early 1966, an unidentified pharmaceutical salesman sat in Coach Jim Acree's office at the Field House. He opened the conversation by saying, "Thank you, Coach, for working me into your busy day."

Acree got right to the reason he agreed to the meeting, "Glad to. I'm hoping to confirm that you'll continue leaving our vitamin B12 shots at the goalposts on Wednesday evenings?"

Salesman, "Actually, I wanted to tell you that we are discontinuing that supplement promotion."

Acree lamented, "What? By giving the shots ourselves, we've saved a lot of money and time."

"That's true, Coach, but company management says we will no longer provide the vitamins."

Acree replied, "But your research shows that B12 improves performance of even Olympic athletes. You know it helps our boy's endurance too."

"Right, and we want to support your football program ..."

Acree interjected, "The UIL doesn't prohibit giving players vitamins. Why the change?"

The salesman stammered, "First, there's no need. Medical services at clinics are more accessible now. The new Medical Arts Clinic in Corsicana is a good example. Secondly, times are changing. Reputation is important. Look what happened in Bonham."

Flabbergasted, Acree responded, "What's wrong with giving vitamins?"

"Nothing, Coach. You'll have to find another way for your players to get shots."

Acree asked, "Are we being singled out?"

"No. I've been meeting with other coaches in my region."

"You must be scheduling a lot of meetings. What's the reaction you're hearing?"

"Some coaches are stopping the practice altogether."

Acree looked incredulous, "Bullshit. The ones that want to win aren't stopping."

The salesman continued, "Others are sending their boys to a local doctor's office for injections."

Acree appealed, "We've worked together for many years. Is there a way we can change your mind on this decision?"

"No, Coach. I'm afraid this is the way it must be."

After the salesman left his office, Acree picked up the phone and called a doctor friend at the Medical Arts Clinic in Corsicana. "Doc, the pharmaceutical salesman just told me they're cutting off our supply of B12 this fall. Our starters must get vitamin shots at the Clinic this year."

* * *

The American wartime attitude of "do what's necessary to win" waned as the mid-'60s ushered in a counter-culture movement. In the general population, hypodermic needles conjured up perceptions of illegal drug use.

When Acree told his wife Rosemary about the meeting with the pharmaceutical salesman, she said, "I think the change is good. We're responsible for the perceptions we create."

"Perceptions aren't reality, Slim," Acree retorted.

Rosemary replied, "That may be true. But people act on them, and that's the problem."

"There's always a set of naysayers that want to drag us down."

"You just make sure you follow UIL rules to the letter of the law."

As the game of football changed, Acree innovated his strategies to surprise an opponent and improve his chances of winning. For example, he incorporated more passing on offense and improved Corsicana's defense by adding blitzes and stunts. Confusing an opponent delighted Acree, but at the same time, his winning pushed competitors and detractors to look for ways to return the heartache of losing. He loved competition, but there was a price for winning.

He dismissed critics. "Doing it right" meant hard work, not quick and easy solutions. He innovated his training techniques but didn't change how he taught what he knew about winning. Acree was Acree. Any suggestion of impropriety went unnoticed. If vitamin shots were part of successful seasons in the past, he would continue giving them in 1966. If boxing improved player toughness, he would continue boxing the boys in 1966. Year after year, he conditioned boys using the same vice-grip of hard work and repetition that helped shape him into a winner.

Winning earned Acree his share of haters. It seems that success breeds resentment. When I asked Coach Edwards about enemies, he knew them by name and spoke from experience, "When you're winning, some people want to get you back down on their level."

Acree identified as a champion. Having established a champion's persona during his playing days in high school and college, his coaching record furthered his "champion" identity.

Importantly, champions desire affiliation with other champions. Hanging around losers is a ticket back to mediocrity. Having a good job and doing his part to make Corsicana a better place in the world would not satisfy Acree if he perceived a change in his ability to win.

With his insistence on using experienced players, winning in 1966 came down to the sixteen juniors on the A-team returning as seniors. Acree's plans rested on their shoulders and the eight seniors returning from the B-team.

After the losses in the '64 season, the ever-competitive Acree gritted his teeth and suffered jibes about not winning a football championship for the first time in his decade-long coaching career. In 1965, he regained his champion status on the legs of Bill Allison and Steve Winn. The seniors that season delighted Acree, but we were gone in '66.

Acree started 1966 happy, planning to turn Corsicana boys into winners again. In general, the town was euphoric with the Tigers' winning ways. Acree had a recent three-year record of 34-3, a AAA State Championship, a AAAA Bi-District championship and a AAAA quarterfinals appearance. Perceiving that Acree might consider other job offers, the School Board voted in the spring to extend his contract through the 1968-69 school year as an incentive for him to stay in Corsicana.

Those dates suited Coach just fine. His oldest daughter Susan was about to graduate and planned to attend a local junior college. His second daughter Debby was set to enter high school and hoped to graduate in 1969. Personally and professionally, he aimed for another championship year in Corsicana. That's what the town expected. It's what he expected of himself.

Acree was content with his choice of teaching high school boys to play football. Speaking to a nearby Blooming Grove Booster Club, he described his situation this way, "I think our athletes are the best product our community can have, bar none. I am glad to be able to work with them in this field because I like sports and I am happy doing exactly what I want to do."

Acree busied himself early in the year, handing out thirty-three letter jackets to members of the '65 state AAAA quarterfinalists team, awarding Bill Allison and Lynn Odom trophies for their selection as outstanding players and giving speeches and lectures at coach's conferences about the Corsicana offense (which he was about to change).

He also introduced THSCA panel sessions on coaching pro-style offense and defense in school-boy football and hosted a conference panel on training junior high coaches. He spent no time advising graduating seniors on where to go to college. He did not want boys to blame him for making wrong choices, He said, "Boys needed to make their own decisions."

Acree was delighted when a record number of ninety-six boys came out for spring training in 1966 (up from fifty-two in 1964). He loved teaching them what he knew about football, especially the ones he perceived as having unshakable determination and an overwhelming desire to win.

Coming from the high-scoring Tigers of the previous year, the question on Corsicana's mind was, "How good would the Tiger offense be in 1966?"

Acree followed all UIL rules regarding practice days, equipment distribution and player involvement. But an exceptionally wet spring and player illnesses hampered workouts, which he assessed as just being "okay."

The team disappointed him. Speaking to the Lions Club, he said, "We are a younger group than last year and more inexperienced, particularly in the backfield."

To finish off spring training, the annual Blue-Gold scrimmage ended in a tie, 22-22. He disliked ties. He'd rather see one of the teams fight to win. The lack of an aggressive attitude from either scrimmage team fostered his angst about the coming season. Would the seniors do what was necessary to win, or were they complacent about what they could achieve?

The names and numbers of players that might be future starters were of interest to fans who filled the bleachers for the scrimmage, but Acree provided no program. Numbers and names were unimportant to him at that point. That was his habit. No doubt, he also wanted to limit information about the team in case the stands also seated scouts from opposing teams.

A fan asked Acree how to recognize if the players had a winning attitude. He replied, "I know it when I see it."

He didn't see ideal replacements for fullback Bill Allison and halfback Steve Winn in the scrimmage. He declared, "We won't have the running game we've had for the past few years."

During the twenty-one days of spring practice, the '66 Tigers appeared to want a championship. They showed up for football practice, put on their uniforms and went through the drills, but their attitude convinced Acree that playing winning football was not their priority. Acree could teach football technique, but he couldn't force boys to develop a desire to play with abandon. Developing courage was part of each boy's journey to becoming a man.

It disappointed him to see half-hearted efforts. A lineman who showed fear when he tip-toed up to his position. A ball carrier who became

329

squeamish at the point of contact. A senior who lingered and failed to step forward to traverse the monkey bars in the fewest number of swings.

Acree could smell desire in the stink of a uniform, hear it in the sound of a hit by a linebacker, see it in the hustle of a blocker racing downfield, feel it in the eagerness of the boys pressing around him to take a knee after practice and taste it in the salt of his mouth when his players gummed their cotton mouth.

Reviewing the scrimmage in the film room with the other coaches, Acree saw a lack of determination when a running back balked at making an extra yard, a receiver didn't strain to catch a bad throw or a defensive lineman failed to sprint from the backside to get in on a tackle.

Quitting did not always mean that a player walked away from the game. Players could give up during a play. Acree turned to Edwards, "Coach, I don't see them having their minds made up to do what they say they want to do."

Edwards replied, "Yes, and do it right. I think Nekuza is our best runner. We need to use him as often as possible."

Ross added, "At fullback, Van Odom has good size, but he seems to have a reputation as a blocker."

On the positive side, Slaughter noted, "Badie Stewart is fast; he can run the ball."

Acree countered, "But we need Stewart at noseguard."

Thinking strategically, Acree speculated, "Getting the boys in the right positions is part of our issues, but our offensive scheme requires speed and experience we just don't have."

Ross suggested, "Move Odom to a tackle position to strengthen the line."

Edwards said, "That's a good idea, but if we did that who would take his place blocking for Nekuza?"

Slaughter pointed out that Tom Rodgers had good size and track speed. By his senior year, he would earn the nickname, "Ramjet."

Acree said, "We can't count on inexperience."

The scrimmage review ended with Acree believing that the current offensive plan would doom this crop of Tigers to a losing season. As if he didn't hear any of the suggestions, he said, "Let's keep the position assignments we have for now. I want to re-evaluate our offensive strategy."

* * *

Later, Acree sat alone in the Field House office and flipped through coaches' magazines contemplating how to solve the problems he saw in the spring scrimmage. He came across an interesting article that spoke to what he believed. After reading it, he decided to teach the Tigers a new offense.

Acree strategized to give his runners a better chance of success by confusing the defense. This was not new for him. He constantly looked for ways to outsmart opponents, and his innovations had managed to keep the Tigers a step ahead of district opponents—most of the time.

He spoke at civic clubs and commented on the possible offensive contributions of selected Tiger players. He candidly noted the team's lack of size and speed, which were standard sportswriter (and fan) requirements for success in football. But he didn't tell anyone of his plans to change the offense to better camouflage play designs to confuse defenses.

Betting on his ability to lead, Acree, the competitor, was thrilled at the thought of the possibilities for success. He loved a good surprise. However, as they moved into the summer off-season work, he perceived that the seniors in the '66 season had yet to make up their minds to play championship football.

He believed a player and a team could be as good as they decided to be. Their hunger and thirst for winning would determine their fate. Moreover, there were no shortcuts to achieving the goal of a championship. The boys had to "do it right."

He could put them through the same rigorous hard work that he had used in the past, but the boys in 1966 were not treating football as if it were a lustful endeavor. Without that, they could not "make a respectable showing on the field."

It became clear that he had to make a more significant change in the offense.

According to Coach Slaughter, Acree decided to attend an offensive coaching clinic on the west coast that summer. He came back all excited about installing a new offense for the fall. He believed he had found a solution to get Nekuza more involved in the running game. Instead of a backfield running game, he'd use a quarterback-based attack. Sweep Nekuza left. Sweep Nekuza right.

Acree wanted to minimize the time competitors had to prepare their defenses, so he kept his plans secret. Talmadge Canant, Sports Editor at the Daily Sun, could only allude to a new scheme in an article about Corsicana's offensive leadership during the Acree years. "If we had to guess, we'd say that a good many offensive changes are in the air."

Coach Ross handled the basketball program in the spring of 1966, disappointing the Tiger basketball team after their success under Coach Matthews. As Athletic Director, Acree hired Coach Jerry Brim as a new basketball coach on July 16, 1966. This allowed Ross, somewhat laid-back as a coach, to focus on football that fall.

Acree continued to try and fill a late October open date in the fall schedule that resulted when the UIL inserted Temple into the north zone of District 13-AAAA. He even advertised for an opponent in Arkansas and Oklahoma but had no takers. He disliked open dates, saying, "I don't feel an open date does much good."

To be around winners, Acree accompanied Bill Allison that summer to Houston to watch him play on the South team in the THSCA All-Star game. Bill was Acree's third All-Star performer since coming to Corsicana. In addition, Acree continued his service on the Board of Directors of the Texas High School Coaches Association.

On August 15, 1966, by UIL rules, Acree issued shoes to seventy-nine football tryouts for the fall season. The players held unorganized workouts until the coaches took over two-a-day practices on August 22. Contact work began on August 26. At a "back to school" rally downtown, Acree reminded fans, "If you don't get behind our ball club, we won't have a good one."

Fan commitment was part of Acree's game plan to keep players motivated. He wanted boys to exhibit a desire for winning, so he needed the town to encourage them to achieve their goals. If players wanted to be champions, citizens in the barber shops, gas stations and grocery stores assumed responsibility to cheer them on as they demonstrated progress by winning football games.

Because of a robust set of seniors on the '65 team, many juniors who became seniors in '66 had never started. Many had little game experience. Reminiscent of the '64 season, the seniors had to compete for starting roles on the '66 team.

Despite the new offense, the spring problems carried over into August. When two-a-day workouts ended, Acree couldn't name a starting lineup, "We just can't tell about some of these positions yet."

Acree juggled players and positions in his new scheme, but success hinged on their mental focus to pick up the new system on offense. For the first time in his tenure in Corsicana, he did not hold a scrimmage on the night of the annual Dads Club BBQ, a tradition to rally fan support.

Instead, he decided to skip it and scout a Bonham scrimmage that night. Bonham was the first scheduled Corsicana opponent.

Rosemary asked, "Jim, how will it look if you are not at the BBQ to introduce the players?"

"I don't think it matters. It's more important for me to see Bonham's defense."

Savvy about football, she replied, "The assistant coaches can scout Bonham. What are you thinking?"

"I've got a new offense, and I want to see what players and personnel they'll line up against us."

"Our home is in Corsicana, not Bonham. Your comments at the BBQ would mean a lot to the boys."

"Slim, Edwards, Ross and I have to be in Sherman for the scrimmage there on Saturday. Slaughter can handle the BBQ."

"You'll have very few Corsicana fans in Sherman."

"I expect that, and fewer scouts too."

Coach Slaughter introduced the players at the BBQ. Acree's absence sent the players a subtle message: "Decide if you want to win this year and show it."

Acree attempted to motivate players to make the most of themselves just as he continuously tried to outsmart competitors. Not having a scrimmage in Corsicana hid his new offense from scouts and the local press.

The attitude of the seniors on the '66 team continued to trouble him. After completing the scrimmage against Sherman, a press article quoted him saying, "The success of any team rests on its leadership, and the seniors must be the leaders. Right now, we don't seem to be willing to pay the price in effort and desire."

He spoke to the Lions Club as the team prepared to play Bonham and predicted the '66 Tigers might end up with a 5-4 record, a losing season to him. Acree's critical eye compared the '66 team to what he had witnessed in previous years and found the boys lacking.

Acree searched for ways the coaches could fix the problem. He confessed, "Perhaps we coaches are not as familiar as we could be with where a boy's best position is."

His core philosophy, however, was based on player desire and determination. He continued, "Sometimes I think that's the hardest part of football coaching—determining which position to play a boy."

Bonham

Bonham was in its second year of UIL probation for allowing football players to receive a 17¢ "church booklet." The '66 Tigers easily defeated the unmotivated Warriors 20-0.

The game served to remove the cloak off Acree's new offense. Canant called it "a fancy-dan offense that had more shifts than a discotheque."

The shifts were designed to confuse Bonham. The win momentarily encouraged Acree who told the Dads, "We have the potential to be a good ball club."

Acree hoped the win would encourage his seniors to focus on beating the next opponent, Jacksonville. Preparing that week, however, his dissatisfaction with the team lingered, "I don't think the boys realize what's coming up. Their mind doesn't seem to be on their business."

Jacksonville

Wanting to prove Acree wrong, the '66 Tigers trounced the Jacksonville Indians, 21-7. But Acree wanted perfection. As if they won by accident, he said, "We're still not aggressive. We still don't have that bunch of hitters we are looking for. We're not consistent in our defensive play."

John Tyler

Preparing for John Tyler, the next opponent, he better framed his concern, "We coaches don't seem to be getting out of them what we should be getting out of them. There's a lot of individual effort, but not enough group effort."

He didn't want to see just one Tiger in on a tackle. He expected two, three or four Tigers to hit a ball carrier simultaneously. Hustling to make such "gang tackling" discouraged opponents.

John Tyler walloped the Tigers in front of a hometown crowd, 6-34, handing them a 28-point loss. A complete team breakdown shocked fans at Tiger Field.

Losing by four touchdowns had not happened since Dallas Samuel beat the Tigers 13-41 seven years earlier. That was 1960, Acree's first year in Corsicana. And the Tigers were AAA. Samuel was a AAAA powerhouse.

The Tigers wallowed in mental mistakes. The referees called an illegal procedure penalty on their first possession. Acree discussed the formation shifts with the officials, but the flap cost the team what poise it had. Executing the new offense, they turned the ball over a half dozen times via fumbles and pass interceptions. Most of these set up easy scores for John Tyler.

Before writing this chapter, I watched the game film, and the fumbles were comical. The Tiger runners coughed up the ball like a cat spits out a hairball. The defeat was an embarrassment, something a winner like Acree wanted to avoid.

Leaving the field after the loss, sophomore quarterback Bobby Morehead trailed Acree running off the field. He overheard Coach say to a fan, "We just don't have it this year."

His perceptions of the team turned into reality. Previous Acree teams created an expectation of winning among fans and competitors. Before the '66 season, Acree's record in Corsicana was 58-11-2. The team collapse against John Tyler in 1966 left most fans speechless.

But not everyone was silent. A winner like Acree had his share of detractors in the town. When I interviewed Coach Edwards, he quickly listed several names of people critical of Acree. Their identities are unimportant now, but their disdain for Acree convinced his detractors that he needed to be humbled.

Another critic not mentioned by Edwards was a local doctor with no connection to the team. It's unclear if the doctor even knew Acree personally. Researching their relationship, I can only put them in one civic meeting together. Nevertheless, this doctor wrote a letter to the Texas State Board of Education complaining about "some of the methods followed by the football coach."

As Rosemary said, right or wrong, people act on their perceptions. Perhaps the doctor believed he could not get a fair hearing if he brought his concerns directly to Acree or the local school board. Or maybe he wanted to create a controversy by suggesting illegal drug use. His letter advised its recipients that "individual football players at Corsicana were being given vitamins or drugs, by mouth or by injection, before football games."

Meanwhile, the margin of the loss to Tyler and the sloppy play had fans shaking their heads. The town found consolation, however. Tyler was a non-district opponent. Zone championship play would start the following week.

Waco Richfield

The Tiger defense came roaring back in their Zone opener against Waco Richfield. As though the team received a slap in the face with red meat, they chewed up the red-shirted Rams, 20-7. As a tribute to the team, Acree said, "The defense started to hit people."

Unfortunately, senior defensive back Ronnie Dosser suffered a broken leg during the game, which ended his season.

Waco High

Even so, the next week away from home in their second Zone outing, the Tigers defeated Waco High, 14-10. The victory came on the strength of a blocked punt by Mike Butler. Badie Stewart scooped up the bouncing ball and returned it 54 yards for the winning touchdown.

Waco University

In their third Zone game, Corsicana fans were joyous when the Tigers obliterated Waco University, 40-0.

Sacking all three Waco schools made the loss to John Tyler just a bad memory. As far as fans were concerned, Tiger winning ways were back or so it seemed.

Meanwhile, the offended doctor's letter worked through the state's regulatory bureaucracy, the Texas Education Agency. The complaint of alleged drug use was forwarded to the UIL in Austin.

Cleburne

In their fourth Zone match of the season, playing at home against the Cleburne Yellow Jackets, the Tigers lost, 15-23. Corsicana lost control of its destiny.

Temple

Fans still had hope, however, until Temple came to town the following week. The Tigers could not mount a consistent run game using the new offense. Nekuza injured a leg. The Tigers stalled without a running game that could deliver first downs to keep drives alive. Tony Haefs led the defense when game circumstances handed the Tigers their only points on two safeties. The Tigers lost, 4-7.

After the loss to Temple, Corsicana had no hope of winning a Zone title. A District Championship was impossible, but Acree wanted to "close out the books a winner."

Bryan

However, on November 11, 1966, the last game of the season, the Bryan Broncos defeated the Tigers, 0-9. The Tiger defense played an excellent game, but the Broncos shut out the new offense.

The ride back to Corsicana from Bryan was worse than the two previous Blue Goose breakdowns on Highway 14. The loss capped the longest losing streak of Acree's tenure in Corsicana.

As Acree predicted, the '66 season ended with a 5-4 record, his worst season since coming to Corsicana. He told the Dads Club, "The Tigers may not have been aware of how much every opponent wanted to beat them."

Football season was over for the Tigers, but the drama for Coach Acree had just begun.

* * *

After receiving the offended doctor's letter, the UIL Executive Committee met on December 15, 1966, over a month after the Tiger season ended and recommended an investigation of Corsicana for an alleged violation of the League's Amateur Rule.

The Investigating Committee contacted the Corsicana doctor who wrote the complaint letter and met with him privately. He wrote a subsequent letter to Dr. Rhea Williams, Executive Director at the UIL. From it, the UIL summarized the Doctor's complaint as Corsicana "Provides medical services for the football team."

Adding to giving players' vitamins, coaches providing medical services *without school administrator supervision* violated Rule 25. Coach

Edwards said, "The UIL investigator, Bailey Marshall made a surprise visit to the Field House and came to the training room."

Marshall asked Edwards rhetorically, "Do you have a medical degree? ... If not, I suggest you stop practicing medicine."

At the time, coaches routinely assisted players with injuries, cleaning scrapes, butterfly taping helmet "pops" and taping knees and ankles. They supervised players' use of whirlpools, gave them ice treatments and treated deep muscle bruises. But coaches quickly sent players to the hospital for more severe injuries requiring x-rays or a doctor's treatment.

Unaware of the UIL proceedings, the Dads Club held their annual meeting on December 20, 1966, and awarded the Tiger coaches appreciation checks as a "thank you" for their extra hours of service to achieve Corsicana's athletic success.

Outstanding by any measure, Acree's seven-season record in Corsicana was 63-15-2. As usual, he held an end-of-season meeting with his assistant coaches to review what went wrong and to learn from their mistakes.

Coach Edwards identified what he thought was the main problem, "Jim, I agree with your assessment about lack of focus, but we just didn't have the power and speed we've had in the past."

Coach Slaughter delivered bad news on a similar line, "Coach, the B-team talent is not what we've had in the past either."

Acree understood that a AAAA classification brought on new requirements for the number of players and increased the importance of player size and speed. Acree said, "It looks like 1967 will be a repeat of 1966."

He had problems with his staff as well. Don Ross and Jerry Brim didn't want to spend as much time coaching as he demanded, so Acree needed to make staff changes.

That evening, he delivered the bad news at home to Rosemary, "Slim, looking down the road, we're not going to have the football talent we need to compete for championships."

She asked him, "Just next year?"

"No. I think it will be two years of losses if we stay in Class AAAA."

"What are the enrollments showing?"

"Corsicana's attendance is not increasing. As the UIL raises their cutlines for diving the schools into classes, we'll likely drop back down to Class AAA in 1968."

"I know you don't want to go backward. What are you thinking?"

Acree opened up, "Dave Smith from SMU called today to remind me about their interest in recruiting Mike Nekuza. SMU is the Southwest Conference champion this year. He also said that if we want to move to the college level, now is the time."

Rosemary debated him, "Jim, Debby is in her first year of high school. I don't want to move her now."

"Slim, I understand, but coaching at SMU would be a promotion for us."

"I realize that, but I don't want to move our girls."

Acree compromised, "I commuted to ETSU for a summer. I can commute to Dallas this spring. We can decide later about relocating."

"Figure something out, but I don't want to move."

Acree pleaded, "It would be awkward to continue making a home in Corsicana if I'm not the football coach."

Rosemary gave him the green light to investigate an opportunity at SMU. Dave Smith, an SMU assistant coach, arranged an interview between

Acree and Head Coach Hayden Fry. Things happened quickly afterward.

* * *

Two weeks into the new year, on January 14, 1967, Jim Acree shocked the community and resigned his position as Athletic Director and Head Coach to take a job as offensive coach at SMU under Hayden Fry. Today, this position is called offensive coordinator.

Corsicana Superintendent Don Bowen issued a public statement saying the Board reluctantly released Acree from his contract, called him an outstanding coach and wished him the best in his new "promotion" and work. Acree resigned. He was not fired or "run out of town."

The previous day, on January 13, 1967, with no Corsicana officials attending, the Investigating Committee of the UIL met in Austin with the Executive Committee. It recommended they set a hearing date on February 2, 1967, to consider the evidence of Corsicana's alleged violation of the Amateur Rule and Rule 25 of the Football Plan.

Unaware of the UIL proceedings, fans congratulated Acree and recognized his success as a coach. He had become friends with many people in Corsicana, and although people were sad to see him leave, they accepted his desire to seek a coaching job at the college level.

I was away in college when my dad called to tell me the news. He said, "I'm surprised that Acree stayed here as long as he did."

It would have been unusual for a high school coach to go directly to a head coaching position at the college level. Acree moving to an assistant coaching position at SMU, a winning school in the prestigious Southwest Conference, made career sense to most fans.

After Acree's resignation and unaware of the UIL investigation, the Corsicana School Board got right to work on finding a replacement.

Football-crazy fans took Acree's departure in stride and began speculating about who would be the next head coach.

Corsicana Athletic Director/Head Coach positions were highly desirable, given its championship culture. According to the Daily Sun, Corsicana quickly received "quite a few" applications for the vacancy left by Acree. It reported that "Many hopefuls had excellent records."

Acree was soon recruiting former players and competitors to SMU. He signed running-back Bill Dietz from Waco Richfield, who was attending Kilgore Junior College, and he signed Mike Nekuza, his quarterback from Corsicana. Also, former assistant Coach Jerry Moore, who had previously jumped to SMU as a scout-team coach, assumed the duties of coaching receivers under Acree.

Various names of applicants for the Corsicana job circulated through the feed store, lumber yard and cotton mill, but surprisingly and hastily, on January 25, 1967, the School Board announced that former assistant coach Raymond Anderson would become the next athletic director and head coach.

Anderson was well known in town, and his appointment pleased many fans. However, as a Sam Houston Elementary School Principal, Anderson had been out of coaching for two years. And having received applications from active coaches with winning records, why would the School Board choose Coach Anderson? And why would it make its decision so quickly? Not even two weeks had passed since Acree's resignation.

A possible reason for the haste was announced the following week, on February 3, 1967, when the UIL placed the football program at Corsicana High School on probation for two years. Corsicana officials met in Austin with the UIL Executive Committee on February 2nd and accepted the terms of the probationary ruling. The Corsicana School Board appeared unaware of the UIL investigation until after Acree's resignation. He did not attend the February meeting in Austin and made no defense of the accusation against him.

Compared to the penalty Bonham received for giving athletes a "church booklet," the UIL was lenient with Corsicana. The press described the ruling as a "slap on the wrist."

Unlike the Bonham ruling, probation allowed Corsicana to still compete for a District title, and it affected no other UIL-regulated activities at the school. Probation meant that the football program in Corsicana was on notice, and another rule violation in the next two years would result in a penalty.

School officials denied any knowledge of the practice of giving players vitamin shots. The League alleged that Coach Acree violated its Amateur Rule when he had a local medical clinic give injections to football players *without the players paying for the service.*

The Amateur Rule stated that players "must not receive any monetary or valuable consideration to compete." Services offered free to players must be available to the entire student body. The vitamin shots, valued at 50¢ each, totaled $4.50 for players who received shots for all nine games in 1966.

The school billed the parents of the players who had received shots (between 16 and 18 starters). New Athletic Director Raymond Anderson agreed to clear all such future activities in advance with the School Board.

The UIL also found that Corsicana violated Rule 25, loss of institutional control for the Superintendent of Schools allowing coaches to perform medical services for players. Perhaps the Dads Club awarding "appreciation checks" to coaches also represented out-of-control booster activity? The amounts exceeded the League's $500 limit. The UIL wanted members not to reward coaches for the success of their football teams. The League believed overcompensation would undermine the educational goals of UIL competition. They bucked a coming trend to pay winning coaches much greater salaries.

On February 7, 1967, Talmadge Canant wrote in his Corsicana Daily Sun column, "It is known that vitamin pills or shots are given players by the majority of schools in Texas, as well as by the majority of colleges."

Canant reported that "Many schools had telephoned to learn the details of the Corsicana case, since they, too, give their players vitamins."

Acree was surprised by the UIL ruling, and Coach Slaughter said, "The doctor's complaint angered him."

To understand the doctor's side of the story, I contacted his family and asked for an interview. The doctor, still living, declined, saying, "not much good can come from it."

Hence, the motivation of the doctor remains unknown. There is no evidence that he wanted Acree out of coaching or that he was on a vendetta to drive Acree out of town. Perhaps he wanted to protect the reputation of the medical profession?

It's unlikely that the doctor would have been able to predict the consequences of his letter. People act on their perceptions established by rumors and sometimes by the facts. The doctor's family had to deal with the blowback from fan perception that the doctor's complaint ran the popular coach "out of town."

Already on the staff at SMU, Acree made no public statements about the matter.

In giving vitamins to players, it appears that Acree did nothing that was not common among other schools in Texas. The UIL didn't object to players receiving vitamins, but players should have paid for the shots.

Acree's critics needed some means to vilify his success. Labeling him as "a rule breaker" tarnished his reputation. From a UIL perspective, Acree had a "target on his back."

While he was in Corsicana in the '60s, Acree never uttered a harsh word to players against the UIL or its rules. Instead, he praised it in public situations.

As an assistant coach, Raymond Anderson helped Acree observe UIL rules. And Anderson saw nothing wrong with offering players vitamins before games or vitamin C tablets during the winter cold season.

Canant summarized the vitamin issue by paraphrasing the title of a jazz song embedded in the culture at that time, "Tain't What You Do (It's the Way That You Do It)."

* * *

The Acree family had grown to love Corsicana and considered it home. However, given the vitamin controversy, Coach and Rosemary decided to move their clan to Richardson, Texas. As a benefit of his affiliation, their daughter, Susan, enrolled in SMU tuition free that spring. Daughters Debby and Nancy were popular teenagers and cheerleaders. Leaving Corsicana unsettled their lives. At age nine, son Felix said, "I was Jim Acree's son in Corsicana, but I was a nobody in Richardson."

The move was unpleasant for the family. Each had to start a process of mending the torn fabric of their social lives. In response to the disappointments, Coach likely said, "That's life."

* * *

In February 1967, Acree entered the coaching suite at SMU and flipped on the lights. As usual, he was the first to arrive and eager to put in a full day's effort. His confidence energized his drive. His experience and understanding gave him insight into the intricacies of the game. He was sure that his focus on creating strategies for winning would work in the future as they had in the past. And he believed talented college players would bend to his will and become champions just as they had when he was a high school coach.

Acree took a moment to admire the trophies encased behind glass in a wall of cabinets. He noted a few of the championships they memorialized. Smiling, he expected more would be added now that he was at SMU.

Behind the glass were also pictures of groups of other coaches, some he had already met. And there was Coach Fry, too. Acree suspected he was a football mastermind. It took one to know one. They would agree completely, he thought. And there was a picture of the defensive coach. A hunch told Acree that conflict between the two would be natural, but that's okay, he thought. His brows furrowed. The thought of a good competitive situation put his mind to work.

Acree turned and walked into his office. He noticed a box of new business cards on the desk and eagerly opened it. He removed a card and examined it closely. As he admired its red and blue colors, he read the name and position on the front. His ears pulled back as his face tightened in a grin. No thought of the troubles behind him in Corsicana worried him.

Admiring the card, he noted his assistant coach position but reminded himself, "I'm going places." Full of desire and determination, he planned to become a head coach again someday. He was just as sure of it as the name on the card, Jim Acree. He was a winner. And winners win.

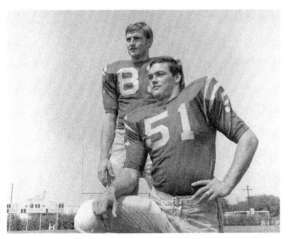

Ronnie Ward (standing), Bruce Butler (kneeling), 1967 at East Texas State University

CHAPTER 13 REMEMBRANCES

"Coach Jim Acree. 'Run it again, men.'"

Statue plaque in Corsicana, Tx

Putting up a life-size statue of Coach Acree in downtown Corsicana was a team effort. He would have wanted it that way. Team members included City employees, players from the '63 State Championship team, and the Acree family—his son, Felix, his daughters, Susan, Debby and Nancy and his brother, Stan Acree. The family signed the football held in the statue's extended left arm.

Coach Acree passed away unexpectedly in 1995. Football championships were the norm in Corsicana during his tenure, 1960-1966. Daughter Susan also signed the football for Rosemary, his wife who passed away in 2011 after an extended battle with cancer.

The '63 team didn't sign the football. Their names are on a plaque at the foot of the statue. The plaque also includes the names of assistant coaches in '63—Raymond Anderson, Jerry Moore, Paul Slaughter and Jerry Matthews. The inscription tells a story. Over a fourteen-game season, the

1963 Corsicana Tigers were the only undefeated, untied University Interscholastic League (UIL) team in Texas. The '63 Tigers captured the Class AAA State Championship. Below the inscriptions are the players' names and two managers (John Elmore and Gene Garrett). The players include fourteen seniors—Sam Cooper, Mark Dawson, Donnie Denbow, Lonnie Elmore, Robert Graham, Jim Hagle, Holly Holstein, Marc Maxwell, Johnny Nelson, David Robinson, Gary Roman, Joe Smith, John Stover and Jim Wood, fifteen juniors—Jerry Anderson, Bruce Butler, Ronald Cottar, Roger Goldesberry, Bill Henson, Don Ivie, Rankin Koch, Rick Libal, Ronnie Rhoads, Stan Rosen, Nick Sanders, Jerry Sheets, Cody Sherrard, Chick Whistler and Danny Wilcox and four sophomores—Bill Allison, Ben, and Glen Smith and Ronnie Ward. Team captains were Jim Wood and Gary Roman.

The statue is on the northwest corner of 6th Avenue and Beaton Street. Coach Acree loved hitting, so the statue's extended left arm protrudes into the sidewalk such that a passerby must dodge it. Otherwise, they'll experience Acree's love for contact. The City Manager didn't plan its placement to have that feature, but it was not surprising to the men Acree coached that hitting would be a consequence of his statue's placement. As players, we knocked heads plenty in his presence.

Payne Lara, the artist who created the statue, had difficulty getting Acree's likeness. I was the project manager, and we had an agreed date for the family to drive to Payne's shop and approve the likeness. On the morning of the approval meeting, I received a phone call at 5 AM from Payne asking to cancel the appointment, "I don't have him yet."

I had briefed Payne on Acree's popularity in football-crazy Corsicana back in the '60s. He later joked about the stress of finding Acree's image saying, "I'd rather work on a President of the United States than a coach of a state championship football team in Texas."

Given Payne's experience placing dozens of other bronze statues, he thought it would take less than thirty minutes to install the Acree bronze. However, after three hours of work to anchor it to the sidewalk, Payne had to re-drill holes in the concrete and move it a few inches. He worked up a sweat and was vexed as we drove to a nearby hardware store for materials to do the installation again. Payne experienced, "Run it again, men."

It tickled me to see Acree's statue testing Payne's desire—did he really want it (installed correctly)? With the help of two City workers, Acree's son Felix and me, we completed the installation and made it ready for the unveiling. Onlookers clapped.

Watching nearby, Assistant Coach Jerry Moore and team Captain Jim Wood laughed at the installation difficulties. "That's just like Acree—hard to please in real life, and now he even makes it hard and painful for those working to install his statue."

That was just the start of the laughs and funny stories shared the next day as hundreds of people gathered in downtown Corsicana inside the remodeled Palace Theater at 10 AM to honor Coach Jim Acree before the unveiling ceremony at 11 AM on March 17, 2017.

Halfback Mark Dawson emceed the gathering from a lectern on stage. Seated in a row were a few players from the '63 team, Donnie Denbow, Jim Hagle, Bill Allison, Jim Wood, Gary Roman and Stan Rosen. Unrehearsed, Mark got the men talking with a proposition. "In 1963, Jim Acree was a man out of his time. He was so deeply steeped in what the game meant, what sports meant, what competition meant that he didn't fit that era of regulation."

The players on stage began thinking of how to respond using the microphones in front of them. Their responses imply they missed Mark's following line, "I propose that Coach Jim Acree never broke a rule in his life, and I mean it."

But sitting in the audience, I heard his proposition. I couldn't nod in agreement or disagreement. To comprehend Mark's conjecture requires an appreciation of 1) how the University Interscholastic League regulations stymied coaches like Acree who played to win, 2) the extent of the football rivalries between Corsicana and neighboring towns, Athens, Cleburne, Ennis, Jacksonville, Palestine, Tyler, Waco and Waxahachie, 3) the regional football competition between Central Texas, East Texas, West Texas, North Texas and South Texas, 4) the rich football talent larger schools mustered against smaller schools, 5) individual player struggles to please Coach Acree, 6) a cultural shift in the '60s to a more leisurely lifestyle, 7) Acree's goals for his players derived from his values, which were forged during the Depression, World War II and service in the Army in Korea and 8) Acree's journey to escape an abusive father and become an exceptional athlete, a championship football coach in Texas, a successful distribution manager in a large company and a final stint in public education before his sudden death at age 67.

During the pre-unveiling gathering at the statue ceremony, Mark Dawson's conjecture referred to Corsicana's "free vitamin shots" controversy and subsequent practicing and "dummy use" violations at Midland Lee. Having players take vitamins was not illegal but giving the vitamins free to players did violate UIL rules at that time. Mark's question highlighted Acree's focus as a coach, his competitive nature and that he was a misfit in an era of over regulation.

Was Acree unsympathetic to rules that weren't part of the game? During the '63 season, Acree specifically gained permission from the UIL to feed players an evening meal for two-a-days in exchange for performing odd jobs around the Field House. As players, he regularly had us work in order to eat together. It would have been easy for Acree to conflate permission to provide a meal with permission to include giving players vitamins. Acree potentially thought, "Here, have some roast beef, a baked potato and green beans covered in honey with a side of vitamin B12."

To Mark's point, it likely didn't occur to Coach Acree that anyone would be concerned about giving vitamins to players. In the changing cultural norms of the '60s, that was a mistake.

Ignoring the vitamin shot issue at the ceremony, Jim Hagle emphasized Acree's focus on football, "He got us ready to play every game, more so than the coaches I played for in college and the NFL." Continuing, Hagle said, "Coach Acree was like the Bill Belichick of that era. He researched everything."

All-State end Donnie Denbow later became superintendent of Corsicana schools and hired Acree to work with seventh-grade boys, "He did some really good things with those kids, and, you know, I'll always be grateful for that latter part of our life, we were golfing buddies."

Donnie painted a picture of Coach Acree playing golf. "I didn't think he knew the right end of a golf club, but he wanted to win every shot, every putt, every hole, every round. I mean, he wanted to win everything he could because that's how competitive he was."

As for Acree's impact on our lives, Mayor Denbow concluded, "And that was what he imparted to all of us, the desire to win, the desire to be successful."

Gary Roman, the quarterback of the '63 team, described his experience with Acree, "I spent a lot of time with Acree being a quarterback. I watched a lot of films, too. I used to think that when I put on my helmet that Coach became deaf because he immediately got right in my face. He put his hand under my shoulder pads and pulled his face next to mine. He pulled right up next to my face guard, and then he would start tapping on my shoulder with his other hand. But he was not someone who screamed and hollered. He taught us how to win and was responsible for winning a state championship. He outcoached every coach that we played against."

All-State fullback Bill Allison described how Acree recruited him into the game. "He came over to Collins Junior High one time in '62. I was out playing grab-ass football, accomplishing nothing, and Acree introduced himself. I said, 'I've heard of you. You're the coach over at high school. I hear you run a lot over there. I don't want to run.'"

Bill continued, "It was then that Acree said, 'Let me tell you something, Bill, you can do much more with your life if you get into sports. You don't have a lot going for you right now.' And I said, 'what do you mean?' He asked, 'do you date?' I hesitated, saying, 'well (I hadn't quite started dating yet).' He said, 'if you play football, you'll have a better chance of getting a date.' I said, 'I'd be on your team, right?' He said 'yes.' I said, 'I'll go get my track shoes right now.' That's the first time I ever met him."

Bill summarized Acree's influence. "If it weren't for him, we wouldn't be what we are today, and I would have never played football." And then Bill made Acree's impact personal, "If it weren't for Jim, I'd be dead or in a Mexican prison."

* * *

For the statue dedication, the city blocked off the intersection of 6th and Beaton, erected a canopy and set up a podium for the speakers with a sound system. Hundreds of people sat in folding chairs under the canopy or stood around the canopy to experience the unveiling. Bill Allison emceed the event and warmed up the crowd of fans on a beautiful morning before introducing the speakers. Reverend Rankin Koch began with an invocation. Mayor Donnie Denbow spoke next, saying, "It's my honor to accept this statue on behalf of the city of Corsicana of Coach James D. Acree."

Mayor Denbow, having played under Coach Acree in Corsicana, coached with him as an assistant at Midland Lee. Later, as school superintendent, he employed Coach Acree and related his unique perspective: "We experienced his devotion to his players and the game itself. His was an example that provided all of us with a blueprint for success." He elaborated, "Jim taught us there were no shortcuts or substitutes for excellence. He believed sincerely that an individual had to discipline his mind and body and extend his abilities to the very limits and beyond to be successful. Coach Acree was a fierce disciple of the concept of team play and a man full of passion for the game. He played with dedication. Coached with dedication. And lived with dedication."

Bill Allison reminded the crowd that Corsicana had two state championships the previous century but that the first one ended in a tie game and was won on penetrations (since neither team scored, the UIL later declared both teams as co-champions). But the 1963 champions had no asterisks, fourteen wins, no losses or ties.

Coach Paul Slaughter who had a long tenure as an assistant coach in Corsicana, not only under Acree but with other head coaches, ascribed the character qualities of the Greatest Generation to Coach Acree, "Jim believed in duty, honor and service. He had great courage; he was thrifty and believed in personal responsibility. He loved his country. And Jim loved his family and his football family, too. And that meant a lot to all of us."

Coach Slaughter told a couple of stories about working with Coach Acree at Collin Street Bakery in the '80s. According to Slaughter, although Acree was out of coaching, he still watched hours and hours of game film.

Another time when both men were refereeing a junior high football game, Slaughter saw Acree coaching a linebacker between plays. UIL rules? He laughed, saying, "I told Jim, as a referee, you can't do that."

Helping a boy improve and grow into a man mattered more to Acree.

Notably, Slaughter reminded the crowd of Acree's diligence, "He used the same skills at the bakery that he used coaching, and he gave 110 percent of himself to his work. And he also expected his employees to do the same."

Coach Jerry Moore reminded the Corsicanans of his long association with Coach Acree. About Acree's move from Oklahoma to begin his coaching career at Bonham, Texas, "I may be the only person here who saw the Acree family when they crossed the Red River into Texas."

As a player for Acree in Bonham, Moore said, "He prepared all of us to play the game." Alluding to his own extremely successful career as a college football coach, Moore said, "and it carried over into the game of life. And it had a great domino effect. I like to think sometimes I was his first domino." Other former players nodded their heads in agreement.

Dr. Stan Acree, Coach's brother, shared several stories about Coach growing up in Maud, Oklahoma. He ended his remarks by saying, "This is a wonderful statue by Payne Lara, a very lasting tribute that makes the Acree families very proud. It represents everything Jim stood for—persistence, determination, dedication and the desire to succeed through hard work. May it become a lasting inspiration for the youth of tomorrow."

Complimenting the artist Payne Laura as the next speaker, Bill Allison quipped, "That statue is so good it could pass a DNA test."

* * *

Payne was a no-show to the dedication ceremony, so I stepped in and began to speak by asking, "Why do we put up a statue to honor a man and a team and a rare achievement by a city?"

"It's said, 'History is why we are who we are, what we are.'"

"When I look at the Acree statue, I remember Coach's impact on my life. He passed on to his players the knowledge that winning was possible if we were determined and persistent. He demonstrated grit, hard work and personal responsibility as keys to success in life.

"Certainly, his beliefs inspired the outstanding achievements of a state championship team and a 14-0-0 season, but the season ended and the games are long over. However, his teaching continues in us because we are still alive. He ingrained his beliefs in us, and we pass them on to those who follow us."

I thanked the city for letting the players and family erect a statue of a beloved Coach and ended with, "The statue reminds me of who I am and where I came from and why I continue to fight to be the man he so eagerly desired for all of us to be."

Working in unison, Acree's children uncovered the statue, and the photo session began. Everyone wanted their picture standing next to Coach, wearing his blue, short-sleeve shirt and black tie. He made us proud champions—the players, the fans and the city.

Former players and coaches from Corsicana and a group of Midland Lee players shared dozens of stories and moments of praise for Acree when their lives intersected his.

Mark Dawson from the '63 team led a roll call naming the '63 players who have passed on, and then everyone joined in singing, "When the Roll is Called up Yonder." Our joy was so complete that it would not have surprised anyone had the statue come to life, walked off the sidewalk and joined us in singing:

When the trumpet of the Lord shall sound and time shall be no more,
And the morning breaks, eternal, bright and fair;
When the saved of earth shall gather over on the other shore,
And the roll is called up yonder; I'll be there.

When the roll is called up yonder,
When the roll is called up yonder,
When the roll is called up yonder,
When the roll is called up yonder, I'll be there.

On that bright and cloudless morning when the dead in Christ shall rise,
And the glory of His resurrection share;
When his chosen ones shall gather to their home beyond the skies,
And the roll is called up yonder; I'll be there.

When the roll is called up yonder,
When the roll is called up yonder,
When the roll is called up yonder,
When the roll is called up yonder, I'll be there.

Let us labor for the Master from the dawn till setting sun;
Let us talk of all His wondrous love and care.
Then when all of life is over, and our work on earth is done,
And the roll is called up yonder; I'll be there.

When the roll is called up yonder,
When the roll is called up yonder,
When the roll is called up yonder,
When the roll is called up yonder, I'll be there.

CONCLUSION

Jim Acree went on from Corsicana to coach at SMU from January 1967 to August 1968. There, he would learn that his coaching strategy needed to change with elite college athletes. He moved to Lubbock to coach at Texas Tech University from August 1968 to February 1970. He was successful but left in the staff turnover after head coach J.T. King retired.

Acree considered a coaching position on the west coast but turned it down for family reasons, as Rosemary didn't want to live in California. He bid for the head coaching job at Baylor but was unsuccessful.

He reentered high school coaching from 1970 to 1977 at Midland Lee. As he did at Bonham and Corsicana, he turned a 0-10 losing program into a winning culture in the toughest UIL district at the time. He recruited Donnie Denbow and Jackie Edwards as assistant coaches.

Coach Edwards related the following story of their first day on the Midland Lee practice field when the boys showed up to meet the coaches. Having just driven into town, Acree and Edwards were wearing street clothes. Thinking that they were meeting Acree so that he could introduce himself and the assistant coaches, the boys showed up in a mix of shorts, t-shirts and street clothes. Without opening remarks, Acree asked Edwards to go down to the 40-yard line. Then, Acree had the boys line up across the goal line and told them to sprint down to Edwards. Some boys were spent after 10 trips. They walked off and quit. After 20 trips, another set of boys stopped. The same happened after 30. After 40 trips, Acree addressed the remaining boys saying, "Men, my name is Coach Acree."

Disagreements with the UIL ensued, and after resigning from Midland Lee, Acree returned to Corsicana to work as a distribution manager at the Collin Street Bakery. After a ten-year hiatus from coaching, Tom Wilson, his quarterback during the 1961 season at Corsicana, recruited Acree as an assistant coach in Palestine. Later, Wilson returned to Corsicana as a head coach, bringing Acree back to Corsicana, where he finished his career in public education.

His name tops the alphabetical list of nominees for the Texas High School Coaches Association's Hall of Honor. Despite his winning record and prolonged service to THSCA, he will likely never be voted into the Hall of Honor. More than one person I interviewed believes Acree was unfairly blackballed.

The scope of this book didn't allow for the presentation of Acree's issues with the UIL at Midland Lee, the THSCA suspension of his membership and a civil case in Corsicana over his alleged rough treatment of a junior-high boy.

Note: Thanks to Lloyd Huffman, the statue unveiling ceremony can be watched here: www.vimeo.com/211227639, videos of the morning and afternoon sessions with the players here: www.vimeo.com/212498764 and www.vimeo.com/213377730.

These three URLs can be easily accessed using these QR codes:

APPENDIX GRAHAM GAME

And so hold on when there is nothing in you
Except the Will which says to them: 'Hold on!'
And—which is more—you'll be a Man, my son!
               If— Rudyard Kipling

Fans of the 1963 Graham Steers entering Arlington's Memorial Stadium for a AAA state semifinals playoff game agree, "We should easily defeat the Corsicana Tigers today."

"Yes, they're from Central Texas District 8-AAA, a wasteland of sorry football teams."

"We couldn't have picked a better opponent!"

"That's right. Our tough, hard-hitting Steers play West Texas football."

West Texas had placed six teams in the last six AAA title games and hadn't lost any. The previous week, Graham defeated Dumas, the reigning two-time AAA State Champion. The Steers held the Demons scoreless, winning 13-0. They broke a Dumas 23-game win streak.

On the other hand, Corsicana squeaked by McKinney, 14-7, in their quarterfinals game, but the newspapers ranked the Tigers number two in the state, above the Steers. The Tigers were undefeated and untied. Graham tied Wichita Falls Ryder to advance into the playoffs on penetrations. They had a non-district season loss to Brownwood, 14-13, by "one measly point."

A Steer fan raves, "After our win over Dumas? The Tiger ranking is nonsense."

Another fan remarks, "Our downtown parade was fantastic! Just a preview of how we'll celebrate after we win state! This is our year! Go, Steers!"

A steady wind on a sunny, cold Saturday, December 14, 1963, sends the chill factor down into the teens. Walking into the stadium, Corsicana fans attempt to encourage one another. "Early in the season, the Steers lost to Brownwood, 14-13. They're not invincible."

"At the Corsicana Dads Club meeting, Coach Acree wasn't optimistic. The Tigers have smaller players, weighing on average ten pounds less than their Steer counterparts."

"We owe Graham a big 'thank you.' We didn't have to drive all the way to Dumas for this semifinal game!"

"They blanked Dumas 13-0, and four other opponents this season."

"Acree said the Steers wanted to win more than the Demons."

Acree never acts like the Tigers are the favorites. Fans knew that was his schtick. They also knew he would look for some way to come out on top. He played to win—always.

The two teams warm up with calisthenics at opposite ends of the field. The yellow-beige grass is dormant for the winter. Steer fans sit high in the eastside bleachers. The light from the bright afternoon sun warms their faces. Many have cowbells, which clang to punctuate their conversations.

"Great seats! From this vantage point, we have the best view. We won't miss a thing. Our Steers are going to play a great game! We're on a stampede to a state championship!"

361

At the team rally, Coach Curry had warned the fans the team must stop Jim Hagle, the Corsicana Tiger's big fullback. Confident it wouldn't be a problem, a fan said, "Middle linebacker Boomer Davis will corral Hagle."

Moreover, the fans didn't think the Tiger defense was a match for the Steers' running game: sweep left, sweep right, run up the middle. They all had tremendous confidence in the Steers' quarterback, P.D. Shabay.

A fan asks, "Who do we play after we beat Corsicana?"

"The game winner between Pharr San Juan Alamo and LaMarque."

"Doesn't matter. Our Steers can saddle either one."

Steer fans have other reasons to be proud. Seven years have passed since their last quarterfinal playoff appearance, but this is their first ever semifinal match, and fans have rallied around their achievement.

"This is the Big Year! Coach Curry complimented us on our team support. He said the team couldn't have won the rough 4-AAA district without our backing. We love our Steers! Our cheering led us into post-season play!"

Clang, clang, clang.

Graham tromped Snyder in their bi-district game, winning 19-0. Holding Snyder scoreless was a considerable accomplishment.

"The way that wind's blowing, Corsicana will be eating West Texas dust today!"

Tiger fans sit low in the shadows of the westside bleachers, near the exit wells, buffeted by the cold north wind. Close to the field, they can see their Tigers shiver while doing jumping jacks to stay warm. With glassy eyes, frozen faces and dry lips, Tiger fans can only hope their winning continues. The Tigers have only five returning senior lettermen, so it has been a surprise to make it this far in the playoffs. Coach Acree has trouble finding boys tough enough for his conditioning drills—tough enough to come out, stay out and play on days like today.

"Look at the size of the Graham players! Giants!"

On the east side of the stadium, accustomed to the cold and the wind, Steer fans smile, tip their hats, shake hands, bear hug and yell in unison, "Go all the way, Steers—win State!"

Tiger coach Jim Acree wears only a blue, short-sleeved shirt, his refusal to acknowledge the cold showing his superstitious side. "It will take more than luck for them to win today." Graham fans laugh. "Who is he anyway? A fugitive from Oklahoma? Someone said he was an All-State linebacker in Maud. We hear he is a graduate of Bud Wilkinson's Sooners and an Orange Bowl champion. Yes, but rumor has it he was third string. Before Corsicana, he was an assistant coach in Bonham. He has a winning record. But not playing our brand of hard-nosed, West Texas football."

Both teams work through pregame drills. Graham fans are amazed as the players come near each other around midfield. "Our Steers are like a herd of prize bulls! Look at how small the Tigers are! Team talent is important, but weight, size and speed matter most in our game. We have the whole package this year."

After the win over Dumas, awards for the Steers came rolling in. Coaches around the State picked quarterback P.D. Shabay and linebacker E.A. Gresham to the All-State team. District coaches named six team members All-District. Four others received Honorable Mention. A third of the team are bona fide All-Stars. On top of that, the School Board just awarded Head Coach Roy Curry a two-year contract extension.

Believing your team will win is essential in any battle. The Graham Reporter urged Steer fans to "Follow the Steers, Quarterfinals Champions!"

As Acree pow-wowed game strategy with his assistant coaches, Jerry Moore and Raymond Anderson, he considered what weaknesses the Tigers might exploit. "Is Graham's strong, fast defense vulnerable to a big play?" Think about it—the winning touchdown by Brownwood came on a 46-yard pass play. Then Rider scored on a 60-yard running play, and the Steers had to come from behind to tie it. Maybe Graham's defense wobbles under pressure like a big, speeding cattle truck that jackknifes after hitting a patch of black ice in a West Texas winter storm.

As they have done all year, Corsicana fans watch Coach Acree work with the boys on the field. They admire his attention to detail. He is a stickler for perfection. He wants their boys to reach their potential, and the parents of the team members feel very fortunate because of it. "Coach Acree merits a 'Coach of the Year' nomination. He prepares for games like no other coach! He keeps the boys late in practice because it takes time to turn boys into men. Acree loves hitting, so we should see some 'leather popping' today. The Daily Sun says he's one of the most feared coaches in Texas. But he's sure got to be cold in that short-sleeved shirt!"

Like pulling warm socks onto cold feet, Graham fans bunch up on a game day with weather like this. They are traveling fans, accustomed to the long drives between towns in West Texas. They know each other and crowd up close in the bleachers. Good spirits underscore their confidence. They high five, bump fists and squeeze together to fill the bleacher seats. "This is a great sign—our Steers are wearing the same uniforms today as when we beat Dumas. We love those sky-blue helmets, red stripes on the shoulders and red leggings. It makes the team look like they are wearing Superman outfits sans capes. All eyes in Texas football are on us today, and rightly so. We have what it takes to be championship Steers. Tame the Bengals! Send them to a taxidermist. LET'S GO, STEERS! Stuff the Tigers!" Clang, clang.

Some football games are just unforgettable. The weather can contribute to memorability, but it will take more than a chill factor in the teens today to impress this experienced group of fans. Graham capped off their regular, ten-game season against Rider in freezing-cold Wichita Falls. They sat wedged together in the stands and cheered for the slightest edge in a typical, rough West Texas football game. They won on penetrations. To defeat Dumas, Graham fans endured an Abilene northerner in Borger, a neutral site. Thirty-six mph winds whipped the field. Today, they warm in the glow of being in the bright spot of the AAA state playoffs. "The Steers are hot like a branding iron! Oh, that win over Dumas was so wonderful. We deserve to win state! Corral the Tigers!"

The Steers work line drills on the north end of the field. The cold wind and sight of the enormous players send chills down the spines of the Tigers at the south end of the field. Acree's quarterback, Gary Roman, tosses the ball downfield to his receivers, Donnie Denbow and Johnny Nelson. Like their fans in the stadium seats, the players tremble in the cold but feel the chill more when they see the size of the Steer players up close. The pre-game scouting report from coaches Jerry Matthews and Paul Slaughter described the size of the players, but the reality is unsettling. Roman exclaims to Hagle, "That looks like a college team warming up. They're giants! What AAA team has a 6'-7", 202-pound defensive guard?"

Hagle responds, "And another defensive guard that's 210-pounds? And a 205-pound linebacker? You've got to be kidding me."

Roman gestures to his 170-pound frame. "Shabay is a 194-pound quarterback!"

To Ronnie Ward, a fifteen-year-old, 155-pound sophomore linebacker for the Tigers, Graham players look as big as Coach Acree, men who walk tall as if they are on stilts, with large faces squeezed into round, bowling ball like helmets. Their heads sit on broad, square shoulders, standing tall like the caprocks of West Texas; their jerseys stretch tight over the pads and muscles beneath. Even more daunting, they seem impervious to the wind. The sounds of their helmets colliding together join their warmup shoulder pops and carry downwind to the nervous Tigers who remind themselves, "The butterflies will go away after the first hit!"

Shouts from the Graham fans encourage the players, "Go, Steers! We are proud of you. Cage the Tigers!" They stand and appear to swagger, moving back and forth into the gusty wind, "CRUSH CORSICANA!"

Corsicana fans are surprised that Acree doesn't have his receivers wearing dark-blue helmets, an offensive innovation he introduced the previous week against McKinney. "Is he off his game? Our boys aren't wearing enough clothing. Their short-sleeve, dark-blue jerseys are not enough protection. They have on white, long-sleeved, cotton undershirts. Some of the players are wearing multiple layers. Why did he do that?"

A Graham fan observes, "The Tigers look plump, like fatted calves, ready for processing. Rope the Tigers! Get those little boys out of the cold."

In the locker room, Acree speaks to the Tigers, "Men, they're big, but they put their jeans on one leg at a time like we do. They only play eleven men at a time, just like us. We are all playing in the same weather. We can win this game if you want it bad enough. Stay focused. Every man here needs to dig deep and think of the work you've put in to come this far. Make up your mind to go out there and win this game!"

Fans on both sides of the stadium cheer when their teams retake the field for the coin toss. Tiger team captains, linebacker Jim Wood at 160 pounds and quarterback Gary Roman at 170 pounds, walk to midfield. Graham fans size them up. "Looks like they are moseying in a funeral procession. More like 'Mutt and Jeff.' They are shorter and skinnier than our captains, Shabay and Gresham."

Shabay and Gresham have been friends since childhood, and their presence on the field inspires confidence and hope in their fans. They win the coin toss, an omen of a good day. Cowbells clang, clang, clang as Steer fans bellow loudly in approval. Graham elects to receive. The only time they have lost the coin toss this season happened at the Brownwood game, that stomach-churning loss by "One measly point!"

Corsicana takes the wind and will defend the north end zone. Winning the coin toss only further boosts the confidence of the Graham fans. "Let's get this rodeo going! We can't lose on a day like this against such a fine opponent!"

First Quarter

The Tigers kick off with the aid of a north wind. It is a weak kick that only makes it to the Steers' 20-yard line. The Steer receiver makes a fantastic catch over his shoulder and returns the ball to the 23. The Steers line up for a power sweep, which goes to the left. Next, fullback "Bulldozer" Ingram runs up the middle.

"Good call, coach! Look at Dozer bowl over those Tigers! Keep them guessing."

Third down, and Shabay passes an 11-yard stab to a receiver on the left side for a first down. The Tigers are out of position and scramble to keep up—another sweep to the right for a gain of 14 yards and another first down.

"Go, Steers, Go!" Things are playing out just the way the Steers fans expect. Ingram tests the Tiger line for a short gain. A deep pass by Shabay falls incomplete.

"What's Coach thinking? Dang, the wind is in our face!"

Acree substitutes two defensive players into the game. Acree anticipates another Graham sweep and orders Tiger defensive stunts by Cody Sherrard, a 5'3", 145-pound noseguard, and tackles Sam Cooper and Don Ivie. Graham fans have complete confidence in their All-State center, E.A. Gresham, and their big tackles, 210-pound George Hays and 202-pound Mike Lochner. Shabay calls a reverse. He takes the snap, fakes to Ingram up the middle and hands it to the halfback running right. The halfback then gives the ball to the wingback coming the other way.

The Tiger noseguard Sherrard erupts into the Steers backfield, almost takes the handoff, and forces a fumble. Multiple Tigers swarm around the mess caused by Sherrard. "Ball!" "Ball!" "Ball!" the Tigers yell as they recover the Steer fumble.

Graham fans lament, "The cold makes the football stiff and hard to hold. We were driving for a touchdown, too! We should be up by seven right now."

Before each game, Acree had a Thursday night team meeting where he drilled his quarterback Roman on plays to call based on down and situation. Acree even prepared Roman during the bus ride to the game. He wanted Roman to call plays as if the two had one mind. Assistant Coach Jerry Moore, an All-State receiver at Bonham who played for Acree, had joined the Corsicana coaching staff after graduating from Baylor. The Tiger passing game improved overnight.

The Tiger offense starts at their 47-yard line. Roman puts Chick Whistler in motion to the right, then rolls right and hits Whistler with a swing pass for 6 yards. Next, Roman throws an unusual quick pass to split end Donnie Denbow, lined up on the left, for a gain of 3 yards. The quick pass spreads out the defense. If the Steer covering Denbow backs off the line too far, Roman will signal Denbow and then throw the quick-pass instead of the play called in the huddle.

A Graham fan just smiles and says, "Hagle is supposed to be running the ball. Acree's players are too small or he'd bring them in tight and go nose-to-nose against us. He thinks that quick pass will wear us down, but we're the Steers, the team who beat the Dumas Demons."

Third down and one. Roman hands off to fullback Jim Hagle who picks up a first down at the Graham 46-yard line. Roman tosses another quick pass to Denbow who is split left again, but he is gang tackled by three

Steers. On second down, Roman floats the ball toward the flat on the right side, where a tall Steer lineman knocks it down.

Clang, clang, the cowbells peal out in a raucous chorus. "WAY TO GO, DEFENSE! They were throwing with the wind, and the ball floated like a leaf."

Coach Acree taught Roman to keep the ball and run if his receivers were covered. On the next play, he rolls right where he has two split receivers racing downfield with Steer defenders matching them stride for stride. Roman keeps the ball and turns the corner to pick up 5 yards. It is now fourth down and five at the Graham 35. Everyone expects Acree to call Hagle's number in a short-yardage situation. Instead, Roman rolls left to pass. He lobs the ball in a high arc like a basketball shot, but it wobbles like a drunk cowboy trying to walk a straight line. The tall Steer defensive linemen bats it away.

The Steer fans gloat. "Poor play calling! We have Acree's passing game figured out! Our defense covered the two split receivers like gnats on plow horses. Plow the Tigers!"

Scoreless, the Graham offense takes over on downs at their 35-yard line. Graham fans furrow their brows and yell out encouragement to their Steers, wanting a sweep to get the offense moving.

Anticipating a sweep, Acree stunts multiple defensive linemen through the gaps like flies swarming a bull's face. This forces the running back to swing deep into the backfield, where the defensive linemen gang tackle him for a 10-yard loss.

"Come ON, Steers! This isn't working!"

On second down, Shabay fakes a pass and hands the ball to the tailback on a counter play for no gain. Third down. Shabay connects on a swing pass which gains 8 yards. Fourth down, so the Steers punt.

After the whistle on the runback, an aggressive Steer defender plows onto Tiger receiver Chick Whistler who is lying on the ground. The referees don't call a penalty. Tiger fans shout and point. Graham fans congratulate the judgment of the refs. "What are the Tigers upset about? Way to go, ref! Even with the sun in our face, we could see that there was no foul on that play!"

Starting on the Tiger 33-yard line, Acree has Roman make a run-action fake to Hagle who has released into the left flat. Roman throws a bullet over Hagle's left shoulder, which he catches and runs for an 11-yard gain.

Graham fans jump to their feet. "KNOCK HIM TO THE GROUND! The fullback is not supposed to catch like a receiver."

Acree prods the Graham fans as he has the Tigers line up in a slot-left formation into the short side of the field. Denbow is tight on the right end, the wide side of the field. Graham fans cheer, "That's it! Rotate our defense right into their strong side!"

Roman fakes a run-action play left to Hagle, then rolls right to the Tigers' weak side. Coach Moore taught Denbow to burst off the line and square out 7 yards downfield. He separates from the Steer covering him, and Roman hits him in the numbers with a pass. Coach Moore had taught Denbow to turn straight up field the moment he makes a catch.

The Steer defensive back comes in fast, but Denbow dances and avoids the tackle like a rodeo clown dodging a bull. "Get him! Tackle him! CATCH HIM! OH NO!"

Denbow scampers 56 yards up the side of the field to the south end zone for 6 points.

"Oh, no! A big play! Look for a flag! What? No flags!" The Tiger cheerleaders jump for joy.

The scoreboard reads Tigers 6, Steers 0. Graham fans sit down and bellow like unweaned calves separated from their mothers. Cold from standing on the sideline, Tiger kicker Ricky Libal sends the extra point try off to the left of the goal posts. There is a collective sigh from the east side bleachers. Streamers on the goal post blow south, reminding Steer fans, "The wind is at the backs of the Tigers."

Graham fans have been behind before this season. "Watch! Our Steers will charge hard to catch up even though we're going into the wind."

A referee calls a late hit on the Tigers on the kickoff return. "Good Call, Ref! A blind heifer could see that one! Acree plays dirty."

The penalty puts the ball at the Steer 40-yard line, starting their third possession in good field position. Curry calls a new formation to open the drive. Both ends and the wing back are split out.

"Go, Steers! Spread the Tigers over the field!"

They run for a 3-yard gain up the middle. "Good call, Coach!"

The Steers hustle out of the huddle and up to the line. Second down. The quick break confuses the Tigers, and the Steers complete a pass over the middle for 5 yards. Third down and 2. Sweep right out of a flanker set is the 'bread-and-butter' play for the Steers in third and short situations. The runner turns the corner and hoofs up the right sideline, "He's headed for the barn. First down!"

"Acree blew it, not calling a stunt. He must be overconfident."

The ball is at the Tiger 35-yard line.

The Steer fans are ecstatic—Clang, clang, clang. "Here we go! Run, Steers, run! We're tearing up the Tiger defense! Hey, our band is on their feet. Stand up to see better. I love those cowbells! In this wind, the Steer cheerleaders sure are jumping high. This is getting good—a score will tie it up, and with the extra point, we'll go ahead 6 to 7."

On first down, the Steer fullback gains 5 yards, a good gain up the middle. On second down, they run a counter play with their tailback for another yard.

"We're confusing Acree good, now!"

Third down, Shabay completes a pass against the wind to the split back on the right side for a first down on the Tiger 23. "Their defense is in the middle of a stampede but doesn't know it."

The Steers run Ingram up the middle again for 3 yards, so now the Steers have a penetration. Fans are confident they won't need it in this game. Second down, the Steers sweep left from a split formation for a gain of 5 yards.

Clang, clang, clang. "We're unstoppable! Buck 'em, Steers!"

On third down, the Steer line opens a hole in the middle of the Tiger defensive line, and Shabay hands the ball to Ingram. The Tigers over pursue. Ingram sees only 15 yards of yellow grass between him and the end zone. He runs in for the score.

"That's West Texas football! Shove it down their throats! Way to go, Steers! Way to dominate this game!" Clang, clang, clang.

"Look at our big Steers jump up and down in the end zone. That evens the game at 6-6. With the extra point, we'll have the lead!"

Acree scrambles on the sideline to send in a play with Chick Whistler. Forgetting the biting cold wind in their faces, Graham fans continue to jump and cheer. Turning from facing the sun's warmth, their vision blurs, looking into the wind. The extra-point kick doesn't make it past the line of scrimmage.

"What the heck just happened?"

Whistler raced around the left end to block the extra-point attempt. The kick ricocheted off his outstretched hands, and the ball spun like a top on the turf. Tiger linebacker Jim Wood picked it up and tried to run with it.

The first quarter ends in a 6-6 tie.

Second Quarter

Graham fans are fired up. "We should have a lead now! Instead, the score is 6-6, and we're tied on penetrations, too. We have the wind this quarter. After that drive, our Steers are ready to bust loose!"

The Steers kick the ball to Corsicana Tiger Chick Whistler. Steer fans yell, "Get him! KNOCK HIM DOWN!" Whistler returns the ball to the Tigers' 37-yard line.

"Dang, we left the gate open on that one! But we still have the momentum."

"Saddle that Tiger!"

Coach Curry orders maximum pressure on the Tigers. Roman tries to freeze the defense with a fake, but the Steer linebacker shoots the gap like a bull coming out of a rodeo chute. He sacks Roman for a 7-yard loss. Second down. Another Steer bursts through the Tiger line, "Roman scampered back left to save his hide."

Roman throws toward the sideline into the wind, but the ball floats like fat on gravy, and the ball is nearly intercepted.

"Defense! Defense!" Clang, clang, clang.

Acree has his arm around guard Jim Wood and sends him in with a play. On third and long, Acree puts the Tigers into a strange formation with two wingbacks, Hagle as the fullback, with Roman behind Hagle. John Stover's snap flies past Hagle to Roman, and he snags the ball and quick kicks it over the heads of the Steer secondary. The ball hits the ground and rolls and rolls. Graham fans yell, "FALL ON IT!"

The ball just keeps rolling and rolling against the wind. "GET IT!"

The ball finally stops on the Steer 17-yard line, a 53-yard punt into the wind! The Tigers gather and dance around the ball, daring a Steer to approach it.

"Must be some Indian ritual Acree learned in Oklahoma."

Acree is playing field position. Graham fans jump to their feet, excited about their first possession with the wind. The Steer tailback sweeps left for a 2-yard gain. "Shouldn't we be passing? We have the wind. Acree won't expect us to pass this deep in our territory."

Second down, Shabay drops to pass, but the Tiger defenders are all over him. Even though the pass hit the receiver in the hands, it goes incomplete.

"Shake it off! They had good coverage as well as pressure on Shabay. Let's go, offense! RUN THAT BALL!"

Third down, Shabay runs a fake draw, then throws a screen pass to the left. Acree's Tigers hustle to the ball like they are hunting in a pack. The play only gains 2 yards. Graham has to punt.

Graham fans anticipate a booming punt with the wind, but the kicker shanks the ball and only travels 35 yards. Hagle hustles forward to catch it on the Tigers' 44-yard line. Acree coached the Tigers to set up a string of blockers, and Hagle ran in the open behind a wall.

Hagle sprints up the sideline in front of the Tiger bench. Dread washes over Graham fans like cowboys sitting high on horses in an open pasture during a lightning storm. "Come on, Steers. Get him. TACKLE HIM!"

Hagle is finally brought down at the Steer 28-yard line. The referees throw a flag and signal a clip.

"Good call, Ref! The Tigers are dirty players. He's walking that ball back. But boy, they still have good field position."

First down. Denbow splits out on the left side and catches a quick pass. Steers bulldog him to the ground for no gain. "Crush the Tigers! We have Acree figured out."

Second down. The Tigers run a razz-ma-tazz reverse play, but the Steer pressure forces skinny David Robinson to give ground. He wants to throw the ball, but the receiver is too deep. Robinson can't throw the ball that far into the wind. It flutters and falls short. Third down, Roman pump fakes, but the Steers trample over the Tiger blockers and force Roman to give ground. He goes back 10 yards and twists to get away.

"HOGTIE HIM! Fumble! Fumble! We got it! We got it! Great job, defense! People in downtown Fort Worth hear us yelling!" Clang, clang, clang.

"It's our ball on the Tiger 19-yard line. Go Steers—SCORE! Make it 6-13!" The last play caused a penetration, so the tie is broken.

First down. Coach Curry calls a sweep left, but Acree has defensive end Bill Henson blitz. He knocks down two of the lead blockers. The tailback slows to hop over the bodies, and the defenders catch him from behind for a 2-yard loss. The ball is on the Tigers' 22-yard line. Second down. Shabay's pass hits the receiver in the hands, but he drops the ball!

"AW, COME ON! Let's go, Steers! That's two drops!"

"Our receiver was in a crowd of Tiger defenders, and they elbowed him like pigs jostling at a feeding trough."

Third down. The Steers run the same play, but the receiver breaks inside. Before he can catch it, a Tiger bats the ball away. The ball is almost intercepted.

Fourth down, a setup for what looks like an easy field goal. "We'll have the lead and the wind, too!" Clang, clang, clang.

A couple of overeager Tigers jump offsides, which moves the ball inside the 10-yard line.

"CRUSH CORSICANA! Let's hope that delay doesn't make the kicker nervous! This will make the score 6-9!"

Graham fans expect three points from such a short kick with the wind but determined Acree calls his kick-block technique again. The fans see the setup and yell to their lineman to watch for it. The Tiger linemen open a gap near the left corner, and Whistler leaps not toward the kicker but back toward the center. He's airborne as if his outstretched arms and body are flying. The Graham kicker lifts his head like a spectator and slices the ball. It flutters off to the right side of the end zone and tumbles to the ground, wiggling and bouncing like a wounded jackrabbit. The score remains tied at 6-6.

"Bummer! Our kicker has gone lame. Our defense just has to hold the Tigers on this possession."

First down at the 20. Roman pitches to tailback Ronnie Rhoads who tries to pass it downfield to end Johnny Nelson.

"Great defense! They got lucky! We almost intercepted that pass! Good coverage, Steers!"

Second down. Hagle runs left for 2 yards. "He hasn't done much in the game, mostly because of our Boomer Davis in the middle."

Third down, Hagle runs right 5 yards, stumbling from hits by the Steers. "Hagle left, Hagle right. That's the Acree offense we expected. Our Steers have stopped him in his tracks every time."

"Way to go, DEFENSE!"

Fourth down, the Tigers punt into the wind, going only 35 yards! Acree coached the Tigers to circle and protect the ball as it rolls. Shabay walks up to it but not looking to grab it and run. A Tiger hits Shabay while the ball is still moving. "So what if the whistle hasn't blown? That's dirty football! Our Steers play right. The Graham Reporter receives many weekly letters citing 'the good conduct and sportsmanship of the Steers.'"

Acree plans and prepares for almost every situation the team faces. He drills the Tigers to be aggressive around the football, to coil into a hitting stance, keep their feet moving like they are in an Indian war dance and pop any opponent who approaches the ball if the whistle has not blown.

The Steer middle linebacker Boomer Davis races toward the rolling ball to protect Shabay. Tiger center John Stover comes out of nowhere and shoulder-pops Davis, knocking him sideways when it is evident that Davis would never grab the ball and run.

A referee standing next to both players sees Davis shove Stover and then take a swing at the Tiger center. No telling what Boomer said, but no one thinks he would have used foul language. The referee throws a flag, calls a personal foul and ejects Davis from the game for unsportsmanlike conduct.

"BAD CALL! That is so unfair! Throw a flag on Stover! Look at him turn his back and jog off like he didn't poke Boomer with a hot iron. The Tigers are dirty players, and Acree is to blame! Let's hope the Graham Reporter won't mention Davis' ejection in the game write-up. That was an unnecessary penalty on a fine player and a good team. Maybe they'll cut it out of the game film, too? We're MAD now, like Steers in a bullfight."

Marking off the penalty, the referee places the ball at the Steers' 23-yard line. Time is growing short, and the fullback goes around the end for a 6-yard gain on first down. He is taken down by a hit from Jim Wood, which could easily have caused a fumble as he put his helmet right in the numbers. Second down. Shabay keeps it and rolls right. He runs sideways, then is taken down by at least five Tigers. He gains only a yard. Third down. Shabay throws over the middle, but the pass is incomplete. The Steers punt.

"Way to try, Steers! Great punt!"

Roman returns the ball to the Tiger's 27-yard line. First down. The Tigers try another trick play that takes too long to develop. The Steers tackle the runner for a loss. Second down, Roman pitches the ball to Hagle, running around the right side.

"STOP HIM! Get him, Steers! Way to go!"

Third down, the Steers hold the Tigers for no gain, so on fourth down, the Tigers punt. The ball rolls on the ground, and the Tigers encircle it, their feet doing a happy dance! They will hit any Steer that dares come near the ball.

"Why don't we just catch it before it hits the ground? That would be tough because the wind is playing tricks with the ball. We still have time to score again."

First down. Starting at the Steer 27-yard line, Ingram runs off the right side. Second down and short yardage. Shabay throws right, but Hagle almost intercepts it. No gain on third down. Fourth down, the game has turned into a punting contest, with a strong wind complicating matters.

Roman fields the kick and returns it for a short gain. The referee throws a penalty flag because a Steer plows into Roman when he is laying on the ground.

"That's not right. He was still wiggling. That was a legal hit!"

The Tigers start at their 37. First down, a handoff to Rhoads on the left side, and he fights for 5 yards. Second down, Hagle tears his way 15 yards through the middle to the Steers' 42-yard line.

"Our Boomer would have stopped him for no gain. Sorry call to eject him from the game! DEFENSE! DEFENSE! It's hard to watch them driving the ball."

Acree tries a counter play up the middle for no gain. Second down, the clock is becoming a factor. Roman drops back and throws deep toward the goal line, but two Steer defenders bat the ball to the ground.

"Why didn't we intercept it? HOLD THE TIGERS!"

Third down, Roman fakes a run action and then makes a pump fake before throwing deep again. The ball is intercepted!

CLANG-CLANG-CLANG. "He tossed it right to our Steer defender at the 10-yard line. We dodged a gopher hole on that one! GO STEERS! What? No flag?"

The Tiger center John Stover hit a Steer in the back who is standing over the pile and no penalty is called.

"Man! Acree has coached those Tigers to play dirty! The interception gives us momentum going into the half. We won it on penetrations, 2-1!"

Fans reassure each other as if everything is OK, but they were supposed to be way ahead by this point.

The score is 6-6 at halftime.

Halftime

Graham fans watch the action on the field. "The Tiger band is playing and marching, but they look clumsy and stiff in the cold as entertainment goes. Our marching band is thrilling. Their uniforms are so colorful. They play such fun tunes, too."

The Director has the band march in rows as straight as those in a West Texas corn field. Their turns are crisp and tight, like pivots around barrels in a rodeo competition. The band and cheerleaders endured a lot this season—the heat of August, the rain and mud of November and the wind and cold of December.

"They are such a fine band. Such fine cheerleaders, too. We are so proud of them. It was terrible that officials canceled their performances after Oswald killed JFK. They had worked so hard. We wanted them to march and play."

Graham fans sample the concessions. "They're good, but not as tasty as ours served back home. The coffee's cold."

Interacting in the concession lines, they chatter about how they beat Snyder in the bi-district game, then raise their voices over the wind so others can hear about their win over Dumas. Recounting these exploits avoids talking about the halftime score. If anyone brings up Brownwood, they say, 'One measly point!' and change the subject to the toughness of West Texas football. They know their Steers will win; they just know it. They recount playing in the mud, the rain, the wind and the cold. Swear words describe the poor calls by the referees in the first half, especially the sorry call to eject Boomer Davis. Nothing can erase that bad call. Nothing.

In the Tiger locker room, Coach Raymond Anderson busies himself re-taping Hagle's knee and Jim Wood's ankle and cleaning and scrubbing tough skin on cut knuckles and elbows. Coach Acree reviews the team's play calling and gives updates to the quarterbacks. Coach Moore briefs the receivers and running backs on route changes to implement in the second half. Finally, Coach Acree addresses the whole team. Some boys stand. Others sit on benches. Most are on one knee, gathered in a circle around him. With the aid of a blackboard and Xs and Os to describe blocking and stunt adjustments, his left hand wields a chalk stick like Zorro slashed and dashed with a sword. Having coached all that is needed, he places his big left hand on Jim Wood, kneeling beside him, and says, "Men. You have to decide if you want to win this game. You decide. The going will be tough this half. They want it bad, but only you can decide if you want it more."

Third Quarter

Graham fans settle back into their seats. The game tied 6-6. "We need to yell louder in this wind."

The Steers kick off with the wind to start the third quarter. The Tigers return the short kick to their 32-yard line. Curry must have given the Steers a good talk at halftime because they are antsy. First down. The Steers charge offsides and the refs throw a flag, giving the Tigers 5 yards they didn't earn.

"These referees are something else. PUSH 'EM BACK! PUSH 'EM BACK!"

First down is played over again. Acree has Roman fake a handoff and pitch the ball to the halfback Rhoads going around the left side. The Steer secondary charges up to make the stop in front of the Tiger bench, but it almost breaks as a big play. The Steers focus on stopping big Jim Hagle. First down. Hagle blasts up the middle for another first down.

"DEFENSE! They are driving the ball too easily. HOLD THE TIGERS!"

At the Tiger 48, Roman fakes a pitch right to Rhoads but keeps the ball and turns upfield for a 5-yard gain. Second down. Roman rolls right and fakes a pitch. A herd of Steers chases him out of bounds for a 2-yard gain. Third down. The Steers are ready to let loose and eight are on the line. Acree calls a pitchout to Hagle as the Steers have anticipated, and he stumbles around the left side for only 2 yards.

The Graham fans are ecstatic. "Way to go, defense! Hagle is not that tough. When is he going to contribute to this game? Certainly, he's not as good as our Bulldozer. He is poorly coached, too. He carries the ball in his right arm when he sweeps left! CRUSH CORSICANA!"

Graham fans are ready for what they have come to expect—the moment when the Steers burst the game wide open.

Third and five at the Steer 40-yard line, they set up in a slot-right formation. Denbow splits left to the wide side of the field. Steers coaches yell to their team from the sidelines to watch for the quick pass. Hagle blocks as Roman rolls right. The Steers pressure Roman and force him deep. He practically falls over backward and throws the ball from one foot. It floats up against the wind and drifts wide, then drops into Shabay's hands like manna from heaven for an interception.

Steer fans jump up, making it hard to see, but they tell each other it looked like the Tiger receiver cinched up to Shabay like he was saddling a bronc. Shabay bobbles the ball and tips it circus-like to Neil Edwards on the outside who takes off sprinting at full speed.

Clang, clang, clang. "Shabay is a master! He is so fun!"

Edwards is so fast with the wind at his back that he sails up the sideline in front of the Steer bench. As if Edwards might forget which direction to run, Graham fans wave their arms right-to-left, directing him toward the south goal. He crosses the goal in front of the Graham cheerleaders who are jumping and screaming, while the fans in the bleachers leap for joy. They excitedly retell each other what just happened. "Did you see that? An interception runback for 60 yards and a TOUCHDOWN! That extra point kick is good. Go, Steers, Go! The scoreboard reads Visitors 6 Home 13. We're going to win this game!" CLANG, CLANG, CLANG!

They jump and high five, hug and holler as if they had just beat Dumas. "Our Steers are tops! The best team in the state, for sure!"

To the drumbeat of the band, they belt out the fight song. Over the wind's noise, they retell what happened to those sitting nearby. They tell it over and over. Each fan is excited as if they individually made the score. "Great run! This game is so exciting! Look at Acree talking to the Tigers. Too late, coach! As a Sooner, you know what it's like to be run over by a charging steer! WAY TO GO, STEERS! Our Steer defense is big and fast and organized. Here we come, State!"

The stunned Corsicana fans have the expression of cowboys upended when a bull bucks them end-over-end coming out of a rodeo chute. They ask each other, "What just happened?"

The shadows grow long on the field, but none of the Graham fans consider leaving to get a head start on the drive back home. They want to to savor the moment. The clock says 8:29 left in the third quarter. The game is not over, but with their heads bowed, a few Corsicana fans trudge toward the stadium exit on the track behind the south goal posts where Graham just scored. The north wind blows goalpost streamers in their direction like a kite's tail rippling back and forth, waving goodbye to those exiting. Graham fans know the sting of losing. "It's sad to see them lose. They never had a chance against a fine team like our Steers. How can they expect to win a playoff football game against a West Texas team with such small players?"

Graham fans watch their kickoff with the wind sail to Hagle who catches it and returns the ball to the Tigers' 30-yard line. First down. Roman and Hagle have an awkward exchange, and the ball falls to the ground. The game would be over if the Steers could have jumped on it. The Tigers recover and only lose a yard. Second down, a blitzing Steer almost takes the handoff, but Hagle manages to pick up 4 yards. Third down and eight.

"The whip is working now! Those poor Tigers look flustered. DEFENSE! DEFENSE!"

The Tigers' pre-snap motion has backs spreading out in every direction, like scared men trying to get away during a Bull Run in Pamplona. Scattering doesn't fool anyone and the Steers down Roman for a 3-yard loss. Fourth down. The Tigers punt and the Steers let it roll to their 36-yard line.

"Why don't we catch the ball? Be careful! Don't go near it! They play dirty if the ball is not whistled dead."

With the lead, Graham fans are perfectly content when the Steers call plays that eat up the clock. They line up in a split formation, and Shabay reverses out from under the center and hands the ball to the fullback

Ingram who carries the ball up the middle. The Tigers meet him in the hole, but he still pushes forward for 4 yards. "WAY TO GO, BULLDOZER!"

Second down, from the same split formation, Shabay pitches to the tailback who sweeps left, rounds the corner, and like a charging bull, puts his head down to make a first down. Tiger linebacker Jim Wood is in on the tackle but comes up limping.

At the Steer 46-yard line, from the same split formation, Shabay hands the ball to Ingram again, and he plunges up the middle to keep the Tigers honest. Second down and ten, from the same split formation, Shabay fakes a handoff to the fullback, then completes a pass to the receiver on the left side. "GOOD PLAY! Did you see that? He could have made a first down if he had run a little deeper route!"

Third and short, the Steers call a wing-set right formation and sweep right to the short side of the field, where the tailback cuts back up the middle to stay inbounds. Jim Wood and the Tigers claw him down short of a first down. Time to punt. The Tigers try for a block but miss it. The ball sails to the Tigers' 14-yard line, where the Steer players down the ball. "Way to HUSTLE Steers!"

Prodding the hind side of a Tiger may cause it to peel its ears back. Graham fans collectively sense the importance of this next series by the Tigers. They stand and cheer. "Defense! DEFENSE!"

Acree inserts Rankin Koch in place of Roman at quarterback. Starting at their 14-yard line and mixing up their formations and ball carriers, the Tigers make three first downs in a series of pitches, reverses, counters and keepers with runs by Robinson, Whistler, Hagle, Rhoads and Koch. At the end of the third quarter, the Tigers are on the Graham 41-yard line, having gained 44 yards in 7 plays. They are driving into the wind and don't call any pass plays.

The third quarter ends with the Tigers behind, 6-13, but they are driving the ball into the wind and that's about to change.

Fourth Quarter

The east side of the stadium is still packed. None of the Graham fans have left. The Tigers now have the wind at their back. On third down, Rankin Koch pitches to Hagle who turns the corner and goes out of bounds at the Steer 34. "GET 'EM STEERS! Boomer would have stopped Hagle when he turned the corner!"

On their feet, Graham fans cheer. "DEFENSE! DEFENSE!" Telling each other, "They need us now."

Hagle runs the ball up the middle for a short gain. Robinson takes a pitch and runs right but only gains short yardage to the Steer 29-yard line. "The Tigers look tired."

Acree rests Hagle and substitutes sophomore fullback, Bill Allison. Third down, Koch calls the play sent in by Acree. He pitches left to Allison. The ball hits Allison's hands, but it tumbles to the ground. He never has control of it. The ball spins on the turf like a wayward top and a Steer falls on it.

CLANG, CLANG, CLANG! "Turnover! Another Tiger mistake!"

The fans stand up to see what happened. The Steer bench jumps, throwing their arms into the air. "WAY TO GO, STEERS! Poor coaching by Acree. Oh well, never look a gift horse in the mouth. Our fine team wouldn't make that mistake."

The clock shows less than 11:00 left in the game. The Steers decide to run time off the clock. Shabay runs a fullback sweep to the left. Acree calls for his right-side tackle Don Ivie to stunt through a gap. Faster than a bull's tail can swat a fly, Ivie tackles the ball carrier behind the line.

"COME ON, STEERS! GET TOUGH!"

Shabay is a steady influence on the Steers. They call his number and he runs a sweep to the 36-yard line. Third down. It's time to fool the Tigers, so they line up in a wing-set left, then run the wing back on a counter to the right. The Steers sense how tired the Tigers are. But Sam Cooper grabs an ankle to tackle the back for no gain. Acree coached his team to stay home if they saw cross-motion. Fourth down. The Steers punt the ball into the wind, and Hagle catches it on a high bounce at his 33. He doesn't let the ball roll on the ground. Acree taught him always to catch the ball if he could. He eagerly plants a foot in the turfless dirt and runs south to the Tigers' 37-yard line.

The clock reads 8:46 left in the game. The Tigers have the wind at their backs but choose not to throw the ball. First down. Roman is back at quarterback and hands off to slotback Whistler on a counter play to the left side to advance the ball to their 42-yard line. Second down. Hagle runs off the left tackle to their 46.

"Defense! DEFENSE!"

Again, on third down, Hagle runs off their left tackle for a first down. Everyone in both stands rises to their feet with a collective gasp. Hagle isn't getting up off the turf. Acree runs out to check on the big fullback. Hagle stands up and limps off the field, Acree in the blue shirt walking next to him. The wind mutes the clapping, muffled by gloves. It looks like the end of the game for Hagle.

"We're sorry to see him leave, but he hasn't made much difference in the game. Not like our 'Bulldozer' Ingram who scored in the first quarter. Our fullback should be All-State."

With 7:37 on the clock, Acree inserts sophomore Allison again, but he doesn't repeat his previous mistake. Roman fakes to Allison and then hands it to Robinson who gets happy feet before floating a high desperation pass downfield. Defenders go up with Denbow, but the pass is just out of his reach.

386

"GOOD JOB, STEERS! Way to cover! The Tigers are so lucky. The ball fell to the ground. It should have been intercepted. Our height advantage paid off!"

Second down. The Steers have eight defensive players on the line and rush all of them. Roman fakes to the fullback and hands it to Robinson, but the rushers immediately corral him for a loss in the backfield, where they practically strip off his jersey.

"The Tigers look as if they are giving up. We are in control of this game now. Call us ringmasters! STUFF THE TIGERS!"

Third down. The Graham fans sense that the Tigers are desperate. The clock reads 7:21, and it's third and 15 yards to go. The ball is on the Tigers' 44-yard line. The defensive linemen don't have to worry about a run, so they barrel in after Roman. He rolls left and locks eyes with Denbow, 7 yards downfield. As Roman throws, the defensive back cuts between the receiver and the flying ball like a hungry steer aiming to be first in line at a feed trough. INTERCEPTION! The Steer runs the ball back to the 50-yard line.

CLANG, CLANG, CLANG. The applause is deafening as the fans scream, their lungs filling with cold air. "Listen to the band. Those drums boom so loud!"

The Graham fans look like jumping jacks with their arms raised high. They yell as loud as any Steer ever will. Only the joy of beating Dumas surpasses this delight.

"Who got the interception? Was Roman throwing to Nelson or Denbow? GO! STEERS! GO! We have complete control of such a fine game. CRUSH CORSICANA!"

6:49 remains in the game, and the fans dance a jig in an air thick with euphoria and jubilation. The band jumps around, the cheerleaders leap and hug and everyone is on their feet congratulating each other.

Corsicana fans are on their feet, too, as they start to leave the stadium. The path along the fence behind the goal post on the south end soon becomes lined with Tiger fans, dejectedly heading toward the southeast exit.

The goal now for the Steers is ball control to run out the clock. Everyone can predict the plays they will call. Pitch to the halfback for a sweep left, and he cuts up the middle and picks up 2. Second down. The team hustles from the huddle to the line, completely energized. The fullback drives up the middle for 3. At the Tiger 45-yard, Shabay sweeps to the right. Fans spot Hagle back in the game at his defensive cornerback position, where he forces Shabay out of bounds at the 42-yard line.

"Shabay should have stayed in bounds to keep the clock running! Don't worry; our Steers are playing good football. That's a mistake. We'll ask him about it at the next Quarterback Club meeting when Coach reviews the game film."

It's fourth down, so the Steers line up in punt formation, but the Tigers continue to self-destruct. Noseguard Cody Sherrard jumps offside.

"CLANG-CLANG-CLANG. Yay, Steers! That penalty gives us a first down. It's disappointing to see a poorly coached opponent beat themselves. But the Tigers deserve to lose this one. Playing dirty. Overly aggressive, as Acree has taught them. Our wonderful Steers play the game right."

As the referee marks the ball down at the Tiger 37-yard line, more Corsicana fans pack up and leave their seats. They try not to make eye contact with anyone. Even a few Graham fans decide to go before the game ends. "Let's find a good restaurant, where we can celebrate."

Unlike the Corsicana fans, Graham fans walking out shake hands and grin at each other, "Congratulations! Victory is sweet! Win STATE!"

It's first and ten at the Tiger 37-yard line, and Shabay pitches to the fullback, but instead of sweeping, he cuts up field through the Tiger line for a gain of 9 yards. The fans cheer his ad-lib play that keeps the clock running. Shabay fakes to Ingram up the middle and spins to follow him through the hole. "He is so delightful to watch. He is such a master quarterback."

Steers on the field smell victory and joyously jump, signaling first down, pointing their arms toward their end zone. Celebrating, the fans mimic the players on the field.

More Corsicana fans walk out of the bleachers and onto the path behind the south goal post. Acree gathers the Tigers on the sideline. "If you can trust yourselves as a team, men, you can win this game."

It's first and ten at the Tiger 25-yard line. The Steer fullback runs up the middle, but he's hit in the backfield and stopped for no gain by limping Jim Wood. Many Corsicana fans are walking out, but the Tiger players are still fighting. The clock says 4:30 left in the game. Second down, Shabay pitches to the fullback and to avoid going out of bounds, he turns up field instead of sweeping right, and is again tackled by Wood.

It's third and seven to go on the Tiger 23. Everyone on the Graham side is on their feet. "RUN! STEERS! RUN! SCORE! SCORE!"

They run the fullback up the middle, where Jim Wood meets him in the hole for a gain of two yards. It's fourth and five to go.

"GO FOR IT! CLANG-CLANG-CLANG."

Starting from a split formation, Shabay pitches to the fullback who sweeps right, but the Tiger defensive line put up a wall to stop his progress. He's tackled from behind by Jim Wood for a loss of 2 yards.

"Oh NO! They get the ball back!"

The ball goes over to the Tigers on downs at their 23-yard line. Wood stands with legs crossed, hands on hips and chest heaving.

"They're beaten. We tamed those Tigers! Corsicana fans are flowing out of the stadium. Even their band is packing up. In a few minutes, it will all be over. The best team will win."

* * *

The clock says 3:03. Graham has the lead, 6-13. Taking the ball over on downs, Acree says to the Tigers, "Keep your heads, men. Each of you, dig down deep. You can win this game." The Tigers start from their 23, with the wind at their backs. Roman fakes to Hagle. Denbow races from his split position downfield to catch a pass from Roman over the middle at the Tiger 46.

Graham fans are on their feet. "DEFENSE! DEFENSE!"

The clock is at 2:21. It's first and ten, and a huge crowd of fans stop to line the fence behind the south goal post. Denbow is split left. Roman drops back and throws to him as he runs a square out to the left. He catches the ball and steps out of bounds at the Graham 46-yard line. The fans lining the fence raise their arms high to show their approval.

The play only took 11 seconds; the clock reads 2:10, and it is second down, two to go. Roman misfires to the split back on the right who looks fatigued and is slow to make the outside break. The clock descends to 2:07. Now, third down and two, it's time for Hagle.

The Graham fans are confident. "We can stop Hagle even without Boomer. We have seven players up front. Watch out for that quick pass to Denbow!"

The Tigers get in a slot-left formation, but the right-side cornerback plays loose. Roman hands off to Hagle, running to the left, where he takes advantage of the slot blocking. The Steer defender meets the blocker at the line of scrimmage, but Hagle runs through him to pick up 4 yards and a first down.

Graham fans wonder, "What's going on? He left the game injured. How can he still run like that?"

Tiger assistant Coach Raymond Anderson knows how to adjust Hagle's trick knee. On the sideline, he has manipulated the torn meniscus out of the joint and re-taped it. Now Hagle can run as if nothing is wrong.

The clock is at 1:54. It's first and ten, and the ball is at the Steer 42-yard line. Acree sends Denbow down the right side; Roman steps up into the pocket, plants both feet and throws deep. While the ball is in the air, Shabay practically tackles Denbow at the 31. Another Steer intercepts the ball. CLANG-CLANG-CLANG.

Overjoyed, the Steer fans excitedly jump and shout as the defender returns the interception deep into Tiger territory.

"A flag? No, that can't be! What a lousy job by the refs!"

The referee closest to the players threw a red flag and called pass interference on Shabay. Two Steer defenders involved in the play talk to each other. Their body language says, 'You screwed up!'

The referee spots the ball at the Graham 31 and signals first down for Corsicana.

The clock is at 1:37. Roman throws high but misses Denbow on a square-out to the left. The incomplete pass sends more fans toward the stadium exit. Corsicana fans line the fence behind the south goal posts five deep to watch the Tigers' last-ditch effort.

Steer fans who left their seats early now pack the high grassy area near the exit and look down on the field. The Steers put eight defenders up front to bull rush the Tigers who have a receiver split wide on each side. The Tiger offensive line starts from the up position to pass block. Acree is constantly innovating. The two split receivers sprint deep, clearing out the Steer secondary. Tiger end Johnny Nelson releases late from his flex position on the left side into the flat, and he is wide open. Roman drops the ball over the outstretched hands of the tall, leaping defender, and Nelson gathers it in. He advances the ball to the 23-yard line, where a Steer upends him.

With 1:25 on the clock, it's third and 3 to go. Acree decides to repeat the previous play to Nelson on the opposite side. The tall defender bats down Roman's toss. "We are so proud of him. He's tall enough to stack hay in the loft without a ladder."

The ball spins around on the ground, and other Steers jump on it as if it were a fumble. Anything to depress the Tigers now. Their misery will soon be over. The incomplete pass stops the clock."

The clock says 1:19, and it is fourth down and 3 to go. This is the ball game. Everyone in the stadium, including the concession workers, knows that Hagle will get the ball. The Tigers are predictable and line up in the same slot-left formation they used when it was third and two earlier in the drive. Denbow splits right into the wide side of the field. It looks like it might be a quick pass. Roman takes the snap and hands it to Hagle, running left toward the slot back. The Steer defender meets him at the line of scrimmage, but Hagle plows through him to the 19-yard line for 4 yards and a first down. The Corsicana fans at the fence jump and cheer.

It is first and ten at the 19-yard line. Acree splits Denbow left, and he races downfield and breaks at the 10-yard line toward the goal post. Roman lays the ball into his breadbasket just ahead of the outstretched arms of the Steer defenders. Denbow catches it between two Steers and fights down to the 1-yard line. The crowd behind the fence raises their arms and jumps, cheering for the Tigers.

Graham fans sit on the cold metal seats feeling uneasy, wishing they were home in a warm place, not watching the clock.

The clock is at 0:43, and it's first and goal from the one. The Steers fans are sure they are going to run Hagle again. Acree has them in the same slot-left formation they've used on the previous two short yardage situations on this drive. It's like Acree has spotted a weakness on the Graham defensive right side. Roman calls the snap and hands it to Hagle who drives left across the goal line into the end zone.

The fans behind the fence go crazy! In the Graham stands, everyone looks at each other in disbelief. The score is 12-13. With the extra-point kick, the score will end tied 13-13. Steer fans quickly remind each other, "We lead on penetrations, 2-1."

Acree plays to win. Coaches Moore and Anderson nod in agreement; he's already decided to go for two.

Like a Tiger's roar freezes its prey, Steer fans watch in silent astonishment after the score is tied. The impending play is just too much for them to believe.

The referee places the ball at the two-and-a-half-yard line. Again, everyone in the stadium knows Hagle will get the ball. The Tigers line up in a wing-set right formation, which Acree has not previously used in the game. Roman starts right and appears to hand off to Hagle who slams into the line. Several Steers collapse onto Hagle like a pack of hungry coyotes, but Roman pulls the ball out at the last second and keeps it. He starts for the corner of the end zone on the right side and turns toward the goal line needing to cover 5 yards to score.

Three Steers angle to cut him off. A Tiger wingback blocker misses the lead defender but forces him wide enough to delay the others for a split second. Roman crosses the goal line into the endzone untouched. He turns to face his teammates, leaps up and throws both hands above his head. The referee near him raises his arms to signal the two-point conversion. Roman tosses the ball to the referee. The scoreboard changes to Visitors 14 Home 13. The fence crowd looks like massive corn kernels popping for joy.

Stunned, the Graham fans sit back down again. They can't watch what is happening. They become quiet. The band becomes silent. The cowbells stop clanging. The cheerleaders slump in their walk, their hands covering their mouths.

The clock reads 0:33, and everyone looks up at the scoreboard. Graham is behind by 'one measly point,' and their hearts sink into silent sadness. The cheerleaders start crying. The band begins packing up to leave. Slowly, ever so slowly, Graham fans start to exit the stadium. They walk away from each other like strays wandering off from a herd.

Acree is on the sidelines, hurriedly giving instructions to the Tiger kicker on how and where to place the kickoff as if it's the first time the player has ever kicked a football. He warns the defense to avoid penalties. With 0:33 on the clock, the Tiger kickoff flies low and fast just over the heads of the first line of the Steers. It hits the ground and bounces like a hot grounder. Shabay snags it and races to the sideline at the Graham 28-yard line to stop the clock at 0:30.

The Tigers know that Shabay must pass, but not where he will throw it. On first and 10, the Steers throw deep against the wind over the middle, not to the sidelines. The receiver is open and leaps up to graze the ball, which is slightly overthrown. Graham fans leap to their feet as the receiver jumps, hoping he will make the catch, but it falls to the ground incomplete. The Steer fans collapse back into their seats and gather their belongings to leave.

With 0:24 on the clock, second and 10, the Steers run a screen pass to the right. The Tigers are playing loose as Acree instructed them. The Steer rambles along to make a first down, but the Tigers keep him on his feet inbounds. When the referee signals first down, Steers on the bench jump hopeful but fail to realize that Acree has coached the Tigers to let the ball carrier amble along to eat up more time. The clock runs down to 0:13.

On first and 10, with the ball at the Steer 41-yard line, Shabay drops back and throws deep down the right side. His strong arm arcs the ball against the wind to the Tiger 25, but it falls incomplete. Deep drops and passes have chewed into the clock, which now reads 0:08.

On second and 10, Shabay repeats the same play but throws deep down the left side. A Tiger almost makes an interception, but the ball drops to the ground. The clock reads 0:02. Tigers on the field congratulate each other on the play.

On third and 10, from the Steer 41-yard line, Shabay throws a bullet over the middle, high and slightly behind the receiver. The ball tumbles around in his hands before it breaks free and falls to the ground.

The clock reads 0:00. And the scoreboard reads Tigers 14, Steers 13.

The shock on the faces of Graham fans is like that of a bull that just got castrated—their mouths hang open, their eyes are wide, but they make no sound.

The remaining Graham fans start for their cars, pickup trucks and buses. The sun is low in the sky. They want to distance themselves from Arlington's Memorial Stadium and the referees who called the game. Some shake their heads. The memory of the game will last longer than the drive home. Never will they forget the referees. "We had it won, but a sorry call stole victory from us. Things would have been different if they hadn't kicked out Boomer Davis. The referees cost us the game."

While the Graham fans exit, the Tigers gather in the middle of the field and take a knee. Surrounded by many fans, assistant coaches and Acree, they sing, "When the Roll is Called Up Yonder. When the Roll is Called up Yonder. When the Roll is Called up Yonder, we'll be there."

As they walk next to the exit, Graham fans fight back the tears. Someone mutters, "One measly point."

* * *

A week later, Corsicana defeated Pharr San Jan Alamo, 7-0, to win the AAA State Championship. Coach Acree never won another state championship. Although Graham's tall players won the basketball AAA State Championship in 1964, the Steers have never won a state football championship. Corsicana and Graham have never played each other again.

P.D. Shabay, E.A. Gresham, Gordon Nees, Boomer Davis and Terry Collins played college football at TCU. Jim Hagle, Donnie Denbow, Jim Wood, Sam Cooper and Bill Henson played at SMU. Gary Roman and Ronnie Rhoads played at Texas Tech. Ricky Libal played at the University of Houston. Many other players from both teams went on to play division two football.

Jerry Moore achieved head coaching acclaim as a three-time National Champion at Appalachian State.

Reverend Eugene Wood, Jim Wood, Coach Jim Acree in 1963 after winning the AAA State Championship (photo used with permission)

SELECTED REFERENCES

Chapter 1

1. Gambling Hall Raided, The Maud Monitor, Maud, Oklahoma, Jan 19, 1928, p. 1
2. City Police Dep't Makes Two Changes, The Maud Monitor, Maud, Oklahoma, Mar 08, 1928, p. 1
3. Frosh Gridders to Tackle Varsity Reserves Today, The Oklahoma Daily, Norman, Oklahoma, Oct 29, 1947, p. 1
4. Squad Hardest Hit at Fullback, The Oklahoma Daily, Norman, Oklahoma, Dec 3, 1947, p. 6
5. Intrasquad Football Game Slated Today on Owen Field, The Oklahoma Daily, Norman, Oklahoma, Apr 17, 1948, p. 6
6. Mentor Divides Squad for Saturday's Contest, The Oklahoma Daily, Norman, Oklahoma, Apr 23, 1948, p. 10
7. OU's Boxers Hear Call to Practice, The Oklahoma Daily, Norman, Oklahoma, Sep 24, 1948, p. 8
8. Sooners Wallop Cyclones, 33-6, The Norman Transcript, Norman, Oklahoma, Oct 31, 1948, p. 6
9. Grid Workouts for Sugar Bowl Game Disappoint Wilkinson, The Norman Transcript, Norman, Oklahoma, Dec 23, 1948, p. 4
10. OU Grid Squad Heads for Drill Site at Biloxi, The Norman Transcript, Norman, Oklahoma, Dec 26, 1948, p. 6
11. Acton Draws Hood Tonight in Tourney, The Daily Oklahoman, Oklahoma City, Oklahoma, Jan 25, 1949, p. 13
12. Wilkinson Names Grid Lettermen for 1948 Season, The Oklahoma Daily, Norman, Oklahoma, Jan 27, 1949, p. 6
13. Central State Ranks High in Golden Gloves, The Edmond Sun, Edmond, Oklahoma, Jan 27, 1949, p. 1
14. Champions Crowned in City District Golden Gloves, The Daily Oklahoman, Oklahoma City, Oklahoma, Jan 27, 1949, p. 30
15. Football? Glovers Play It, Too, The Daily Oklahoman, Oklahoma City, Oklahoma, Feb 04, 1949, p. 39
16. Seminole Legion Fighters Meet Maud Club Here Saturday Night, Seminole Producer, Seminole, Oklahoma, Feb 04, 1949, p. 5

17. Golden Gloves Ready for Finals, The Ponca City News, Ponca City, Oklahoma, Feb 11, 1949, p. 9

18. Acree Gets Nod, The Oklahoma Daily, Norman, Oklahoma, Feb 11, 1949, p. 11

19. State Gloves Meet in Finals Tonight, The Ponca City News, Ponca City, Oklahoma, Feb 15, 1949, p. 11

20. State's Golden Glovers Mix in Finals Tonight, Seminole Producer, Seminole, Oklahoma, Feb 15, 1949, p. 4

21. Brownrigg Upset Washburn in Gloves Finals; Acree is Beaten, Seminole Producer, Seminole, Oklahoma, Feb 16, 1949, p. 5

22. Legion's Fighters Will Battle Maud, Seminole Producer, Seminole, Oklahoma, Feb 17, 1949, p. 5

23. 90 Hopefuls Out for First Football Practice Session, The Oklahoma Daily, Norman, Oklahoma, Mar 10, 1949, p.6

24. Sooner Athletes Will Have a Full Day, The Oklahoma Daily, Norman, Oklahoma, Mar 12, 1949, p. 7

25. St Louis, The Daily Oklahoman, Oklahoma City, Oklahoma, May 29, 1949, p. 59

26. OU Mitt Men to Fight OC Team Tonight, The Oklahoma Daily, Norman, Oklahoma, Nov 22, 1949, p. 9

27. OU Punchers--Jim Acree Slams His Way to TKO Over Mack McNutt, The Oklahoma Daily, Norman, Oklahoma, Nov 23, 1949, p. 16

28. Sooner Boxers Trim City, 6-2, The Daily Oklahoman, Oklahoma City, Oklahoma, Nov 24, 1949, p. 52

29. IMA-IFC Teams Will Play Sunday, The Oklahoma Daily, Norman, Oklahoma, Dec 03, 1949, p. 1

30. OU Glovers Face Texans This Friday, The Oklahoma Daily, Norman, Oklahoma, Dec 06, 1949, p. 8

31. Return of Bradley, Acree Bolsters OU, The Daily Oklahoman, Oklahoma City, Oklahoma, Dec 07, 1949, p. 25

32. Seven OU Clouters Set for WKY Bout, The Oklahoma Daily, Norman, Oklahoma, Dec 17, 1949, p. 6

33. OU Fighters to Appear on Benefit Card, The Norman Transcript, Norman, Oklahoma, Dec 18, 1949, p. 6

34. Benefit Fight-Card Set, The Oklahoma Daily, Norman, Oklahoma, Dec 20, 1949, p. 9

35. College Boxers to Trade Blows for BOQ Relief, The Norman Transcript, Norman, Oklahoma, Dec 21, 1949, p. 4

36. Sooner Boxers Travel to City, The Norman Transcript, Norman, Oklahoma, Jan 10, 1950, p. 6

37. Watchin'...with Watchman, The Oklahoma Daily, Norman, Oklahoma, Jan 20, 1950, p. 9

38. Acree to Lead Boxers to State Glove Meet, The Oklahoma Daily, Norman, Oklahoma, Feb 01, 1950, p. 8

39. Jim Acree, Maud Ace Stays in Contest, Seminole Producer, Seminole, Oklahoma, Feb 05, 1950, p. 5

40. Sooner Glovers Will Weigh in for State Meet, The Norman Transcript, Norman, Oklahoma, Feb 06, 1950, p. 6

41. Acree Forced Out of Glovers' Meet, The Norman Transcript, Norman, Oklahoma, Feb 09, 1950, p. 6

42. Acree Loses Semi-Final Bout in AAU Tourney, The Norman Transcript, Norman, Oklahoma, Feb 22, 1950, p. 6

43. Bud Singing Those Old Fashion Football Blues, The Oklahoma Daily, Norman, Oklahoma, Sep 13, 1950, p. 8

44. 14 Try Out for OU Boxing Team, The Norman Transcript, Norman, Oklahoma, Sep 27, 1950, p. 5

45. Sooners Will Have Former Glovers on Team in '52, The Oklahoma Daily, Norman, Oklahoma, Sep 26, 1952, p. 6

46. OU Boxers Will Meet Cameron J.C. Thursday, The Oklahoma Daily, Norman, Oklahoma, Dec 03, 1952, p. 6

47. Sooner Duo Trim Tournament Foes in Tulsa, The Oklahoma Daily, Norman, Oklahoma, Dec 19, 1952, p. 6

48. Three Ponca Indian Boxers Lose Out in Golden Gloves, The Ponca City News, Ponca City, Oklahoma, Feb 11, 1953, p. 13

49. Club Initiation Set for Varsity Lettermen, The Oklahoma Daily, Norman, Oklahoma, Feb 18, 1953, p. 1

50. Fine Welters in AAU Event, The Daily Oklahoman, Oklahoma City, Oklahoma, Feb 22, 1953, p. 18

51. Sooners Slate Football Drills, The Norman Transcript, Norman, Oklahoma, Feb 25, 1953, p. 7

52. Acree Annexes AAU State Title, The Daily Oklahoman, Oklahoma City, Oklahoma, Mar 02, 1953, p. 40

53. Fans Await Tough Schedule, The Oklahoma Daily, Norman, Oklahoma, Aug 05, 1953, p. 58

54. Welcome on Dad's Day, The Oklahoma Daily, Norman, Oklahoma, Oct 17, 1953, p. 12

55. Probable Starting Lineups, The Norman Transcript, Norman, Oklahoma, Nov 27, 1953, p. 5

56. OU Leather Pushers to Battle Cameron College Here Tonight, The Norman Transcript, Norman, Oklahoma, Dec 02, 1953, p. 11

57. OU Boxers Play Host to Cameron, The Oklahoma Daily, Norman, Oklahoma, Dec 03, 1953, p. 6

58. Sooner Scrappers End Fights Early with Host of TKOs, The Norman Transcript, Norman, Oklahoma, Dec 04, 1953, p. 23

59. Oklahoma Boxers Meet Cameron, The Oklahoma Daily, Norman, Oklahoma, Dec 10, 1953, p. 7

60. OU Boxers to Compete in T-Town, The Oklahoma Daily, Norman, Oklahoma, Jan 14, 1954, p. 5

61. Boxers Enter 'Gloves', The Oklahoma Daily, Norman, Oklahoma, Feb 09, 1954, p. 9

62. Spring Drills Start Tuesday for Gridders, The Oklahoma Daily, Norman, Oklahoma, Mar 06, 1954, p. 5

63. Fast Grid Session Greets 100 Men at Sooner Turnout, The Norman Transcript, Norman, Oklahoma, Mar 10, 1954, p. 8

64. Alumni, The Oklahoma Daily, Norman, Oklahoma, Apr 10, 1954, p. 3

65. NHS Post May Go to Acree, The Norman Transcript, Norman, Oklahoma, May 12, 1954, p. 9

66. Hats Off to the 1954 Seniors, The Oklahoma Daily, Norman, Oklahoma, May 26, 1954, p. 6

67. Magee, Jerry, The Transcribe, The Norman Transcript, Norman, Oklahoma, May 28, 1954, p. 7

68. Purple Warriors Coaching Staff, The Bonham Daily Favorite, Bonham, Texas, Sep 03, 1954, p. 1

69. Dairy Queen, The Bonham Daily Favorite, Bonham, Texas, May 02, 1958, p. 4

70. James Acree Moved Up to Head Coach; Anderson Top Aide, The Bonham Daily Favorite, Bonham, Texas, May 30, 1958, p. 8

71. Acree Says Grid Outlook for '58 is Question Mark, Bonham Daily Favorite, Bonham, Texas, Aug 20, 1958, p. 1

72. PTA Installation Slated Thursday, The Bonham Daily Favorite, Bonham, Texas, May 06, 1959, p. 3

73. Jim Acree Submits Coach Resignation, The Bonham Daily Favorite, Bonham, Texas, Jan 04, 1960, p. 1

74. Canant, Talmadge, Comments by Canant, Corsicana Daily Sun, Corsicana, Texas, Jan 05, 1960, p. 7

75. Dave Smith Resigns as Assistant, Corsicana Daily Sun, Corsicana, Texas, Jan 13, 1960, p. 7

76. New Athletic Director Here Assumes Duties on Tuesday, Corsicana Semi-Weekly Light, Corsicana, Texas, Jan 29, 1960, p. 12

77. Jim Acree Has Moved Family to Corsicana, Corsicana Daily Sun, Corsicana, Texas, Feb 01, 1960, p. 5

78. Schools, Corsicana Daily Sun, Corsicana, Texas, Feb 10, 1960, p. 10

79. Story on Change Branded Untrue, The Bonham Daily Favorite, Bonham, Texas, Feb 12, 1960, p. 1

Chapter 2

1. Postpone Junior High Gridiron Work To Monday, Corsicana Daily Sun, Corsicana, Texas, Mar 09, 1960, p. 6

2. Palestine is the Goal of Many Track Entries, Corsicana Daily Sun, Corsicana, Texas, Mar 10, 1960, p. 15

3. Tigers Finish Second in Practice Meet, Corsicana Daily Sun, Corsicana, Texas, Mar 25, 1960, p. 6

4. No Places for Tigers Saturday at Commerce, Corsicana Daily Sun, Corsicana, Texas, Mar 28, 1960, p. 6

5. Junior High Grid Tilts Set, Corsicana Daily Sun, Corsicana, Texas, Mar 29, 1960, p. 7

6. Grimmett, Richard, Grins and Groans, Corsicana Daily Sun, Corsicana, Texas, Mar 30, 1960, p. 4

7. Junior Football Tilt Rosters Announced, Corsicana Daily Sun, Corsicana, Texas, Mar 30, 1960, p. 4

8. Junior High Elevens End Drills Thursday, Corsicana Daily Sun, Corsicana, Texas, Apr 01, 1960, p. 6

9. Grimmett, Richard, Grins and Groans, Corsicana Daily Sun, Corsicana, Texas, Apr 04, 1960, p. 6

10. Jim Acree Speaks at Dads Club Wednesday, Corsicana Daily Sun, Corsicana, Texas, Apr 07, 1960, p. 17

11. Football Rosters are Released, Corsicana Daily Sun, Corsicana, Texas, Apr 28, 1960, p. 17

12. Canant, Talmadge, Comments by Canant, Corsicana Daily Sun, Corsicana, Texas, Apr 30, 1960, p. 7

13. Best in 8-AAA, Corsicana Daily Sun, Corsicana, Texas, May 14, 1960, p. 7

14. Kilgore-Nacogdoches Victor Meets Tigers, Corsicana Daily Sun, Corsicana, Texas, May 16, 1960, p. 8

15. Canant, Talmadge, Comments by Canant, Corsicana Daily Sun, Corsicana, Texas, Jun 16, 1960, p. 15

16. Canant, Talmadge, Comments by Canant, Corsicana Daily Sun, Corsicana, Texas, Jul 02, 1960, p. 7

17. Dads Select New Officers, Corsicana Daily Sun, Corsicana, Texas, Jul 06, 1960, p. 8

18. Canant, Talmadge, Comments by Canant, Corsicana Daily Sun, Corsicana, Texas, Jul 09, 1960, p. 7

19. Canant, Talmadge, Comments by Canant, Corsicana Daily Sun, Corsicana, Texas, Jul 19, 1960, p. 7

20. Canant, Talmadge, Comments by Canant, Corsicana Daily Sun, Corsicana, Texas, Jul 21, 1960, p. 13

21. Tigers Will Attend Grid Tilt Saturday, Corsicana Daily Sun, Corsicana, Texas, Jul 22, 1960, p. 7

22. Acree, Corsicana Staff to Attend Coach School, Corsicana Daily Sun, Corsicana, Texas, Jul 30, 1960, p. 7

23. Canant, Talmadge, Comments by Canant, Corsicana Daily Sun, Corsicana, Texas, Aug 05, 1960, p. 9

24. Football Drills ar Corsicana High Near, Corsicana Daily Sun, Corsicana, Texas, Aug 11, 1960, p. 13

25. Tigers Begin Grid Practice, Corsicana Daily Sun, Corsicana, Texas, Aug 16, 1960, p. 7

26. Canant, Talmadge, Comments by Canant, Corsicana Daily Sun, Corsicana, Texas, Aug 16, 1960, p. 7

27. Canant, Talmadge, Comments by Canant, Corsicana Daily Sun, Corsicana, Texas, Aug 18, 1960, p. 13

28. Bengals Begin Second Week of Football Drills, Corsicana Daily Sun, Corsicana, Texas, Aug 22, 1960, p. 6

29. Tiger Coaches Talk Monday to Kiwanis Club, Corsicana Semi-Weekly Light, Corsicana, Texas, Aug 23, 1960, p. 3

30. Grimmett, Richard, Grins and Groans, Corsicana Daily Sun, Corsicana, Texas, Aug 24, 1960, p. 7

31. Grid Coach is Rotary Speaker Wednesday, Corsicana Daily Sun, Corsicana, Texas, Aug 24, 1960, p. 9

32. Canant, Talmadge, Comments by Canant, Corsicana Daily Sun, Corsicana, Texas, Aug 27, 1960, p. 7

33. Grimmett, Richard, Grins and Groans, Corsicana Daily Sun, Corsicana, Texas, Aug 29, 1960, p. 6

34. Fans Observe Tigers at Barbeque, Corsicana Daily Sun, Corsicana, Texas, Sep 01, 1960, p. 17

35. Canant, Talmadge, Comments by Canant, Corsicana Daily Sun, Corsicana, Texas, Sep 03, 1960, p. 7

36. Football Hitting High Gear, Corsicana Daily Sun, Corsicana, Texas, Sep 05, 1960, p. 7

37. Corsicana-Waco Battle Set, Corsicana Daily Sun, Corsicana, Texas, Sep 08, 1960, p. 13

38. Bengal Elevens Are Squared Off, Corsicana Daily Sun, Corsicana, Texas, Sep 09, 1960, p. 7

39. Tigers Lose Grid Opener to Waco, Corsicana Daily Sun, Corsicana, Texas, Sep 10, 1960, p. 7

40. Grimmett, Richard, Grins and Groans, Corsicana Daily Sun, Corsicana, Texas, Sep 12, 1960, p. 6

41. Mistakes Hurt CHS Says Acree, Corsicana Daily Sun, Corsicana, Texas, Sep 13, 1960, p. 6

42. Grimmett, Richard, Grins and Groans, Corsicana Daily Sun, Corsicana, Texas, Sep 14, 1960, p. 6

43. Tigers Warned of Palestine, Corsicana Daily Sun, Corsicana, Texas, Sep 15, 1960, p. 17

44. Tigers Put 13-6 Bite on Palestine, Corsicana Daily Sun, Corsicana, Texas, Sep 17, 1960, p. 7

45. Tigers Can Beat Cleburne--Acree, Corsicana Semi-Weekly Light, Corsicana, Texas, Sep 23, 1960, p. 10

46. Corsicana Bengals Swat Jackets, Corsicana Daily Sun, Corsicana, Texas, Sep 24, 1960, p. 7

47. Grimmett, Richard, Grins and Groans, Corsicana Daily Sun, Corsicana, Texas, Sep 26, 1960, p. 6

48. Week's Outlook in 8-AAA Bleak, Corsicana Daily Sun, Corsicana, Texas, Sep 26, 1960, p. 6

49. Bulldogs Warned, Corsicana Daily Sun, Corsicana, Texas, Sep 27, 1960, p. 7

50. Bengals Not Impressive Wednesday, Corsicana Daily Sun, Corsicana, Texas, Sep 29, 1960, p. 13

51. Jacksonville Blanks Corsicana, Corsicana Daily Sun, Corsicana, Texas, Oct 01, 1960, p. 5

52. Spartan Fans Will Follow Team Friday, Corsicana Daily Sun, Corsicana, Texas, Oct 05, 1960, p. 6

53. Westminster Men Enjoy Grid Program at Banquet Wednesday, Corsicana Daily Sun, Corsicana, Texas, Oct 06, 1960, p. 20

54. Samuell Spartans Hack Corsicana, Corsicana Daily Sun, Corsicana, Texas, Oct 08, 1960, p. 7

55. Canant, Talmadge, Comments by Canant, Corsicana Daily Sun, Corsicana, Texas, Oct 11, 1960, p. 7

56. Tigers at Lufkin Friday, Corsicana Daily Sun, Corsicana, Texas, Oct 13, 1960, p. 17

57. 27 Register by Draft Board in September, Corsicana Semi-Weekly Light, Corsicana, Texas, Oct 14, 1960, p. 7

58. Tigers Rebound to Blank Lufkin, Corsicana Daily Sun, Corsicana, Texas, Oct 15, 1960, p. 6

59. Dads Watch Films of Lufkin Tilt, Corsicana Daily Sun, Corsicana, Texas, Oct 18, 1960, p. 7

60. Four Teams See Battles; Waxa in Open Date, Corsicana Daily Sun, Corsicana, Texas, Oct 19, 1960, p. 7

61. Tiger Fans to Follow Team to Ennis Tonight, Corsicana Daily Sun, Corsicana, Texas, Oct 21, 1960, p. 6

62. Tigers Overcome Early Lion Lead, Corsicana Daily Sun, Corsicana, Texas, Oct 22, 1960, p. 7

63. Tigers, Hornets Lead 8-AAA Grid Circuit, Corsicana Daily Sun, Corsicana, Texas, Oct 25, 1960, p. 7

64. Tigers Squeeze Past Aroused Waxahachie, Corsicana Daily Sun, Corsicana, Texas, Oct 29, 1960, p. 7

65. First Methodists Receive Four New Members, Corsicana Daily Sun, Corsicana, Texas, Oct 31, 1960, p. 3

66. Tigers Prepare for Next Week, Corsicana Daily Sun, Corsicana, Texas, Nov 04, 1960, p. 6

67. Grimmett, Richard, Grins and Groans, Corsicana Daily Sun, Corsicana, Texas, Nov 07, 1960, p. 8

68. 8-AAA Elevens Battle Friday, Corsicana Daily Sun, Corsicana, Texas, Nov 08, 1960, p. 7

69. Hawkeye Coach Defends Modern Gridiron Game, Corsicana Daily Sun, Corsicana, Texas, Nov 09, 1960, p. 6

70. Late Tiger Tallies Bury Athens Hornets, Corsicana Daily Sun, Corsicana, Texas, Nov 12, 1960, p. 7

71. Grimmett, Richard, Grins and Groans, Corsicana Daily Sun, Corsicana, Texas, Nov 14, 1960, p. 8

72. Gridiron Chase Closing Friday in 8-AAA Loop, Corsicana Daily Sun, Corsicana, Texas, Nov 16, 1960, p. 6

73. Skeeters, Tigers Battle Tonight, Corsicana Daily Sun, Corsicana, Texas, Nov 18, 1960, p. 7

74. Jacksonville Comes Here for Playoff, Corsicana Daily Sun, Corsicana, Texas, Nov 19, 1960, p. 7

75. Tigers Turn Back Mesquite, Corsicana Daily Sun, Corsicana, Texas, Nov 19, 1960, p. 7

76. Tiger, Indian Coaches Scan Game Movies, Corsicana Daily Sun, Corsicana, Texas, Nov 21, 1960, p. 12

77. Dads Club Sees Mesquite Films Monday Night, Corsicana Daily Sun, Corsicana, Texas, Nov 22, 1960, p. 7

78. Special Film Rotary Program Wednesday Noon, Corsicana Daily Sun, Corsicana, Texas, Nov 23, 1960, p. 2

79. Corsicana, Jacksonville Elevens Poised for Battle, Corsicana Daily Sun, Corsicana, Texas, Nov 24, 1960, p. 14

80. Corsicana, Jacksonville Fight to 7-7 Standoff, Corsicana Daily Sun, Corsicana, Texas, Nov 26, 1960, p. 7

81. Deadlock was Not Expected, Corsicana Daily Sun, Corsicana, Texas, Nov 26, 1960, p. 8

82. Tiger Mentor Speaks Monday Kiwanis Club, Corsicana Daily Sun, Corsicana, Texas, Dec 05, 1960, p. 5

83. Grimmett, Richard, Grins and Groans, Corsicana Daily Sun, Corsicana, Texas, Dec 07, 1960, p. 6

84. CHS Gridders Get Awards for 1960 Season, Corsicana Semi-Weekly Light, Corsicana, Texas, Dec 09, 1960, p. 10

85. Cash Gift Will Go To Coaches, Corsicana Daily Sun, Corsicana, Texas, Dec 10, 1960, p. 7

86. Tiger Football Slate for 1961 Set, Corsicana Daily Sun, Corsicana, Texas, Dec 15, 1960, p. 17

87. James Acree Under Knife, Corsicana Daily Sun, Corsicana, Texas, Dec 20, 1960, p. 9

88. Coach Making Quick Recovery, Corsicana Daily Sun, Corsicana, Texas, Dec 22, 1960, p. 14

89. Fans Fete District Champions, Corsicana Daily Sun, Corsicana, Texas, Jan 24, 1961, p. 7

90. Tewes Signs at Houston, Corsicana Semi-Weekly Light, Corsicana, Texas, Mar 02, 1962, p. 2

Chapter 3

1. Acree Talks to Eleventh Ave Methodist Men, Corsicana Daily Sun, Corsicana, Texas, Feb 22, 1961, p. 7

2. CHS Trackmen Schedule Meets, Corsicana Daily Sun, Corsicana, Texas, Feb 24, 1961, p. 7

3. Junior High Gridiron Work in Full Swing, Corsicana Daily Sun, Corsicana, Texas, Mar 03, 1961, p. 7

4. Junior Elevens Scrimmage Friday, Corsicana Daily Sun, Corsicana, Texas, Mar 07, 1961, p. 7

5. Circuit Nixes CHS Golf Plea, Corsicana Daily Sun, Corsicana, Texas, Apr 06, 1961, p. 16

6. 120 Graduate from Drane in Largest Class in History, Corsicana Semi-Weekly Light, Corsicana, Texas, Jun 02, 1961, p. 5

7. Canant, Talmadge, Comments by Canant, Corsicana Daily Sun, Corsicana, Texas, Jun 03, 1961, p. 7

8. Harkrider to Coach at Moody, Corsicana Daily Sun, Corsicana, Texas, Jun 27, 1961, p. 4

9. Canant, Talmadge, Comments by Canant, Corsicana Daily Sun, Corsicana, Texas, Jul 10, 1961, p. 9

10. Canant, Talmadge, Comments by Canant, Corsicana Daily Sun, Corsicana, Texas, Jul 13, 1961, p. 15

11. Lloyd Nichols Has Accepted Grapevine Job, Corsicana Daily Sun, Corsicana, Texas, Jul 25, 1961, p. 7

12. Raymond Anderson Resigns as Coach to Accept Smiley Post, Corsicana Daily Sun, Corsicana, Texas, Jul 26, 1961, p. 3

13. Former Baylor Captain New Assistant Tiger Mentor, Corsicana Daily Sun, Corsicana, Texas, Jul 28, 1961, p. 8

14. Kiwanis Club Hears of New Tiger Stadium, Corsicana Daily Sun, Corsicana, Texas, Jul 31, 1961, p. 11

15. Canant, Talmadge, Comments by Canant, Corsicana Daily Sun, Corsicana, Texas, Aug 02, 1961, p. 7

16. Local Coaches Will Atten Coaching School, Corsicana Daily Sun, Corsicana, Texas, Aug 05, 1961, p. 7

17. Dads Club Slates Appreciation Barbeque Aug. 18, Corsicana Daily Sun, Corsicana, Texas, Aug 08, 1961, p. 5

18. Tigers Fall Out Monday, Corsicana Daily Sun, Corsicana, Texas, Aug 12, 1961, p. 7

19. Bengals Work Twice Daily, Corsicana Daily Sun, Corsicana, Texas, Aug 14, 1961, p. 6

20. 62 Attend Opening Workouts, Corsicana Daily Sun, Corsicana, Texas, Aug 15, 1961, p. 7

21. Grid Games Scheduled, Corsicana Daily Sun, Corsicana, Texas, Aug 16, 1961, p. 7

22. Tigers Near End of Second Drill Week, Corsicana Daily Sun, Corsicana, Texas, Aug 24, 1961, p. 16

23. Bengals Drill in Henderson, Corsicana Daily Sun, Corsicana, Texas, Aug 26, 1961, p. 7

24. Bengals Need More Conditioning--Acree, Corsicana Daily Sun, Corsicana, Texas, Aug 28, 1961, p. 8

25. Bulldog, Tiger Grid Players Work Over Dummies in Drills, Corsicana Daily Sun, Corsicana, Texas, Aug 31, 1961, p. 16

26. Rotary Club Hears Coach Jim Acree Talk, Corsicana Daily Sun, Corsicana, Texas, Sep 06, 1961, p. 5

27. Cubs and Panthers in Mexia, Corsicana Daily Sun, Corsicana, Texas, Sep 07, 1961, p. 14

28. Corsicana, Waco Stage 6-6 Standoff, Corsicana Daily Sun, Corsicana, Texas, Sep 09, 1961, p. 7

29. Tigers Get to Work, Corsicana Daily Sun, Corsicana, Texas, Sep 12, 1961, p. 7

30. Canant, Talmadge, Comments by Canant, Corsicana Daily Sun, Corsicana, Texas, Sep 12, 1961, p. 7

31. Tigers Overtake, Pass Palestine, Corsicana Daily Sun, Corsicana, Texas, Sep 16, 1961, p. 7

32. Jim Acree at Kiwanis Club Monday Noon, Corsicana Daily Sun, Corsicana, Texas, Sep 18, 1961, p. 13

33. Canant, Talmadge, Comments by Canant, Corsicana Daily Sun, Corsicana, Texas, Sep 19, 1961, p. 7

34. Canant, Talmadge, Comments by Canant, Corsicana Daily Sun, Corsicana, Texas, Sep 20, 1961, p. 6

35. Tigers Felled by Cleburne, Corsicana Daily Sun, Corsicana, Texas, Sep 23, 1961, p. 7

36. Indians Are Tough Says Coach, Corsicana Daily Sun, Corsicana, Texas, Sep 26, 1961, p. 7

37. Heavy Rain at Tiger Field Postpones Game, Corsicana Daily Sun, Corsicana, Texas, Sep 28, 1961, p. 8

38. Bengals Turn Back Jacksonville, Corsicana Daily Sun, Corsicana, Texas, Sep 30, 1961, p. 7

39. Bisons are Deep and Big, Corsicana Daily Sun, Corsicana, Texas, Oct 03, 1961, p. 7

40. Canant, Talmadge, Comments by Canant, Corsicana Daily Sun, Corsicana, Texas, Oct 03, 1961, p. 7

41. Canant, Talmadge, Comments by Canant, Corsicana Daily Sun, Corsicana, Texas, Oct 04, 1961, p. 6

42. Corsicana Tigers Claw Sunset High Bison Eleven, 7-0, Corsicana Daily Sun, Corsicana, Texas, Oct 07, 1961, p. 7

43. Dads View Movies of Bison Tilt, Corsicana Daily Sun, Corsicana, Texas, Oct 10, 1961, p. 7

44. Tigers Get by Late-Starting Weatherford, 14-8, Corsicana Daily Sun, Corsicana, Texas, Oct 14, 1961, p. 7

45. District Play Arrives in 8-AAA, Corsicana Daily Sun, Corsicana, Texas, Oct 17, 1961, p. 6

46. Bengals, Lions to Battle, Corsicana Daily Sun, Corsicana, Texas, Oct 20, 1961, p. 6

47. Corsicana Eleven Turns Back Ennis Bid, 27-8, Corsicana Daily Sun, Corsicana, Texas, Oct 21, 1961, p. 7

48. Indians on War Path, Acree Says, Corsicana Daily Sun, Corsicana, Texas, Oct 24, 1961, p. 7

49. Tiger Cubs Host Waxa Thursday, Corsicana Daily Sun, Corsicana, Texas, Oct 25, 1961, p. 8

50. Bengals Expecting the Worst, Corsicana Daily Sun, Corsicana, Texas, Oct 27, 1961, p. 7

51. Tigers Put Down Waxa Indian Uprising, 19-2, Corsicana Daily Sun, Corsicana, Texas, Oct 28, 1961, p. 7

52. Bengals Easing Up a Little, Corsicana Daily Sun, Corsicana, Texas, Oct 31, 1961, p. 10

53. Athens Aims for Win Over Tigers, Corsicana Daily Sun, Corsicana, Texas, Nov 10, 1961, p. 7

54. Corsicana Whips Athens in District Tilt, 18-2, Corsicana Daily Sun, Corsicana, Texas, Nov 11, 1961, p. 7

55. Tigers Need Good Effort, Corsicana Daily Sun, Corsicana, Texas, Nov 14, 1961, p. 7

56. Bengals Blank Skeeters, 11-0, Corsicana Daily Sun, Corsicana, Texas, Nov 18, 1961, p. 7

57. Tigers Prepare for Carthage, Corsicana Daily Sun, Corsicana, Texas, Nov 21, 1961, p. 6

58. Corsicana Tigers Repeat Winners of District 8-AAA Vs. Mesquite, Corsicana Semi-Weekly Light, Corsicana, Texas, Nov 21, 1961, p. 8

59. Corsicana and Carthage Face Grid Decision, Corsicana Daily Sun, Corsicana, Texas, Nov 24, 1961, p. 7

60. Tigers Tumble Bulldogs, 19-6, in Bi-District Tilt, Corsicana Daily Sun, Corsicana, Texas, Nov 25, 1961, p. 7

61. Gainesville is Rugged, Corsicana Daily Sun, Corsicana, Texas, Nov 28, 1961, p. 8

62. The Numbers Game, Corsicana Daily Sun, Corsicana, Texas, Nov 29, 1961, p. 7

63. Corsicana, Gainesville Poised for Collision, Corsicana Daily Sun, Corsicana, Texas, Nov 30, 1961, p. 15

64. Catfight Set Tonight, Corsicana Daily Sun, Corsicana, Texas, Dec 01, 1961, p. 9

65. Quarterfinals Tilt Sees Bengals Losing in a Score Fest, Corsicana Daily Sun, Corsicana, Texas, Dec 02, 1961, p. 7

66. Corsicana Dads See Game Movies, Corsicana Daily Sun, Corsicana, Texas, Dec 05, 1961, p. 7

67. Acree Reveals Several Tigers District Picks, Corsicana Daily Sun, Corsicana, Texas, Dec 06, 1961, p. 1

68. Rotary, Corsicana Daily Sun, Corsicana, Texas, Dec 06, 1961, p. 7

69. Coaches Select Stellar Eleven, Corsicana Daily Sun, Corsicana, Texas, Dec 07, 1961, p. 20

70. Tewes Makes All-State Grid Outfit, Corsicana Daily Sun, Corsicana, Texas, Dec 07, 1961, p. 20

71. Corsicana Dads Thank Coaches, Corsicana Daily Sun, Corsicana, Texas, Dec 12, 1961, p. 7

72. Canant, Talmadge, Comments by Canant, Corsicana Daily Sun, Corsicana, Texas, Dec 26, 1961, p. 7

73. 33 Tigers Win "C's", Corsicana Daily Sun, Corsicana, Texas, Jan 03, 1962, p. 21

74. Canant, Talmadge, Comments by Canant, Corsicana Daily Sun, Corsicana, Texas, Jan 11, 1962, p. 13

75. Weather Hampers Track Workouts, Corsicana Daily Sun, Corsicana, Texas, Jan 25, 1962, p. 13

76. Jon Tewes Named on Star Team, Corsicana Semi-Weekly Light, Corsicana, Texas, Jan 26, 1962, p. 2

77. Corsicana Honors Tigers at Annual Banquet, Corsicana Daily Sun, Corsicana, Texas, Jan 26, 1962, p. 18

78. Wilson Inks Raider Pact, Corsicana Daily Sun, Corsicana, Texas, Feb 23, 1962, p. 19

Chapter 4

1. National, American Leagues Each Have Six Teams Trying for Title, Corsicana Daily Sun, Corsicana, Texas, Jun 04, 1959, p. 7

2. Junior Teenage Roster is Listed, Corsicana Daily Sun, Corsicana, Texas, Jul 01, 1959, p. 13

3. American Orange, National Green Freshman are Thursday Winners, Corsicana Daily Sun, Corsicana, Texas, Jul 08, 1960, p. 9

4. List Collins Art Winners, Corsicana Daily Sun, Corsicana, Texas, Feb 07, 1962, p. 4

5. CHS Coaches Attend Clinic, Corsicana Daily Sun, Corsicana, Texas, Feb 16, 1962, p. 7

6. Panel Talks Scheduled at First Methodist, Corsicana Daily Sun, Corsicana, Texas, Feb 17, 1962, p. 13

7. Juniors Open Grid Practice, Corsicana Daily Sun, Corsicana, Texas, Feb 19, 1962, p. 7

8. Collins, Drane Scrimmage Due Wednesday, Corsicana Daily Sun, Corsicana, Texas, Mar 03, 1962, p. 17

9. Murray to be Collins Head Coach, Corsicana Daily Sun, Corsicana, Texas, Jun 23, 1962, p. 22

10. Cougars Get Grid Call, Corsicana Daily Sun, Corsicana, Texas, Aug 14, 1962, p. 17

11. Cougars To Kick Off Grid Drills Saturday, Corsicana Daily Sun, Corsicana, Texas, Aug 30, 1962, p. 15

12. Canant, Talmadge, Comments by Canant, Corsicana Daily Sun, Corsicana, Texas, Aug 31, 1962, p. 20

13. Cougars, Panthers to Open Play This Week, Corsicana Daily Sun, Corsicana, Texas, Sep 11, 1962, p. 17

14. Cougars Blank Garland, Corsicana Daily Sun, Corsicana, Texas, Sep 12, 1962, p. 21

15. Collins Downs Terrell Thursday Night, 34-14, Corsicana Daily Sun, Corsicana, Texas, Sep 21, 1962, p. 7

16. Cougars in First Setback, Corsicana Daily Sun, Corsicana, Texas, Sep 28, 1962, p. 8

17. Cougars Defeated by Mesquite, 15-8, Corsicana Daily Sun, Corsicana, Texas, Oct 05, 1962, p. 4

18. Collins Council is Installed, Corsicana Daily Sun, Corsicana, Texas, Oct 12, 1962, p. 5

19. Collins Drops 12-10 Loss to Highland Park, Corsicana Daily Sun, Corsicana, Texas, Oct 12, 1962, p. 11

20. Cougars Outpoint Athens Juniors, Corsicana Daily Sun, Corsicana, Texas, Oct 26, 1962, p. 9

21. Cubs, Panthers, Cougars Facing Gridiron Challenges This Week, Corsicana Daily Sun, Corsicana, Texas, Oct 30, 1962, p. 7

22. Collins Cougars Fall to Cleburne Gridders, Corsicana Daily Sun, Corsicana, Texas, Nov 02, 1962, p. 10

23. Canant, Talmadge, Comments by Canant, Corsicana Daily Sun, Corsicana, Texas, Nov 06, 1962, p. 7

24. 4 Emergencies at Memorial, Corsicana Daily Sun, Corsicana, Texas, Nov 07, 1962, p. 3

25. Cougars Sock Ennis Juniors, 30-0, Corsicana Daily Sun, Corsicana, Texas, Nov 09, 1962, p. 7

26. Collins Blank Waxa Juniors Eleven, 22-0, Corsicana Daily Sun, Corsicana, Texas, Nov 16, 1962, p. 7

27. Collins-Drane Clash Due 7:30 Tuesday, Corsicana Daily Sun, Corsicana, Texas, Nov 19, 1962, p. 14

28. Rain Stops Junior High Grid Tilt, Corsicana Daily Sun, Corsicana, Texas, Nov 21, 1962, p. 7

29. Panthers Take Cougars, 22-8, Corsicana Daily Sun, Corsicana, Texas, Nov 28, 1962, p. 8

30. Collins Lettermen are Announced, Corsicana Daily Sun, Corsicana, Texas, Dec 04, 1962, p. 7

31. Collins Football Team Feted Saturday Night by Cougarette Group, Corsicana Daily Sun, Corsicana, Texas, Dec 03, 1962, p. 4

32. Collins Cagers Jump into Play Wednesday, Corsicana Daily Sun, Corsicana, Texas, Dec 04, 1962, p. 8

33. Collins Junior High 'Cougar' Issued Recently, Corsicana Daily Sun, Corsicana, Texas, Jan 03, 1963, p. 26

34. Collins Junior Good Citizens Are Announced, Corsicana Daily Sun, Corsicana, Texas, Jan 17, 1963, p. 4

35. Kiwanis Club Meets Monday at Lee School, Corsicana Daily Sun, Corsicana, Texas, Mar 04, 1963, p. 13

36. Science Fair Winners Local Schools Have Been Announced, Corsicana Daily Sun, Corsicana, Texas, Mar 07, 1963, p. 24

37. Joel Lusk From Athens Speaker at Kiwanis Club, Corsicana Daily Sun, Corsicana, Texas, Mar 25, 1963, p. 13

Chapter 5

1. Social Revue, Corsicana Daily Sun, Corsicana, Texas, Aug 23, 1956, p. 5

2. Students of Lee, Houston to Hear Dallas Symphony, Corsicana Daily Sun, Corsicana, Texas, Jan 24, 1958, p. 5

3. Scout Court of Honor is Slated Tuesday Evening, Corsicana Daily Sun, Corsicana, Texas, Apr 21, 1958, p. 7

4. Ten Enroll in "Y" Lifesaving, Corsicana Daily Sun, Corsicana, Texas, May 06, 1958, p. 8

5. Seven Complete Lifesaving Course, Corsicana Daily Sun, Corsicana, Texas, May 20, 1958, p. 9

6. Fellowship Groups Inducts Officers at Westminster, Corsicana Daily Sun, Corsicana, Texas, Jun 30, 1958, p. 8

7. Junior Grid Drills Under Way, Corsicana Daily Sun, Corsicana, Texas, Feb 20, 1959, p. 6

8. Westminster in Sunday Rites, Corsicana Daily Sun, Corsicana, Texas, May 16, 1959, p. 2

9. Panthers Plan to Fling Ball Thursday Night, Corsicana Daily Sun, Corsicana, Texas, Sep 09, 1959, p. 7

10. Panthers and Palestine Play Here, Corsicana Daily Sun, Corsicana, Texas, Oct 20, 1959, p. 9

11. Boy Gets Help from Khrushchev, Corsicana Daily Sun, Corsicana, Texas, Nov 28, 1959, p. 1

12. Court of Honor Set Tuesday at Westminster, Corsicana Daily Sun, Corsicana, Texas, Jul 11, 1960, p. 5

13. Panthers to Invade Mesquite, Corsicana Daily Sun, Corsicana, Texas, Sep 22, 1960, p. 14

14. Collins and Drane Grid Clash Set, Corsicana Daily Sun, Corsicana, Texas, Nov 17, 1960, p. 15

15. Seven Scouts Due to Receive Eagle Award, Corsicana Semi-Weekly Light, Corsicana, Texas, Apr 11, 1961, p. 1

16. Seven Eagles, Corsicana Daily Sun, Corsicana, Texas, Apr 17, 1961, p. 14

17. Canant, Talmadge, Comments by Canant, Corsicana Daily Sun, Corsicana, Texas, Feb 24, 1962, p. 17

18. Acree in Austin, Corsicana Daily Sun, Corsicana, Texas, Mar 14, 1962, p. 8

19. Board Decides to Improve Campuses, Corsicana Daily Sun, Corsicana, Texas, Mar 16, 1962, p. 1

20. Trustees Re-Elect Executives, Plan Beautify School Campuses, Corsicana Semi-Weekly Light, Corsicana, Texas, Mar 20, 1962, p. 2

21. Dads Elect Officers, Corsicana Daily Sun, Corsicana, Texas, Apr 10, 1962, p. 17

22. Mrs. M. Boyd to Head Staff of Drane PTA, Corsicana Daily Sun, Corsicana, Texas, Apr 24, 1962, p. 4

23. Three Seniors on District Title Outfit, Corsicana Daily Sun, Corsicana, Texas, Apr 26, 1962, p. 17

24. Athletics are Great Teacher, Says Acree, Corsicana Daily Sun, Corsicana, Texas, May 03, 1962, p. 43

25. Gridiron Great Speaks Monday Kiwanis Club, Corsicana Daily Sun, Corsicana, Texas, May 14, 1962, p. 11

26. School Board Deplores Hazing, Names Instructors for 1962-1963, Corsicana Semi-Weekly Light, Corsicana, Texas, May 15, 1962, p. 2

27. Olsen, Settle Captain Tigers for This Fall, Corsicana Daily Sun, Corsicana, Texas, May 16, 1962, p. 8

28. Canant, Talmadge, Comments by Canant, Corsicana Daily Sun, Corsicana, Texas, May 21, 1962, p. 7

29. Tiger Water Party Has Need for Boat Rigs, Corsicana Daily Sun, Corsicana, Texas, May 23, 1962, p. 20

30. Canant, Talmadge, Comments by Canant, Corsicana Daily Sun, Corsicana, Texas, May 24, 1962, p. 15

31. Rotary Program, Corsicana Daily Sun, Corsicana, Texas, May 29, 1962, p. 11

32. Canant, Talmadge, Comments by Canant, Corsicana Daily Sun, Corsicana, Texas, May 30, 1962, p. 9

33. Rotarians Hear Jim Acree at Noon Luncheon, Corsicana Daily Sun, Corsicana, Texas, May 30, 1962, p. 23

34. Canant, Talmadge, Comments by Canant, Corsicana Daily Sun, Corsicana, Texas, May 31, 1962, p. 15

35. Officers Named for Two Classes, Corsicana Daily Sun, Corsicana, Texas, Jun 01, 1962, p. 4

36. Canant, Talmadge, Comments by Canant, Corsicana Daily Sun, Corsicana, Texas, Jun 04, 1962, p. 22

37. Canant, Talmadge, Comments by Canant, Corsicana Daily Sun, Corsicana, Texas, Jun 16, 1962, p. 17

38. Paul Slaughter Moves to High School Staff, Corsicana Daily Sun, Corsicana, Texas, Jun 21, 1962, p. 36

39. Canant, Talmadge, Comments by Canant, Corsicana Daily Sun, Corsicana, Texas, Jul 11, 1962, p. 21

40. Cage Coach Named for TIgerland, Corsicana Daily Sun, Corsicana, Texas, Jul 13, 1962, p. 21

41. Canant, Talmadge, Comments by Canant, Corsicana Daily Sun, Corsicana, Texas, Jul 14, 1962, p. 7

42. Canant, Talmadge, Comments by Canant, Corsicana Daily Sun, Corsicana, Texas, Jul 31, 1962, p. 7

43. Coaches Off to Lubbock, Corsicana Daily Sun, Corsicana, Texas, Aug 06, 1962, p. 8

44. Wade Fills Tiger Staff, Corsicana Daily Sun, Corsicana, Texas, Aug 11, 1962, p. 8

45. Dads Club Plan for Upcoming Grid Season, Corsicana Daily Sun, Corsicana, Texas, Aug 14, 1962, p. 17

46. District 8-AAA Meets in Ennis, Corsicana Daily Sun, Corsicana, Texas, Aug 15, 1962, p. 11

47. Ratliff, Harold, V., Sports Shots, Corsicana Daily Sun, Corsicana, Texas, Aug 16, 1962, p. 32

48. Tigers on the Mark, Corsicana Daily Sun, Corsicana, Texas, Aug 16, 1962, p. 31

49. Bengals Begin Gridiron Grind with Two-A-Day, Corsicana Daily Sun, Corsicana, Texas, Aug 20, 1962, p. 21

50. Tiger Football Under Way, Corsicana Daily Sun, Corsicana, Texas, Aug 21, 1962, p. 7

51. Rotarians Hear Coach Acree of Corsicana High, Corsicana Daily Sun, Corsicana, Texas, Aug 22, 1962, p. 11

52. Tigers at Henderson, Corsicana Daily Sun, Corsicana, Texas, Aug 27, 1962, p. 25

53. Dads Ready Grid Party Barbeque, Corsicana Daily Sun, Corsicana, Texas, Aug 29, 1962, p. 8

54. Tigers Ease Up, Barbeque Slated, Corsicana Daily Sun, Corsicana, Texas, Aug 30, 1962, p. 15

55. Canant, Talmadge, Comments by Canant, Corsicana Daily Sun, Corsicana, Texas, Aug 30, 1962, p. 40

56. Barbeque Party Set Tonight, Corsicana Daily Sun, Corsicana, Texas, Aug 31, 1962, p. 8

57. Dads Fete Tigers at Barbeque, Corsicana Daily Sun, Corsicana, Texas, Sep 01, 1962, p. 17

58. Robinson Has Surgery; CHS Resumes Work, Corsicana Daily Sun, Corsicana, Texas, Sep 03, 1962, p. 21

59. Tigers Seek a Foe, Corsicana Daily Sun, Corsicana, Texas, Sep 07, 1962, p. 9

60. 3 Emergencies at Memorial, Corsicana Daily Sun, Corsicana, Texas, Sep 08, 1962, p. 10

61. Coach Acree is Lions Speaker Tuesday Noon, Corsicana Daily Sun, Corsicana, Texas, Sep 11, 1962, p. 2

62. Dads View Tiger Grid Pictures, Corsicana Daily Sun, Corsicana, Texas, Sep 11, 1962, p. 7

63. Corsicana to Face a Good, Big Waco Eleven, Corsicana Daily Sun, Corsicana, Texas, Sep 12, 1962, p. 9

64. 8-AAA Ready for Friday's Grid Opening, Corsicana Daily Sun, Corsicana, Texas, Sep 13, 1962, p. 11

65. Tigers Battle Waco Tonight, Corsicana Daily Sun, Corsicana, Texas, Sep 14, 1962, p. 21

66. Waco Outlasts Corsicana Grid Club, 28-13, Corsicana Daily Sun, Corsicana, Texas, Sep 15, 1962, p. 7

67. Football Coach Speaker Monday Kiwanis Club, Corsicana Daily Sun, Corsicana, Texas, Sep 17, 1962, p. 11

68. Jim Acree Tells Dads Palestine Big, Fast, Corsicana Daily Sun, Corsicana, Texas, Sep 18, 1962, p. 7

69. Bulldogs, Tigers at Home, Corsicana Daily Sun, Corsicana, Texas, Sep 19, 1962, p. 7

70. Gray-Y Football Practice Opens, Corsicana Daily Sun, Corsicana, Texas, Sep 19, 1962, p. 17

71. Sick Football Player Leaves Plane, Corsicana Daily Sun, Corsicana, Texas, Sep 19, 1962, p. 17

72. Stopping Nichols, a Tiger Task, Corsicana Daily Sun, Corsicana, Texas, Sep 20, 1962, p. 40

73. Tiger Lineup, Corsicana Daily Sun, Corsicana, Texas, Sep 21, 1962, p. 7

74. Tigers Trim Palestine for First Win, Corsicana Daily Sun, Corsicana, Texas, Sep 22, 1962, p. 17

75. Tyler Will be Tough Says Coach, Corsicana Daily Sun, Corsicana, Texas, Sep 26, 1962, p. 10

76. Canant, Talmadge, Comments by Canant, Corsicana Daily Sun, Corsicana, Texas, Sep 28, 1962, p. 25

77. Tyler Squeezes by Corsicana, 12-8, Corsicana Daily Sun, Corsicana, Texas, Sep 29, 1962, p. 17

78. Friday Foes are Tough, Corsicana Daily Sun, Corsicana, Texas, Oct 02, 1962, p. 7

79. Tigers ready for Grid War Party, Corsicana Daily Sun, Corsicana, Texas, Oct 04, 1962, p. 15

80. Corsicana Throttles Jacksonville, Corsicana Daily Sun, Corsicana, Texas, Oct 06, 1962, p. 7

81. Canant, Talmadge, Comments by Canant, Corsicana Daily Sun, Corsicana, Texas, Oct 08, 1962, p. 9

82. Gridders Hunt for Dry Place, Corsicana Daily Sun, Corsicana, Texas, Oct 09, 1962, p. 7

83. Weatherford is Next for Tigers, Corsicana Daily Sun, Corsicana, Texas, Oct 16, 1962, p. 4

84. School Board Considers Various Proposals, Corsicana Semi-Weekly Light, Corsicana, Texas, Oct 16, 1962, p. 6

85. Weatherford Next for CHS, Corsicana Daily Sun, Corsicana, Texas, Oct 18, 1962, p. 15

86. Tigers Bring Home a Kangaroo Hide, 6-0, Corsicana Daily Sun, Corsicana, Texas, Oct 20, 1962, p. 7

87. Ennis Can Make Trouble, Corsicana Daily Sun, Corsicana, Texas, Oct 23, 1962, p. 7

88. Westminster Men Honor Gridiron Players in Wednesday Night Fete, Corsicana Daily Sun, Corsicana, Texas, Oct 25, 1962, p. 15

89. Tigers Escape with Lives at Ennis, 21-14, Corsicana Daily Sun, Corsicana, Texas, Oct 27, 1962, p. 7

90. Tigers Turn Back Waxa in Scorefest, 35-22, Corsicana Daily Sun, Corsicana, Texas, Nov 03, 1962, p. 7

91. A Typical Game with Cleburne, Corsicana Daily Sun, Corsicana, Texas, Nov 06, 1962, p. 7

92. Tigers Wind Up Workouts, Corsicana Daily Sun, Corsicana, Texas, Nov 08, 1962, p. 14

93. Tigers Overtake Cleburne, Win 21-6 Decision Corsicana Daily Sun, Corsicana, Texas, Nov 10, 1962, p. 7

94. Canant, Talmadge, Comments by Canant, Corsicana Daily Sun, Corsicana, Texas, Nov 10, 1962, p. 8

95. Dads See Grid Films on Monday, Corsicana Daily Sun, Corsicana, Texas, Nov 13, 1962, p. 7

96. Corsicana, Terrell Face Tricky Hurdles, Corsicana Daily Sun, Corsicana, Texas, Nov 15, 1962, p. 13

97. Corsicana Blunts Athens Gridiron Bid, 21-3, Corsicana Daily Sun, Corsicana, Texas, Nov 17, 1962, p. 7

98. 8-AAA Showdown, Friday Clash Settles It, Corsicana Daily Sun, Corsicana, Texas, Nov 20, 1962, p. 7

99. Terrell an All-Around Power, Can Hit the Homerun, Says Scribe, Corsicana Daily Sun, Corsicana, Texas, Nov 21, 1962, p. 7

100. Corsicana Ready for Title Game, Corsicana Daily Sun, Corsicana, Texas, Nov 23, 1962, p. 7

101. Canant, Talmadge, Comments by Canant, Corsicana Daily Sun, Corsicana, Texas, Nov 23, 1962, p. 7

102. Bengals Stop Terrell, Take District Title, Corsicana Daily Sun, Corsicana, Texas, Nov 24, 1962, p. 7

103. CHS Readying for Jacksonville Club, Corsicana Daily Sun, Corsicana, Texas, Nov 26, 1962, p. 7

104. Indians Improved Tiger Coach Says, Corsicana Daily Sun, Corsicana, Texas, Nov 27, 1962, p. 7

105. The Second Verse, Corsicana Daily Sun, Corsicana, Texas, Nov 29, 1962, p. 16

106. Congratulations Corsicana Tigers and Coaches, Corsicana Daily Sun, Corsicana, Texas, Nov 29, 1962, p. 11

107. A Salute to The Corsicana Tigers, their Coaches, Cheerleaders, Drum Majors and Band, Corsicana Daily Sun, Corsicana, Texas, Nov 30, 1962, p. 5

108. Bengals, Braves Ready for War, Corsicana Daily Sun, Corsicana, Texas, Nov 30, 1962, p. 8

109. Tigers Fall to Jacksonville Indians, 14-13, Corsicana Daily Sun, Corsicana, Texas, Dec 01, 1962, p. 7

110. Canant, Talmadge, Comments by Canant, Corsicana Daily Sun, Corsicana, Texas, Dec 03, 1962, p. 11

111. No Alibis for Loss, Acree, Corsicana Daily Sun, Corsicana, Texas, Dec 04, 1962, p. 7

112. Canant, Talmadge, Comments by Canant, Corsicana Daily Sun, Corsicana, Texas, Dec 05, 1962, p. 8

113. Stellar Club Selected, Corsicana Daily Sun, Corsicana, Texas, Dec 10, 1962, p. 9

114. Kiwanis Club Hears Acree Monday Noon, Corsicana Daily Sun, Corsicana, Texas, Dec 10, 1962, p. 8

115. Tiger Coaches Feted, Corsicana Daily Sun, Corsicana, Texas, Dec 11, 1962, p. 7

116. Canant, Talmadge, Comments by Canant, Corsicana Daily Sun, Corsicana, Texas, Dec 17, 1962, p. 9

117. CHS Sports Pinnacle...1962, Corsicana Daily Sun, Corsicana, Texas, Dec 20, 1962, p. 15

118. Kiwanians Will Man SA Kettles on Saturday, Corsicana Daily Sun, Corsicana, Texas, Dec 21, 1962, p. 2

119. Corsicana Grid Letter Winners are Announced, Corsicana Daily Sun, Corsicana, Texas, Jan 12, 1963, p. 17

120. Corsicana Fetes 1962 District Championship Eleven, Corsicana Daily Sun, Corsicana, Texas, Jan 23, 1963, p. 7

121. Oklahoma State Signs Hap Settle, Corsicana Daily Sun, Corsicana, Texas, Feb 14, 1963, p. 35

122. Canant, Talmadge, Comments by Canant, Corsicana Daily Sun, Corsicana, Texas, Feb 15, 1963, p. 11

123. Henkel Becomes a Raider, Corsicana Daily Sun, Corsicana, Texas, Feb 20, 1963, p. 17

Chapter 6

1. New Trial for Richland Tax Case Ordered, Corsicana Semi-Weekly Light, Corsicana, Texas, Jun 26, 1962, p. 6

2. Delinquent Tax Suit Filed, Corsicana Semi-Weekly Light, Corsicana, Texas, Aug 07, 1962, p. 5

3. Richland Voters for Abolishing School District, Corsicana Daily Sun, Corsicana, Texas, Sep 15, 1962, p. 11

4. Delay Canvass Richland Vote, Corsicana Daily Sun, Corsicana, Texas, Sep 17, 1962, p. 1

5. Richland, Corsicana Daily Sun, Corsicana, Texas, Sep 18, 1962, p. 2

6. Corsicana Due Richland Pupils, Corsicana Semi-Weekly Light, Corsicana, Texas, Sep 28, 1962, p. 1

7. Richland, Corsicana Semi-Weekly Light, Corsicana, Texas, Sep 28, 1962, p. 3

8. Corsicana Accepts Richland Students, Corsicana Daily Sun, Corsicana, Texas, Sep 28, 1962, p. 17

9. Acree to Talk at Regional Coaches Meet, Corsicana Daily Sun, Corsicana, Texas, Jan 24, 1963, p. 13

10. Canant, Talmadge, Comments by Canant, Corsicana Daily Sun, Corsicana, Texas, Jan 30, 1963, p. 9

11. Local Schools Feel Impact of Varied Sickness, Corsicana Daily Sun, Corsicana, Texas, Mar 11, 1963, p. 1

12. Mrs. O.E. Bounds Rites Sunday, Corsicana Daily Sun, Corsicana, Texas, Apr 15, 1963, p. 17

13. Dads Elect Stover New President, Corsicana Daily Sun, Corsicana, Texas, Apr 16, 1963, p. 7

14. Canant, Talmadge, Comments by Canant, Corsicana Daily Sun, Corsicana, Texas, Apr 25, 1963, p. 16

15. Jim Miller to Accept Place at Jacksonville, Corsicana Daily Sun, Corsicana, Texas, May 23, 1963, p. 30

16. Canant, Talmadge, Comments by Canant, Corsicana Daily Sun, Corsicana, Texas, May 24, 1963, p. 19

17. Canant, Talmadge, Comments by Canant, Corsicana Daily Sun, Corsicana, Texas, May 30, 1963, p. 14

18. Collins, Drane Junior High Schools Graduate Over 300 to CHS, Corsicana Semi-Weekly Light, Corsicana, Texas, Jun 04, 1963, p. 3

19. Canant, Talmadge, Comments by Canant, Corsicana Daily Sun, Corsicana, Texas, Jun 15, 1963, p. 17

20. Canant, Talmadge, Comments by Canant, Corsicana Daily Sun, Corsicana, Texas, Jul 11, 1963, p. 31

21. Canant, Talmadge, Comments by Canant, Corsicana Daily Sun, Corsicana, Texas, Jul 23, 1963, p. 17

22. Ratliff, Harold V., Sports Shots, Corsicana Daily Sun, Corsicana, Texas, Aug 01, 1963, p. 3

23. Canant, Talmadge, Comments by Canant, Corsicana Daily Sun, Corsicana, Texas, Aug 01, 1963, p. 40

24. Local Coaches Will Attend THSCA School, Corsicana Daily Sun, Corsicana, Texas, Aug 03, 1963, p. 8

25. Grid Coaches Get Ready, Corsicana Daily Sun, Corsicana, Texas, Aug 12, 1963, p. 26

26. Dads Club Begins Work, Corsicana Daily Sun, Corsicana, Texas, Aug 13, 1963, p. 19

27. Canant, Talmadge, Comments by Canant, Corsicana Daily Sun, Corsicana, Texas, Aug 14, 1963, p. 7

28. Canant, Talmadge, Comments by Canant, Corsicana Daily Sun, Corsicana, Texas, Aug 15, 1963, p. 38

29. Revision of Tie Rule Made in 8-AAA Meet, Corsicana Daily Sun, Corsicana, Texas, Aug 16, 1963, p. 7

30. Parents Meet Grid Coaches, Corsicana Daily Sun, Corsicana, Texas, Aug 17, 1963, p. 7

31. Tigers Join Gridiron Work Twice Daily, Corsicana Daily Sun, Corsicana, Texas, Aug 19, 1963, p. 7
32. Tigers Open Gridiron Work, Corsicana Daily Sun, Corsicana, Texas, Aug 20, 1963, p. 7
33. Canant, Talmadge, Comments by Canant, Corsicana Daily Sun, Corsicana, Texas, Aug 21, 1963, p. 21
34. Observers See Tiger Grid Work, Corsicana Daily Sun, Corsicana, Texas, Aug 22, 1963, p. 13
35. Bengals Close with Scrimmage, Corsicana Daily Sun, Corsicana, Texas, Aug 24, 1963, p. 17
36. First Methodist Church School Teachers Feted Tuesday Night Banquet, Corsicana Daily Sun, Corsicana, Texas, Aug 29, 1963, p. 31
37. Scrimmage and Barbeque Party Scheduled, Corsicana Daily Sun, Corsicana, Texas, Aug 30, 1963, p. 9
38. Clarke, Doug, Tiger Defense Dominant, Corsicana Daily Sun, Corsicana, Texas, Aug 31, 1963, p. 7
39. Canant, Talmadge, Comments by Canant, Corsicana Daily Sun, Corsicana, Texas, Sep 02, 1963, p. 21
40. Canant, Talmadge, Comments by Canant, Corsicana Daily Sun, Corsicana, Texas, Sep 04, 1963, p. 10
41. Tiger Offense Still Lagging, Corsicana Daily Sun, Corsicana, Texas, Sep 04, 1963, p. 9
42. Schools, Corsicana Daily Sun, Corsicana, Texas, Sep 05, 1963, p. 9
43. Corsicana High Adjusting to Peak Enrollment, Corsicana Daily Sun, Corsicana, Texas, Sep 05, 1963, p. 22
44. Local Schools Show Increase in Enrollment, Corsicana Semi-Weekly Light, Corsicana, Texas, Sep 06, 1963, p. 8
45. Bryan to Scrimmage CHS Tonight, Corsicana Daily Sun, Corsicana, Texas, Sep 06, 1963, p. 22
46. Clarke, Doug, From the Shoulder, Corsicana Daily Sun, Corsicana, Texas, Sep 06, 1963, p. 21
47. Enrollment in Public Schools Continues Rise, Corsicana Daily Sun, Corsicana, Texas, Sep 09, 1963, p. 17
48. Corsicana, Waco Continue Feud, Corsicana Daily Sun, Corsicana, Texas, Sep 13, 1963, p. 7
49. Corsicana Outlasts Waco Felines, 35-6, Corsicana Daily Sun, Corsicana, Texas, Sep 14, 1963, p. 7
50. Palestine to be a Toughie, Corsicana Daily Sun, Corsicana, Texas, Sep 17, 1963, p. 17
51. Canant, Talmadge, Comments by Canant, Corsicana Daily Sun, Corsicana, Texas, Sep 18, 1963, p. 20
52. Tigers Work on Mistakes, Corsicana Daily Sun, Corsicana, Texas, Sep 19, 1963, p. 39
53. Tigers Invade Palestine, Corsicana Daily Sun, Corsicana, Texas, Sep 20, 1963, p. 7
54. Mike Russell Loses Hand in Meat Grinder, Corsicana Daily Sun, Corsicana, Texas, Sep 20, 1963, p. 1
55. Canant, Talmadge, Comments by Canant, Corsicana Daily Sun, Corsicana, Texas, Sep 23, 1963, p. 8
56. Clarke, Doug, From the Shoulder, Corsicana Daily Sun, Corsicana, Texas, Sep 24, 1963, p. 21

57. 1963 Tigers, Corsicana Daily Sun, Corsicana, Texas, Sep 25, 1963, p. 8

58. Four League Clubs Remain Unbeaten Now, Corsicana Daily Sun, Corsicana, Texas, Sep 25, 1963, p. 8

59. Ground Game, Defense Contribute to Victory, Corsicana Daily Sun, Corsicana, Texas, Sep 28, 1963, p. 17

60. Canant, Talmadge, Comments by Canant, Corsicana Daily Sun, Corsicana, Texas, Sep 30, 1963, p. 11

61. Tigers Face Tough Friday, Corsicana Daily Sun, Corsicana, Texas, Oct 01, 1963, p. 8

62. Bengals Sharpen Claws, Corsicana Daily Sun, Corsicana, Texas, Oct 03, 1963, p. 18

63. Tiger-Indian Tussle Looms, Corsicana Daily Sun, Corsicana, Texas, Oct 04, 1963, p. 7

64. Canant, Talmadge, Comments by Canant, Corsicana Daily Sun, Corsicana, Texas, Oct 14, 1963, p. 7

65. Under New Alignment, Corsicana Semi-Weekly Light, Corsicana, Texas, Oct 15, 1963, p. 2

66. New District Sets Session in Waco, Corsicana Semi-Weekly Light, Corsicana, Texas, Oct 15, 1963, p. 4

67. 18 Registrants at Draft Board in September, Corsicana Semi-Weekly Light, Corsicana, Texas, Oct 15, 1963, p. 6

68. Ratliff, Harold, Sports Shots, Corsicana Daily Sun, Corsicana, Texas, Oct 24, 1963, p. 15

Chapter 7

1. Continental Inn Plans $250,000 Expansion, Victoria Advocate, Victoria, Texas, Jan 17, 1963, p. 2

2. Corsicana Tigers Stomp Ennis Eleven, 56-8, Corsicana Daily Sun, Corsicana, Texas, Oct 26, 1963, p. 7

3. Canant, Talmadge, Comments by Canant, Corsicana Daily Sun, Corsicana, Texas, Oct 30, 1963, p. 8

4. Nippy Weather, Grid Pageantry Make Waxahachie Tilt Pleasant, Corsicana Daily Sun, Corsicana, Texas, Nov 02, 1963, p. 8

5. Tiger Line, Ground Attack Dominate Tilt, Corsicana Daily Sun, Corsicana, Texas, Nov 09, 1963, p. 7

6. Title Tie Clinched in Friday Clash, Corsicana Daily Sun, Corsicana, Texas, Nov 16, 1963, p. 7

7. Palestine Bi-District Playoff Battle Site, Corsicana Semi-Weekly Light, Corsicana, Texas, Nov 19, 1963, p. 1

8. Bengals Win Chilly 53-16 Tilt, Corsicana Daily Sun, Corsicana, Texas, Nov 23, 1963, p. 9

9. Corsicana, Palestine Getting Ready, Corsicana Daily Sun, Corsicana, Texas, Nov 25, 1963, p. 13

10. Tigers Place Seven Players on News Team, Corsicana Daily Sun, Corsicana, Texas, Nov 27, 1963, p. 7

11. Victory Grin, Corsicana Daily Sun, Corsicana, Texas, Nov 27, 1963, p. 7

12. Bengals, Wildcats are Ready, Corsicana Daily Sun, Corsicana, Texas, Nov 29, 1963, p. 8

13. Tigers Blunt Palestine Bid With 21-14 Victory Friday, Corsicana Daily Sun, Corsicana, Texas, Nov 30, 1963, p. 7
14. Tigers Hit McKinney Lions 14-7, Corsicana Daily Sun, Corsicana, Texas, Dec 09, 1963, p. 11
15. Go Tigers Beat Graham, Corsicana Daily Sun, Corsicana, Texas, Dec 13, 1963, p. 8
16. Bengals Claw into State Grid Finals, Corsicana Daily Sun, Corsicana, Texas, Dec 16, 1963, p. 7
17. Tigers Need One More Victory, Corsicana Daily Sun, Corsicana, Texas, Dec 16, 1963, p. 8
18. Victoria Site of Title Bout on Saturday, Corsicana Semi-Weekly Light, Corsicana, Texas, Dec 17, 1963, p. 5
19. Corsicana Preps for Saturday Gridiron Job, Corsicana Daily Sun, Corsicana, Texas, Dec 18, 1963, p. 7
20. Scenes from Victory that Sent Tigers into State Football Finals, Corsicana Daily Sun, Corsicana, Texas, Dec 19, 1963, p. 16
21. "Tiger Nite" Due Monday, Corsicana Daily Sun, Corsicana, Texas, Dec 19, 1963, p. 16
22. Clarke, Doug, From the Shoulder, Corsicana Daily Sun, Corsicana, Texas, Dec 20, 1963, p. 9
23. Go Tigers Beat Pharr-San-Juan-Alamo, Corsicana Daily Sun, Corsicana, Texas, Dec 20, 1963, p. 8
24. Schoolboy Grid Chips go on the Line, Corsicana Daily Sun, Corsicana, Texas, Dec 20, 1963, p. 7
25. B Tiger Team Shares Success with State Finalist Eleven, Corsicana Semi-Weekly Light, Corsicana, Texas, Dec 20, 1963, p. 9
26. The Weather, Victoria Advocate, Victoria, Texas, Dec 21, 1963, p. 1
27. P-SJ-A, Corsicana Collide Today, Victoria Advocate, Victoria, Texas, Dec 21, 1963, p. 9
28. Corsicana Tops Pharr for Title in Class AAA, Victoria Advocate, Victoria, Texas, Sun, Dec 22, 1963, p. 12
29. A Salute to the Corsicana AAA State Champion Team, Corsicana Daily Sun, Corsicana, Texas, Dec 23, 1963, p. 9
30. AAA Crown Climaxes August-December Grind, Corsicana Daily Sun, Corsicana, Texas, Dec 23, 1963, p. 11
31. Other Voices Singing, Corsicana Daily Sun, Corsicana, Texas, Dec 23, 1963, p. 14
32. Everybody is Invited Out to Celebrate, Corsicana Daily Sun, Corsicana, Texas, Dec 23, 1963, p. 1
33. Fake Field Goal Tally Brings Win, Corsicana Daily Sun, Corsicana, Texas, Dec 23, 1963, p. 1
34. Jim Acree at Kiwanis Club, Shows Film, Corsicana Daily Sun, Corsicana, Texas, Dec 23, 1963, p. 15
35. Corsicana Thanks Bengals, Coaches, Corsicana Daily Sun, Corsicana, Texas, Dec 24, 1963, p. 7
36. Clarke, Doug, From the Shoulder, Corsicana Daily Sun, Corsicana, Texas, Dec 24, 1963, p. 7
37. It's Great to be a State Champ, Corsicana Semi-Weekly Light, Corsicana, Texas, Dec 24, 1963, p. 6

38. Four Tigers Listed on All-State Grid Squad, Corsicana Daily Sun, Corsicana, Texas, Dec 26, 1963, p. 13

39. Tiger Totals Reflect Championship Season, Corsicana Daily Sun, Corsicana, Texas, Dec 27, 1963, p. 7

40. Champs Club to Induct Friday, Corsicana Daily Sun, Corsicana, Texas, May 12, 1964, p. 9

Chapter 8

1. Local Boxers Lose Matches in GG Tourney, Corsicana Daily Sun, Corsicana, Texas, Feb 05, 1963, p. 17

2. Stevens, Eric C., Why boxing is the most difficult sport, Jul 14, 2014, https://breakingmuscle.com/fitness/why-boxing-is-the-toughest-sport, last accessed Aug 28, 2022

3. The Encyclopedia of Oklahoma History and Culture, Boxing, https://www.okhistory.org/publications/enc/entry.php?entry=BO029, last accessed Aug 28, 2022

4. Dyreson, Mark, and Jaime Schultz, American National Pastimes - A History, Prize Fighting, Routledge, Dec 10, 2014, p. 208

Chapter 9

1. Canant, Talmadge, Comments by Canant, Corsicana Daily Sun, Corsicana, Texas, Feb 06, 1963, p. 8

2. Canant, Talmadge, Comments by Canant, Corsicana Daily Sun, Corsicana, Texas, Feb 08, 1963, p. 10

3. Ratliff, Harold V., Sports Shots, Corsicana Daily Sun, Corsicana, Texas, Feb 21, 1963, p. 40

4. Garland's Chuck Curtis High Grid Coach of the Year, Fort Worth Star-Telegram, Fort Worth, Texas, Sun, Jan 05, 1964, p. 24

5. Acree to Lecture at Clinic, Corsicana Semi-Weekly Light, Corsicana, Texas, Jan 07, 1964, p. 6

6. Chamber, Coaches Praised, Corsicana Daily Sun, Corsicana, Texas, Jan 10, 1964, p. 5

7. Corsicana Thanks Champion Tigers, Corsicana Daily Sun, Corsicana, Texas, Jan 22, 1964, p. 7

8. Change Royal's Speaking Date, Corsicana Daily Sun, Corsicana, Texas, Jan 22, 1964, p. 19

9. Acree and Other Coaches at Grid Clinic, Corsicana Daily Sun, Corsicana, Texas, Jan 24, 1964, p. 17

10. Trull, Royal To Get Awards, Fort Worth Star-Telegram, Fort Worth, Texas, Sun, Feb 09, 1964, p. 24

11. Spring Football for Tigers, Corsicana Daily Sun, Corsicana, Texas, Feb 13, 1964, p. 13

12. Fifty-two Boys Taking Part in Daily Drills, Corsicana Daily Sun, Corsicana, Texas, Feb 25, 1964, p. 7

13. CHS Gridiron Schedule Set, Corsicana Daily Sun, Corsicana, Texas, Feb 25, 1964, p. 7

14. Awards Continued, Royal Gets Another, Fort Worth Star-Telegram, Fort Worth, Texas, Feb 26, 1964, p. 28

15. Canant, Talmadge, Comments by Canant, Corsicana Daily Sun, Corsicana, Texas, Feb 27, 1964, p. 13

16. UT Scrubbed of Probation Blame by Fry, Fort Worth Star-Telegram, Fort Worth, Texas, Feb 28, 1964, p. 37

17. Canant, Talmadge, Comments by Canant, Corsicana Daily Sun, Corsicana, Texas, Mar 02, 1964, p. 8

18. Tigers Enter Second Week, Corsicana Daily Sun, Corsicana, Texas, Mar 03, 1964, p. 21

19. Canant, Talmadge, Comments by Canant, Corsicana Daily Sun, Corsicana, Texas, Mar 07, 1964, p. 8

20. Blue, Gold Teams Getting Ready, Corsicana Daily Sun, Corsicana, Texas, Mar 10, 1964, p. 7

21. Acree to Tutor the South, Corsicana Daily Sun, Corsicana, Texas, Mar 11, 1964, p. 7

22. Cage, Grid Pilots OKd for School, Fort Worth Star-Telegram, Fort Worth, Texas, Mar 12, 1964, p. 16

23. Tiger Gridiron Squad Divided, Corsicana Daily Sun, Corsicana, Texas, Mar 13, 1964, p. 9

24. Tiger Spring Practice Finale Slated Tonight, Corsicana Daily Sun, Corsicana, Texas, Mar 14, 1964, p. 7

25. 14 Emergencies Treated at Memorial During Past Weekend, Corsicana Daily Sun, Corsicana, Texas, Mar 16, 1964, p. 12

26. Whites Whip Blue Eleven, Corsicana Daily Sun, Corsicana, Texas, Mar 16, 1964, p. 7

27. Canant, Talmadge, Comments by Canant, Corsicana Daily Sun, Corsicana, Texas, May 06, 1964, p. 12

28. All-Star Twosome Potent, Fort Worth Star-Telegram, Fort Worth, Texas, Sun, Jul 05, 1964, p. 26

29. Jim Acree is Speaker Rotary Wednesday Noon, Corsicana Daily Sun, Corsicana, Texas, Jul 22, 1964, p. 2

30. All-Star Gridmen, Fort Worth Star-Telegram, Fort Worth, Texas, Sun, Jul 26, 1964, p. 25

31. Acree's South has Some Good Linemen, Corsicana Daily Sun, Corsicana, Texas, Jul 30, 1964, p. 31

32. South Chances are Good, Corsicana Daily Sun, Corsicana, Texas, Jul 31, 1964, p. 21

33. Stopping the South Main Concern for North Eleven, Fort Worth Star-Telegram, Fort Worth, Texas, Jul 31, 1964, p. 17

34. Football Coaches, Fort Worth Star-Telegram, Fort Worth, Texas, Sun, Aug 02, 1964, p. 23

35. Hagle, McVea Impress; Acree Picks Starters for South Grid Club, Corsicana Daily Sun, Corsicana, Texas, Aug 03, 1964, p. 21

36. Canant, Talmadge, Comments by Canant, Corsicana Daily Sun, Corsicana, Texas, Aug 04, 1964, p. 7

37. Coaching School Slate, Fort Worth Star-Telegram, Fort Worth, Texas, Aug 05, 1964, p. 29

38. North Prevails, 23-14 as Records Tumble in Schoolboy Grid Clash, Corsicana Daily Sun, Corsicana, Texas, Aug 07, 1964, p. 17

39. Coach Acree Speaker Monday Kiwanis Club, Corsicana Daily Sun, Corsicana, Texas, Aug 17, 1964, p. 12

40. Corsicana Tigers Start 1964 Grid Work Friday, Corsicana Daily Sun, Corsicana, Texas, Aug 25, 1964, p. 7

41. Gridders Don Shorts, Shirts for First Work, Corsicana Daily Sun, Corsicana, Texas, Aug 28, 1964, p. 7

42. Cloudy Skies a Break for Bengals, Corsicana Daily Sun, Corsicana, Texas, Aug 29, 1964, p. 7

43. It's Like This, Corsicana Daily Sun, Corsicana, Texas, Aug 31, 1964, p. 7

44. Make Believe Practice, Corsicana Daily Sun, Corsicana, Texas, Aug 31, 1964, p. 21

45. Tigers are Lagging, Corsicana Daily Sun, Corsicana, Texas, Sep 04, 1964, p. 21

46. Barbeque Party Set Tonight, Corsicana Daily Sun, Corsicana, Texas, Sep 04, 1964, p. 21

47. Canant, Talmadge, Comments by Canant, Corsicana Daily Sun, Corsicana, Texas, Sep 07, 1964, p. 8

48. Corsicana, Sherman Scrimmage Saturday Night, Corsicana Daily Sun, Corsicana, Texas, Sep 07, 1964, p. 7

49. Dads Prepare for Football-time, Corsicana Daily Sun, Corsicana, Texas, Sep 08, 1964, p. 17

50. Revamped Wall Faces Bonham Grid Challenge, Corsicana Daily Sun, Corsicana, Texas, Sep 09, 1964, p. 19

51. Friday Starters for Tigers Not Definite, Corsicana Daily Sun, Corsicana, Texas, Sep 10, 1964, p. 13

52. Bengals, Warriors to Swap Blows Tonight, Corsicana Daily Sun, Corsicana, Texas, Sep 11, 1964, p. 8

53. Bengals Overtake Bonham Warriors, 21-14, Corsicana Daily Sun, Corsicana, Texas, Sep 12, 1964, p. 7

54. Cowtown Club Burly, Corsicana Daily Sun, Corsicana, Texas, Sep 17, 1964, p. 12

55. Corsicana, Ft Worth Elevens Clash Tonight, Corsicana Daily Sun, Corsicana, Texas, Sep 18, 1964, p. 8

56. Tigers Ground Carter-Riverside Eagles, 17-7, Corsicana Daily Sun, Corsicana, Texas, Sep 19, 1964, p. 7

57. Canant, Talmadge, Comments by Canant, Corsicana Daily Sun, Corsicana, Texas, Sep 21, 1964, p. 9

58. Tyler Eleven Formidable, Corsicana Daily Sun, Corsicana, Texas, Sep 22, 1964, p. 19

59. Friday a Tough Nite, Says Acree, Corsicana Daily Sun, Corsicana, Texas, Sep 24, 1964, p. 19

60. Tyler Ekes by Corsicana, Snaps String, 7-6, Corsicana Daily Sun, Corsicana, Texas, Sep 26, 1964, p. 7

61. Canant, Talmadge, Comments by Canant, Corsicana Daily Sun, Corsicana, Texas, Sep 28, 1964, p. 11

62. Indians Ready for Corsicana, Corsicana Daily Sun, Corsicana, Texas, Sep 29, 1964, p. 19

63. Corsicana Overtakes Jacksonville, 9-8, Corsicana Daily Sun, Corsicana, Texas, Oct 03, 1964, p. 7

64. Corsicana Eleven Belts Ennis Lions, 28-3, Corsicana Daily Sun, Corsicana, Texas, Oct 10, 1964, p. 7

65. 1964 Bengals, Corsicana Daily Sun, Corsicana, Texas, Oct 13, 1964, p. 9

66. Jackets Visit Tiger Field Tonight as Loop Gridiron Play Begins, Corsicana Daily Sun, Corsicana, Texas, Oct 16, 1964, p. 8

67. Corsicana Wins 35-22 Grid Scorefest from Cleburne, Corsicana Daily Sun, Corsicana, Texas, Oct 17, 1964, p. 7

68. Canant, Talmadge, Comments by Canant, Corsicana Daily Sun, Corsicana, Texas, Oct 17, 1964, p. 7

69. Corsicana-Waco Tilt Headliner in 13-AAAA North Zone Play, Corsicana Daily Sun, Corsicana, Texas, Oct 22, 1964, p. 13

70. Corsicana Shuts Out Brazos Bengals, 20-0, Corsicana Daily Sun, Corsicana, Texas, Oct 24, 1964, p. 7

71. Tigers Stampede Broncos, 17-7, Lead North Zone, Corsicana Daily Sun, Corsicana, Texas, Oct 31, 1964, p. 7

72. Canant, Talmadge, Comments by Canant, Corsicana Daily Sun, Corsicana, Texas, Nov 02, 1964, p. 9

73. Corsicana Whips Scrappy Bryan Outfit with Passes, Field Goal, Corsicana Semi-Weekly Light, Corsicana, Texas, Nov 03, 1964, p. 6

74. University Trojans Challenge Corsicana Eleven Here Tonight, Corsicana Daily Sun, Corsicana, Texas, Nov 06, 1964, p. 8

75. Corsicana Tigers Slash Waco Trojans, 41-14, Corsicana Daily Sun, Corsicana, Texas, Nov 07, 1964, p. 7

76. Tigers Could Lose Any Day Now, Corsicana Daily Sun, Corsicana, Texas, Nov 10, 1964, p. 7

77. North Zone Decides a Champion Friday, Corsicana Daily Sun, Corsicana, Texas, Nov 11, 1964, p. 7

78. Richfield Wants the Game, Too, Corsicana Daily Sun, Corsicana, Texas, Nov 12, 1964, p. 14

79. No Cannon Boom to be Heard at Waco Friday, Corsicana Daily Sun, Corsicana, Texas, Nov 12, 1964, p. 8

80. Beat Richfield, Corsicana Daily Sun, Corsicana, Texas, Nov 13, 1964, p. 9

81. Richfield Up for Corsicana Club Tonight, Corsicana Daily Sun, Corsicana, Texas, Nov 13, 1964, p. 10

82. Rams Batter Tigers in Area Showdown, 29-15, Corsicana Daily Sun, Corsicana, Texas, Nov 14, 1964, p. 9

83. Screen Shows Dads Bengal Grid Errors, Corsicana Daily Sun, Corsicana, Texas, Nov 17, 1964, p. 8

84. Jim Acree is Speaker for Rotary Club, Corsicana Daily Sun, Corsicana, Texas, Nov 25, 1964, p. 2

85. Blunt Questions asked by Turk Visitors on Visit to Corsicana, Corsicana Daily Sun, Corsicana, Texas, Nov 25, 1964, p. 2

86. Dads Thank Coaches, Tigers at Reception, Corsicana Daily Sun, Corsicana, Texas, Dec 01, 1964, p. 9

87. Tiger Stats Impressive, Corsicana Daily Sun, Corsicana, Texas, Dec 04, 1964, p. 8

88. Tigers Put Seven on Zone Team, Corsicana Daily Sun, Corsicana, Texas, Dec 07, 1964, p. 13

89. Jim Acree is Speaker Monday Kiwanis Club, Corsicana Daily Sun, Corsicana, Texas, Dec 21, 1964, p. 10

90. Ivie Named to Stellar Grid Club, Corsicana Daily Sun, Corsicana, Texas, Dec 28, 1964, p. 14

91. Rhoads, Ivie Win Outstanding Player Nominations by Ballot, Corsicana Semi-Weekly Light, Corsicana, Texas, Feb 02, 1965, p. 5

92. Libal Inks Grid Pact, Corsicana Daily Sun, Corsicana, Texas, May 31, 1965, p. 6

93. Picador Stalwart – Don Ivie, Corsicana Daily Sun, Corsicana, Texas, Nov 09, 1965, p. 20

94. Potter, Lloyd, Demographic Briefing, House Committee on Business and Industry, Feb 19, 2013

Chapter 10

1. Spring Football at CHS Opening, Corsicana Daily Sun, Corsicana, Texas, May 03, 1965, p. 26

2. Tiger Football Hopefuls Bump Heads, Corsicana Daily Sun, Corsicana, Texas, May 04, 1965, p. 17

3. Canant, Talmadge, Comments by Canant, Corsicana Daily Sun, Corsicana, Texas, May 10, 1965, p. 10

4. Canant, Talmadge, Comments by Canant, Corsicana Daily Sun, Corsicana, Texas, May 14, 1965, p. 21

5. Dads Elect, Plan Grid Tilt, Blue and Gold Game Set for Saturday Nite, Corsicana Daily Sun, Corsicana, Texas, May 18, 1965, p. 17

6. Canant, Talmadge, Comments by Canant, Corsicana Daily Sun, Corsicana, Texas, May 19, 1965, p. 7

7. Blue and Gold Rosters Announced, Corsicana Daily Sun, Corsicana, Texas, May 20, 1965, p. 41

8. Tigers Await Clash, Starters are Listed, Corsicana Daily Sun, Corsicana, Texas, May 21, 1965, p. 17

9. White Eleven Spring Game Winner, 25-14, Corsicana Daily Sun, Corsicana, Texas, May 24, 1965, p. 7

10. In the Clear and Pardon My Arm, Corsicana Daily Sun, Corsicana, Texas, May 25, 1965, p. 21

11. Canant, Talmadge, Comments by Canant, Corsicana Daily Sun, Corsicana, Texas, May 25, 1965, p. 21

12. Canant, Talmadge, Comments by Canant, Corsicana Daily Sun, Corsicana, Texas, May 26, 1965, p. 7

13. Canant, Talmadge, Comments by Canant, Corsicana Daily Sun, Corsicana, Texas, Jun 28, 1965, p. 10

14. Canant, Talmadge, Comments by Canant, Corsicana Daily Sun, Corsicana, Texas, Jul 09, 1965, p. 8

15. Canant, Talmadge, Comments by Canant, Corsicana Daily Sun, Corsicana, Texas, Jul 14, 1965, p. 10

16. Fit Grid Shoes, Corsicana Daily Sun, Corsicana, Texas, Aug 18, 1965, p. 7
17. Coaches Join Tiger Staff, Corsicana Daily Sun, Corsicana, Texas, Aug 20, 1965, p. 19
18. Tiger Roster Numbers 70, Corsicana Daily Sun, Corsicana, Texas, Aug 21, 1965, p. 16
19. All Schoolboy Teams Out Now, Corsicana Daily Sun, Corsicana, Texas, Aug 23, 1965, p. 9
20. Canant, Talmadge, Comments by Canant, Corsicana Daily Sun, Corsicana, Texas, Aug 25, 1965, p. 19
21. Contact Starts Friday, Corsicana Daily Sun, Corsicana, Texas, Aug 26, 1965, p. 35
22. Tuesday Ends Two-A-Day Schedule, Corsicana Daily Sun, Corsicana, Texas, Aug 31, 1965, p. 7

Chapter 11

1. CHS Has New Coaching Look, Corsicana Daily Sun, Corsicana, Texas, Jul 19, 1965, p. 7
2. Matthews Resigns Cage Post, Corsicana Daily Sun, Corsicana, Texas, Jul 31, 1965, p. 16
3. Jerry Moore Leaves for SMU, Corsicana Daily Sun, Corsicana, Texas, Aug 09, 1965, p. 8
4. Tigers Start Early Monday; Pillans Shaken, Corsicana Daily Sun, Corsicana, Texas, Aug 30, 1965, p. 25
5. Grid Barbeque Nears, Corsicana Daily Sun, Corsicana, Texas, Aug 31, 1965, p. 7
6. Corsicana, Sherman Elevens Scrimmage Before Barbeque, Corsicana Daily Sun, Corsicana, Texas, Sep 04, 1965, p. 16
7. Corsicana, Sherman Scrimmage, Corsicana Daily Sun, Corsicana, Texas, Sep 06, 1965, p. 7
8. Starters are Listed, Corsicana Daily Sun, Corsicana, Texas, Sep 09, 1965, p. 30
9. Tigers Claw Bonham, 26-14, Corsicana Daily Sun, Corsicana, Texas, Sep 11, 1965, p. 20
10. Canant, Talmadge, Comments by Canant, Corsicana Daily Sun, Corsicana, Texas, Sep 14, 1965, p. 10
11. Carter-Riverside to Run Power Football, Corsicana Daily Sun, Corsicana, Texas, Sep 14, 1965, p. 10
12. CHS Lineup to be Same for Eagles, Corsicana Daily Sun, Corsicana, Texas, Sep 16, 1965, p. 14
13. Tigers, Eagles in FW Clash, Corsicana Daily Sun, Corsicana, Texas, Sep 17, 1965, p. 8
14. Corsicana Belts Carter-Riverside Eagles, 33-0, Corsicana Daily Sun, Corsicana, Texas, Sep 18, 1965, p. 7
15. Tiger Blocking Cited; Tough Tyler Comes Up, Corsicana Daily Sun, Corsicana, Texas, Sep 21, 1965, p. 7
16. Tigers, Rams in Tough Tasks, Corsicana Daily Sun, Corsicana, Texas, Sep 22, 1965, p. 7
17. Corsicana Outscraps John Tyler Friday, 14-12, Corsicana Daily Sun, Corsicana, Texas, Sep 25, 1965, p. 8
18. Jacksonville Indians are Always Tough, Acree Advises Dads Club, Corsicana Daily Sun, Corsicana, Texas, Sep 28, 1965, p. 17
19. Corsicana Felines in Jacksonville Invasion, Corsicana Daily Sun, Corsicana, Texas, Oct 01, 1965, p. 20
20. Corsicana Hits Jacksonville Eleven, 33-0, Corsicana Daily Sun, Corsicana, Texas, Oct 02, 1965, p. 16

21. Ennis Big and Tough, Corsicana Daily Sun, Corsicana, Texas, Oct 05, 1965, p. 7

22. Airborne Lions Are Dangerous, Corsicana Daily Sun, Corsicana, Texas, Oct 07, 1965, p. 13

23. Corsicana, Ennis Clash Tonight, Corsicana Daily Sun, Corsicana, Texas, Oct 08, 1965, p. 9

24. Corsicana Shatters Ennis Lion Gridders, 49-0, Corsicana Daily Sun, Corsicana, Texas, Oct 09, 1965, p. 17

25. Cleburne Good, Acree Tells Dads, Corsicana Daily Sun, Corsicana, Texas, Oct 12, 1965, p. 17

26. Tiger-Jacket Tilt to Headline Zone Action, Corsicana Daily Sun, Corsicana, Texas, Oct 13, 1965, p. 10

27. Tigers are Prepared, Corsicana Daily Sun, Corsicana, Texas, Oct 14, 1965, p. 14

28. Tigers and Jackets Face Showdown, Corsicana Daily Sun, Corsicana, Texas, Oct 15, 1965, p. 7

29. Corsicana Belts Cleburne in North Zone, 22-0, Corsicana Daily Sun, Corsicana, Texas, Oct 16, 1965, p. 17

30. Wacoans Can be Tough, Corsicana Daily Sun, Corsicana, Texas, Oct 19, 1965, p. 7

31. Waco Has The "Bomb", Corsicana Daily Sun, Corsicana, Texas, Oct 21, 1965, p. 36

32. Corsicana is Favorite in Old Time Feud, Corsicana Daily Sun, Corsicana, Texas, Oct 22, 1965, p. 19

33. Corsicana Felines Claw Waco High Eleven, 26-7, Corsicana Daily Sun, Corsicana, Texas, Oct 23, 1965, p. 7

34. Canant, Talmadge, Comments by Canant, Corsicana Daily Sun, Corsicana, Texas, Oct 25, 1965, p. 6

35. Broncos Better Than Record, Acree Warns, Corsicana Daily Sun, Corsicana, Texas, Oct 26, 1965, p. 18

36. North Zone Grid Teams Prep for Third Round of Action, Corsicana Daily Sun, Corsicana, Texas, Oct 27, 1965, p. 7

37. Zone Lead is at Stake, Corsicana Daily Sun, Corsicana, Texas, Oct 28, 1965, p. 39

38. Corsicana Shreds Bryan Grid Defense, 34-3, Corsicana Daily Sun, Corsicana, Texas, Oct 30, 1965, p. 17

39. Line Performance Key to Tiger Grid Success, Corsicana Daily Sun, Corsicana, Texas, Nov 02, 1965, p. 7

40. Canant, Talmadge, Comments by Canant, Corsicana Daily Sun, Corsicana, Texas, Nov 03, 1965, p. 13

41. Tigers Ready for Trojan Tiff, Corsicana Daily Sun, Corsicana, Texas, Nov 04, 1965, p. 17

42. Trojans Bar Tiger Grid Title Route, Corsicana Daily Sun, Corsicana, Texas, Nov 05, 1965, p. 19

43. Late Touchdown Saves Bengals from Tie by Aroused University, Corsicana Daily Sun, Corsicana, Texas, Nov 06, 1965, p. 8

44. Friday's Games Tell Tale, Corsicana Daily Sun, Corsicana, Texas, Nov 08, 1965, p. 8

45. Canant, Talmadge, Comments by Canant, Corsicana Daily Sun, Corsicana, Texas, Nov 08, 1965, p. 25

46. Rams Aim for Tigers, Corsicana Daily Sun, Corsicana, Texas, Nov 09, 1965, p. 8

47. Tiger-Rams Duel Nears, Corsicana Daily Sun, Corsicana, Texas, Nov 11, 1965, p. 11

48. Richfield Rams Invade Tigerland, Corsicana Daily Sun, Corsicana, Texas, Nov 12, 1965, p. 19

49. Grid Spirit Engulfs Corsicana, Corsicana Daily Sun, Corsicana, Texas, Nov 12, 1965, p. 21

50. Tigers Maul Rams, 26-0; Annex Zone Title, Corsicana Daily Sun, Corsicana, Texas, Nov 13, 1965, p. 17

51. Canant, Talmadge, Comments by Canant, Corsicana Daily Sun, Corsicana, Texas, Nov 16, 1965, p. 7

52. Fortson, Jane, Tiger Tales, Corsicana Daily Sun, Corsicana, Texas, Nov 18, 1965, p. 41

53. Reb Record Misleading, Corsicana for of Saturday Night Can Be Tough, Corsicana Daily Sun, Corsicana, Texas, Nov 18, 1965, p. 13

54. Tigers, Rebs in Title Tiff, Aggieland is Site of Grid Tilt at 8 P.M., Corsicana Daily Sun, Corsicana, Texas, Nov 19, 1965, p. 7

55. Corsicana Takes Loop Title, 34-12, Corsicana Daily Sun, Corsicana, Texas, Nov 20, 1965, p. 7

56. Corsicana, Alice Play Saturday Night in Austin, Corsicana Daily Sun, Corsicana, Texas, Nov 22, 1965, p. 33

57. "Beat Alice" on Telephone is Requested, Corsicana Daily Sun, Corsicana, Texas, Nov 23, 1965, p. 2

58. Canant, Talmadge, Comments by Canant, Corsicana Daily Sun, Corsicana, Texas, Nov 23, 1965, p. 9

59. Bengals Go Back to Practice for Alice Encounter, Corsicana Daily Sun, Corsicana, Texas, Nov 24, 1965, p. 7

60. Fortson, Jane, Tiger Tales, Corsicana Daily Sun, Corsicana, Texas, Nov 25, 1965, p. 2

61. CHS Ends Work for Alice Club, Corsicana Daily Sun, Corsicana, Texas, Nov 26, 1965, p. 17

62. Austin Revisitation Due, Corsicana Daily Sun, Corsicana, Texas, Nov 29, 1965, p. 9

63. Tigers Repel Alice, 17-14, Corsicana Daily Sun, Corsicana, Texas, Nov 29, 1965, p. 8

64. Dads View Tiger Win on Film, Corsicana Daily Sun, Corsicana, Texas, Nov 30, 1965, p. 18

65. Corsicana Studying Vols High Powered Offense, Corsicana Daily Sun, Corsicana, Texas, Nov 30, 1965, p. 17

66. Eight Teams Alive in Each Class as Schools Reach Quarterfinals, Corsicana Daily Sun, Corsicana, Texas, Nov 30, 1965, p. 17

67. Tigers Get the Message, Corsicana Semi-Weekly Light, Corsicana, Texas, Nov 30, 1965, p. 5

68. Canant, Talmadge, Comments by Canant, Corsicana Daily Sun, Corsicana, Texas, Dec 01, 1965, p. 24

69. Coach's Wife Gives View of Behind Scenes in Busy Season, Corsicana Daily Sun, Corsicana, Texas, Dec 01, 1965, p. 18

70. Fortson, Jane, Tiger Tales, Corsicana Daily Sun, Corsicana, Texas, Dec 02, 1965, p. 40

71. Canant, Talmadge, Comments by Canant, Corsicana Daily Sun, Corsicana, Texas, Dec 02, 1965, p. 13

72. Figures Pointing to Offensive Duel Saturday Night, Corsicana Semi-Weekly Light, Corsicana, Texas, Dec 03, 1965, p. 6

73. Canant, Talmadge, Comments by Canant, Corsicana Daily Sun, Corsicana, Texas, Dec 03, 1965, p. 19

74. GO Tigers GO, Corsicana Daily Sun, Corsicana, Texas, Dec 03, 1965, p. 8

75. Tigers Work as Usual Thursday: Close Drills, Corsicana Daily Sun, Corsicana, Texas, Dec 03, 1965, p. 7

76. Thousands Trail Felines to Quarterfinals, Corsicana Daily Sun, Corsicana, Texas, Dec 04, 1965, p. 8

77. Canant, Talmadge, Comments by Canant, Corsicana Daily Sun, Corsicana, Texas, Dec 04, 1965, p. 8

78. Telegrams Got Longer, Corsicana Daily Sun, Corsicana, Texas, Dec 06, 1965, p. 21

79. 14 Emergencies Get Treatment During the Weekend, Corsicana Daily Sun, Corsicana, Texas, Dec 06, 1965, p. 22

80. Highlights, Sidelights Given on Corsicana Trip to Quarterfinals, Corsicana Daily Sun, Corsicana, Texas, Dec 06, 1965, p. 12

81. Lee Vols Bag Tigers in Quarterfinals, 26-21, Corsicana Daily Sun, Corsicana, Texas, Dec 06, 1965, p. 18

82. Corsicana Salutes Coaches, Corsicana Daily Sun, Corsicana, Texas, Dec 07, 1965, p. 17

83. Future Tiger - Felix Acree, Corsicana Daily Sun, Corsicana, Texas, Dec 08, 1965, p. 19

84. Gridiron Receipts Tabulated, Corsicana Daily Sun, Corsicana, Texas, Dec 10, 1965, p. 19

85. A Salute to the Corsicana Tiger Football Team, Corsicana Daily Sun, Corsicana, Texas, Dec 10, 1965, p. 5

86. Autos Collide on Highway 22, Corsicana Daily Sun, Corsicana, Texas, Dec 17, 1965, p. 4

87. Four Corsicana High Gridders are Named on All-District Elevens, Corsicana Daily Sun, Corsicana, Texas, Dec 20, 1965, p. 29

88. Letter 37 Tigers for 1965 Season, Corsicana Daily Sun, Corsicana, Texas, Dec 23, 1965, p. 17

89. Canant, Talmadge, Comments by Canant, Corsicana Daily Sun, Corsicana, Texas, Dec 24, 1965, p. 11

90. Canant, Talmadge, Comments by Canant, Corsicana Daily Sun, Corsicana, Texas, Jan 01, 1966, p. 7

91. Ronnie Ward Signs for ASC Scholarship, Corsicana Daily Sun, Corsicana, Texas, May 18, 1966, p. 17

Chapter 12

1. Canant, Talmadge, Comments by Canant, Corsicana Daily Sun, Corsicana, Texas, Jan 27, 1966, p. 31

2. Board Approves Year Extension Acree Contract, Corsicana Daily Sun, Corsicana, Texas, Apr 15, 1966, p. 1

3. Canant, Talmadge, Comments by Canant, Corsicana Daily Sun, Corsicana, Texas, Apr 25, 1966, p. 26

4. Spring Football to Open Monday, Corsicana Daily Sun, Corsicana, Texas, Apr 27, 1966, p. 9

5. Corsicana High Gridders in Soggy Start, Corsicana Daily Sun, Corsicana, Texas, May 02, 1966, p. 9
6. First Grid Drill Held Inside Gym, Corsicana Daily Sun, Corsicana, Texas, May 03, 1966, p. 8
7. Canant, Talmadge, Comments by Canant, Corsicana Daily Sun, Corsicana, Texas, May 06, 1966, p. 9
8. Colds Bothering Tigers, Corsicana Daily Sun, Corsicana, Texas, May 12, 1966, p. 13
9. Canant, Talmadge, Comments by Canant, Corsicana Daily Sun, Corsicana, Texas, May 19, 1966, p. 35
10. Tiger Elevens in 22-22 Tie, Corsicana Daily Sun, Corsicana, Texas, May 23, 1966, p. 7
11. Coach Acree is Jaycee Speaker Thursday Noon, Corsicana Daily Sun, Corsicana, Texas, Jun 16, 1966, p. 29
12. Tiger Grid Plans Set, Corsicana Daily Sun, Corsicana, Texas, Jul 07, 1966, p. 33
13. Canant, Talmadge, Comments by Canant, Corsicana Daily Sun, Corsicana, Texas, Aug 15, 1966, p. 21
14. Athletic Director, Corsicana Daily Sun, Corsicana, Texas, Aug 17, 1966, p. 17
15. Corsicana Tigers Begin 1966, Corsicana Daily Sun, Corsicana, Texas, Aug 23, 1966, p. 6
16. Tigers End Two-A-Day Workouts, Corsicana Daily Sun, Corsicana, Texas, Aug 31, 1966, p. 6
17. Bengals in Hard Work, Corsicana Daily Sun, Corsicana, Texas, Sep 01, 1966, p. 11
18. Grid Barbeque a Hit, Corsicana Daily Sun, Corsicana, Texas, Sep 03, 1966, p. 8
19. Younger Tigers, Lions Program Topic Tuesday, Corsicana Daily Sun, Corsicana, Texas, Sep 06, 1966, p. 11
20. Corsicana Blanks Bonham Warriors Grid Debut, 20-0, Corsicana Daily Sun, Corsicana, Texas, Sep 10, 1966, p. 16
21. Jacksonville is Next Tiger Gridiron Foe, Corsicana Daily Sun, Corsicana, Texas, Sep 13, 1966, p. 6
22. Corsicana Complacent, says Acree, Corsicana Daily Sun, Corsicana, Texas, Sep 15, 1966, p. 31
23. Tigers Put Down Jacksonville Threat, 21-7, Corsicana Daily Sun, Corsicana, Texas, Sep 17, 1966, p. 6
24. Tiger Defense Lagging, Corsicana Daily Sun, Corsicana, Texas, Sep 20, 1966, p. 5
25. John Tyler Lions Claw Corsicana High Eleven 34-6, Corsicana Daily Sun, Corsicana, Texas, Sep 24, 1966, p. 6
26. Canant, Talmadge, Comments by Canant, Corsicana Daily Sun, Corsicana, Texas, Sep 27, 1966, p. 6
27. Corsicana Claws Waco Felines, 14-10, Corsicana Daily Sun, Corsicana, Texas, Oct 8, 1966, p. 6
28. Corsicana, Cleburne Ready, Corsicana Daily Sun, Corsicana, Texas, Oct 27, 1966, p. 6
29. Temple Edges Past Corsicana, Corsicana Daily Sun, Corsicana, Texas, Nov 5, 1966, p. 9
30. Bryan Broncos Unseat Corsicana, Corsicana Daily Sun, Corsicana, Texas, Nov 12, 1966, p. 6
31. Dads View Bryan Film, Corsicana Daily Sun, Corsicana, Texas, Nov 15, 1966, p. 6

32. Tiger Basketball is Outlined, Corsicana Daily Sun, Corsicana, Texas, Nov 22, 1966, p. 6

33. Tiger Coaches Feted, Corsicana Daily Sun, Corsicana, Texas, Dec 20, 1966, p. 8

34. Minutes of the Meeting of the UIL State Executive Committee, Corsicana Alleged Violating the Amatuer Rule, Dec 15, 1966

35. Minutes of the Meeting of the UIL State Executive Committee, Corsicana Alleged Violating the Amatuer Rule, Jan 13, 1967

36. Jim Acree Quits, Corsicana Daily Sun, Corsicana, Texas, Jan 14, 1967, p. 8

37. Canant, Talmadge, Comments by Canant, Corsicana Daily Sun, Corsicana, Texas, Jan 17, 1967, p. 6

38. Canant, Talmadge, Comments by Canant, Corsicana Daily Sun, Corsicana, Texas, Jan 19, 1967, p. 1

39. Canant, Talmadge, Comments by Canant, Corsicana Daily Sun, Corsicana, Texas, Jan 20, 1967, p. 6

40. Canant, Talmadge, Comments by Canant, Corsicana Daily Sun, Corsicana, Texas, Jan 21, 1967, p. 10

41. New Coach, Corsicana Daily Sun, Corsicana, Texas, Jan 25, 1967, p. 6

42. Canant, Talmadge, Comments by Canant, Corsicana Daily Sun, Corsicana, Texas, Jan 28, 1967, p. 7

43. Minutes of the Meeting of the UIL State Executive Committee, Article VIII, Sec. 8, Amatuer Rule, Rule 25, Football Plan: Provides Medical Services for Football Team, Feb 2, 1967

44. Reshuffle for Ponies, The Waco News-Tribune, Waco, Texas, Feb 02, 1967, p. 25

45. Gibbs, Dick, Gibbs Gab, Corsicana Daily Sun, Corsicana, Texas, May 09, 1971, p. 24

Chapter 13

1. Kirk, Deanna, Tribute to Acree: Beloved coach is honored with life-size bronze, Corsicana Daily Sun, Mar 11, 2017, https://www.corsicanadailysun.com/news/tribute-to-acree-beloved-coach-is-honored-with-life-size/article_d9c5ef40-05e2-11e7-92fd-abcAAAc90319b.html, (last accessed Aug 30, 2022)

2. Maud Grad to Have Statue Unveiled in Texas, Shawnee News-Star, Mar 07, 2017, http://www.news-star.com/sports/20170307/maud-grad-to-have-statue-unveiled-in-texas, (last accessed Mar 08, 2017)

3. McGathey, Chris and Ron Farmer, Honoring Acree: Legendary '63 CHS football coach honored with statue, Corsicana Daily Sun, Mar 21, 2017, https://www.corsicanadailysun.com/news/honoring-acree-legendary-63-chs-football-coach-honored-with-statue/article_423f9826-0e41-11e7-b0f5-43c2cdd594f0.html, (last accessed Aug 30, 2022)

4. Coach Jim Acree - Corsicana, TX - Statues of Historic Figures, https://www.waymarking.com/waymarks/WMXKNP_Coach_Jim_Acree_Corsicana_TX, (last accessed Aug 30, 2022)

5. Famed Corsicana football coach Jim Acree will be honored with statue, The Dallas Morning News, Mar 15 2017, https://www.dallasnews.com/high-school-sports/2017/03/15/famed-

corsicana-football-coach-jim-acree-will-be-honored-with-statue/, (last accessed Aug 30, 2022)

6. Coach Jim Acree Statue Ceremony, Mar 08, 2017, https://www.facebook.com/watch/live/?ref=watch_permalink&v=1461860623832211, (last accessed Aug 30, 2022)

7. Corsicana Bronze Statue Tour, B2 Jim Acree, https://visitcorsicana.com/bronzes-2/, (last accessed Aug 30, 2022)

Conclusion

1. Ratliff, Harold V., Sports Shots, Corsicana Daily Sun, Corsicana, Texas, Feb 14, 1963, p. 36
2. Ratliff, Harold, Sports Shots, Corsicana Daily Sun, Corsicana, Texas, Mar 10, 1966, p. 36
3. Laird, John, Sports Soapbox, The Odessa American, Odessa, Texas, Sun, Jun 01, 1975, p. 18
4. Midland-Lee Barred from Playoffs, Abilene Reporter-News, Abilene, Texas, Aug 25, 1977, p. 103
5. Rule Change Catches Lee Coach 'Unaware', Lubbock Avalanche-Journal, Lubbock, Texas, Aug 26, 1977, p. 54
6. Lawler, Art, Rocky 5-AAAA Start, Abilene Reporter-News, Abilene, Texas, Sep 01, 1977, p. 29

Appendix Graham Game

1. Shabay, P.D., Graham Steer Football: 1963 Quarterfinal and Semifinal Games [Film], Dec 14, 1963
2. Settle, Happy, Corsicana 14 Vs. Graham 13 Semi-Finals 1963 [Film], Dec14,1963
3. Controversial Football Film Scheduled Tonight, The Graham Leader, Dec 19, 1963
4. Phillips, Mike, '63 Tigers: 'It Was Magical,' Corsicana Daily Sun, Oct 21, 2013, https://www.corsicanadailysun.com/news/local_news/63-tigers-it-was-magical/article_d139b5e0-e323-5492-83fb-6951e20edf1a.html (last accessed Aug 31, 2022)

AFTERWORD

In 2013, players from the Corsicana AAA State Championship team and assistant coaches held a 50th-anniversary celebration. A writer retained to write the story of the '63 Tigers also attended. He heard the stories and conducted some interviews but failed to produce anything. He never followed through. It was heartbreaking to Jim Wood and disappointing the rest of us.

In 2017, when the team put up a statue of Coach Acree, conversation about a book resumed. Many former players believed Acree's impact on football, the teams and the town of Corsicana needed to be written.

Having managed the statue project to successful completion, and in honor of Jim Wood, I volunteered to explore writing a book. I had experience writing academic research papers, so I began developing the idea of a creative non-fiction book written in a narrative style.

After researching newspaper accounts, I wanted to write more literature-like, so I began by telling the story of how I got into football. This work became Chapter 4 here. As a structural aid, I used the first chapter of Elmore Leonard's **Viva Cuba Libre**! I shared the draft with family members and the Acree family. The feedback was lukewarm.

Being Acree trained, I pushed ahead and wrote a draft of what became Chapter 10 in this book. For structural guidance, I used Virginia Woolf's short story, **Mrs. Dalloway in Bond Street**. I shared the result with several former players and friends, and one player's comment impressed me. He said, "Reading it, I felt like I ran to the Green House again."

I decided that a book to help readers "experience Acree" might work. After conducting interviews with former players, I wrote what is Chapter 2 in the book. I used **Axolotl** by Julio Cortazar to structure how Acree transformed the boys in 1960 into champions. I shared it with former players on the 1960 team and they felt it captured what they experienced under Acree.

When I interviewed Jim Hagle, he told me the story of the Henderson scrimmage in 1962, so I wrote Chapter 5 loosely structured using Flannery O'Connor's short story, **A Good Man is Hard to Find**. Robert Graham served as a literary foil. Following it, I wrote Chapter 8 using **The Elevator** by William Sleator for help to create the dread of the boxing room in the Field House. I shared drafts of these chapters with former players and the Acree family. Their comments confirmed the book's direction to convey "experiencing Acree" in a narrative form.

Having personally experienced the Graham game in 1963, I wrote the story, **One Measly Point** using **Miss Brill** by Katherine Mansfield for structural help. A version of that story appeared in *The Nav-Co Chronicle*, but a better-edited version appears in the Appendix here.

I decided to summarize Coach Acree's life before Corsicana in Chapter 1. After researching it, I structured his story using Blake Snyder's **Save the Cat! Beat Sheet**. It was troubling to dig through the past of a person I respected and also write accurately in a biographical sense. I almost gave up the project because my quest to "find the story" had an unavoidable tragic ending—he was forced out of coaching. I decided to limit the book to just Acree's tenure as head coach in Corsicana.

Due to encouragement from others, I wrote the remaining chapters detailing various seasons highlighting the players. No Acree story would be worthwhile if it omitted his impact on the lives of those who played for him. Every man I interviewed could tell his own story. Mine is not special. Including it serves only as an example.

ACKNOWLEDGMENTS

The author is grateful to Dr. Stan Acree, Susan Acree Hansen and Felix Acree for their encouragement and support in writing this book. Stan Hansen, Susan and Felix read rough drafts and patiently coached the author on Acree family history. They graciously provided photos and answered many questions.

Others who read early drafts and provided inspiration and encouragement were Jim Hagle, Ronnie Ragsdale, Warren Ivie, Bob Garlington, Gary Roman, Carrie Dils, Jan Ward, Jerry Moore, Margaret Moore and John Stover.

The author is indebted to Talmadge Canant, former sports editor of the Corsicana Daily Sun, for his articles about football in Corsicana. Many direct quotes attributed to Jim Acree came from quotes captured by Mr. Canant and are preserved in Newspapers.com.

The author appreciates interviews granted by numerous former players and assistant coaches including Jerry Moore, Paul Slaughter and Jackie Edwards. Their insights added richness in nostalgia and a level of human depth that could not be manufactured.

Finally, the author wants to thank the editors, Isabel Pettibone, James Anthony, Dan Hays, Amanda Jensen, Jan Ward and Holly Smith who also served as beta readers.

Even with significant help, errors may remain, but they don't change the significance of Acree's impact on the lives of the boys he coached.

Made in the USA
Coppell, TX
27 September 2023

22093614R00256